WORKSHOPS IN COMPUTING
Series edited by C. J. van Rijsbergen

W0107439

Also in this series

continued on back page...

Yves Deville (Ed.)

Logic Program Synthesis and Transformation

Proceedings of LOPSTR 93,
International Workshop on Logic
Program Synthesis and Transformation,
Louvain-la-Neuve, Belgium,
7–9 July 1993

Published in collaboration with the
British Computer Society

Springer-Verlag
London Berlin Heidelberg New York
Paris Tokyo Hong Kong
Barcelona Budapest

Yves Deville
Unité d'Informatique
Université Catholique de Louvain
Place Sainte-Barbe 2
B–1348 Louvain-la-Neuve, Belgium

ISBN-13:978-3-540-19864-2   e-ISBN-13:978-1-4471-3234-9
DOI: 10.1007/978-1-4471-3234-9

British Library Cataloguing in Publication Data
Logic Program Synthesis and Transformation : Proceedings of LOPSTR 93,
International Workshop on Logic Program Synthesis and Transformation,
Louvain-la-Neuve, Belgium, 7–9 July 1993. – (Workshops in Computing Series)
    I. Deville, Yves II. Series
    005.1
ISBN-13:978-3-540-19864-2

Library of Congress Cataloging-in-Publication Data
A catalog record for this book is available from the Library of Congress

Typesetting: Camera ready by contributors

34/3830-543210 Printed on acid-free paper

Foreword

This volume contains extended versions of papers presented at the Third International Workshop on Logic Program Synthesis and Transformation (LOPSTR 93) held in Louvain-la-Neuve in July 1993. Much of the success of the workshop is due to Yves Deville who served as Organizer and Chair.

Many people believe that machine support for the development and evolution of software will play a critical role in future software engineering environments. Machine support requires the formalization of the artifacts and processes that arise during the software lifecycle. Logic languages are unique in providing a uniform declarative notation for precisely describing application domains, software requirements, and for prescribing behavior via logic programs. Program synthesis and transformation techniques formalize the process of developing correct and efficient programs from requirement specifications. The natural intersection of these two fields of research has been the focus of the LOPSTR workshops.

The papers in this volume address many aspects of software development including: deductive synthesis, inductive synthesis, transformations for optimizing programs and exploiting parallelism, program analysis techniques (particularly via abstract interpretation), meta-programming languages and tool support, and various extensions to Prolog-like languages, admitting non-Horn clauses, functions, and constraints. Despite the progress represented in this volume, the transition from laboratory to practice is fraught with difficulties. Some of the challenges that researchers face include (1) the development of techniques for handling more complex and realistic problems, (2) wider availability of implemented systems that can support experiments and education, and (3) support for software evolution. In future LOPSTR workshops we can look forward to continued progress in these areas and signs that the field is fulfilling its promise of radical improvements to software engineering practice.

Palo Alto   Douglas R. Smith
October 1993

Preface

LOPSTR 93, held from 7–9 July 1993, in Louvain-la-Neuve, Belgium, is the third in a series of International Workshops on Logic Program Synthesis and Transformation. The aim of these meetings is to present recent work and to discuss new ideas and trends in logic program synthesis and transformation, as well as related fields. This year, the LOPSTR workshop was held jointly with the Program Development Area Meeting of Compunet, the Esprit Network in Computational Logic.

The workshop brought together 55 researchers from 12 different countries, and 28 talks were presented. This volume contains 19 original contributions in logic program synthesis and transformation, including an invited paper from Douglas R. Smith. Our thanks to all the contributors to the workshop who made LOPSTR 93 a success.

We would like to thank the other Program Committee members for their contribution and fruitful collaboration during the preparation of the workshop and the selection of papers. We thank them and the other referees for their detailed and timely refereeing of the submitted papers.

We are most grateful to the Esprit Network in Computational Logic, and the Belgian National Fund for Scientific Research for their financial support. Special thanks to Vincent Lombart for his help in organizing the workshop and preparing these proceedings.

Louvain-la-Neuve   Yves Deville
October 1993

Contents

Toward the Synthesis of Constraint Propagation Algorithms *

Douglas R. Smith

Kestrel Institute

3260 Hillview Avenue

Palo Alto, California 94304 USA

1 Introduction

Within the last decade logic programming has developed into constraint logic programming. One motivation for this development has been the need to handle richer data structures in a manner consistent with the nondeterministic and relational style of logic programming. It was realized early on that ordinary unification was equation solving over trees. From there it was a natural step to allow equation solving over more complex structures (e.g. lists, booleans, integers) and further to allow constraint solving in various theories (e.g. monoids, boolean algebras, real closed fields). From another point of view, constraint logic programming languages, such as PROLOG III [2], CLP(R) [5], and CHIP [4], can be seen as attempts to integrate the best features of logic programming and work on constraint satisfaction algorithms in Artificial Intelligence and Operations Research. See [1] for an overview of constraint logic programming.

In a constraint program, a constraint set partially characterizes the objects of interest and their relationships. Constraint propagation is one of the key operations on constraints in constraint logic programming. As committments are made that further characterize some object, consequences of those committments are inferred and added as new constraints. Efficiency concerns drive us to look closely at (1) the representation of constraints, (2) inference procedures for solving constraints and deriving consequences, and (3) the capture of inferred consequences as new constraints.

It is natural to begin to consider the problem of synthesizing constraint logic programs. We report here on our current efforts at developing automated methods for deriving problem-specific constraint propagation code. This effort is part of a broader development of automated tools for transforming formal specifications into efficient and correct programs. The KIDS system [8] serves as the testbed for our experiments and provides tools for performing deductive inference, algorithm design, expression simplification, finite differencing, partial evaluation, data type refinement, and other transformations. We have used KIDS to derive over 60 algorithms for a wide variety of application domains, including scheduling, combinatorial design, sorting and searching, computational geometry, pattern matching, and mathematical programming.

A transportation scheduling application motivated our constraint propagation work [11]. The problem is NP-complete and is partly characterized by

---

*This research was supported in part by ARPA/Rome Laboratories under Contract F30602-91-C-0043, in part by the Office of Naval Research under Grant N00014-90-J-1733, and in part by the Air Force Office of Scientific Research under Contract F49620-91-C-0073.

discrete variables and disjunctive constraints. We used KIDS semiautomatically to derive a global search (backtrack) scheduler. The derivation included inferring pruning conditions and deriving constraint propagation code. The resulting code is given in [10] and has proved to be dramatically faster than other programs running the same data. The pruning and constraint propagation are so strong that the program often does not backtrack on the data we have tried. For example, on a transportation problem involving 15,460 movement requirements obtained from the US Transportation Command, the scheduler produces a complete feasible schedule in about one minute. A naive constraint network formulation based on this problem data would have over 31,000 variables and 120,125,000 constraints. Incorporating some of the structure of the problem, such as the linearity of time, allows reformulating this to a system of about 108,700 constraints. However, this is still a such large formulation that it seems an implicit representation is necessary to find feasible schedules efficiently.

What kind of support is needed to incorporate constraints into logic programming? First, constraints are expressed in the language of some theory (e.g. linear arithmetic with inequalities) and there must be a representation of constraints[1]. Second, in that theory there must be procedures for solving constraints and extracting solutions. Third, there must be a procedure for inferring consequences of constraints and capturing their content in a new constraint (perhaps by weakening or approximation). Fourth, there must be a way to compose two constraints (e.g. to assimilate a new constraint). Current constraint logic programming systems effectively carry out these operations via representations and operations specialized to the theory of the constraint language. For the sake of efficiency it may be necessary to design representations and operations that exploit not only the general background theory, but the intrinsic structure of the particular problem being solved.

2 Global Search Theory

Our studies of constraint propagation take place within a formal model of a class of programs called *global search*. Global search generalizes the well-known algorithm concepts of binary search, backtrack, and branch-and-bound [7].

The basic idea of global search is to represent and manipulate sets of candidate solutions. The principal operations are to *extract* candidate solutions from a set and to *split* a set into subsets. Derived operations include (1) *filters* which are used to eliminate sets containing no feasible or optimal solutions, and (2) constraint propagators that are used to eliminate nonfeasible elements of a set of candidate solutions. Global search algorithms work as follows: starting from an initial set that contains all solutions to the given problem instance, the algorithm repeatedly extracts solutions, splits sets, eliminates sets via filters and propagates constraints until no sets remain to be split. The process is often described as a tree (or DAG) search in which a node represents a set of candidates and an arc represents the split relationship between set and subset. The filters and constraint propagators serve to prune off branches of the tree that cannot lead to solutions.

---

[1] We will not distinguish constraints and constraint sets, since a constraint set usually denotes the constraint that is a conjunction of the constituent constraints.

The sets of candidate solutions are often infinite and even when finite they are rarely represented extensionally. Thus global search algorithms are based on an abstract data type of intensional representations called *space descriptors* (denoted by hatted symbols). The space descriptors can be thought of as constraints or representations of constraints.

Global search can be expressed axiomatically via a global search theory [7] which we elide here. In the following we present just those parts needed to discuss the formal derivation of constraint propagation code.

A problem can be specified by presenting an *input domain D*, an *output domain R*, and an *output condition* $O : D \times R \rightarrow boolean$. If $O(x, z)$ then we say z is a *feasible* solution with respect to input x. In other words, the output condition defines the conditions under which a candidate solution is feasible or acceptable. Global search theory extends the components of a problem with a datatype of *space descriptors* (constraint representations) $\hat{R}$ and a predicate *Satisfies* : $R \times \hat{R} \rightarrow boolean$ that gives the denotation of space descriptors; if $Satisfies(z, \hat{r})$ then z is in the set of candidate solutions denoted by $\hat{r}$ and we say that z satisfies $\hat{r}$. $\hat{R}$ contains a distinguished space descriptor $\hat{r}_0$ that contains all feasible solutions. A basic global search program scheme follows:

$$F(x, z) \; : - \; F\_gs(x, \hat{r}_0(x), z)$$

$$F\_gs(x, \hat{r}, z) \; : - \; Extract(z, \hat{r}), \; O(x, z)$$

$$F\_gs(x, \hat{r}, z) \; : - \; Split(x, \hat{r}, \hat{s}), \; F\_gs(x, \hat{s}, z)$$

It can be proved within global search theory that this scheme is correct (see e.g. [7]), so that any instance of it can be used to enumerate all feasible solutions to a given problem. For details of the procedure for constructing global search theories for given problems see [7, 8, 9].

One version of the transportation scheduling problem can be specified as follows. The input is a set of movement requirements and a collection of transportation resources. A movement requirement is a record listing the type of cargo, its quantity, port of embarkation, port of debarkation, due date etc. Schedules are represented as maps from resources to sequences of trips, where each trip includes earliest-start-time, latest-start-time, port of embarkation, port of debarkation, and manifest (set of movement requirements). The type of schedules has the invariant (or subtype characteristic) that for each trip, the earliest-start-time is no later than the latest-start-time. A partial schedule is a schedule over a subset of the given movement records.

Twelve constraints characterize a feasible schedule for this problem:

1. *Consistent POE and POD* – The POE and POD of each movement requirement on a given trip of a resource must be the same.

2. *Consistent Resource Class* – Each resource can handle only some movement types. For example, a C-141 can handle bulk and oversize movements, but not outsize movements.

3. *Consistent PAX and Cargo Capacity* – The capacity of each resource cannot be exceeded.

4. *Consistent Initial Time* – The start time of the first trip of a transportation asset must not precede its initial available date, taking into account any time needed to position the resource in the appropriate POE.

5. *Consistent Release Time* – The start time of a trip must not precede the available to load dates of any of the transported movement requirements.

6. *Consistent Arrival time* – The finish time of a trip must not precede the earliest arrival date of any of the transported movement requirements.

7. *Consistent Due time* – The finish time of a trip must not be later than the latest arrival date of any of the transported movement requirements.

8. *Consistent Trip Separation* – Movements scheduled on the same resource must start either simultaneously or with enough separation to allow for return trips. The inherently disjunctive and relative nature of this constraint makes it more difficult to satisfy than the others.

9. *Consistent Resource Use* – Only the given resources are used.

10. *Completeness* – All movement requirements must be scheduled.

These constraints are expressed concisely as quantified first-order sentences.

A simple global search theory of transportation scheduling has the following form. A set of schedules is represented by a partial schedule. The split operation extends the partial schedule by adding one movement requirement in all possible ways. The initial set of schedules is described by the empty partial schedule – a map from each available resource to the empty sequence of trips. A partial schedule is extended by first selecting a movement record *mvr* to schedule, then selecting a resource *r*, and then a trip *t* on *r* (either an existing trip or a newly created one). Finally the extended schedule has *mvr* added to the manifest of trip *t* on resource *r*. The alternative ways that a partial schedule can be extended naturally gives rise to the branching structure underlying global search algorithms. The formal version of this global search theory of scheduling can be found in [10].

When a partial schedule is extended it is possible that some problem constraints are violated in such a way that further extension to a complete feasible schedule is impossible. In global search algorithms it is crucial to detect such violations as early as possible. The next two subsections discuss two general mechanisms for early detection of infeasibility and techniques for mechanically deriving them.

2.1 Pruning Mechanisms

Pruning tests are derived in the following way. Let x be a problem input and $\hat{r}$ be a space descriptor. The test

$$\exists (z : R) \ (Satisfies(z, \hat{r}) \ \wedge \ O(x, z)) \tag{1}$$

decides whether there exist any feasible solutions satisfying $\hat{r}$. If we could decide this at each node of a global search algorithm then we would have perfect search – no deadend branches would ever be explored. In practice it

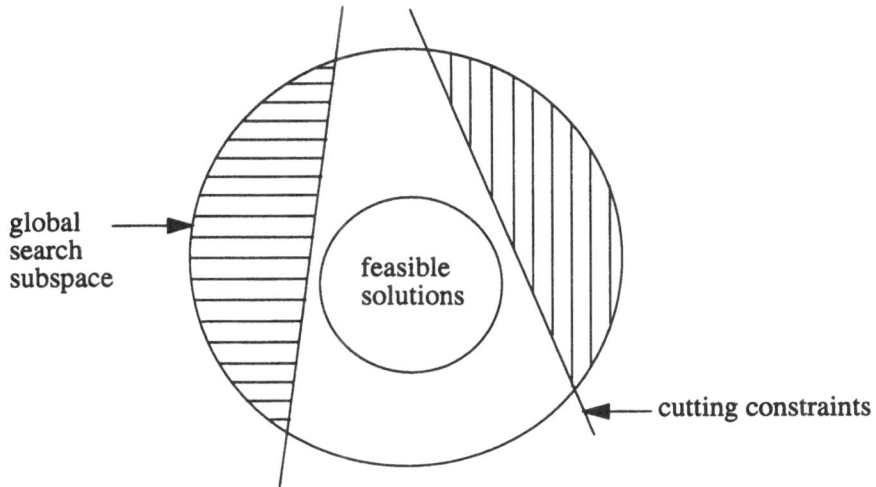

Figure 1: Global Search Subspace and Cutting Constraints

would be impossible or horribly complex to compute it, so we rely instead on an inexpensive approximation to it. In fact, if we approximate (1) by weakening it (deriving a necessary condition of it) we obtain a sound pruning test. That is, suppose we can derive a test $\Phi(x, \hat{r})$ such that

$$\exists(z : R)\,(Satisfies(z, \hat{r}) \wedge O(x, z)) \implies \Phi(x, \hat{r}). \tag{2}$$

By the contrapositive of (2), if $\neg\Phi(x, \hat{r})$ then there are no feasible solutions satisfying $\hat{r}$, so we can eliminate $\hat{r}$ from further consideration. More generally, necessary conditions on the existence of feasible (or optimal) solutions below a node in a branching structure underlie pruning in backtracking and the bounding and dominance tests of branch-and-bound algorithms [7].

Pruning is incorporated into the basic global search program scheme as follows:

$$F(x, z) \; :- \; \Phi(x, \hat{r}_0(x), z), \; F\_gs(x, \hat{r}_0(x), z)$$

$$F\_gs(x, \hat{r}, z) \; :- \; Extract(z, \hat{r}), \; O(x, z)$$

$$F\_gs(x, \hat{r}, z) \; :- \; Split(x, \hat{r}, \hat{s}), \; \Phi(x, \hat{s}(x), z), \; F\_gs(x, \hat{s}, z).$$

It appears that the bottleneck analysis advocated in the constraint-directed search projects at CMU [3, 6] leads to a semantic approximation to (1) that is neither a necessary nor sufficient condition. Such a *heuristic* evaluation of a node is inherently fallible, but if the approximation to (1) is close enough it can provide good search control with relatively little backtracking.

In KIDS, a filter Φ is derived using a general-purpose first-order inference system. The inference of Φ takes place within the theory of the specified problem. Potentially, any special problem structure captured by the axioms and theorems of this theory can be exploited to obtain strong problem-specific pruning mechanisms. Analogous comments apply to the constraint propagation mechanisms discussed next. For details of deriving pruning mechanisms for various problems see [7, 8].

2.2 Cutting Constraints and Constraint Propagation

Pruning has the effect of removing a node (set of solutions) from further consideration. In contrast, constraint propagation has the effect of changing the space descriptor so that it denotes a smaller set of candidate solutions. Constraint propagation is based on the notion of *cutting constraints* which are necessary conditions $\Psi(x, z, \hat{r})$ that a candidate solution z satisfying $\hat{r}$ is feasible:

$$\forall(x : D, z : R, \hat{r} : \hat{R}) \ (Satisfies(z, \hat{r}) \wedge O(x, z) \implies \Psi(x, z, \hat{r})). \qquad (3)$$

By the contrapositive of (3), if $\neg\Psi(x, z, \hat{r})$ then z cannot be a feasible solution satisfying $\hat{r}$. So we can try to incorporate Ψ into $\hat{r}$ to obtain a new descriptor, without losing any feasible solutions. See Figure 1.

Once the inference system has been used to derive a cutting constraint Ψ, we specify an operation, called *Cut*, that maps $\hat{r}$ to a new descriptor $\hat{s}$ such that

$$Satisfies(z, \hat{s}) \iff (Satisfies(z, \hat{r}) \wedge \Psi(x, z, \hat{r})).$$

If $Satisfies(z, \hat{r}) \wedge \Psi(x, z, \hat{r}) \iff false$ then *Cut* returns the descriptor of the empty space denoted $\perp$. Constraint propagation is the iteration of *Cut* until we reach a fixpoint $Cut(x, \hat{i}) = \hat{i}$ (See Figure 2). The challenge in implementing constraint propagation is scheduling this iteration in order to minimize unnecessary work. This involves analyzing the dependencies between variables at design time and generating the control structure needed to reestablish a fixpoint when the *Split* operation causes the value of some variable to change.

Propagation is incorporated into the global search program scheme as follows:

$$F(x, z) \ :- $$
$$\qquad \Phi(x, \hat{r}_0(x)),$$
$$\qquad Propagate(x, \hat{r}_0(x), \hat{r}_0'(x)),$$
$$\qquad \hat{r}_0'(x) \neq \perp,$$
$$\qquad F\_gs(x, \hat{r}_0'(x), z)$$

$$F\_gs(x, \hat{r}, z) \ :- \ Extract(z, \hat{r}), \ O(x, z)$$

$$F\_gs(x, \hat{r}, z) \ :- $$
$$\qquad Split(x, \hat{r}, \hat{s}),$$
$$\qquad \Phi(x, \hat{s}),$$
$$\qquad Propagate(x, \hat{s}, \hat{s}'),$$
$$\qquad \hat{s}' \neq \perp,$$
$$\qquad F\_gs(x, \hat{s}', z).$$

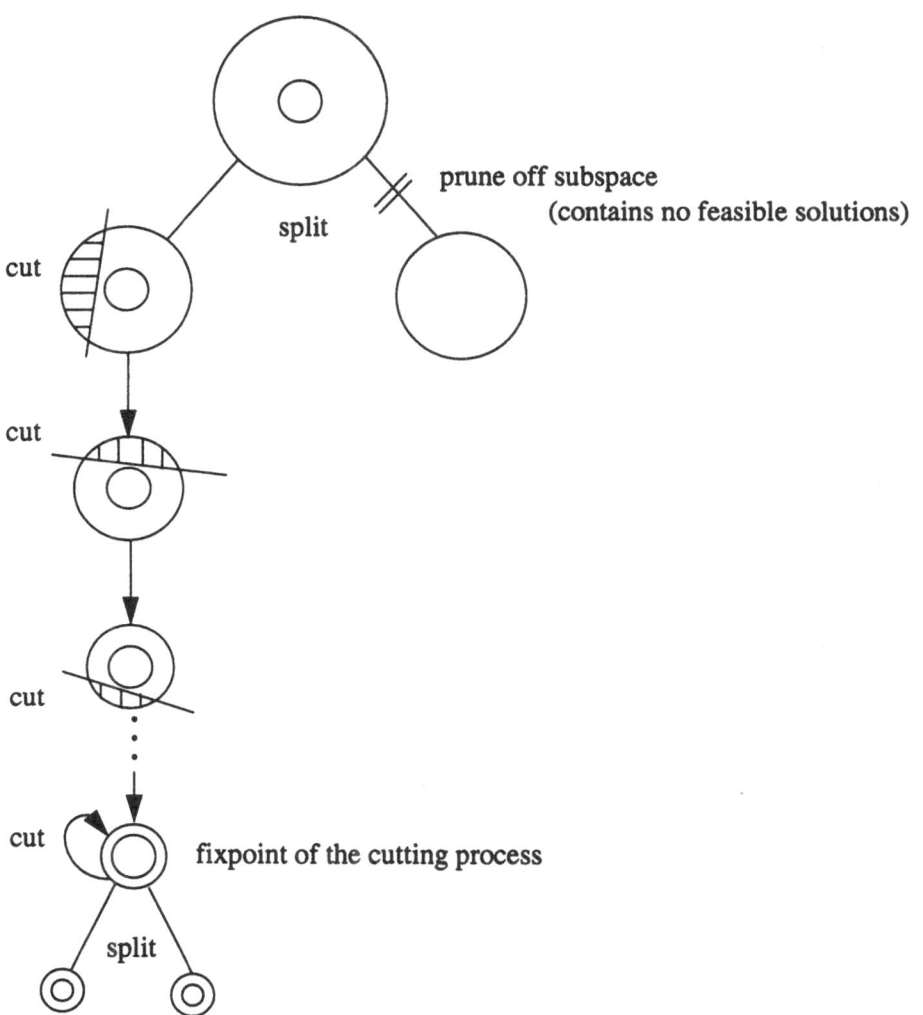

Figure 2: Pruning and Constraint Propagation

$$Propagate(x, \hat{r}, \hat{r}) \; :- \; Cut(x, \hat{r}) = \hat{r}$$

$$\begin{aligned}
Propagate(&x, \hat{r}, \hat{t}) \; :- \\
& Cut(x, \hat{r}) = \hat{s}, \\
& \hat{r} \neq \hat{s}, \\
& Propagate(x, \hat{s}, \hat{t}).
\end{aligned}$$

The effect of constraint propagation is to propagate information through the subspace descriptor resulting in a tighter descriptor and possibly exposing infeasibility. There are several reasons for constraint propagation. First, it shrinks the space of candidate solutions and may thus reduce the branching required to explore it. Second, the generated descriptors may fail the pruning tests and thus allow early termination.

The mechanism for deriving cutting constraints is similar to (in fact a generalization of) that for deriving pruning mechanisms. For transportation scheduling, the derived Cut operation has the following form, where est_i denotes the earliest-start-time for trip i and est_i' denotes the earliest-start-time for trip i after applying Cut (analogously, lst_i denotes latest-start-time), and $roundtrip_i$ is the roundtrip time for trip i on resource r. For each resource r and the ith trip on r,

$$est_i' = max \left\{ \begin{array}{l} est_i \\ est_{i-1} + roundtrip_i \\ max{-}release{-}time(manifest_i) \end{array} \right.$$

$$lst_i' = min \left\{ \begin{array}{l} lst_i \\ lst_{i+1} - roundtrip_i \\ min{-}finish{-}time(manifest_i) \end{array} \right.$$

Here $max{-}release{-}time(manifest_i)$ computes the max over all of the release dates of movement requirements in the manifest of trip i and $min{-}finish{-}time(manifest_i)$ computes the minimum of the finish times of movement requirements in the same manifest. Boundary cases must be handled appropriately.

The effect of iterating this Cut operation after adding a new movement record to some trip will be to shrink the $\langle earliest{-}start{-}time, latest{-}start{-}time \rangle$ window of each trip on the same resource. If the window becomes negative for any trip, then the partial schedule is necessarily infeasible and it can be pruned.

3 Concluding Remarks

Except for constraint propagation, the global search design tactic has been implemented in KIDS and extensively tested [8]. The tactic has been recently extended to derive cutting constraints for various problems, including transportation scheduling. A further extension of the tactic to derive $Propagate$ is currently under development.

Constraint propagation can be viewed as run-time inference. From this view emerges the issue of how to design specialized inference procedures. Global search theory provides a natural setting in which to explore constraint propagation algorithms. The resulting code is naturally expressed in constraint logic programming languages.

References

[1] COHEN, J. Constraint logic programming languages. *Communications of the ACM 33*, 7 (1990), 52–68.

[2] COLMERAUER, A. An introduction to PROLOG III. *Communications of the ACM 33*, 7 (1990), 69–90.

[3] FOX, M. S., SADEH, N., AND BAYKAN, C. Constrained heuristic search. In *Proceedings of the Eleventh International Joint Conference on Artificial Intelligence* (Detroit, MI, August 20–25, 1989), pp. 309–315.

[4] HENTENRYCK, P. V. *Constraint Satisfaction in Logic Programming*. Massachusetts Institute of Technology, Cambridge, MA, 1989.

[5] JAFFAR, J., MICHAYLOU, S., STUCKEY, P., AND YAP, R. The CLP(R) language and system. *ACM Transactions on Programming Languages and Systems 14*, 3 (July 1992), 339–395.

[6] SADEH, N. Look-ahead techniques for micro-opportunistic job shop scheduling. Tech. Rep. CMU-CS-91-102, Carenegie-Mellon University, March 1991.

[7] SMITH, D. R. Structure and design of global search algorithms. Tech. Rep. KES.U.87.12, Kestrel Institute, November 1987. to appear in *Acta Informatica*.

[8] SMITH, D. R. KIDS – a semi-automatic program development system. *IEEE Transactions on Software Engineering Special Issue on Formal Methods in Software Engineering 16*, 9 (September 1990), 1024–1043.

[9] SMITH, D. R. Constructing specification morphisms. Tech. Rep. KES.U.92.1, Kestrel Institute, January 1992. to appear in Journal of Symbolic Computation, Special Issue on Automatic Programming, 1993.

[10] SMITH, D. R. Transformational approach to scheduling. Tech. rep., Kestrel Institute, November 1992.

[11] SMITH, D. R. Transformational approach to transportation scheduling. In *Proceedings of the Eighth Knowledge-Based Software Engineering Conference* (Chicago, IL, September 1993).

A Formal View of Specification, Deductive Synthesis and Transformation of Logic Programs

Kung-Kiu Lau

Department of Computer Science, University of Manchester
Oxford Road, Manchester M13 9PL, United Kingdom
kung-kiu@cs.man.ac.uk

Mario Ornaghi

Dipartimento di Scienze dell'Informazione
Universita' degli studi di Milano
Via Comelico 39/41, Milano, Italy
ornaghi@imiucca.csi.unimi.it

Abstract

We view logic programs as (first-order) axiomatisations, and deductive synthesis and transformation as operations on mathematical systems composed of axioms and "logical" systems such as SLD and SLDNF. In this framework, we distinguish between specification, deductive synthesis and transformation and discuss their inter-relationships.

1 Introduction

LOPSTR 92 concluded with a discussion on the distinction (if any) between synthesis and transformation. Most people accepted that the two areas were distinct (if not disjoint). However, it was not clear whether the distinction is mainly based on pragmatic considerations or on more fundamental reasons.

In this paper, we will propose and formalise a distinction between *specification*, *synthesis*, and *transformation*. This distinction is based on a formal framework described in [7] and [8]. In this framework, we view logic programs as (first-order) axiomatisations. Specification, synthesis and transformation are operations on mathematical systems which are composed of axioms and logical systems such as Classical Logic (*CL*), *SLD* and *SLDNF*. The distinction between specification, synthesis and transformation arises from the different behaviours of the mathematical systems involved in these operations.

However, we will also show that despite this distinction, there are close inter-relationships between specification, synthesis, and transformation via *deductive synthesis*. In this approach, the specification is given in the form of a set of axioms, and the synthesis process systematically derives a set of clauses which are logical consequences of these axioms.[1] Examples of deductive synthesis methods include [4, 5, 6].

---

[1] Note that Manna and Waldinger [10] use *deductive synthesis* to mean *proofs-as-programs*.

In Section 2 we give an informal overview of our terminology and our proposed distinction. In Section 3 we summarise the formal terminology for our formal framework described in Section 4. Then we give a formalisation of deductive synthesis in Section 5, which provides a basis for our accounts of specification in Section 6, synthesis in Section 7, transformation in Section 8, and their inter-relationships in Section 9.

2 Overview

In this section we give an informal overview of our terminology and our proposed distinction. The formal terminology will be explained in the next section.

2.1 Specification

A *specification* is a triple

$$\langle S \cup D, Ans(G), CL \rangle$$

where CL, S, D and $Ans(G)$ have the following meaning.

CL is some inference system for first order classical logic. It indicates the *logic system* employed at the specification level.

S is a set of (first-order) axioms, called a *specification framework*. It should be as rich and complete as possible, to codify our knowledge of the problem domain, to define in a natural way many problems and to prove properties relevant for program synthesis. In this context, various induction schemas for instance are very useful.

D is an axiom defining in S the relation to be computed, G is a *set of goal formulas* involving such a relation and $Ans(G)$ is the set of the *possible answers* of G. By D we single out one of the problems definable in S, while by $Ans(G)$ we specify the following behaviour of the logic program that we wish to synthesise: "for every goal $g \in G$, search for the formulas of $Ans(g)$ provable in S".[2]

An example specification might be

$$\langle S_{list} \cup D_{prefix}, Ans(\{prefix(M, n) \mid n \text{ is ground}\}), CL \rangle \tag{1}$$

where S_{list} is a (sufficiently rich) theory of lists, for instance containing identity axioms, axioms for list operations, induction schema on lists, etc; D_{prefix} is the *definition axiom* (called a *logic description* in [1]):

$$prefix(L, M) \leftrightarrow \forall i \leq length(L). L[i] = M[i] ;$$

Ans is the function associating with every goal $prefix(M, n)$ the set of formulas of the form $prefix(\tau, n)$ (τ being any term). Not every possible answer is a valid answer. For example, $prefix(M, nil)$ has possible answers $prefix(nil, nil)$, $prefix(a.nil, nil)$, $prefix(b.a.nil, nil)$, and so on, but only the first one is an answer.

---

[2]By G and *Ans* we can specify things like directionality [1], pre- and post-conditions, and other possible requirements.

2.2 Synthesis

Synthesis is defined as getting a logic program P from $\langle S, Ans(G), CL \rangle$ such that

$$\langle S, Ans(G), CL \rangle \asymp \langle Ax(P), Ans(G), SLD \rangle$$

i.e. a formula of $Ans(G)$ has a proof in S using CL iff it has a proof in $Ax(P)$ using SLD. Here, $Ax(P)$ denotes the axiomatisation that corresponds to P, and we use SLD in a non-standard manner to denote a logical system (see Section 4.2).

For example, from the specification (1), we can get (somehow) the program P

$$\begin{aligned}
prefix(nil, M) &\leftarrow \\
prefix(X.L_1, X.L_2) &\leftarrow prefix(L_1, L_2)
\end{aligned}$$

such that

$$\begin{aligned}
&\langle S_{list} \cup D_{prefix}, Ans\{prefix(M,n) \mid n \text{ ground}\}, CL \rangle \\
\asymp\ &\langle Ax(P), Ans\{prefix(M,n) \mid n \text{ ground}\}, SLD \rangle
\end{aligned}$$

Thus we view a specification $\langle S, Ans(G), CL \rangle$ as the definition of a problem in a general (possibly infinite) framework S, from which by synthesis we get $Ax(P)$ as a *small* (finite) subsystem, just sufficient to (efficiently) compute the required answers of the goal formulas. That is, S 'properly contains' $Ax(P)$ in an informal sense.

In general, specification frameworks are infinite first order axiomatisations; then every synthesised program is necessarily a smaller subsystem. This fact and the stronger incompleteness result of [8] show that specifications and programs are different[3] and that synthesis is a process of specialisation.

2.3 Transformation

Transformation is defined as getting a program P_2 from a given program P_1, such that P_1 and P_2 are equivalent programs. Then transformation maps programs into programs. Moreover, while synthesis extracts a small subsystem, transformation often goes through systems *equivalent* in CL, i.e. such that

$$\langle Ax(P_1) \cup D, CL \rangle \asymp \langle Ax(P_2) \cup D, CL \rangle$$

where D is a set of definition axioms, linking the predicate symbols of the two programs.

For example, from the program P_1 (to compute Fibonacci numbers)

$$\begin{aligned}
f(0, s(0)) &\leftarrow \\
f(s(0), s(0)) &\leftarrow \\
f(s(s(I)), Z) &\leftarrow f(I, Z_1), f(s(I), Z_2), +(Z_1, Z_2, Z)
\end{aligned}$$

using the definition axiom

$$D\ :\ \forall x, y, z.(ff(x,y,z) \leftrightarrow f(x,y) \wedge f(s(x),z))$$

---

[3]Note that if S is finite, then there exists a logic program P whose completion is equivalent to S (see, e.g. [9, 11]) and this difference disappears.

we can get the program P_2

$$ff(0, s(0), s(0)) \leftarrow$$
$$ff(s(I), A, B) \leftarrow ff(I, H, A), +(I, H, B)$$
$$f(X, A) \leftarrow ff(X, A, B)$$

such that P_1 and P_2 compute the same relation f. Note that

$$\langle Ax(P_1) \cup D, CL \rangle \asymp \langle Ax(P_2) \cup D, CL \rangle$$

i.e. in this example, transformation yields an axiomatisation $Ax(P_2)$ equivalent (using D) to the starting one.

Of course, there may be transformations that work as program specialisation, as discussed in the next subsection.

2.4 Partial Evaluation

Although we shall not discuss partial evaluation in this paper, it is interesting to see where it fits in our scheme of things. We define *partial evaluation* as follows: for a given program P_1 and a chosen goal I, using I as an input for partial evaluation, get a program P_2 such that

$$\langle Ax(P_1), Ans(I), SLD \rangle \asymp \langle Ax(P_2), Ans(I), SLD \rangle$$

i.e. for the answers of the chosen goal I, P_1 and P_2 should be 'equivalent'. In general $\langle Ax(P_2), CL \rangle$ is a proper subsystem of $\langle Ax(P_1), CL \rangle$. Thus we view partial evaluation as a form of *program specialisation*.

If we use *spec* and *prog* to denote sets of all specifications and programs respectively, we have

$$
\begin{array}{rcl}
\text{specification } \textit{specialisation} & \equiv & \textit{spec} \rightarrow \textit{prog} \\
& \equiv & \text{program synthesis} \\
\text{program } \textit{specialisation} & \equiv & \textit{prog} \rightarrow \textit{prog} \\
& & \text{e.g. partial evaluation} \\
\text{program } \textit{transformation} & \equiv & \textit{prog} \rightarrow \textit{prog}
\end{array}
$$

Thus we regard partial evaluation as program transformation rather than as program synthesis.

Note that we also have

$$\text{specification } \textit{transformation} \equiv \textit{spec} \rightarrow \textit{spec}$$

even though here we do not deal with specification transformation at all.

3 Formal Terminology

In this section we present a brief summary of the basic terminology for logical and mathematical systems.[4]

A *logical system* $\mathcal{L}$ is characterised by the set $\mathbf{P}_{\mathcal{L}}$ of the *proofs derivable in* $\mathcal{L}$. Every proof $\pi \in \mathbf{P}_{\mathcal{L}}$ has the attributes a, c where

---

[4] For the sake of simplicity, we assume that all our systems work on formulas of first-order logic with equality.

- $a(\pi)$ is a set of formulas called the *assumptions* of π;

- $c(\pi)$ is a formula called the *consequence* of π.

For example, in a sequent system, if $A_1, \ldots, A_n \Rightarrow B_1, \ldots, B_m$ is the end sequent of a proof π, then $a(\pi) = \{A_1, \ldots, A_n\}$, $c(\pi) = B_1 \vee \cdots \vee B_n$.

For two logical systems $\mathcal{L}_1$ and $\mathcal{L}_2$, $\mathcal{L}_1$ is a *subsystem* of $\mathcal{L}_2$, or $\mathcal{L}_1 \sqsubseteq \mathcal{L}_2$,[5] iff there is a function

$$\rho \,:\, \mathbf{P}_{\mathcal{L}_1} \to \mathbf{P}_{\mathcal{L}_2}$$

such that for every $\pi \in \mathbf{P}_{\mathcal{L}_1}$:

$$a(\pi) = a(\rho(\pi)) \ \text{ and } \ c(\pi) = c(\rho(\pi)) \,.$$

$\mathcal{L}_1$ and $\mathcal{L}_2$ are *equivalent*, or $\mathcal{L}_1 \asymp \mathcal{L}_2$, iff $\mathcal{L}_1 \sqsubseteq \mathcal{L}_2$ and $\mathcal{L}_2 \sqsubseteq \mathcal{L}_1$.

A set of formulas Γ *proves* C in a logical system $\mathcal{L}$, or $\Gamma \vdash_{\mathcal{L}} C$, iff there is at least a proof $\pi \in \mathbf{P}_{\mathcal{L}}$ such that

$$a(\pi) \subseteq \Gamma \ \text{ and } \ C = c(\pi) \,.$$

Note that if $\mathcal{L}_1 \sqsubseteq \mathcal{L}_2$, then $\Gamma \vdash_{\mathcal{L}_1} C$ implies that $\Gamma \vdash_{\mathcal{L}_2} C$.

A *mathematical system* is a pair $\langle M, \mathcal{L} \rangle$, where M is a set of mathematical axioms[6] of a first-order language L_M (the signature of L_M contains the relation and function symbols axiomatised by M) and $\mathcal{L}$ is a logical system. We say that π is a *proof* in $\langle M, \mathcal{L} \rangle$ iff π is a proof in $\mathcal{L}$ and $a(\pi) \subseteq M$. We shall use $\mathbf{P}_{\langle M, \mathcal{L} \rangle}$ to denote the set of the proofs in $\langle M, \mathcal{L} \rangle$.

The consequence $c(\pi)$ of a proof in $\langle M, \mathcal{L} \rangle$ will be called a *theorem* of $\langle M, \mathcal{L} \rangle$. To indicate that a formula H is a theorem of $\langle M, \mathcal{L} \rangle$, we will write $\langle M, \mathcal{L} \rangle \vdash H$.

For two mathematical systems $\langle M_1, \mathcal{L}_1 \rangle$ and $\langle M_2, \mathcal{L}_2 \rangle$ with (possibly) different languages L_{M_1} and L_{M_2}, $\langle M_1, \mathcal{L}_1 \rangle$ is *representable* in $\langle M_2, \mathcal{L}_2 \rangle$, or $\langle M_1, \mathcal{L}_1 \rangle \sqsubseteq \langle M_2, \mathcal{L}_2 \rangle$,[7] if there is a translation ρ_L of L_{M_1} into L_{M_2} and a function

$$\rho \,:\, \mathbf{P}_{\langle M_1, \mathcal{L}_1 \rangle} \to \mathbf{P}_{\langle M_2, \mathcal{L}_2 \rangle}$$

such that, for every $\pi \in \mathbf{P}_{\langle M_1, \mathcal{L}_1 \rangle}$, $\rho_L(c(\pi)) = c(\rho(\pi))$. Of course, the relation between the two systems depends on the properties of ρ_L. We will consider only functions ρ_L such that, for every $H \in L_{M_1} \cap L_{M_2}$, $\rho_L(H) = H$. This implies that, in the common language, every theorem of the first system is also a theorem of the second one.

$\langle M_1, \mathcal{L}_1 \rangle$ and $\langle M_2, \mathcal{L}_2 \rangle$ are *equivalent*, or $\langle M_1, \mathcal{L}_1 \rangle \asymp \langle M_2, \mathcal{L}_2 \rangle$, iff $\langle M_1, \mathcal{L}_1 \rangle \sqsubseteq \langle M_2, \mathcal{L}_2 \rangle$ and $\langle M_2, \mathcal{L}_2 \rangle \sqsubseteq \langle M_1, \mathcal{L}_1 \rangle$. This implies that, in the common language, the two systems have the same set of theorems.

Two relevant and remarkable examples of equivalence are:

$$M \vdash_{CL} N \Rightarrow \langle M \cup N, CL \rangle \asymp \langle M, CL \rangle \tag{2}$$

$$\langle M \cup \{\forall x. (r(x) \leftrightarrow F(x))\}, CL \rangle \asymp \langle M, CL \rangle \,. \tag{3}$$

(2) and (3) are well-known examples of *conservative extensions*.[8]

---

[5] The relation $\sqsubseteq$ is reflexive and transitive.

[6] A mathematical axiom is any closed formula that is not a logical axiom.

[7] The relation $\sqsubseteq$ is reflexive and transitive.

[8] In (3), $\forall x. (r(x) \leftrightarrow F(x))$ is a *definition axiom* which introduces a new relation symbol $r(x)$.

Finally we shall use

$$\langle M, \mathcal{A}, \mathcal{L} \rangle$$

(where $\mathcal{A}$ is a set of formulas), to denote the subsystem of $\langle M, \mathcal{L} \rangle$ such that: π is a proof in $\langle M, \mathcal{A}, \mathcal{L} \rangle$ iff π is a proof in $\langle M, \mathcal{L} \rangle$ and $c(\pi) \in \mathcal{A}$. In other words, the proofs in $\langle M, \mathcal{A}, \mathcal{L} \rangle$ are just the proofs in $\langle M, \mathcal{L} \rangle$ of formulas in $\mathcal{A}$. We call $\langle M, \mathcal{A}, \mathcal{L} \rangle$ the *restriction* of $\langle M, \mathcal{L} \rangle$ to $\mathcal{A}$.[9]

Restrictions of systems will be called *restricted systems*. For such systems, the definitions of $\sqsubseteq$ and $\asymp$ are as before.

4 A Formal Framework for Deductive Synthesis

In this section, we summarise our framework for deductive synthesis of logic programs in [7, 8]. For logic programming notation, we shall follow [9] closely. Atoms will be denoted by $A, A_1, \ldots$, literals by $L, L_1, \ldots$, clauses by $C, C_1, \ldots$, and substitutions by $\sigma, \theta, \ldots$ However, goals will be denoted by $\leftarrow G, \leftarrow G_1, \ldots$, where $G, G_1, \ldots$ are sequences of atoms or literals.

4.1 Logic Programs as Axiomatisations

In our formal framework, logic programs are regarded as (first-order) axiomatisations.

For a *definite* program P_D, the corresponding (finite) set of axioms, denoted by $Ax(P_D)$, is given by

$$Ax(P_D) = \{ Ax(C) \mid C \text{ is a clause of } P_D \}$$

where[10]

$$
\begin{aligned}
Ax(A \leftarrow) &= \forall(A) \\
Ax(A \leftarrow A_1, \ldots, A_k) &= \forall(A_1 \wedge \cdots \wedge A_k \rightarrow A) \,.
\end{aligned}
$$

For a *normal* program P_N, the corresponding axiomatisation is just its completion $Comp(P_N)$. However, for our purposes it will be more convenient, as will become evident later, to use a set of axioms which is logically equivalent to $Comp(P_N)$. We shall call this equivalent set $Comp^*(P_N)$, it contains:

- *Equality axioms.*[11]

- *Success axioms.* For every normal clause C of P_N, $Ax(C)$ (as defined above) is a success axiom of $Comp^*(P_N)$.

- *Default axioms.* For every predicate symbol $p(\underline{x})$, if there is no clause of P_N containing p in its head, then $\forall \underline{x}. \neg p(\underline{x})$ is a default axiom of $Comp^*(P_N)$.

---

[9] Note that some formulas in $\mathcal{A}$ may not have proofs in $\langle M, \mathcal{L} \rangle$ at all. In a specification, $\mathcal{A}$ is $Ans(G)$.

[10] We shall use $\forall(F)$ to denote the universal closure of a formula F.

[11] See the equality theory on p. 79 in [9].

- *Failure axioms.* For every predicate symbol $p(\underline{x})$ occurring in the head of some clause, if

$$\forall \underline{x}. \, (p(\underline{x}) \leftrightarrow E_1 \vee \cdots \vee E_k)$$

is the completed definition of $p(\underline{x})$, then

$$\forall \underline{x}. \, (\neg E_1 \wedge \cdots \wedge \neg E_k \rightarrow \neg p(\underline{x}))$$

belongs to $Comp^*(P_N)$. We call this the failure axiom of $p(\underline{x})$.

Equality axioms, success axioms, default axioms, and failure axioms are the only formulas which belong to $Comp^*(P_N)$.

4.2 Mathematical Systems in CL, SLD and SLDNF

We will consider logic program synthesis in the framework of mathematical systems based on the following (first-order) logical systems: classical logic CL, SLD-logic and $SLDNF$-logic.

A mathematical system based on CL is denoted by $\langle S, CL \rangle$, where S is a set of first-order mathematical axioms [12] and CL a deductive logical system for classical logic. S will be assumed to be *finite* or *recursive*. In examples, proofs in systems $\langle S, CL \rangle$ will be developed in an informal way, but it will be clear that they can be formalised.

Mathematical systems based on SLD-logic and $SLDNF$-logic are denoted by $\langle Ax(P_D), SLD \rangle$ and $\langle Comp^*(P_N), SLDNF \rangle$ respectively. For our purposes, we formalise the proofs in SLD and $SLDNF$ logical systems as follows:[13]

The set $\mathbf{P}_{SLD}$ of SLD-proofs and the set $\mathbf{P}_{SLDNF}$ of $SLDNF$-proofs are respectively the sets of "proofs" of the forms

$$Ax(P_D) \Rightarrow_\Gamma G_D\theta \quad \text{and} \quad Comp^*(P_N) \Rightarrow_{\Gamma'} G_N\theta'$$

where P_D is a definite program, G_D a definite goal, and Γ is a SLD-refutation of $\leftarrow G_D$ with program P_D and computed answer θ; P_N is a normal program, G_N a normal goal, and Γ' is a $SLDNF$-refutation of $\leftarrow G_N$ with program P_N and computed answer θ'. For SLD-proofs and $SLDNF$-proofs, the *assumptions* are $Ax(P_D)$ and $Comp^*(P_N)$, and the *consequence* is $\bigwedge(G_D\theta)$ and $\bigwedge(G_N\theta')$, respectively.[14]

5 Deductive Synthesis of Logic Programs

Now we introduce our model of deductive synthesis of logic programs from logic specifications.

---

[12] That is, first-order closed formulas of some first-order language.

[13] We do not need to consider any precise representation of SLD- or $SLDNF$-refutations.

[14] We use $\bigwedge\{F_1, \ldots, F_n\}$ to denote $F_1 \wedge \cdots \wedge F_n$.

5.1 The Initial Specification

First of all, we have to build the logic specification. We assume that we want to compute a relation expressed by a formula R of a specification framework $\langle S, CL \rangle$. The first step is to introduce a new relation symbol r through the definition axiom $\forall (r \leftrightarrow R)$. Using r, we give the set G of the goals to be answered and the set $Ans(G)$ of the related possible answers. In this way, we build a restricted mathematical system:

$$\langle S \cup D_0, Ans(G), CL \rangle \tag{4}$$

where $D_0 = \{\forall (r \leftrightarrow R)\}$. We call (4) the *initial specification*. Every $g \in G$ will be called a *goal* and every $g^* \in Ans(g)$ will be called a *possible answer* of g.

If the specification framework completely defines the relation r,[15] the valid answers can be defined as follows. A possible answer is a valid *answer* iff it is provable in $\langle S \cup D_0, CL \rangle$.

For example, consider the problem to decide whether or not a natural number is even and, if it is, to compute its integer half. An adequate specification framework is first-order Peano Arithmetic PA, containing the usual axioms for $=, s, +, \cdot$, and the first-order induction schema. The relation "Z is half of a natural number X" is defined in PA by the formula $Z + Z = X$; so we introduce the definition axiom D_0:

$$\forall Z, X. (half(Z, X) \leftrightarrow Z + Z = X)$$

and build the specification[16]

$$\langle PA \cup \{D_0\}, Ans_g(\{half(Z, n) \mid n \text{ is a numeral}\}), CL \rangle$$

where $Ans_g(half(Z, n)) = \{half(m, n) \mid m \text{ is a numeral}\}$[17]. Note that Ans_g specifies the desired behaviour; indeed, if no (valid) answer exists, then n is odd; otherwise there is a unique valid answer $h(m, n)$, containing the integer half m of n.

5.2 The Synthesis Process

Starting from an initial specification $\langle S \cup D_0, Ans(G), CL \rangle$, the aim of a deductive synthesis process is to find a logic program P such that[18]

$$\langle Ax(P), Ans(G), SLD \rangle \asymp \langle S \cup D_0, Ans(G), CL \rangle .$$

Now in order to answer the goals of G, we may have to use some relation expressed (in the language of S) by some non-atomic formula H. Since clauses contain only atomic formulas, we represent H by a new relation symbol h, introduced by a *definition axiom* $\forall (h \leftrightarrow H)$. Thus the synthesis process can be formalised as a sequence of the form

$$\langle S \cup D_0, Ans(G), CL \rangle \Rightarrow \langle S \cup D_1 \cup Ax(P_1), Ans(G), CL \rangle \Rightarrow \cdots$$
$$\Rightarrow \langle S \cup D_n \cup Ax(P_n), Ans(G), CL \rangle$$

---

[15] That is, a tuple $t_1, \ldots, t_n$ is in r iff $r(t_1, \ldots, t_n)$ is provable. One can consider also parametric or loose specifications; this case will be briefly discussed in Section 6.

[16] A numeral is a ground term of the form $s(s(\ldots s(0)\ldots))$.

[17] That is, g in Ans_g stands for *ground*

[18] For the sake of simplicity, we shall assume that P is a definite program.

where $D_0 \subseteq D_1 \subseteq \cdots \subseteq D_n$ are definition axioms, $P_1 \subseteq \cdots \subseteq P_n$ are logic programs, and

$$S \cup D_k \cup Ax(P_k) \vdash_{CL} Ax(P_{k+1}), \quad \text{for } 1 \leq k < n .\tag{5}$$

By insisting on (5) (and using (2) and (3)) we can prove the *partial correctness* of every P_h (see [7, 8] for details), but not total correctness. A synthesis process *correctly halts* when the final program P_n is *totally correct*, i.e. when the following holds:[19]

$$\langle Ax(P_n), Ans(G), SLD \rangle \asymp \langle S \cup D_0, Ans(G), CL \rangle .$$

Note that for total correctness, we do not require that $Ax(P_n)$ and S_0 are equivalent, but only that they are equivalent as systems *restricted* to $Ans(G)$.[20]

In order to have a practical criterion for total correctness which will enable us to know when to stop the synthesis process, we shall make use of *failure axioms*: we will stop as soon as we can prove that

$$\langle S \cup D_n \cup Ax(P_n), CL \rangle \vdash Fax_n$$

where Fax_n contains the failure axioms of the relations defined in D_n, according to the synthesised program P_n.

If the above condition holds, *termination* implies *total correctness*.[21] Of course, we need also some method to state halting, but this does not concern us here and we will only deal with examples where halting is obvious.

The above criterion works in the cases where the specification framework completely defines the relations involved in the synthesis process. But it can be extended to parametric specifications: here one has to prove the failure axioms only for the non-parametric relations. A deeper study of failure axioms in program synthesis will be given in a subsequent paper.

Finally, we can extend our model to $SLDNF$ to obtain a final program P such that

$$\langle Comp^*(P), Ans(g), SLDNF \rangle \asymp \langle S_0, Ans(g), CL \rangle .$$

Because the synthesis process is an incremental one, here we have to avoid non-monotonicity. When we add a clause C to our current program, we introduce (and prove) only its *success* axiom $Ax(C)$ in our axiomatisation. We only introduce a *default* axiom $\forall x. \neg p(x)$ if we can prove it.

Furthermore, we only introduce the *failure* axiom of a predicate p when we have introduced *all* the clauses having p in their heads. In addition, to ensure partial correctness, we need to prove all the failure axioms that we introduce. This implies that if in intermediate synthesis steps there are failure axioms which cannot be proved, then partial correctness does not hold. However, as soon as all the failure axioms become provable, then partial correctness is 'restored'.

We conclude this section with an example to illustrate our model of deductive synthesis.

---

[19]Note that $\langle Ax(P_n), Ans(G), SLD \rangle \asymp \langle Ax(P_n), Ans(G), CL \rangle$.

[20]In general, $\langle Ax(P_n), CL \rangle$ is a proper subsystem of $\langle S_0, CL \rangle$, even if P_n is totally correct. We will use this fact in our distinction between synthesis and transformation.

[21]By termination we mean that for every goal of G, we obtain a positive or a negative answer. Since failure axioms guarantee that negative answers are correct answers, we have a program that is totally correct with respect to G.

Example 5.1 We start from the initial specification considered in Subsection 5.1:

$$\langle PA \cup \{D_0\}, Ans(\{half(Z,n) \,|\, n \text{ is a numeral}\}), CL \rangle \;.$$

We can get a clause for $half(0,X)$ from D_0:[22]

$$half(0,X) \leftrightarrow 0+0 = X \leftrightarrow X = 0 \;.$$

This first step of the synthesis process gives:

$$\langle PA \cup \{D_0, Ax(half(0,X) \leftarrow X = 0)\}, \{half(Z,n) \,|\, n \text{ is a numeral}\}, CL \rangle \;.$$

The corresponding failure axiom is

$$\forall Z, X. \, (\neg Z = 0 \wedge \neg X = 0 \rightarrow \neg half(Z,X)) \;.$$

We can prove its negation in $PA \cup D_0$, and therefore our current program $half(0,X) \leftarrow X = 0$ is only partially, but not totally, correct. So we have to search for some other clause.

Suppose we try to find a clause for $half(s(I),X)$ as follows:

$$
\begin{aligned}
half(s(I),X) \quad &\leftrightarrow \quad s(I) + s(I) = X \\
&\leftrightarrow \quad s(s(I+I)) = X \\
&\leftrightarrow \quad \exists W. \, (s(s(W)) = X \wedge half(I,W))
\end{aligned}
$$

and so we get

$$
\begin{aligned}
\langle PA \cup \{D_0, \\
Ax(half(0,X) \leftarrow X = 0), Ax(half(s(I),X) \leftarrow s(s(W)) = X, half(I,W))\}, \\
\{half(Z,n) \,|\, n \text{ is a numeral}\}, CL \rangle \;.
\end{aligned}
$$

Now the failure axiom is

$$
\begin{aligned}
\forall Z, X. \, ((\neg(X = 0 \wedge Z = 0) \wedge \neg \exists W, I. \, (s(s(W)) = X \wedge Z = s(I) \wedge \\
half(I,W)) \rightarrow \neg half(Z,X))
\end{aligned}
$$

and it can be proved. So our program is totally correct, since it halts for all the goals considered. ◇

6 Specification

In this section, we discuss the activity of constructing a specification for deductive synthesis of logic programs. In general, specification is of course only an informal process of translating an informal, and hence loose and often incomplete statement of some problem into a precise specification, which could be formal or informal. Clearly there is no formal method for proving the correctness of specifications.

In our framework, the aim of the specification phase is to build up a *logical* specification, formalised as a restricted mathematical system of the form $\langle S, \mathcal{G}, CL \rangle$.[23] The *specification framework S* may be completely given, though

---

[22] This is provable in $PA \cup D_0$.

[23] Although we only consider CL, in general we may have different kinds of logics, such as modal, temporal or higher order logics.

more usually it has to be built and maintained (i.e. added to whenever necessary). We shall discuss two ways of constructing such a specification.

Firstly, if we start with an informal (but precise) idea of the problem and know nothing about S, we can use a process similar to deductive (program) synthesis, and build up the specification, i.e. S and $\mathcal{G}$, in a stepwise manner. The idea is that if we can construct a clause set, i.e. a logic program P, which represents the problem we have in mind, then we can use $Ax(P)$ as S. Thus, we get a specification together with a program that satisfies it. However, in our framework, this process is not program synthesis, since every step gives rise to new axioms which add to the current incomplete specification of the problem in question. We will call it *specification synthesis* to distinguish it from program synthesis. Our specification synthesis corresponds to the construction of logic descriptions of [1]. We now give a simple example of specification synthesis.

Example 6.1 Consider the problem of finding all the prefixes of a list L. The first step of formalising the problem is to state a logic language for lists and its intended interpretation.

Suppose we choose the following language. It is many-sorted, with sorts *Els* (elements) and *Lists* (finite lists of elements), and its symbols are:

- the constant *nil* (the empty list) and the function symbol '.' such that $X.L$ is the list with head X and tail L;

- the (polymorphic) identity relation symbol $=$ on *Lists* and *Els*.

Now, to specify our problem, we introduce the relation $prefix(L_1, L_2)$, meaning "L_1 is a prefix of L_2, i.e. L_2 is of the form $L_1 \ldots$", and try and find a set of clauses characterising *prefix* according to its intended meaning.

Suppose we try to define *prefix* by using the clause:

$$prefix(X.L_1, X.L_2) \leftarrow prefix(L_1, L_2) .$$

Now $Ax(prefix(X.L_1, X.L_2) \leftarrow prefix(L_1, L_2))$ agrees with our intended interpretation. However, the failure axiom

$$\forall(\neg \exists X, L_1, L_2 : (A = X.L_1 \land B = X.L_2 \land prefix(L_1, L_2)) \rightarrow \neg prefix(A, B))$$

imposes, for instance, that $prefix(A, B)$ is *false* if $A = nil$, contrary to the intended meaning of *prefix*. So we add the clause

$$prefix(nil, L) \leftarrow$$

where $Ax(prefix(nil, L))$ is valid in our intended interpretation.

Again, we analyse the failure axiom. It is now

$$\forall(\neg A = nil \land \neg \exists X, L_1, L_2 : (A = X.L_1 \land B = X.L_2 \land$$
$$prefix(L_1, L_2)) \rightarrow \neg prefix(A, B))$$

and agrees with our intended interpretation.

At this point, we have synthesised both a program and an axiomatisation. Of course, the program is correct with respect to the axiomatisation, by construction.[24]   ◇

---

[24] However, it is worth repeating that there is no formal way of proving the correctness of the axiomatisation with respect to our intended meaning.

Secondly, we can construct a specification, i.e. S and $\mathcal{G}$, in the framework of a given well-understood and expressive formal system, which we shall call a *specification framework*. In this situation, we can define *prefix* by a definition axiom, say D, directly in terms of the axioms of the specification framework SF, to yield the logical specification $\langle SF \cup D, Ans(prefix), CL \rangle$. Of course, such a situation is the norm in our framework.[25] We now illustrate with an example.

Example 6.2 Suppose we have to specify the *prefix* problem, but this time we are given the following specification framework for lists, which we denote by S_{list}. It contains the usual identity axioms and the axioms characterising the basic operations on lists, as follows:

- $\forall X, L. (\neg X.L = nil)$

- $\forall X_1, X_2, L_1, L_2. (X_1.L_1 = X_2.L_2 \rightarrow X_1 = X_2 \wedge Y_1 = Y_2)$

- induction schema on lists, for every formula H:

$$H(nil) \wedge \forall X, L. (H(L) \rightarrow H(X.L)) \rightarrow \forall L. H(L) .$$

Suppose S_{list} also contains, among other things,[26] the relation $occ(L, i, X)$, which means that X occurs at place i in L, characterised by the following axioms:

- $\forall L, X, Y, i. (occ(L, i, X) \wedge occ(L, i, Y) \rightarrow X = Y)$

- $\forall X, i. \neg occ(nil, i, X)$

- $\forall L, X, i. occ(X.L, 0, X)$

- $\forall L, X, Y, i. (occ(X.L, s(i), Y) \leftrightarrow occ(L, i, Y))$

Then in S_{list}, we can define *prefix* by the following *definition axiom*:

$$D_{prefix} : \quad prefix(L, M) \leftrightarrow \forall i, X. (occ(L, i, X) \rightarrow occ(M, i, X)) \tag{6}$$

and the initial specification for the *prefix* problem is

$$\langle S_{list} \cup D_{prefix}, Ans(\{prefix(M, n), n \text{ is ground}\}), CL \rangle$$

◇

The specification constructed in Example 6.2 will be the starting point for (deductive) program synthesis. In contrast, the specification constructed in Example 6.1 above directly represents a program. This would seem to suggest that it would always be advantageous to use our deductive synthesis approach to do specification synthesis. However, this is not the case. In fact, there are many advantages doing program synthesis. For example, consistency problems can be avoided using program synthesis methods which preserve consistency. Furthermore, starting from the same specification, we can synthesise many

---

[25] It is what we assumed in our model of deductive synthesis of programs.

[26] Such as the sort *Nat* of natural numbers and the language *LN* and the axioms of *PA*.

different algorithms. Moreover, using correct synthesis methods, all the synthesised programs are correct with respect to the specification. Consequently, once we have evidence that our starting specification agrees with our intended meaning,[27] the correctness of programs is no longer a problem. Finally, during the synthesis, we can use all the knowledge developed in the specification framework.

Of course, the two methods for constructing specification can be mixed. For instance, it may happen that, while synthesising programs to compute the relations in question, we may discover that we need to add new axioms. In this way, we can enrich the given specification framework, thus obtaining a new one. We will discuss this further in Section 9.

To conclude this section, we now briefly discuss *parametric specification frameworks*.

Frameworks like *PA* are not parametric. For a non-parametric framework S,[28] we assume that there is an intended term model, i.e. a model whose elements can be represented by suitable ground "normal" terms (e.g. in *PA* natural numbers are represented by numerals). We say that S completely defines a relation R by a formula $F_R(\underline{X})$ iff the following holds: for every normal $\underline{t}$, if $\underline{t}$ is in R, then $F_R(\underline{t})$ is provable in S, otherwise $\neg F_R(\underline{t})$ is provable. This definition is very close to the notion of correctness in [1] and allows us to use negation in an appropriate way.

In general, parametric specifications cannot be used to completely define relations. For example, if in S_{list} the sort *Els* is a parameter, we have no ground terms for this sort. Then no relation containing some non-empty list in its domain can be completely defined, since we do not have ground terms denoting non-empty lists. Another example is the use of parametric relation symbols. For instance, we may assume some partial ordering relation without completely defining it (i.e. we give only the axioms of partial ordering).

An instance of a parametric framework S is a set of axioms $S_I \supset S$ completely characterising the parameters. Now, consider a class $\mathcal{R}$ of relations, containing a relation R_I for each possible instance S_I of S; we say that a formula $F_{\mathcal{R}}(\underline{X})$ *parametrically defines* $\mathcal{R}$ in S iff, for every instance S_I, $F_{\mathcal{R}}(\underline{X})$ completely defines (in S_I) the relation R_I. For example, in lists with parametric sort *Els*, for every instance I of *Els* we have a corresponding relation $prefix_I(X,Y)$, i.e. we have a class of relations; one can see that the definition axiom D_{prefix} parametrically defines this class. Synthesis from parametric definitions works as in the complete ones, using failure axioms as a sufficient criterion to stop synthesis. A deeper analysis of this will be one of our future research topics.

7   (Deductive) Program Synthesis

In this section, we will use the model of deductive synthesis described in Section 5 to illustrate the difference between specification synthesis and program synthesis for the *prefix* problem. We shall assume that the initial specification is given in a general specification framework (as in Example 6.2), and

---

[27] The problem of the correctness of the formal specification with respect to the informal problem remains, but it can now be studied once for all.

[28] For the sake of simplicity, we omit the logical system *CL* here.

use our deductive synthesis model to synthesise a program for *prefix* from this specification.

Example 7.1 The initial specification is

$$\langle S_{list} \cup D_{prefix}, \{prefix(m,n) \mid n \text{ is ground}\}, CL \rangle$$

as defined in Example 6.2.

In order to compare program synthesis with specification synthesis, we choose synthesis steps that are identical to the ones in Example 6.1. The first step is to prove (in $S_{list} \cup D_{prefix}$):[29]

$$
\begin{aligned}
prefix(X.L_1, X.L_2) \quad &\leftrightarrow \quad \forall i, Y. (occ(X.L_1, i, Y) \rightarrow occ(X.L_2, i, Y)) \\
&\leftrightarrow \quad \forall i, Y. (occ(L_1, i, Y) \rightarrow occ(L_2, i, Y)) \\
&\leftrightarrow \quad prefix(L_1, L_2)
\end{aligned}
$$

and so the result of this first step is the same as that of the first step in Example 6.1. However, here we have a formal proof of partial correctness in S_{list}.

Moreover, we can prove the negation of the failure axiom of the clause synthesised. Therefore total correctness does not hold, and we go on with a further synthesis step, which is:

$$
\begin{aligned}
prefix(nil, M) \quad &\leftrightarrow \quad \forall i, X. (occ(nil, i, X) \rightarrow occ(M, i, X)) \\
&\leftrightarrow \quad true
\end{aligned}
$$

At this point we can prove in S_{list} the failure axiom. Since our program now halts for the goals considered, we have a totally correct program P_{prefix} and we stop the synthesis. ◇

The difference with respect to specification synthesis is that here the correctness of every synthesis step has been proved in the specification framework S_{list}.

Furthermore, we can easily see that the mathematical systems

$$\langle Ax(P_{prefix}), CL \rangle$$

(corresponding to the extracted program P_{prefix}) is a *very small sub-theory* of the initial specification.[30] This sums up our view on (deductive) program synthesis: it extracts a small sub-theory (formalised as a logic program) which specialises the initial specification to just the goals specified.

In contrast, as we shall see in the next section, *program transformation* means transformation of a small (mathematical) system, representing a logic program only (but not a specification framework), into an equivalent system, representing another program.

---

[29] In particular, the second bi- implication is a useful theorem of S_{list} which could be added to our specification framework, thus enriching our knowledge base.

[30] Even considering the completion $\langle Comp^*(P_{prefix}), CL \rangle$, we obtain a proper subsystem.

8 Program Transformation

Program transformation starts from a program and gives rise to another program. In our framework, both logic programs and specifications are formalised as mathematical systems. However, mathematical systems for programs employ the logical system SLD whilst those for specifications employ CL.[31] If we consider CL as a logical computing mechanism, just as SLD, then specifications are "programs" using CL as the (inefficient) computing mechanism, and any distinction between logic specifications and logic programs, and hence between program synthesis and program transformation, can only be based on pragmatic considerations rather than logical ones.

However, we think that a distinction can be proposed that is based not on the distinction between CL and SLD, nor on the way of doing synthesis or transformation. Such a distinction can be based on a classification of mathematical systems into those which are *specifications* and those which represent logic programs. Clearly, the latter is a subclass of the former.

We say that a mathematical system $\langle S, CL \rangle$ *represents a program* iff $S = Ax(P)$, for some program P, or it is *equivalent* to some logic program P. Different equivalence notions may be considered. Two of them are, for example, the following ones.

$\langle S, CL \rangle$ is equivalent to P if there are definition axioms D such that[32]

$$\langle S \cup D, CL \rangle \asymp \langle Ax(P) \cup D, CL \rangle \tag{7}$$

and every definite goal provable in $Ax(P) \cup D$ is provable also in $Ax(P)$, i.e. no solution is lost by omitting D.

In the second definition, instead of (7), we require

$$\langle S \cup D, CL \rangle \asymp \langle Comp^*(P), CL \rangle \, .$$

In this case every finite axiomatisation represents a program. Indeed, S can be transformed into an equivalent $Comp^*(P)$ according to [9].

Thus deriving a program P from S does not extract a small part of S (as in the case of deductive program synthesis), but an *equivalent* axiomatisation. Rather it can be seen as a *transformation* of a "program" S, specified using the inefficient computing mechanism CL, into a program P such that, by the completeness of SLD, the (efficient) computing mechanism SLD can be used instead of CL.

In our framework, we regard (*deductive*) *program synthesis* as deriving a program from a mathematical system representing a *specification*; whereas deriving a program from a mathematical system representing a program is considered as *program transformation*. It is worth repeating that, in our framework, program synthesis derives a (very) small sub-theory of the initial specification, while program transformation derives an axiomatisation equivalent to that of the initial program.

For program transformation it is possible to apply techniques which cannot be applied, in general, to synthesis. Total correctness is not an issue here, since

---

[31] Our considerations hold for any specification logic and any logic programming system.

[32] We compare the two axiomatisations not as systems restricted to any kind of goals, but as unrestricted mathematical systems based on CL. A translation ρ_L may be involved, corresponding to the definition axioms of the relations computed by P.

any adequate notion of equivalence should imply it. The main problem for transformation is then to preserve the equivalence of the mathematical systems involved, using CL or, at least, SLD.

Here we consider a transformation method working in CL, and based on the general model of Section 5 but with the following difference. Instead of proving total correctness, we prove (7) by proving[33]

$$\langle Ax(P_n) \cup D_n, CL \rangle \vdash S . \tag{8}$$

and we then show that no solution is lost by omitting D_n.

Let us explain with two simple examples.

Example 8.1 This example is a transformation involving SLD programs. Therefore the logic programming system remains the same, and transformation modifies the programs. We start from the following program P_{fib} to compute Fibonacci numbers (we omit the usual clauses for $+$):

$$
\begin{aligned}
f(0, s(0)) &\leftarrow \\
f(s(0), s(0)) &\leftarrow \\
f(s(s(I)), Z) &\leftarrow f(I, Z_1), f(s(I), Z_2), +(Z_1, Z_2, Z)
\end{aligned}
$$

Of course, the corresponding mathematical system

$$\langle Ax(P_{fib}), CL \rangle$$

represents a program. We can transform it into a more efficient program in the usual way. First of all, we introduce a new relation ff, by the following definition axiom D_{ff}:

$$D_{ff} \; : \; ff(X, A, B) \leftrightarrow f(X, A) \wedge f(s(X), B) .$$

The transformation is carried out as deductive synthesis, but here, instead of total correctness, we test for the condition (8).

In the first transformation steps, we can prove, in $Ax(P_{fib}) \cup D_{ff}$, the axioms

$$Ax(ff(0, s(0), s(0)) \leftarrow) , \; Ax(ff(s(I), A, B) \leftarrow ff(I, H, A), +(I, H, B)) . \tag{9}$$

However, no goal in f can be solved by $Ax(P_{fib})$, since there are no clauses for f. So we add the axiom:

$$Ax(f(X, A) \leftarrow ff(X, A, B)) . \tag{10}$$

Let P_{ff} be the program containing the clauses in (9) and (10). To prove that no solution is lost by omitting D_{ff}, we can prove for instance that it is true in the minimum Herbrandt model. Hence we have our final equivalent program.

$\diamond$

In the above example, transformation involves definite programs, and the computing mechanism is not changed. In the next example, we transform an equational program into a logic one. Transformation is carried out in CL, which contains both the starting equational system and the target SLD system.

---

[33] Of course, this cannot be proved in program synthesis, since in general $Ax(P_n) \cup D_n$ (and even $Comp^*(P_n) \cup D_n$) is properly contained in $S \cup D_n$.

Example 8.2 The initial "program" S is the following equational theory for computing + for numerals (the usual axioms for identity will be assumed):

$$\{\forall x.\, x + 0 = x, \forall x, y.\, x + s(y) = s(x + y)\}$$

and the corresponding mathematical system is $\langle S, REW \rangle$, where REW is a rewriting system for example.

The first step to transform this equational system into a relational one is to introduce the definition axiom

$$D_0 \ : \ \forall x, y, z.\,(sum(x, y, z) \leftrightarrow x + y = z)\,.$$

Then to perform the transformation on S, we start a deductive synthesis process from the initial specification:

$$\langle \{\forall x.\, x + 0 = x, \forall x, y.\, x + s(y) = s(x + y)\} \cup$$
$$\{\forall x, y, z.\,(sum(x, y, z) \leftrightarrow x + y = z)\},$$
$$\{sum(m, n, Z) \,|\, m, n \text{ are numerals}\}, CL\rangle$$

where the equational goals have been mapped into relational ones.
The first step is to derive:

$$sum(X, 0, Z) \ \leftrightarrow \ X + 0 = Z \ \leftrightarrow \ X = Z$$

and we obtain a program P_0 containing the clause $sum(X, 0, X) \leftarrow$. At this point, however, we can prove only one of the axioms of S, i.e.

$$\langle \{Ax(sum(X, 0, X) \leftarrow), D_0\}\rangle \vdash \forall x.\, x + 0 = x\,.$$

So we go on as follows:

$$sum(X, s(I), Z) \ \leftrightarrow \ X + s(I) = Z \ \leftrightarrow \ s(X + I) = Z$$
$$\leftarrow \ \exists W.\,(Z = s(W) \wedge X + I = W)^{34}$$
$$\leftrightarrow \ \exists W.\,(Z = s(W) \wedge sum(X, I, W))$$

and get the clause

$$sum(X, s(I), s(W)) \leftarrow sum(X, I, W)\,.$$

Now it can be proved easily that:

$$\langle \{Ax(sum(X, s(I), s(W)) \leftarrow sum(X, I, W)), D_0\}, CL\rangle$$
$$\vdash \ \forall x, i.\, x + s(i) = s(x + i)\,.$$

To prove that no solution is lost by omitting D_0, we can show for instance that in the minimum Herbrandt model $sum(X, Y, Z)$ defines a total function $Z = f(X, Y)$. Therefore we have obtained our final logic program that is equivalent to the original equational one. $\diamond$

---

[34] The implication follows from identity axioms. A bi-implication does not hold, since S_0 does not contain axioms for successor s.

9 Mixing Specification with Synthesis and Transformation

Although in the previous sections we have made clear and formal distinctions between specification, synthesis and transformation, we have at the same time also hinted at their close inter-relationships by applying our deductive synthesis model to both specification and transformation. Indeed, to emphasise this, we will now give examples of how in methodological terms it may be desirable and possible to mix specification with synthesis and transformation respectively.

9.1 Specification and Synthesis

First we discuss specification and its relation with synthesis. In our deductive synthesis model, we assume that a specification is constructed using a (given) specification framework. The idea is that a specification framework is based on a well consolidated set of axioms. We assume that new specifications are always introduced by *definition axioms*, and synthesis gives rise to conservative extensions. Consequently, we have no consistency problems. Moreover, synthesis gives rise to extensions where the properties of the old relations are not affected by the new axioms. The latter point is important, since adding new programs does not affect the correctness of the old ones.

Of course, ideally we would want to be given specification frameworks that are expressive and powerful. In practice, however, often we have to build specification frameworks ourselves. In such a situation, we can imagine that we start from an inadequate axiomatisation and go through an initial experimental phase, whereby this axiomatisation is changed or enriched. In our framework, this phase may be performed as specification synthesis (as we saw in Section 6), during which experimental attempts are made at specifying new relations or synthesising new programs. Let us see some examples.

Example 9.1 The specification framework S_{list} of Section 6 may be seen as an initial stage in the process of building up a specification framework for lists. Let us try to define the permutation relation $perm(L_1, L_2)$. An obvious way is to say that every element X has the same number of occurrences in both L_1 and L_2. However, we cannot express the relation "number of occurrences" by a definition axiom. So this is a primitive relation (which we shall call $nocc(X, L, N)$) characterised by *new* axioms, which can be obtained for example by the following specification synthesis steps:

$$nocc(X, nil, 0) \leftarrow \qquad \text{(Failure axiom wrong.)}$$
$$nocc(X, X.L, s(I)) \leftarrow nocc(X, L, I) \qquad \text{(Failure axiom wrong.)}$$
$$nocc(X, Y.L, I) \leftarrow \neg(X = Y), nocc(X, L, I) \text{ (Failure axiom correct.)}$$

and the corresponding success and failure axioms characterise *nocc*.
At this point, we can define the relation $perm(L_1, L_2)$ as follows:

$$\forall(perm(L_1, L_2) \leftrightarrow$$
$$\forall X, N, M. (nocc(X, L_1, N) \land nocc(X, L_2, M) \rightarrow N = M)) .$$

Now we have a richer specification context and we can go on with our specification. $\Diamond$

Example 9.2 Suppose we want to specify sorting problems. To do so, we require an ordering relation $\leq$ on the sort *Els*. This relation introduces a *constraint* on the parameter *Els*. To avoid constraint propagation in previously developed programs, it is better to introduce a new specification framework S_{olist}. It is equal to S_{list}, but the language now contains the new relation symbol $\leq$. Even if we do not give axioms on $\leq$, we can specify ordered lists for instance as follows:

$$\forall(ord(L) \leftrightarrow (occ(L, I, X) \wedge occ(L, s(I), Y) \rightarrow X \leq Y)) .$$

It is easy to see that we can synthesise a program for deciding *ord*. Now, we can specify *sort* as follows:

$$\forall(sort(L, M) \leftrightarrow (ord(M) \wedge perm(L, M))) .$$

However, if we try to synthesise a sorting algorithm, we discover that $\leq$ must be a total ordering, and we have to add the corresponding axioms to our specification framework. Again such axioms introduce new constraints on the parameter *Els*, which are not needed, for example for the program deciding the predicate *ord*. Therefore it is better to introduce a new specification framework S_{tolist} containing the total ordering axioms on $\leq$, and carry on in this new framework.

$$\diamond$$

In the above example, S_{olist} is a subclass of S_{list} which inherits all the programs already developed in S_{list}. S_{tolist} is, in turn, a subclass of S_{olist} and inherits from S_{olist}. In contrast, in Example 9.1, we added the new relation *nocc* without introducing a new subclass, and just by updating S_{list}. This amounts to a pragmatic choice to ensure that the starting framework should be strong enough to define all the properties we consider basic for any kind of lists: length, concatenation, permutation, reverse, and so on. On the other hand, ordering is related to properties of the elements, and hence characterises particular kinds of lists, corresponding to subclasses.

Examples 9.1 and 9.2 show how abstract data types, classes and inheritance (as introduced in [3] for example) can be managed in logic program synthesis. Moreover, synthesis methods can be used both in program and in specification synthesis, so that we have a framework where synthesis and specification can be mixed in very natural way, without confusing one with the other. We believe that the study of methodologies using specification frameworks is an important issue in logic program synthesis.

9.2 Specification and Transformation

As well as mixing specification with synthesis, we can mix specification with transformation. We now give a simple example. In this example, we transform a program into another by first augmenting the specification framework with an axiom that enables the transformation to be performed. Note that the starting program and the target one are not equivalent systems; the transformation preserves correctness but not equivalence.

Example 9.3 Suppose we have the following axioms, defining a map *set* from lists into sets:

$$
\begin{aligned}
set(nil) &= \emptyset \\
set(X.L) &= \{X\} \cup set(L) .
\end{aligned}
$$

We can add the above axioms and some suitable axiomatisation of finite sets to S_{list} to get $S_{listset}$. Suppose we specify the relation "list union" lu as follows:

$$\forall(lu(A, B, C) \leftrightarrow set(A) \cup set(B) = set(C)) .$$

¿From this, we may infer or synthesise for instance the following program P_1 which is obviously correct:

$$\begin{aligned}
lu(A, nil, A) &\leftarrow \\
lu(nil, A, A) &\leftarrow \\
lu(X.A, Y.B, X.Y.C) &\leftarrow lu(A, B, C)
\end{aligned}$$

However, P_1 computes only part of the relation lu. For example, we know that $lu(a.nil, a.nil, a.nil)$ holds, but P_1 computes only $lu(a.nil, a.nil, a.a.nil)$. Even though we cannot prove the failure axioms of lu, nevertheless we may be satisfied if our aim is to find only one of the possible outputs.

On the other hand, we may wish to improve P_1 by transforming it. One way to do so would be to add the axiom (which we can prove)

$$\forall(lu(X.A, X.B, X.C) \leftrightarrow lu(X.A, X.B, X.X.C))$$

to our specification framework, and then use this axiom to transform P_1 into the following program P_2:

$$\begin{aligned}
lu(A, nil, A) &\leftarrow \\
lu(nil, A, A) &\leftarrow \\
lu(X.A, X.B, X.C) &\leftarrow lu(A, B, C) \\
lu(X.A, Y.B, X.Y.C) &\leftarrow \neg X = Y, lu(A, B, C)
\end{aligned}$$

The two programs P_1 and P_2 represent *equivalent* systems in the following sense:

$$\forall(lu(X.A, X.B, X.C) \leftrightarrow lu(X.A, X.B, X.X.C)) \vdash Ax(P_1) \leftrightarrow Ax(P_2) .$$

In other words equivalence holds not in pure logic, but in our augmented specification framework, where we can prove

$$\forall(lu(X.A, X.B, X.C) \leftrightarrow lu(X.A, X.B, X.X.C)) .$$

$\diamond$

10   Conclusion

We have presented a formal mathematical framework for deductive synthesis of logic programs. In this framework, logic programs are viewed as axiomatisations, and specification, (deductive) synthesis and transformation are regarded as operations on mathematical systems made up of axiomatisations and logical systems such as classical logic, SLD and $SLDNF$. We have proposed a distinction based on the behaviour of the mathematical systems involved in these operations.

Program specification may be constructed in two different ways: the first is to build up an axiomatisation of the problem in hand (using our deductive synthesis model), the second is to define the problem by a formula in a given specification framework. The resulting specification is a restricted mathematical system $\langle S, \mathcal{G}, CL \rangle$. The correctness of a specification can only be stated informally.

Program synthesis starts from a specification $\langle S, \mathcal{G}, CL \rangle$, and extracts a program. This program represents a small sub-system of the initial specification, specialised to solve just the goals being considered. The correctness of the program can be formally established.

Program transformation works on small systems representing programs instead of specifications, and transforms them into equivalent systems. The equivalence can also be formally proved.[35]

This distinction naturally leads to an ideal scenario, where we start by specifying abstract data types and classes, and then synthesise and optimise (by transformation) logic programs. However, in practice, it is often desirable and possible to mix specification with synthesis and transformation.

With respect to classes, there is a natural notion of subclass (as a stronger specification framework), and subclasses inherit programs synthesised in superclasses. We believe that an important step is to develop a methodology not only for program derivation, but also for managing specification frameworks.

Finally, we have considered classical logic only. However, our model works equally well with different logics. Using suitable representation functions ρ and ρ_L, we can translate problems specified in a modal logic for example into computation problems which can be solved in SLD. Thus the notion of representation of mathematical systems provides a means to extend the above scenario to specifications based on logics different from classical logic.

Acknowledgements

We would like to thank the referees for their valuable comments which have improved this paper considerably. We are also grateful to LOPSTR 93 participants for making our workshop presentation a lively 'interactive' session.

References

[1] Y. Deville. *Logic Programming: Systematic Program Development.* Addison-Wesley, 1990.

[2] A. Eriksson, A.-L. Johansson and S.-Å.Tärnlund. Towards a Derivation Editor. In M. van Caneghem and D.H.D. Warren, editors, *Logic Programming and its Applications*, pages 117–126. Ablex Publ. Co., 1986. 1990.

[3] J.A. Goguen and J. Meseguer. Unifying functional, object-oriented and relational programming with logical semantics. In B. Shriver and P. Wegner, editors, *Research Directions in Object-Oriented Programming*, pages 417–477. MIT Press, 1987. 283,

---

[35] In [2], program synthesis and transformation are respectively classified as (i) a derivation from a definition D_d of data structures and a definition D_r about relations or functions; and (ii) a derivation from a program and the definitions D_d and D_r. Such a distinction is really very similar to ours in spirit.

[4] Å. Hansson and S.-Å. Tärnlund. A natural programming calculus. In *Proc. IJCAI-79*, pages 348–355, 1979.

[5] C.J. Hogger. Derivation of logic programs. *Journal of the ACM*, **28**, 372–392, 1981.

[6] K.K. Lau and S.D. Prestwich. Top-down synthesis of recursive logic procedures from first-order logic specifications. In D.H.D. Warren and P. Szeredi, editors, *Proc. 7th Int. Conf. on Logic Programming*, pages 667–684. MIT Press, 1990.

[7] K.K. Lau and M. Ornaghi. Towards a formal framework for deductive synthesis of logic programs. Technical Report UMCS-92-11-2, Department of Computer Science, University of Manchester, November 1992.

[8] K.K. Lau and M. Ornaghi. An incompleteness result for deductive synthesis of logic programs. In D.S. Warren, editor, *Proc. 10th Int. Conf. on Logic Programming*, pages 456–477, MIT Press, 1993.

[9] J.W. Lloyd. *Foundations of Logic Programming*. Springer-Verlag, 2nd edition, 1987.

[10] Z. Manna and R. Waldinger. A deductive approach to program synthesis. *ACM TOPLAS*, 2(1):90–121, Jan 1980.

[11] J.C. Shepherdson. Negation in Logic Programming. in J. Minker, editor, *Foundations of Deductive Databases and Logic Programming*, pages 19-88. Morgan Kaufmann, 1988.

Reachability Analysis
for the Extension Procedure
— A Topological Result —

Gerd Neugebauer

Intellektik, Informatik, Technische Hochschule Darmstadt

Alexanderstr. 10, D-64283 Darmstadt (Germany)

Net: gerd@intellektik.informatik.th-darmstadt.de

Abstract

Starting from a clausal representation of a program — not necessarily Horn — it is a small step to a program utilizing Prolog technology. In the Prolog program provisions have to be made for various ways to enter a clause, i.e. contrapositives, and the necessity of a context, i.e. the ancestors. A static analysis of the program can detect situations where contrapositives or contextual information are not required. This analysis imitates the deduction mechanism to a certain depth thus it depends to a certain amount on the underlying deductive apparatus.

Such an analysis is presented for the extension procedure which is based on the connection method. The analysis can lead to a translation which leaves Horn programs as (nearly identical) Prolog programs. Situations requiring non-Horn support are identified and a new topological result is presented showing how non-Horn regions can be located in the initial program.

1 Introduction

Given a program as set of Horn clauses it is quite natural to use Prolog technology to solve it. We can give a simple transformation into Prolog namely the identical transformation — if we make no provisions to cope with the missing occurs check[1] and the depth-first search strategy.

Now we consider full first order programs. For this purpose it is sufficient to deal with programs given in clausal form. Those clausal form programs are not necessarily Horn. This means we allow classical negation in our programs which goes beyond the capabilities of Prolog.

To deal with full first order programs we will use the extension procedure. The extension procedure is an affirmative calculus based on the connection method [Bibel, 1987]. The extension procedure consists of two basic operations — the extension and the reduction. The extension step takes the current subgoal L and a complementary literal $\neg L'$ in one clause (after unification). The remaining literals in (a new instance of) the clause containing $\neg L'$ have to be solved within the context containing L. The context is called path and is initially empty.

The second operation of the extension procedure is the reduction step. This reduction step solves a subgoal by unifying it with a complementary element

---

[1] Most Prolog systems nowadays still use unification without the occurs check.

of the path. This step can not be found in Prolog execution since it is easy to see that Horn programs do not need this step.

We are focusing on Prolog since we are aiming at a compilation of the program using Prolog technology. This will be done in the same way used in [Stickel, 1988] to implement the model elimination calculus — a near relative of the connection method. The transformation can be described shortly as follows. The Prolog execution mechanism is used to emulate extension steps. Provisions have to be made for the reduction steps. This is done by adding arguments to each literal to containing the set of ancestors which is called path. This path has to be lengthened for each extension step. The reduction step is implemented as extra clause which tries to find a complementary literal on the path.

In [Stickel, 1988; Stickel, 1989] provisions are made to cope with unsound unification of Prolog and the depth first search strategy of Prolog which is replaced by iterative deepening search. Those points are of minor interest for this paper.

Let us come back to the reduction step. If we have a Horn program we are forced to start with a positive clause[2]. At each extension step a positive literal is added to the path since we are entering each clause at the single negative literal (of the head). Thus we can be sure that no reduction step is required since there are no negative literals on the path which would be required by the reduction step.

This simple analysis led to the relative efficiency of Horn clause logic — as used in Prolog — in contrast to full first order logic. Not only that no reduction steps with the path checking are required but also techniques like tail recursion optimization can only be applied if the last element of the path (i.e. the current stack frame) is known not to be needed anymore.

To overcome the deficiency of requiring the path for reduction steps — or reduction steps at all — several attempts have been made to generalize the argumentation given for Horn programs to the non-Horn case. Those attempts resulted in a analysis of the reachability of literals in the set of clauses. This reachability relation can be used to determine where reduction steps are super-fluous and thus can be omitted. Variants of this idea can be found in [Poole & Goebel, 1986; Wakayama & Payne, 1990; Sutcliffe, 1992]

The novelty in this paper are considerations about the topology of non-Horn regions. This leads to the insight that the hard part of a program lies at the beginning, i.e. near the goal. As soon as this part is left behind "simple" Horn technology can be used and no other hard region will be met.

The following sections of this paper are organized as follows. In section 2 basic preliminaries are presented. Some terminology and an example of an extension proof are presented. Since the analysis of reachability starts from goal clauses we have to explain which clauses have to be considered as goals. Finally, we rely on the use of contrapositives which are also introduced in this section. In section 3 we formally introduce the reachability graph and show how superfluous reduction steps can be identified. In section 4 we take a look at non-Horn region. We prove that non-Horn regions cluster around goals. We end the paper with concluding remarks.

---

[2]Note that we are using connection method terminology — the goal is positive and the facts are negative.

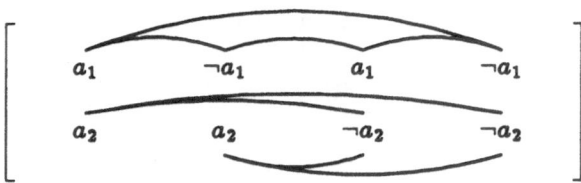

Figure 1: The complete matrix in two propositions

2 Basics

2.1 The Extension Procedure

As we need connection method terminology we will briefly mention some basic terms and results in this section. Additionally we will present a short proof illustrating the extension procedure.

For our purposes we are considering formulae in clausal form. Such a set of clauses $\{C_1, \ldots, C_n\}$ is called matrix (in normal form). Since the extension procedure is affirmative a matrix can be interpreted as disjunction of clauses.

A clause C is a set of literals $C = \{L_1, \ldots, L_m\}$. The clauses can be seen as conjunction of literals. A literal can be either positive or negative. The literal $\neg L$ is negative. We say that $\neg p$ is the predicate symbol of $\neg L$ if p is the predicate symbol of the un-negated literal L. A clause is called positive or negative if it contains only positive or negative literals respectively.

We represent a matrix two-dimensionally by writing the clauses as columns. An example can be seen in figure 1. This propositional matrix contains four clauses with two literals each. The arcs between complementary literals are connections. In figure 1 all connections are drawn.

As we have seen in section 1 the extension procedure essentially applies two operations — extension and reduction steps. Those operations are applied to open subgoals, i.e. those subgoals not already processed. Each subgoal consists of a literal which is augmented by a set of literals (the ancestors) which is called path. Initially a goal clause has to be selected. Each literal of this goal clause is augmented with the empty path to constitute the initial subgoals.

The reduction step tries to find a complementary literal for a subgoal on its path. If this succeeds the subgoal is solved. The extension step tries to find a complementary literal for a subgoal in the matrix. A new instance of the containing clause is drawn. The remaining literals of the new instance — after deletion of the complementary one — together with a new path are left as open subgoals. The new path consists of the subgoal we started with and its path.

The proof succeeds if nothing is left to do. Since at each step various possibilities may exist this search space has to be explored, e.g. by using backtracking.

Let us sketch a proof of the matrix given in figure 1. Suppose we have the first clause as initial goal. The first literal a_1 is selected to be solved. There are two possible extension steps for this subgoal. The one to the first literal of the second clause is taken. Now the second clause contains one open subgoal, namely a_2, with the path $\{a_1\}$. Another extension to the second literal of the fourth clause leaves the subgoal $\neg a_1$ with the path $\{a_1, a_2\}$. A reduction step closes this branch since the subgoal is already on the path.

There is only one subgoal left, namely the second literal of the first clause. The extension procedure completes the proof analogously with two extensions and one reduction. Thus the matrix in figure 1 is proven valid.

Initially a goal had to be selected to start the proof process. At first sight each clause could have been used as a goal clause. Thus alternative goal clauses would have to be tried if a proof attempt fails. How this goal selection can be restricted is shown next.

2.2 Goal Selection

In Horn clause programs there is one determined goal. This goal has two interesting properties. First, the proof process is started with the goal. Second, in the spirit of *Logic Programming* the user might be interested in the result of the proof process, i.e. the bindings of variables occurring in the goal. In this sense we can speak of the computation of a result by a logic program.

We want to carry over these properties to full first-order logic, at least partially. In general, a (clausal) proof problem is of the form $\Psi \vdash \varphi$ where φ is a disjunction of goals and Ψ is a conjunction of premises. Thus in first-order logic there might be more than one potential goal and we have to consider several clauses as starting point for a proof attempt.

Considering the form $\Psi \vdash \varphi$ we can see that there are two ways to prove a goal. First we can try to find a direct proof of φ and second we can show the inconsistency of Ψ. This inconsistency check is performed by selecting a clause from Ψ and show that its negation is a direct consequence of Ψ. Thus we potentially need to consider each clause as a goal.

We want to lift the notion of computation of a result to full first-order logic. Thus we allow the user to declare any subset of the clauses to be goals. These goals are preferred when starting a proof attempt. If they do not succeed other clauses may have to be taken into account too. The following well-known result allows us to restrict the clauses we have to consider as initial goals.

Theorem 1
Each proof of a matrix M involves at least one positive and one negative clause of M.

We can exploit this theorem in the following way. It is sufficient to take into account only positive clauses since there is a proof starting from a positive clause.[3]

Considering the proof process as a computation the user may be interested in the results, i.e. bindings of variables of a goal clause. Such a goal clause is not necessarily positive. Thus we will allow the user to specify an arbitrary set of goals and add to this set all positive clauses. This procedure is inspired by the idea that the user may primarily be interested in a direct proof of a certain goal. This is in contrast to an indirect proof where a contradiction in the premises has to be established.

---

[3]The theorem is symmetric and allows us to consider the dual version as well, i.e. taking into account only negative clauses.

In general we want to reduce the number of clauses we have to consider as goals without loosing completeness. This leads to the following definition.

Definition 1
Let M be a matrix and $\mathcal{G}$ a subset of clauses of M. $\mathcal{G}$ is called a complete *set of goals of M if any proof of M involves at least one clause of $\mathcal{G}$.*

It is obvious that the whole set of clauses constitutes a complete set of goals. On the other side we can get as corollary of theorem 1 the result that all positive clauses as well as all negative clauses constitute complete sets of goals.

Using this insight we can sketch the selection of goal clauses as follows. First of all we take the clauses given by the user. This set of goal clauses is enlarged to contain all positive or negative clauses of the matrix. Thus we have a complete set of goal clauses. It is sufficient for the further proof attempt to use only clauses of this set as initial clauses.

Reconsider our example given in figure 2. Since there is only one positive clause we — as the user — select this positive first clause to be in the set of goals. This set is already complete. Thus it suffices to start proof attempts from this initial goal.

2.3 Contrapositives

To overcome the problem of various entry points into a single clause a well-known technique is to fan out the clause into its contrapositives. A contrapositive is the representation of a clause with one distinguished literal (the entry point). In Prolog like notation a contrapositive can be written as implication with exactly one head literal.

These contrapositives represent the clause but each contrapositive has only a single entry point. The contrapositives allow a fast procedural implementation using Prolog technology. The disadvantage of contrapositives is their large number. Consider the clause $C = L_1 \wedge \ldots \wedge L_n$. This clause can be represented in n different ways:[4]

$$\neg(\neg L_e \leftarrow L_1 \wedge \ldots \wedge L_{e-1} \wedge L_{e+1} \wedge \ldots \wedge L_n) \tag{1}$$

In this formula e can take the values $1, \ldots, n$ resulting in n contrapositives. Each of these contrapositives can be seen as the special case of the clause C when the extension step enters an instance of this clause at the literal L_e. Thus the literal L_e is called the entry point.

Prolog itself requires only one of those contrapositives — namely the one with the head as entry point — since it can be shown in advance that the others can not be used during a proof. The argumentation used for this purpose relies on the fact that Prolog works on Horn clauses. The selection of the goal as well as the signs of head and body literals force the use of a single contrapositive out of n.

We will try to carry over the advantages of contrapositives to the non-Horn case.

---

[4] The inner implication should indicate the close relation to Prolog clauses. The outer negation stems from the affirmative point of view taken by the connection method.

2.4 Transforming Logic to Prolog

We want to show one context in which the reachability analysis presented in section 3 can be applied. Thus we shortly present the transformation similar to the one presented in [Stickel, 1988]. This transformation takes a program (and a set of goals) and produces a Prolog program (and a single goal) which has the same set of solutions.

We suppose that we have given a program P which is not necessarily Horn as a matrix. Some of the clauses of P are marked as goal clauses as discussed in section 2.2.

To describe the transformation we need some basic terminology. We define ν to be the operator which translates a literal by adding the negation to the predicate name (note that we implicitly assume that double negation is eliminated):

$$\nu(L) = \begin{cases} not\_p(t_1, \ldots, t_m) & \text{if } L = \neg p(t_1, \ldots, t_m) \\ L & \text{else} \end{cases} \tag{2}$$

Additionally we need the operation of adding arguments to a literal. This is denoted by appending the additional arguments enclosed in parentheses. Thus $p(t_1, \ldots, t_m)(P, D) = p(t_1, \ldots, t_m, P, D)$.

Consider a contrapositive of the form (1). First of all we consider the head. We have to guarantee that each variable in the head is unique, i.e. does not occur more than once. Thus we replace a multiply occuring variable x by new variable x' and collect unification problems of the form $unify(x, x')$.[5] Let L'_e be the transformed head L_e without multiple variables and γ the (Prolog) conjunction of the unification problems gathered during the transformation. Then the contrapositive of the form (1) is transformed into a Prolog clause of the following form.

$$\begin{aligned} \nu(\neg L'_e)(P, D) \quad :- \quad & \alpha(D, D_1), \beta(P, P_1), \gamma, \\ & \nu(L_1)(P_1, D_1), \ldots, \nu(L_{e-1})(P_1, D_1), \\ & \nu(L_{e+1})(P_1, D_1), \ldots, \nu(L_n)(P_1, D_1). \end{aligned} \tag{3}$$

In (3) P denotes the additional path argument, i.e. a list of the ancestor literals. D denotes a depth argument which is used to turn the depth first search of Prolog into iterative deepening search. $\alpha(D, D_1)$ is a sequence of Prolog calls to check and decrement the depth bound: $D > 0, D_1$ is $D - 1$. $\beta(P, P_1)$ adds the current literal to the path: $P_1 = [\nu(\neg L_e) \mid P]$.

Up to now we have described the transformation on the clause level, i.e. each clause is transformed into a set of contrapositives. Those contrapositives are transformed into a set of Prolog clauses. Now we have to perform an additional transformation on the level of Prolog procedures. A Prolog procedure is characterized by the predicate of the head literals. Let q be the predicate symbol and sign of a head literal of a contrapositive and m its arity. For each such pair q/m the following clause is added:

$$\nu(q(x_1, \ldots, x_m))(D, P) :- sound\_member(\nu(\neg q(x_1, \ldots, x_m)), P). \tag{4}$$

---

[5] $unify/2$ is assumed to be a Prolog predicate which performs sound unification.

where $x_1, \ldots, x_m$ are new variables. The Prolog predicate *sound_member*/2 is assumed to be a sound implementation of the member predicate, i.e. it performs an occurs check.

The transformation of the contrapositives according to (3) implements extension steps whereas the transformation (4) implements reduction steps. The additional efforts are necessary to deal with the occurs check problem and the modified search strategy.

Now we have to translate the goal. Let $\mathcal{G} = \{G_1, \ldots, G_g\}$ be a complete set of goals. Let $v_1, \ldots, v_v$ be the variables in $\mathcal{G}$ and *goal* a new predicate symbol. The each $G_i = \{L_1, \ldots, L_n\}$ is translated into a clause

$$goal(v_1, \ldots, v_v)(D) :\!- \nu(L1)([\,], D), \ldots, \nu(L_n)([\,], D). \tag{5}$$

Finally the overall goal which produces the same solutions as the initial program is added:

$$goal(v_1, \ldots, v_v) :\!- generate(D), goal(v_1, \ldots, v_v)(D). \tag{6}$$

where $generate(D)$ is a predicate which generates — upon backtracking — increasing numbers, i.e. the depth limit.

Our aim in this context is to see in advance where the reduction step, i.e. clause (4) or the additional path argument can be omitted. We are approaching this aim in section 3.

3   The Set of Connections and Reachability

To start with we consider the set of connections to be used during a proof. Connections are defined to be complementary pairs of literals. Note that in contrast to the definition in [Bibel, 1987] connections need not to be contained in *different* clauses. These connections can be seen as simple edges in a symmetric (i.e. undirected) graph. In addition to the information about the possible connection partners of a literal we want to take into account also the direction induced by the proof.

We usually start a proof with the selection of a goal clause. Afterwards extension and reduction steps are applied until no further open subgoal is left. We will take into account this procedure to build up a graph of possible connections. This graph is called reachability graph. In contrast to the mere set of possible connections the reachability graph is directed. The reachability graph is defined with respect to a set of goal clauses. In fact we are only interested in a reachability graph w.r.t. a complete set of goals. Nevertheless this is not part of the following definition.

Definition 2
Let $M = \{C_1, \ldots, C_n\}$ be a matrix in normal form. Let $\mathcal{G}$ be a set of goal clauses. We inductively define the reachability graph as follows:

- *Each literal in one of these goal clauses is reachable.*

- *If a literal L is reachable and there exists a connection from L to a literal L' then all literals in the clause containing L' except L' are also reachable. The arc from L to L' is contained in the reachability graph $\mathcal{R}_g$ w.r.t. $\mathcal{G}$.*

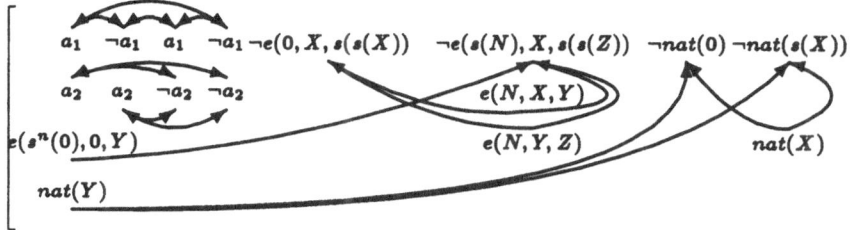

Figure 2: $\mathcal{E}_2(n)$

As an example let us reconsider the matrix given in figure 2. For the moment we ignore the arrows contained therein. The matrix is the combination of four parts. The first part is the complete matrix which we have already seen in figure 1. The second part consists of the clauses 5 and 6. These clauses define a relation e which essentially relates a term $s^n(0)$ in the first argument with a similar term in the third argument — but this term has exponentially many functor symbols s. The third part consists of the last two clauses. The relation nat defined here describes terms of the form $s^n(0)$. Finally, those three parts are connected by two additional subgoals in the first clause.

To be precise we have to explain the notion $s^n(0)$ used in the matrix. This means that n times the function s is applied, for a natural number $n > 0$. In fact this is a parameter and we have described a family of matrices. The other parameter is the size of the complete submatrix. But we will not consider other sizes as 2 in this paper.

Now consider the matrix $\mathcal{E}_2(n)$ given in figure 2. As set of goals we take the set containing the first clause only. This set of goals is complete since there is only one positive clause and this clause is in the set of goals.

Initially we only know that the literals in the goal clause are reachable. Let us start with a_1. There are two complementary literals. This leads to two arcs going into the clauses 2 and 4. We follow the arc into clause 2. We have to consider the literals other than $\neg a_1$, i.e. a_2. There are two possibilities, namely the arcs to $\neg a_2$ in the clauses 3 and 4. We consider the arc into clause 4. From there we can come back to the first literal of clause 1. Thus we have a arc from a_1 to $\neg a_1$ and vice versa. If we explore all possibilities we get such double links for any complementary pair of literals in the complete submatrix.

Now consider the third literal of the first clause. From there we come to the first literal of clause 6. Note that the fifth clause is no alternative since this literal is not unifiable with $e(s^n(0), 0, Y)$ for $n > 0$. The recursion in clause 6 produces arcs back into this clause and finally into the terminating unit clause 5. We see that there is no way back into the first clause. Thus we have single arcs instead of double links.

Continuing the process of adding arcs finally leads to the reachability graph $\mathcal{R}_g$ given in figure 2. It is easy to see that the reachability graph is uniquely defined, i.e. for any matrix any set of goals there is exactly one reachability graph.

What we have seen is that the construction of the reachability graph in some way mimics the behavior of a prover applying extension or reduction steps. But this is done only in a very restricted manner. No instances are used and the unifier is not kept. Nevertheless all possible connections leading to a proof are found.

Theorem 2
Let M be a matrix. If there exists a proof with the extension procedure for M then all its connections are contained in the reachability graph of M.

We can use this theorem to reduce the number of connections. This preselection mechanism is superior to the weak unification[6] proposed in [Eder, 1985] and used in SETHEO [Letz et.al., 1992]. This can be seen in our example if we assume an additional independent part of the matrix. This part should be without positive clauses and sufficiently full. E.g. we can take another complete matrix without the positive clause. The propositional variables have to be chosen different from existing ones. The weak unifications in this submatrix would be considered useful whereas they are not part of the reachability graph because they can not be reached.

The other observation we can make is that the reachability graph mimics the proof procedure well enough to determine the points where the clauses are entered. This means we can restrict ourself to consider only those contrapositives where the head literal is also an entry point in the reachability graph.

Next we have a look at the reduction steps during a proof. We want to avoid testing reduction steps whenever we can determine in advance if such a step will not succeed.

During an extension step the negated entry point is appended to the current path. This is the only place where the path is expanded. The reduction step tries to find a complementary literal on the path (via unification). Each arc in the reachability graph represents a possible extension or reduction step. So we can determine for which procedures reduction steps are appropriate.

Theorem 3
Let $\mathcal{R}_\mathcal{G}$ be the reachability graph of a matrix M w.r.t. a set of goals $\mathcal{G}$. Let L be an entry point in a clause. If there is no entry point which is connected to L with an arc in $\mathcal{R}_\mathcal{G}$ then no reduction step for this entry point is required.

This theorem shows how to avoid reduction steps for single contrapositives. We want to cluster all contrapositives into procedures. Any procedure should try a reduction step only once. This can be achieved when using theorem 3 to verify that each entry point of a procedure does not require a reduction step.

In the case of Horn clauses each clause has exactly one entry point. Thus no entry point can be connected to another literal via an arc in $\mathcal{R}_\mathcal{G}$. Thus we can conclude that in the case of Horn clauses no reduction step is required at all. This property is already know.

As another special case we consider Horn clauses and consistently negate predicate symbols. The resulting matrix has essentially the same properties. Especially the reachability graph carries over. Thus we can use a Horn theorem prover. Nevertheless the Horn property is formally not fulfilled and common approaches would consider the general case of first-order formulae.

---

[6]Two literals L_1 and L_2 are called weak unifyable if new instances of them are unifyable. The overall unifier is not taken into account.

4 Non-Horn Clusters

One question remains. How graceful is the ascent from Horn to first-order logic? In our terminology this means to answer the question how dense the reachability graph is. The hope is that it turns out that there are small islands of non-Horn procedures and the rest can be treated in the usual Prolog fashion. But this hope is destroyed by the following observations.

The non-Horn procedures can be characterized by entry points which are starting points of arcs in the reachability graph. We have called such a literal double linked. Each literal in the complete submatrix of $\mathcal{E}_2(n)$ has this property, i.e. each entry point (end node of an arc in the reachability graph) is also a starting point of an arc.

If we talk about clusters in the reachability graph we have in mind two kinds of connectives. The first one is the connectivity in a clause, i.e. literals in one clause are considered to be in a cluster. The other kind of connectivity is given by the double linked literals. Thus we can build equivalence classes, i.e. clusters, w.r.t. these two connectives.

We can find one cluster in the example given in figure 2. This cluster consists of the clauses 1 to 4. The other parts of the matrix do not belong to any non-Horn cluster, i.e. one which contains no double linked literals. This is already the general case. In general there is at most one non-Horn cluster which contains the set of goals. Formulated as a theorem this reads as follows.

Theorem 4
Let $\mathcal{R}_\mathcal{G}$ be the reachability graph of the matrix M w.r.t. the set of goals $\mathcal{G}$. Let L be a double linked literal. Then each literal which is on a path from L to a literal in $\mathcal{G}$ is double linked.

Proof 4
The proof is done by contradiction. Suppose there is a path from a goal literal to a double linked literal L such that no literal on this path is double linked. Let L' be the literal on the path just before L and connected to L. Since L is double linked there is another entry point into the clause of L. By construction of the reachability graph L is starting point of arcs pointing to all complementary and unifyable literals in the matrix. Because the arc from L' to L is in the reachability graph L' and L have this property. Thus the arc from L to L' is in the reachability graph as well. This contradicts our assumption and shows that each island of double linked literals contains a goal literal. □

The best we can hope for are separated clusters starting from independent goal clauses. This means we can refine our analysis and consider reachability graphs for each goal clause separately. We do not follow this route any further in this paper.

On the other side we can look at the far end of the non-Horn cluster. As soon as there are descendants which are not double linked we can start to apply further improvements. We can skip code to maintain and carry around a path since it is not required. The theorem 4 and its proof has shown us that if a literal L is not double linked then each literal in the contrapositive with entry point L is also not double linked.

As a consequence we can combine our results into a transformation taking a matrix and a (complete) set of goals. The result is a set of procedures. For each procedure we can determine whether or not a reduction test is required. As a special case we have pure Horn clauses which can be compiled as indicated by the well-known WAM technology.

The other extreme are matrices where all contrapositives are needed. In this case we also come to the results already obtained by theorem provers like PTTP and SETHEO. What we have gained is a uniform procedure which also handles gently the cases between the two extremes.

Finally we want to mention the complexity of the operations proposed. The building of the reachability graph can be performed with a greedy type algorithm in quadratic time (on the number of literals). Given the appropriate representation the check for double linked literals can be performed in constant time. Thus it can be determined in linear time whether a reduction step for a procedure is obsolete. This low cost analysis is done statically avoiding dynamic tests which might be needed over and over again.

5 Conclusion

In this paper we have studied a preliminary analysis of the deduction process. The analysis resulted in the reachability graph which is a directed refinement of the connection graph.

The reachability graph allows us to determine superfluous contrapositives. Thus we can avoid to generate all contrapositives when they are not required. Another advantage is in determining where a reduction step is needed. If we can determine in advance — at compile time — that the reduction step will fail we do not have to introduce instructions to perform it.

Since the reduction step requires the current path we are in general not allowed to perform last-call-optimization, otherwise we would loose elements of the path. The reachability graph enables us to use last-call optimization in cases where we know in advance that no reduction step will be used and thus no corresponding element of the path is required. Thus the reachability graph can be seen as a means to add smoothly Horn supporting functionality to a deduction procedure utilizing Prolog technology.

One novelty of this paper is the insight about the topology given in theorem 4. This theorem allows us to use Horn technology as soon as we have left a non-Horn cluster. In this case we do not need the path any more.

Similar results as obtained by the reachability graph can be found in [Poole & Goebel, 1986]. Their solution is massively inspired by Prolog and logic programming where we are aiming towards theorem prover applications. Their definition of "potentially relevant" and "potentially askable" literals correspond to starting points and end points of arcs in the reachability graph respectively.

In [de Waal, 1993] the result of [Poole & Goebel, 1986] is achieved by applying partial evaluation to a simple theorem prover in Prolog. With this technique the obsolete reduction steps (ancestor checks) have been identified automatically. The further insight about the topology and the superfluous path arguments is not present there.

The way taken in [Wakayama & Payne, 1990] is to guarantee that no reduction is required in the whole matrix. This is a subset of the application domain of the method described in this paper.

n	t_0	t_1
2	17	0
3	17	0
4	33	16
5	117	100
6	417	383
7	1550	1484
8	6050	5900

Table 1: Times for $\mathcal{E}_2(n)$
The times were measured in milliseconds on a SparcStation 1. A compilation to Quintus Prolog has been used. t_0 denotes the time without the reachability graph. I.e. all entry points have reduction steps. t_1 is the time with reachability graph, i.e. reduction steps for *nat* and *e* are turned off.

In [Sutcliffe, 1992] the starting point is also a criterion to avoid reduction steps completely. Additionally two refinements are developed. Nevertheless the author seems not to be aware of the importance of the initial goal nor the topological relation developed in this paper.

The reachability graph turns out to be a general purpose tool which can be used within several calculi like model elimination and connection method. However it is useful only in situations where contrapositives are used. Other approaches like e.g. [Loveland, 1991; Plaisted, 1988] avoid explicit contrapositives by applying case analysis. These methods do not easily profit from the reachability graph.

The reachability graph has been implemented within several experimental theorem provers written in Prolog. These theorem provers are based on program transformations which take a program in clausal form and produce an executable Prolog program. In table 1 we can see some experimental results for our example given in figure 2. The improvements are noticeable even so not dramatic.

The advantage of the reachability graph lies in the uniform identification of Horn and non-Horn parts of the program. It is an real alternative to the use of the connection graph.

Acknowledgements

I wish to thank W. Bibel, G. Große and other members of the Darmstadt Intellectics group as well as P. Baumgartner, U. Furbach, and anonymous referees for comments on earlier versions of the paper.

References

[Bibel, 1987] Wolfgang Bibel. *Automated Theorem Proving*. Vieweg Verlag, 1987.

[de Waal, 1993] D.A. de Waal. The power of partial evaluation. In *Proceedings of LOPSTR'93*, 1993.

[Eder, 1985] Elmar Eder. Properties of substitutions and unifications. *Journal of Symbolic Computation*, 1:31–46, 1985.

[Letz et.al., 1992] Reinhold Letz, Johannes Schumann, Stephan Bayerl, and Wolfgang Bibel. SETHEO — A high-performance theorem prover. *Journal of Automated Reasoning*, 8(2):183–212, 1992.

[Loveland, 1991] Donald W. Loveland. Near-Horn Prolog and beyond. *Journal of Automated Reasoning*, 7:1–26, 1991.

[Plaisted, 1988] David A. Plaisted. Non-Horn clause logic programming without contrapositives. *Journal of Automated Reasoning*, 4:287–325, 1988.

[Poole & Goebel, 1986] David L. Poole and Randy Goebel. Gracefully adding negation and disjunction to Prolog. In Ehud Shapiro, editor, *Proceedings of the third International Conference on Logic Programming, London, July 1986*, pages 635–641. Springer Verlag, Berlin, Heidelberg, New-York, 1986. LNCS 225.

[Stickel, 1988] Mark E. Stickel. A Prolog Technology Theorem Prover: Implementation by an extended Prolog compiler. *Journal of Automated Reasoning*, 4:353–380, 1988.

[Stickel, 1989] Mark E. Stickel. A Prolog Technology Theorem Prover: A new exposition and implementation in Prolog. Technical Report 464, SRI International, Menlo Park, CA 94025, June 1989.

[Sutcliffe, 1992] Geoff Sutcliffe. Linear-input subset analysis. In D. Kapur, editor, *Proceedings of the 11th Conference on Automated Deduction, Saratoga Springs, NY, USA, June 1992*, pages 268–280. Springer Verlag, Berlin, Heidelberg, New-York, 1992.

[Wakayama & Payne, 1990] Toshiro Wakayama and T.H. Payne. Case-free programs: An abstraction of definite Horn programs. In M.E. Stickel, editor, *Proceedings of the 10th Conference on Automated Deduction, Kaiserslautern, Germany, July 1990*, pages 87–101. Springer Verlag, Berlin, Heidelberg, New-York, 1990.

Inductive Synthesis of Logic Programs and Inductive Logic Programming

Francesco Bergadano

Università di Catania

via A. Doria 6/A, 95100 Catania, Italy

bergadan@mathct.cineca.it

Daniele Gunetti

Università di Torino

corso Svizzera 185, 10149 Torino, Italy

gunetti@di.unito.it

Abstract

Inductive Logic Programming deals with the problem of generating logic programs from examples, normally given as ground atoms. We briefly survey older methods (Shapiro's MIS and Plotkin's least general generalizations) which have set the foundations of the field and inspired more recent top-down and bottom-up approaches, respectively. Recent research has suggested that practical program induction requires a hypothesis space which is restricted a priori. We show that, if this trend is brought to the extreme consequence of requiring a well-defined and finite set of allowed clauses, efficient induction procedures can be devised to produce programs which are consistent and complete with the examples. On this basis, we suggest that "Examples + Hypothesis Space" can become an alternative way to specify a logic program. Software can be developed and reused by adding or modifying examples, and by refining the set of allowed clauses. Inductive synthesis is then proposed as a software engineering tool for the development, reuse and testing of logic programs.

1 Introduction

A new research area is emerging under the name of Inductive Logic Programming (ILP) [9], which is concerned with the inductive synthesis of Horn clauses, but also represents a tool for developing, specifying, debugging and testing logic programs. Early methods of inductive synthesis were mainly devoted to the AI goal of showing that machines could "learn" programs from examples. This is still a goal of recent ILP research, but certainly not the only one.

It is now commonly believed that programs can be generated inductively in an efficient and practical way only if the user can provide strong constraints on the allowed inductive hypotheses, i.e. if the kinds and the basic structure of the program to be learned is determined beforehand [1]. Recent ILP methods normally require some input of this kind, including type and mode of the variables, clause skeletons, rule models, clause antecedent grammars and integrity constraints. Such constraints are not wired into the induction procedure, but are provided as a separate and explicit information. Examples + Constraints can then be seen as an alternative way of specifying a logic program: an inductive specification.

In this paper we show that, if the constraints take the extreme form of a finite and well defined set of allowed clauses, some major problems of top-down ILP methods can be solved by completing the set of given examples. Moreover we describe a simple method of inductive synthesis that does not require unnecessary examples and is appropriate for typical logic programming applications.

Finally, we suggest that efficient ILP systems can become a useful software engineering tool. Logic programs can be developed incrementally by adding examples or modifying the constraints. If a program P is found to produce (not to produce) an incorrect (a correct) ground fact, this is simply added to the negative (positive) examples: the induction procedure will then modify P so that it is consistent with the new information. Clearly, this is also related to the goal of debugging logic programs [13]. If the induction procedure is too inefficient, the constraints need to be made stronger by restricting the set of allowed clauses. If no allowed program that is consistent with the examples is found, then the constraints need to be relaxed, so that additional clauses can be considered. We also show how this framework can be adapted to the problem of reusing and testing logic programs.

2 Early approaches to the induction of logic programs

Early work on issues now developed within the ILP area are well represented by Plotkin's study on least general generalizations [11] and Shapiro's Model Inference System [13]. The former is related to the problem of generalizing clauses, as a basis for the bottom-up induction of logic formulas: the least general generalization of a number of examples will serve as a compressed description. The latter is based on the top-down specialization of clauses, until a logic program which is consistent with the available examples is produced. Both approaches provide a foundation for Inductive Logic Programming as well as the basis for recent developments.

2.1 Plotkin's least general generalizations

Even if there is not a total agreement in the field of Machine Learning about the meaning of generalization, intuitively we can say that a statement S_1 is a generalization of a statement S_2 if whatever is true on the basis of S_2 is also true for S_1, but not vice versa. In a logical framework, this may be made precise in a number of different ways, e.g. $S_1 \models S_2$, $S_1 \vdash S_2$ or even $S_1 \vdash_{SLD} S_2$. In other words, to generalize means to go from the specific (e.g. a set of examples) to the general (e.g. a set of rules entailing those, and perhaps other, examples), and this is the common assumption of all bottom up ILP methods, no matter which generalizing operation is in use.

Plotkin [11] was the first to rigorously analyze the notion of generalization based of θ-subsumption. He did not restrict himself to Horn clause logic; in fact Logic Programming did not yet exist at that time.

In Plotkin's framework, we say that a clause C θ-subsumes (or is a generalization of) a clause D, if there exists a substitution θ such that $C\theta \subseteq D$. Usually this is written C $\preceq$ D. If S is a set of clauses, C is a generalization of S if, $\forall$ D $\in$ S, C $\preceq$ D. We say that C is a least general generalization (lgg) of D if C $\preceq$ D and, for every other E such that E $\preceq$ D it is also the case that E $\preceq$ C. In a similar way we define the lgg of a set of clauses (see [11] for the Plotkin's method to build lggs).

We are mostly interested in lgg relative to a background knowledge (rlgg), for example a set of Horn clauses. This case is important for ILP, because we may have available a partial logic program P, and need to refine it by adding other clauses that would allow to derive new examples.

An atom A is a lgg of atom B w.r.t. a theory Σ, if there is a σ such that $\Sigma \vdash A\sigma \equiv B$. We write A $\preceq_\Sigma$ B. A clause C is a lgg of a clause D w.r.t. theory Σ, if $\Sigma \vdash C\theta \rightarrow$ D for some substitution θ. This is equivalent to $C\sigma \subseteq E$ for some σ and $\Sigma \vdash D \equiv E$.

In practice, suppose we are given a logic program P and two examples (two ground atoms) E_1 and E_2 such that $P \not\vdash E_1$ and $P \not\vdash E_2$. We want to build the lgg C of E_1 and E_2 w.r.t. the program P such that $P \wedge C \vdash E_1 \wedge E_2$. We can proceed as follows [9]:

$$P \wedge C \vdash E_1$$
$$C \vdash P \rightarrow E_1$$
$$\vdash C \rightarrow (\neg P \vee E_1)$$
$$\vdash C \rightarrow ((\neg p_1 \vee \neg p_2 \vee \ldots) \vee E_1)$$

where P is replaced by the ground atoms p_1, p_2, ... representing a model of P. Similar steps can be done for E_2. Now, if we let C_1 and C_2 be $((\neg p_1 \vee \neg p_2 \vee \ldots) \vee E_1)$ and $((\neg p_1 \vee \neg p_2 \vee \ldots) \vee E_2)$, respectively, we have: $\vdash C \rightarrow lgg(C_1, C_2)$. This is obtained by letting $C = lgg(C_1, C_2)$. This procedure allows us to learn a logic program from examples by adding to external and built-in clauses the rlgg of those examples.

2.2 Shapiro's Model Inference System (MIS)

The model inference system is so called because it infers a finite axiomatization of an unknown model M from the ground facts that are true in M. This finite axiomatization is described by means of Horn clauses. As such, MIS is concerned with the inductive synthesis of logic programs. The method is *incremental*, in the sense that it maintains a current inductive hypothesis (a logic program P), and modifies it as new examples are provided:

repeat
read a new example
while P is not consistent with the available examples do
       if P $\vdash$ a and a is a negative example, then make P weaker
       if P $\not\vdash$ a and a is a positive example, then make P stronger
forever

Weakening P is accomplished by means of a "contradiction backtracing" algorithm. If a is a negative example, it will be represented as :-a. From this and P, we obtain the empty clause, since P⊢a. The proof tree for the empty clause is then processed as follows:

start from the root (the empty clause);
at any node, query the user for the atom resolved upon;
if it is true, move to the clause containing the atom in the body
       otherwise move to the clause having the atom as its head;
repeat the above, until a leaf is reached;
remove the corresponding clause from P.

The rationale for this procedure is that, if the atom resolved upon is true, then the clause having this atom as its head is not necessarily wrong. By contrast, as the resolvent is wrong, the clause using this true atom in its body must be wrong. If it is a leaf, it must be removed, otherwise the mistake must be found higher up in the proof tree leading to this clause.

Strengthening P is done by "refining" some previously removed clause. If P ⊬ Q(k1, ..., kn) and Q(k1, ..., kn) is a positive example, then the refining process is triggered and a clause having a head that matches this atom is selected from among the ones removed by the contradiction backtracing algorithm. If no such clause is found, the most general clause Q(X1, ..., Xn) is used. The selected clause is refined by making it weaker (e.g. adding a literal to its body). After producing every refined clause, MIS will check whether it covers the example Q(k1, ..., kn) which triggered the whole process. In order to do so, MIS has to evaluate the clause body, after substituting k1, ..., kn to X1, ..., Xn. Usually this is done asking the user for the truth value of each literal occurring in the antecedent, after the substitution [13]. If all literals are marked as true, then the example is covered and the refinement process can stop after adding the refined clause to the program P. Shapiro has shown [13] that MIS will identify a restricted class of logic programs in the limit [6].

3   Restricting the hypothesis space

The early work described in the previous section has set the foundations of Inductive Logic Programming and has guided much of the recent research. Plotkin's idea of least general generalizations of logic formulas has inspired later work on "inverse resolution" [8, 15] while providing the basis for most bottom-up approaches to the induction of logic programs [9]. Shapiro's use of a refinement operator is a natural reference for recent top-down clause induction methods [3, 12, 4, 10], although most recent approaches are not incremental, and require all examples to be given at the beginning. For this reason they are called *one step* methods.

The most serious problem of earlier approaches is that, if we want to be assured that any kind of program can be learned, then we need to search a very large space of clauses, and the induction method is not practical. Recent work has tried to overcome this problem in two ways: heuristics and "explicit bias". Heuristic approaches (e.g. [12]) keep a large space of possible clauses, so that any program can virtually be generated, but search this space selectively, on the basis of general purpose heuristic criteria (e.g. clauses that derive less negative examples are considered first, and are specialized in order to produce a consistent program). Alternatively, we can keep on requiring that the whole search space is analyzed, but reduce this space to a manageable size on the basis of a priori information. Methods based on this principle (e.g. [10]) define which clauses are allowed, depending on syntactic requirements (e.g. input variables of all literals must occur earlier in the clause body). Heuristic methods may be faster, but are not guaranteed to find a solution. Explicit bias is well suited for demonstrating strong completeness and consistency properties for the synthesized program.

If we go further in the direction of restricting the hypothesis space, we come to the extreme consequence of defining a finite set of allowed clauses. With this assumption we may define efficient and provably reliable induction procedures, which may be proposed as a useful tool for logic programming. The requirement of having a set of permitted clauses which is finite may seem too strong a restriction. However, all inductive synthesis systems are practically limited by the high complexity of the problem, and the number of clauses that they are able to consider is not only finite, but usually quite small. Determining beforehand a limited set of clauses to be examined has a number of important advantages, which are discussed in the rest of this section.

First, the user will have an extremely clear and explicit way of controlling the induction procedure: the allowed clauses could be virtually listed in a file, some that are unnecessary could be deleted, others could be added on an individual basis. This should be contrasted with the wired-in preference criteria of older methods and even with more recent forms of explicit inductive bias, which usually only define general principles, e.g., "input variables should be instantiated".

Second, a finite set of allowed clauses prompts a method for completing the available examples as a preprocessing step, so that problems related to the extensional interpretation of literals are solved. This point deserves a more detailed discussion.

Intuitively, a program P generated inductively is acceptable if it is consistent and complete

Definition 1 *Given a set E+ of positive examples and a set E- of negative examples, a program P is consistent if ($\forall$e-$\in$E-) P $\not\vdash$ e-. P is complete if ($\forall$e+$\in$E+) P $\vdash$ e+.*

If we regard inductive synthesis as a tool for the development of logic programs, the above condition is extremely important, as the user will expect the synthesized program to behave as indicated on the given examples. However, this is not always the case with existing ILP systems. Consider a clause
C: s(X,Y) :- p(X,Z), q(Z,W), r(W,Y).
where, for s, p, q and r, the first argument's mode is input and the second argument's mode is output. We need to decide whether to add this clause to the program being generated. For efficiency reasons most systems, including MIS, GOLEM and FOIL, adopt an extensional interpretation of clauses:
the clause C is said to extensionally cover the example s(a,b) if there are two constants d and f such that p(a,d), q(d,f), r(f,b) are positive examples.
However, since in general, not all examples of all predicates may be given as an

input to the induction procedure, the extensional interpretation is not equivalent to the run-time behavior of the generated program P. This may cause two problems: (1) P may be inconsistent and (2) even if there is an allowed program P' which is consistent and complete, still the induction procedure may be unable to generate it, because some of its clauses may not cover (extensionally) any positive example [2].

However, if the set of allowed clauses is finite, the examples may be "completed" so as to avoid the above problems. If we limit ourselves to functional logic programs, (i.e. programs computing - and built up using - only functional relations [4]), the following completion procedure can be used to query the user for missing examples.

Consider the clause C (this procedure is run for every allowed clause).
For every positive example $s(a,b)$,
  query the user for the value $Z=z1$ (if any) such that $p(a,z1)$ is true.
  Add $p(a,z1)$ to E+
  query the user for the value $W=w1$ (if any) such that $q(z1,w1)$ is true.
  Add $q(z1,w1)$ to E+.
  Finally, query the user for the truth value of $r(w1,b)$. If it is true put
it in E+.

The above completion procedure terminates if all programs belonging to the hypothesis space are guaranteed to terminate, i.e. if the recursive clauses that are allowed can be associated to a well-ordering literal in their body [4]. We may now define an exhaustive induction procedure M which uses only positive examples. Negative examples are implicitly assumed to be all the ones having the same input values as the positive examples but different outputs:

complete the examples with the above completion procedure
examine every clause C
for every (positive) example $s(a,b)$
  If, for some constants d and f, there exist in E+ examples $p(a,d)$, $q(d,f)$
and $r(f,b)$
    then add C to P

In [4] we prove the following:

Theorem 1 -
(1) M produces a complete and consistent program,
(2) if a complete and consistent program can be formed with the allowed clauses, then M will produce one such program.

Observe that the restriction to functional programs does not affect the expressive power, as any computable function can be represented by a functional logic program. Moreover, the result can be easily extended to a wide variety of ILP methods, both top-down and bottom up. A similar technique of example completion via queries is used by the MIS system. However, MIS is an incremental system and does not do that as a preprocessing step. As a consequence, the answer to a query may force the system to retract some clause that was previously generated. By contrast, systems which fit the scheme of M consider every clause only once: when a clause is generated, it will be kept in the final program.

Finally, even if an oracle for answering queries is not available, still a finite set of clauses S (forming a terminating program) allows us to learn a consistent and complete program, whenever it exists. This is shown below with a simple induction procedure, which is adequate for typical logic programming applications and can be easily implemented in Prolog.

P ← []
For each e+∈E+ such that S ⊢$_{SLD}$ e+ do
       find P1 ⊆ S such that P1 ⊢$_{SLD}$ e+ (a backtracking point)
       P ← P ∪ P1
       if ∃e-∈E- such that P ⊢$_{SLD}$ e- then backtrack
output the clauses listed in P

Clearly, if a subset P of S is found, it is consistent and complete w.r.t. the given examples.
If there exists an e+ such that S ⊬$_{SLD}$ e+, the procedure is still applicable, but P will not be complete w.r.t. the given set E+.
Observe that, unlike extensional methods, here clauses cannot be learned one at a time and independently. A partial program P being learned, which is consistent w.r.t. the given examples, can become inconsistent because a new clause is added, and then backtracking is required. For example, suppose we want to learn *member*. Let S be:

(1) member(X,Y) :- tail(Y,Z), null(Z).
(2) member(X,Y) :- head(Y,X).
(3) member(X,Y) :- head(Y,H), tail(Y,T), member(X,T).

The given positive and negative examples are: member(a,[a]), member(a,[b,a]), notmember(a,[]), notmember(a,[b,c]).
Now, using the above procedure, clause (1) derives member(a,[a]), and no negative examples, so P ← {(1)}. Member(a,[b,a]) is derived using (1) and (3), but P will now cover the negative example notmember(a,[b,c]), and we must backtrack. Member(a,[b,a]) is also derived using (2) and (3), but again P derives a negative example, so we must backtrack to the first positive example. Because (2) covers member(a,[a]) and no negative examples, we put P ← {(2)}. Now, member(a,[b,a]) is derived using (2) and (3), and P = {(2), (3)}. Now P derives all the positive examples and no negative examples, and represents a legal program for *member*.
This simple example show two things. First, the order of the clauses appearing in S is fundamental for the efficiency of the procedure. If the first clause in S is put at the third place, a program for *member* can be discovered without backtracking. The position of the clauses in S can then be modified by the user if he or she "feels" that a particular order can improve the efficiency of the learning process. Obviously this is possible only if the whole hypothesis space is finite and available to the user, as it is the case for a finite set of clauses. Second, backtracking can be used not only to learn a single consistent program, but even to to discover different equivalent programs consistent and complete w.r.t. the given examples. These programs can then be confronted

for efficiency or any other required characteristic.

4 Inductive development, reuse and testing of logic programs

In this section, we propose inductive synthesis as a tool for developing logic programs. We have presented a class of reliable methods for generating programs from (1) examples of true and false ground atoms and (2) a hypothesis space described as a finite set of allowed clauses. Here we would like to suggest that "examples + hypothesis space" can be seen as an inductive *specification* of the desired program.

In fact, if there is only one allowed program that is consistent and complete, then the examples and the space of allowed clauses specify precisely which computation rule is sought. The same holds if the complete and consistent programs belonging to the hypothesis space are all equivalent. If this is not the case, then "examples + hypothesis space" can be seen as the intermediate product of a process of *incremental program development*. Software development is, in general, a process that is never completely finished. Inductive specifications acknowledge this fact to a greater degree than traditional programming. We start with an approximate hypothesis space, which may need improving for two reasons: it may be too large (and cause the inductive synthesis to be unacceptably slow) or it may exclude the "correct" program. Software development will then proceed in three ways: allowed clauses are forbidden, new clauses are allowed, positive or negative examples are added. Ideally, this process stops when only one program is complete and consistent. In practice, one may stop before having reached that point, because the complete and consistent programs, even if they are many and different, behave similarly on usual inputs.

We briefly illustrate the idea with the problem of specifying inductively a program for merging two lists. Let us define the allowed clauses as having "merge(X,Y,Z)" as their heads, while the bodies are formed with any combination of the following literals:

null(X), null(Y), X=Z, Y=Z, head(X,X1), head(Y,Y1), tail(X,X2), tail(Y,Y2), X1<Y1, X1=Y1, X1>Y1, X1≤Y1, X1≥Y1, merge(X2,Y,W), merge(X,Y2,W), W=Z, cons(X1,W,Z), cons(Y1,W,Z).

The predicates listed above are defined externally as follows:
head([X|_],X). tail([_|X],X). cons(X,Y,[X|Y]). null([]).
The user will also provide an initial set of examples, e.g.:

merge([],[],[]), merge([],[1],[1]), merge([1],[2],[1,2]),
not merge([],[1],[]), not merge([1],[2],[1]), not merge([1],[2],[2]),
not merge([1],[2],[2,1]), not merge([1],[2],[]).

(Obviously, this example is, in some way, artificial, because the given literals are simply chosen from the required program. Even in this case, the hypothesis space contains, in principle, 2^{18} clauses. Applying various general constraints, such as type and mode of variables, forbidden conjunctions of literals, forcing outputs to be produced once and only once, and to be used, a very small hypothesis space is in fact produced. Moreover, specializations of clauses which do not cover any example are not considered. In general, experiments have shown to us that it is possible to obtain a significant and practically useful restriction of the hypothesis space by applying stronger and stronger constraints). At this point the induction procedure is called. Our implementation of the procedure M described in the previous section has produced the following program:

merge(X,Y,Z) :- null(Y), X=Z.
merge(X,Y,Z) :- null(X), Y=Z.
merge(X,Y,Z) :- head(X,X1), tail(X,X2), merge(X2,Y,W), cons(X1,W,Z).

which is complete and consistent w.r.t. the given examples, though still not a correct version of *merge*. However, the program can be used as is, until an error is detected. For instance, merge([2,1],[1],Z) yields Z=[2,1,1], while the desired output Z=[1,2] is not obtained. The user can then add the following examples: merge([2,1],[1],[1,2]), not merge([2,1],[1],[2,1,1]). The program is corrected automatically by running again the induction procedure. If this is too slow, the user can delete some allowed clauses using stronger constraints. In this case a large number of unnecessary clauses can be forbidden by removing the literals $X1 \leq Y1$ and $X1 \geq Y1$ from the list of atoms that are allowed to occur in the antecedents. Program specification, incremental development and debugging are unified in the same process of adding examples and refining the hypothesis space by adding and removing allowed clauses.

Inductive specifications are also appealing for software *reusability*. In fact, they can often be reused for a new problem simply by changing some of the examples. For instance, if we wanted to merge lists that are ordered in descending order (e.g. [5,3,2]), we can keep the same hypothesis space as above, and change the examples as follows:
merge([],[],[]), merge([],[1],[1]), merge([1],[2],[2,1]), etc.
This is appropriate for reusability, as the need for changing an existing program is often based on some concrete case, and is best described on the corresponding examples.

Inductive synthesis also suggests a general technique for *testing* logic programs. Suppose M is an induction procedure, taking as input a set of examples E and a finite set of allowed clauses AC, and P is the logic program we want to test. The following procedure generates a set E of test cases adequate for P:

$T \leftarrow \emptyset$
repeat $P' \leftarrow M(E,AC)$
find an atom A such that $P \vdash A$ and $P' \nvdash A$
$E \leftarrow E \cup \{A\}$
find an atom B such that $P' \vdash A$ and $P \nvdash A$
$E \leftarrow E \cup \{not\ A\}$
until $P \equiv P'$

In words, examples derived with P are added until P is the program which is obtained inductively from those examples. As the examples somehow identify P from among a set of alternatives, they should also be meaningful for determining whether P is correct. The idea is related to Weyuker's notion of inductively adequate test cases [14], and also to more recent approaches to mutation-based testing (e.g., [5]). As the condition P≡P' is undecidable, we approximate it with a time-bounded test (which, obviously, gives a program neither correct nor complete). An example will end this section. Suppose we are given the following program P for testing:

merge(X,Y,Z) :- null(X), Y=Z.
merge(X,Y,Z) :- null(Y), X=Z.
merge(X,Y,Z) :- head(X,X1), head(Y,Y1), tail(X,X2),
                X1≤Y1, merge(X2,Y,W), cons(X1,W,Z).
merge(X,Y,Z) :- head(X,X1), head(Y,Y1), tail(Y,Y2),
                X1>Y1, merge(X,Y2,W), cons(Y1,W,Z).

There is an error related to the third clause: the comparison X1≤Y1 should be replaced by X1<Y1, and another clause should be inserted for the case X1=Y1. The effect of this error is that elements occurring in both input lists X and Y are repeated in the output Z. Suppose also that the set of allowed clauses is defined as above. Again, we used our implementation of the induction procedure M defined in the previous section. As *merge* computes a function, though, negative examples can be replaced by the following *integrity constraint*:
merge(X,Y,Z) ∧ merge(X,Y,W) ∧ W≠Z → false.

The test case generation procedure will start with an empty set E_1 of examples, and call the induction procedure M. The empty program P_1' is then consistent and complete. We now enumerate pairs of lists X and Y, so that
$P_1' \vdash$ merge(X, Y, Z'), P ⊢ merge(X, Y, Z) and Z ≠ Z'
The first such pair that was found is <X,Y>=<[],[]>; for this input, P_1' produces no output and P outputs Z=[]. The new test set is then E_2 = {merge([],[],[])}.

M is called again, yielding P_2':
merge(X,Y,Z) :- X=Z.
We now enumerate pairs of lists X and Y, so that
$P_2' \vdash$ merge(X, Y, Z'), P ⊢ merge(X, Y, Z) and Z ≠ Z'
The first such pair that was found is <X,Y>=<[],[1]>. The new test set is then $E_3 = E_2 \cup$ {merge([],[1],[1])}. M is called again, yielding P_3':
merge(X,Y,Z) :- Y=Z.

$E_3 = E_2\cup$ {merge([1],[],[1])}.
P_4':
merge(X,Y,Z) :- head(X,X1), X=Z
merge(X,Y,Z) :- head(Y,Y1), Y=Z
merge(X,Y,Z) :- null(X), Y=Z

$E_4 = E_3\cup$ {merge([1],[2],[1,2])}
P_5':
merge(X,Y,Z) :- head(X,X1), tail(X,X2), merge(X2,Y,W), cons(X1,W,Z).
merge(X,Y,Z) :- null(Y), X=Z
merge(X,Y,Z) :- null(X), Y=Z

$E_5 = E_4 \cup \{merge([2],[1],[1,2])\}$
P'_6:
merge(X,Y,Z) :- head(X,X1), head(Y,Y1), tail(X,X2),
  X1<Y1, merge(X2,Y,W), cons(X1,W,Z).
merge(X,Y,Z) :- head(X,X1), head(Y,Y1), tail(Y,Y2),
  X1>Y1, merge(X,Y2,W), cons(Y1,W,Z).
merge(X,Y,Z) :- null(Y), X=Z
merge(X,Y,Z) :- null(X), Y=Z

$E_6 = E_5 \cup \{merge([1],[1],[1,1])\}$
P'_7:
merge(X,Y,Z) :- head(X,X1), head(Y,Y1), tail(X,X2),
  X1<Y1, merge(X2,Y,W), cons(X1,W,Z).
merge(X,Y,Z) :- head(X,X1), head(Y,Y1), tail(Y,Y2),
  X1>Y1, merge(X,Y2,W), cons(Y1,W,Z).
merge(X,Y,Z) :- head(X,X1), head(Y,Y1), tail(X,X2),
  X1=Y1, merge(X2,Y,W), cons(X1,W,Z).
merge(X,Y,Z) :- null(Y), X=Z
merge(X,Y,Z) :- null(X), Y=Z

As $P'_7 \equiv P$, we stop. T_6 is adequate, and it contains an input, namely X=[1] and Y=[1], that demonstrates the error of P, giving Z=[1,1] as output. The correct output would be Z=[1].

Only seven examples were necessary to individuate the error, while many more would have been required by random testing, if there are many possible element values with respect to the average list length. Functional testing would succeed easily, if the rather usual criterion of having equal elements in input lists and vectors is adopted [7]. Nevertheless, we view this not as a general criterion, but as a specific hypothesis about typical programming errors, that is made explicit by our finite set of allowed clauses. Even error-based methods would have problems with the above program. The reason is that the correct program is not a simple mutation of the program P to be tested: it requires one simple modification, and the addition of one entire clause. In an imperative programming language, this would correspond to having a conditional or a similar piece of code to be added to P, in order to obtain the correct mutant. Most approaches to mutation based testing, instead, are only able to generate minor and syntactically simple modifications.

5 Conclusions

In this paper we have argued that ILP can be used as a valid tool for the development, testing and reusing of logic programs, and we believe that this is particularly true if it is possible to restrict the hypothesis space to a finite set of clauses. In this case we can have efficient induction procedures and the developed programs can be made consistent and complete w.r.t the specifications (i.e. they will behave in the way they are expected to).
At these conditions, we believe that inductive synthesis techniques cannot re-

main limited to "toy" examples, but can become useful for the software engineering of real (i.e. large and complex) logic programs.

References

[1] F. Bergadano. The Problem of Induction and Machine Learning. In *Proc. Int. Joint Conf. on Artificial Intelligence*, pages 1073–1079, Sydney, Australia, 1991.

[2] F. Bergadano. Inductive Database Relations. *IEEE Trans. on Data and Knowledge Engineering*, 5(6), 1993.

[3] F. Bergadano, A. Giordana, and L. Saitta. Automated Concept Acquisition in Noisy Environments. *IEEE Transactions on Pattern Analysis and Machine Intelligence*, 10(4):555–578, 1988. New York.

[4] F. Bergadano and D. Gunetti. An interactive system to learn functional logic programs. In *Proc. 13th Int. Joint. Conf. on Artificial Intelligence*, pages 1044–1049, Chambery, France, 1993. Morgan Kaufmann.

[5] R. A. DeMillo and A. J. Offutt. Constraint-Based Automatic Test Data Generation. *IEEE Trans. on Software Engineering*, 17(9):900–910, 1991.

[6] M. E. Gold. Language Identification in the Limit. *Information and Control*, 10:447–474, 1967.

[7] W. E. Howden. Functional Program Testing. *IEEE Trans. on Software Engineering*, 6(2):162–169, 1980.

[8] S. Muggleton. Machine Invention of First Order Predicates by Inverting Resolution. In *Proc. of the Fifth Int. Conf. on Machine Learning*, pages 339–352, Ann Arbor, MI, 1988.

[9] S. Muggleton. Inductive Logic Programming. *New Generation Computing*, 8(4):295–318, 1991.

[10] M. Pazzani and D. Kibler. The Utility of Knowledge in Inductive Learning. *Machine Learning*, 9:57–94, 1992.

[11] G. Plotkin. A note on Inductive Generalization. In B. Meltzer and D. Michie, editors, *Machine Intelligence 5*, pages 153–163, 1970.

[12] R. Quinlan. Learning Logical Definitions from Relations. *Machine Learning*, 5:239–266, 1990.

[13] E. Y. Shapiro. *Algorithmic Program Debugging*. MIT Press, 1983.

[14] E. J. Weyuker. Assessing Test Data Adequacy through Program Inference. *ACM Trans. on Programming Languages and Systems*, 5(4):641–655, 1983.

[15] R. Wirth. Completing logic programs by inverse resolution. In *Proc. European Working Sessions on Learning*, pages 239–250, Montpellier, France, 1989. Pitman.

Induction of Prolog programs with Markus

Marko Grobelnik

Jožef Stefan Institute

Artificial Intelligence Laboratory

Jamova 39, 61000 Ljubljana, Slovenia

E-mail: Marko.Grobelnik@ijs.si

Abstract

This paper describes empirical Inductive Logic Programming system MARKUS, which was designed as a shell for experimenting in different real-life domains. The current version of the system uses as its basis 'covering' paradigm (also used by some other systems, e.g. Quinlan's FOIL). Within this paradigm, the development of single program clauses is performed by iterative deepening search of optimally generated refinement graphs (also used in Shapiro's Model Inference System). The system was successfully applied to several nontrivial learning tasks: construction of qualitative models, program verification, formula invention and construction of some typical Prolog programs, the most difficult being the quick-sort.

Keywords: machine learning, inductive logic programming, program synthesis

1 Introduction

This paper describes a system called MARKUS[1], which aimed to be an improvement of Shapiro's Model Inference System (MIS). [12, 13]. At the time when MIS was invented, it represented a significant step in machine learning and particularly in induction of logic programs. However, nowadays some recent systems like FOIL[10], GOLEM[8], LINUS[7] and others are achieving comparable or better results in the area of induction of logic programs within a framework of new research area called Inductive Logic Programming (ILP)[8]. Although the original MIS implementation is quite inefficient in solving nontrivial problems, the underlying ideas still have the potential to be competitive to the present methodologies and systems in ILP.

In the paper we present a system MARKUS[2], which has its main basis in Shapiro's MIS, but extends it in several directions. Main improvements are:

- optimal generation of the refinement graph,
- controllability of the search space with several parameters,
- use of iterative deepening search,
- use of all positive and negative facts at once[3],

---

[1]Last version of program code (written in standard Prolog) is available by sending an e-mail to the author.

[2]The name MARKUS remains from the initial idea of using Markovian Neural Networks in ILP.

[3]This feature extends the idea of MIS to the empirical ILP framework.

- removing of incorrect and redundant clauses, and
- use of negation.

As the main goal, we tried to build a system, competitive to current empirical ILP systems. Experimental results show that this goal was achieved. For example, MARKUS induces the classical quick-sort Prolog program from 7 facts in 40 CPU seconds on SUN-4 running on SICSTUS-PROLOG.

The following section briefly describes the MIS algorithm with short comments on the weaknesses of its original implementation. Section 3 describes the MARKUS algorithm. Next section presents the results obtained with MARKUS. The final section concludes the presentation with a short discussion.

2   The Model Inference System

The Model Inference System infers Prolog programs from examples and counterexamples of its behaviour. E.g., after interactively giving to the system the facts

$member(a, [a]), true$
$member(b, [a, b]), true$
$member(a, [x]), false$
$member(b, [a, x]), false$

it induces the program

$member(X, [X|Y]) \leftarrow true.$
$member(X, [Y|Z]) \leftarrow member(X, Z).$

The algorithm of MIS which generates such an output is as follows.

Given:
> Definitions of background knowledge predicates to be called by the target concept.

Set target concept P to a (possibly empty) set of Prolog clauses.
repeat
> Read next fact (positive or negative example of the target concept behaviour).
> **repeat**
>> **if** P covers a negative fact **then**
>>> Identify and remove responsible clause from P.
>> **if** P doesn't cover a positive fact **then**
>>> With breath-first search of the refinement graph develop the clause
>>> which covers this fact and add it to P.
>> **until** Neither of the **if**s is entered.
> **output** P
forever

The main step of the above algorithm lies in the second **if** statement of the internal **repeat** loop which searches a new clause of the target predicate such that it covers some uncovered positive example and none of the negative examples. When searching for the correct clause, a refinement graph is used to generate possible clause candidates. MIS starts from the most general clause of the target predicate and develops in the breadth-first manner more specific derivatives until it finds the correct clause. There are three main problems in the realization of refinement graphs in MIS:

1. generation of duplicate nodes in the refinement graph (affects mainly time complexity),

2. no control of the search space (causes unadaptability to concrete problem domains), and

3. use of the breadth-first search (results in enormous space usage).

3 Markus

The basic MARKUS algorithm is as follows:

Given:
> Definitions of background knowledge predicates to be called by the target concept.
> Positive (Pos) and negative (Neg) facts of the target concept behaviour.
> Function $covers(P, Facts)$ which returns the set of facts from $Facts$ which are true in P (P is a set of Prolog causes).

Set the target concept P to a (possibly empty) set of Prolog clauses.
From concept P delete incorrect clauses.
From concept P delete redundant clauses.
while P is incomplete ($covers(P, Pos) \neq Pos$) **or** inconsistent ($covers(P, Neg)$ $\neq \emptyset$) **do**
> With iterative deepening search of the refinement graph develop the clause which covers at least one unmarked (new) positive example w.r.t. P and no negative example and add it to P.
> Mark newly covered positive examples in Pos.
> Delete redundant clauses from P.
endwhile
output P.

Clause C in P is *incorrect* if it is responsible for P to be inconsistent, i.e., if $covers(P, Neg) \neq \emptyset$ and $covers(P - \{C\}, Neg) = \emptyset$. Clause C in P is *redundant* if it does not affect the coverage of P, i.e., if $covers(P, Pos) = covers(P - \{C\}, Pos)$. In MIS, redundant clauses are not eliminated which results in larger and less understandable target programs.

Search of the refinement graph is performed by the iterative deepening technique as follows:

> $Lookahead := 0$
> **loop**
>> **for each** generated clause C (conforming to control parameters) at $Lookahead$ level of the refinement graph **do**
>>> **if** $\exists E \in Pos : covers(P, \{E\}) = \emptyset$ **and** $covers(P \cup C, \{E\}) = \{E\}$
>>> **then**
>>>> $P := P \cup \{C\}$; **exit from loop**

```
        endif
     endfor
     Lookahead := Lookahead + 1
     if Lookahead > MaxLookahead then
         abort( "No clauses found" )
     endif
  endloop
```

Parameters, used to control the generation of a clause, are the following:
- maximal number of free variables (new variables in the body of a clause),
- maximal number of goals in clause body,
- maximal number of goals added at one refinement step[4],
- maximal depth of arguments in the head of a clause,
- maximal number of all modifications in the development of the clause.

One of the major problems in MIS is that duplicate nodes appear in the refinement graph; this causes an unnecessarily large search space. Huntbach's improvement of MIS [5] partly solves this problem by ordering refinement operations. However, duplicate nodes (clauses) may still appear within one refinement operation, for example, when adding goals to the body. MARKUS generates an optimal (a minimal) refinement graph by further ordering of modifications which are performed within one refinement operation (e.g., instantiation of input arguments is first performed on the first argument, then on the second argument, etc.).

MARKUS allows for simple modification of refinement operators. In the built-in general refinement operator, borrowed from MIS, a modification was introduced. The 'add goals' operation can add both positive or negative goals. However, negative goals can be added only in the case that all arguments of the goal are input arguments.

4   Experimental results

The system MARKUS V1.0 is written in standard Prolog. It consists of cca. 2100 lines of code (80kBytes) and runs without source code modifications on QUINTUS-PROLOG (VAX), SICSTUS-PROLOG (SUN) and ARITY-PROLOG (IBM-PC).

The following experiments were made on SUN-4 with SICSTUS-PROLOG V2.1. In the experiments several typical Prolog programs were induced. The table shows the CPU time (in seconds) and the minimal number (manually

---

[4] In optimal generation of a refinement graph, which contains no duplicate nodes, several goals may need to be added to a clause in one refinement step.

determined) of facts needed to induce the target program.

target predicate	no. of facts	CPU time in seconds
integer addition	3	3
integer multiplication	3	10
list membership	3	1
list concatenation	3	3
reverse list (naive)	4	2
reverse list (using difference lists)	4	2
insertion-sort	4	2
insert (for insertion-sort)	5	9
quick-sort (naive)	7	40
quick-sort (using difference lists)	5	107
partition (for quick-sort)	7	33

Probably the most interesting of the above experiments is the induction of naive quick-sort predicate definition. This experiment is also mentioned in [9] and [11]. In the above experiment, MARKUS needed just 7 facts (4 positive and 3 negative):

$qsort([], []), true$
$qsort([b, a], [b, a]), false$
$qsort([a], []), false$
$qsort([d, f, b, e, c, g, a], [a, b, c, d, e, f, g]), true$
$qsort([b, c, a], [a, b, c]), true$
$qsort([f, e, g], [e, f, g]), true$
$qsort([a, c, b], [a, c, b]), false$

The result was the following predicate definition for quick-sort:

$qsort([], [])$.
$qsort([X|L1], L6) \leftarrow$
    $partition(L1, X, L2, L3),$
    $qsort(L2, L4), qsort(L3, L5),$
    $cons(X, L5, XL5), append(L4, XL5, L6).$

were the definition of the $cons/3$ is:

$cons(X, L, [X|L])$.

MARKUS was also applied to solve some other nontrivial learning tasks. It constructed qualitative models[2] as proposed in [1]. Furthermore, it was used as submodule in automatic program verification methodology described in [3]. Its role was to induce loop invariant (which is the hardest part of the automatic program verification) by learning from loop instances generated through loop execution. Finally, MARKUS was also used for induction of mathematical formulas which were induced as a relation between argument- and result-numbers expressed via given arithmetic operators. E.g., from the facts

$40 = f(7, 9, 3, 19)$
$-234 = f(23, 45, 17, 6)$

MARKUS induces the formula

$f(X, Y, Z, V) = (X - Z) * (V - Y)$

5 Discussion

MARKUS can be viewed as an ILP shell which provides for experimenting with different refinement operators and different settings of control parameters. Different improvements of the MIS algorithm in MARKUS result in an effective ILP algorithm which is comparable to the state-of-the-art empirical ILP systems. However, compared to GOLEM and FOIL, MARKUS provides for a more elegant use of compound terms and use of background knowledge in the form of predicate definitions and not only as sets of ground facts (the same as in LINUS). To restrict the search space, GOLEM and FOIL use determinate literals [11] and LINUS used DHDB clauses; MARKUS can restrict the search space by using different refinement operators, and, in addition, by using different settings of control parameters.

In further work, MARKUS will be used to induce multiple alternative definitions of a target predicate. Furthermore, it will be extended with other search techniques (e.g. stohastic search) and stopping criteria aimed at handling noisy data. Finally, maybe the most promising direction for the further development seems to be introduction of schemes[4, 14] (also called skeletons[6]).

References

[1] Bratko, I., Muggleton, S. and Varšek, A. (1991) Learning qualitative models of dynamic systems. Proceedings of First International Inductive Logic Programming Workshop, Viana de Castelo, Portugal, March 1991.

[2] Bratko, I. (1992) - personal communication.

[3] Bratko, I., Grobelnik, M. (1992) Inductive Learning Applied to Program Construction and Verification. Proceedings of AIFIPP Workshop, Madrid, September 1992.

[4] Flener, P., Deville, Y. (1992) Logic Program Synthesis from Incomplete Specifications. Research Report RR 92-22, Université Catholique de Louvain, UNITE D'INFORMATIQUE, 1992.

[5] Huntbach, M. (1986) An improved version of Shapiro's Model Inference System. Third International Conference On Logic Programming. London, UK: Springer-Verlag.

[6] Kirschenbaum, M., Sterling, L.S. (1991) Refinement Strategies for Inductive Learning Of Simple Prolog Programs. Proceedings of 12. IJCAI, Melbourne (1991).

[7] Lavrač, N., Džeroski, S. and Grobelnik, M. (1991) Learning nonrecursive definitions of relations with LINUS. Fifth European Working Session on Learning, EWSL 91. Porto, Portugal: Springer-Verlag.

[8] Muggleton, S.H. (1991) Inductive logic programming. New Generation Computing 8 (4), 295-318.

[9] Muggleton, S.H. and Feng, C. (1990) Efficient induction of logic programs. First Conference on Algorithmic Learning Theory. Tokyo: Ohmsha.

[10] Quinlan, J.R. (1990) Learning logical definitions from relations. Machine Learning 5 (3), 239-266.

[11] Quinlan, J.R. (1991) Determinate Literals as an Aid in Inductive Logic Programming.

[12] Shapiro, E.Y. (1983) Algorithmic program debugging. Cambridge, MA: MIT Press.

[13] Shapiro, E.Y. (1981) Inductive Inference of Theories From Facts. TR 192, Department of Computer Science, Yale University.

[14] Tinkhman, N.L. (1990) Induction of Schemata for Program Synthesis. PhD thesis, Research Report CS-1990-14, Duke University (NC, USA), 1990.

A General Technique for Automatically Generating Efficient Programs Through the Use of Proof Planning*(Abstract)

Peter Madden

Department of Artificial Intelligence, University of Edinburgh
Edinburgh, Scotland, UK

Jane Hesketh

Department of Artificial Intelligence, University of Edinburgh
Edinburgh, Scotland, UK

Ian Green

Department of Artificial Intelligence, University of Edinburgh
Edinburgh, Scotland, UK

Alan Bundy

Department of Artificial Intelligence, University of Edinburgh
Edinburgh, Scotland, UK

A general framework for synthesizing efficient programs, using tools such as higher-order unification (henceforth HOU), has been developed and holds promise for encapsulating an otherwise diverse, and often ad hoc, range of transformation techniques. A prototype system has been implemented. *Proof plans* – formal outlines of constructive proofs – are used to control the (automatic) synthesis of the efficient programs from standard definitional equations [1,6,5]. Programs are specified in the standard equational form within the logic of the OYSTER proof refinement system. The construction of the improved functions is automatically controlled using the CLAM proof planner [2].

For the purposes of this paper we shall consider only *fusion optimizations* using the proof-planning approach. Fusion involves the merging of composed expressions to eliminate intermediate data constructs and function calls. We compare the proof-planning approach with the important *deforestation* technique for obtaining fusion optimizations.

Proof plans are used to control the (automatic) synthesis of functional programs, specified in a standard equational form, $\mathcal{E}$, by using the proofs as programs principle. The goal is that the program extracted from a constructive proof of the specification is an optimization of that defined solely by $\mathcal{E}$. Thus the theorem proving process is a form of program optimization allowing for the construction of an efficient, *target*, program from the definition of an inef-

*This research was supported by SERC grant GR/H/23610 and a SERC Postdoctoral Fellowship to the first author.

ficient, *source*, program. Our main concern lies with optimizing the recursive behaviour of programs through the use of proof plans for inductive proofs. Thus we exploit the *induction-recursion* duality historically accounted for by the *Curry-Howard isomorphism* [3,4].

The general technique for controlling the syntheses of efficient programs involves using $\mathcal{E}$ to specify the target program and then, in some cases, introducing a new sub-goal into the proof of that specification. Different optimizations are achieved by placing different characterizing restrictions on the form of this new sub-goal and hence on the subsequent proof. Meta-variables and HOU are used in a technique called *middle-out reasoning* (henceforth MOR) to circumvent eureka steps concerning, amongst other things, the identification of recursive data-types, and unknown constraint functions.

Such *identification problems* typically require user intervention in existing program synthesis and/or transformation systems. MOR provides complete automation regarding such problems. Meta-variables are employed at the meta-level planning phase which allow the planning to proceed even though certain object-level objects are (partially) unknown. Subsequent planning then provides the necessary information which, together with the original definitional equations, allows for the instantiation of such meta-variables through HOU procedures.

General advantages of the proof-planning approach include a correctness guarantee, termination, automatability, and the ease with which semantic laws can be applied during program construction. The selection of rewrites during plan formation is governed by matching syntactic properties of the rules and of the developing equations. This leads to a very low search branching rate. Specific advantages of using the proof-planning approach for fusion, as compared to the deforestation technique, include the ease with which semantic laws can be applied during program construction, and the broad class of programs that can be optimized.

References

[1] A. Bundy, A. Stevens, F. van Harmelen, A. Ireland, and A. Smaill. Rippling: A heuristic for guiding inductive proofs. Research Paper 567, Dept. of Artificial Intelligence, Edinburgh, 1991. In the Journal of Artificial Intelligence.

[2] A. Bundy, F. van Harmelen, C. Horn, and A. Smaill. The Oyster-Clam system. Research Paper 507, Dept. of Artificial Intelligence, Edinburgh, 1990. Appeared in the proceedings of CADE-10.

[3] H.B. Curry and R. Feys. *Combinatory Logic*. North-Holland, 1958.

[4] W.A. Howard. The formulae-as-types notion of construction. In J.P. Seldin and J.R. Hindley, editors, *To H.B. Curry; Essays on Combinatory Logic, Lambda Calculus and Formalism*, pages 479–490. Academic Press, 1980.

[5] P. Madden, I. Green, and A. Bundy. A General Technique for Optimizing Programs by using Proof Plans. Technical Report in preperation, Dept. of Artificial Intelligence, University of Edinburgh, 1993.

[6] P. Madden, J. Hesketh, I. Green, and A. Bundy. A general technique for automatically optimizing programs through the use of proof plans. Research Paper 608, Dept. of Artificial Intelligence, Edinburgh, 1993.

Guiding Synthesis Proofs

Vincent Lombart*
Unité d'Informatique, Université Catholique de Louvain
Louvain-la-Neuve, Belgium

Geraint Wiggins[†]
Department of Artificial Intelligence, University of Edinburgh
Edinburgh, Scotland

Yves Deville[‡]
Unité d'Informatique, Université Catholique de Louvain
Louvain-la-Neuve, Belgium

Abstract

In this paper, we present a basic set of methods to guide a proof in the Whelk logic program synthesis system. Starting from the methods used in the Oyster/CLAM system, designed for a functional context, we developed some proof "critics" to solve the cases in which those methods are blocked in a relational context. The application of those methods and proof critics is illustrated by an example, the delete predicate synthesis.

1 Introduction

In this paper, we present a basic set of methods to guide a proof in the Whelk logic program synthesis system. Those methods have been elaborated to free the user from most of its routine work, letting him concentrate on the important design decisions in a synthesis process.

Whelk is based on the constructive synthesis approach, it synthesizes logic programs from proofs: a conjecture (called a *synthesis conjecture*) is interactively proven in a constructive way, and Whelk automatically generates the corresponding program. One drawback of this approach is the long-windedness of the proofs necessary to synthesize a program. This raises the need to (at least partially) automate the proofs.

Whelk is designed to be interfaced with the CLAM proof planner [Bundy 88, Bundy *et al* 90b]. This could be a solution to the automation problem if the methods and tactics used in CLAM, developed in a functional context, were usable in a relational context. Actually, they are partially usable but some methods, such as the rippling method, have their best performance when applied to expressions with a high level of function nesting, which does not appear in a relational context. We present here, after some methods we had to specifically design for Whelk's logic and the existing methods, two specialized

*Email: vl@info.ucl.ac.be
[†]Email: geraint@ed.ac.uk
[‡]Email: yde@info.ucl.ac.be

methods we have developed, in the form of proof "critics" [Ireland 92], to fill this gap between the functional and the relational methods. The set of methods, once enhanced by the patching ability of our new proof critics, is able to guide significant parts of proofs in Whelk.

In the following sections, we will first introduce the framework and the necessary notations (section 2). We will then present the methods used to partially automate a proof (section 3). Finally, we present an example of application (section 4) where the methods developed are able to automatically guide the whole proof.

2 Preliminaries

2.1 The Whelk System

Whelk is a proof development system. Under certain conditions, Whelk is able to extract a logic program from a developed proof. This makes it a valuable tool in the logic program synthesis and transformation domain.

Whelk is based on a Gentzen Sequent Calculus, and uses a first order, typed, constructive logic with equality. To derive a logic program from a proof in Whelk, the *proofs-as-programs* paradigm, which usually synthesizes functional programs, has been adapted to the synthesis of logic programs. This adaptation raised two important problems, due to the differences between functional and relational programs:

- There is more than one way to use a relational program (multidirectionality).

- For a given directionality, there are potentially many – or no – outputs.

A solution to those problems is to consider only the all-ground directionality. The predicate can then be seen as a boolean valued function. This is the key idea to transform *proofs-as-functional-programs* into *proofs-as-relational-programs* [Bundy *et al* 90a].

The form of a synthesis conjecture to prove is largely a matter of taste. In Whelk a new operator, ∂, has been introduced with the meaning "It is decidable whether..." [Wiggins *et al* 91, Wiggins 92]. With this operator, to synthesize a program with vector of arguments $\overline{a}$ of type $\overline{\tau}$ and specification $S(\overline{a})$, we must prove a synthesis conjecture of the form

$$\vdash \forall \overline{a}{:}\overline{\tau}.\ \partial S(\overline{a}) \tag{1}$$

For instance, in section 4, we will synthesise the **delete** predicate, where delete(Old, X, New) holds iff New is Old with one occurrence of X deleted. We have the specification

$$\text{delete}(\text{Old}, X, \text{New}) \leftrightarrow$$
$$(\exists L_1.\ \exists L_2.\ \text{Old} = \text{app}(L_1, [X|L_2]) \wedge \text{New} = \text{app}(L_1, L_2)) \tag{2}$$

(where app is append) and the synthesis conjecture to prove is thus:

$$\vdash \forall \text{Old}.\ \forall X.\ \forall \text{New}.$$
$$\partial(\exists L_1.\ \exists L_2.\ \text{Old} = \text{app}(L_1, [X|L_2]) \wedge \text{New} = \text{app}(L_1, L_2)) \tag{3}$$

2.2 Object-Level Notation

The type "integer" will be notated nat, and the type "list of integers" $lnat$. The axioms on integers and lists of integers in Whelk can then be written:

$$\forall X{:}nat.\ \forall Y{:}nat. \qquad X = Y \vee \neg X = Y \tag{4}$$

$$\forall K{:}lnat.\ \forall L{:}lnat. \qquad K = L \vee \neg K = L \tag{5}$$

$$\forall L{:}lnat. \qquad L = [] \vee \exists Hd{:}nat.\ \exists Tl{:}lnat.\ L = [Hd|Tl] \tag{6}$$

$$\cdots$$

The proofs will be presented as they are built in Whelk, in refinement style. In other words, when a rule such as

$$\frac{B \quad C}{A}$$

is used, it is done backwards: If A has to be proven, when using the rule, we are then left with B and C to prove. How these rules are used by Whelk to extract a program is explained in [Wiggins 92]. In this paper, the automatically generated (by Whelk) predicate names will be renamed to improve readability.

A sequent with hypotheses $H_1 \ldots H_n$ and conclusion C can be written horizontally or vertically (or mixed):

$$H_1 \ldots H_n \vdash C \qquad \text{or} \qquad \begin{array}{c} H_1 \\ \vdots \\ H_n \\ \vdash C \end{array}$$

To help the reader, when new hypotheses are introduced, they are marked with a star on their left.

2.3 Meta-Level Notation

Meta-level annotations, which are automatically generated to control the use of rewrite rules in ClAM, are given in the following way. A *wave front*, which surrounds the part of a conjecture which must be moved away to allow matching with a hypothesis, is surrounded by a box. Any subexpression of that part which is required for the match, the *wave hole*, is underlined. The wave front is superscripted with a direction, $\uparrow$ when the front is to move out, and $\downarrow$ when it is to move in. Finally, universally quantified variables in the hypothesis are marked in the conclusion as $\lfloor sinks \rfloor$ — these are targets towards which inward wave fronts can be *rippled*.

An example of a step case sequent with an out-going wave-front — the list constructor and V_0 — a corresponding wave hole — V_1 — and a sink — SupL — is

$\star$ $V_0{:}nat, V_1{:}lnat,$

$\star$ $\forall SupL{:}lnat.\ \partial(\forall X{:}nat.\ X \in V_1 \rightarrow X \in SupL)$

     $\vdash \forall SupL{:}lnat.\ \partial(\forall X{:}nat.\ X \in \boxed{[V_0|\underline{V_1}]}^{\uparrow} \rightarrow X \in \lfloor SupL \rfloor)$

This conclusion might be rewritten — rippled — by the application of the following *wave rule*, which is automatically derived and annotated from the definition of $\in$.

$$X \in \boxed{[Y_0 | \underline{Y_1}]}^{\uparrow} \quad \Rightarrow \quad \boxed{X = Y_0 \vee \underline{X \in Y_1}}^{\uparrow}$$

Application of this rule will yield the conclusion

$$\vdash \forall SupL:\text{lnat. } \partial(\forall X:\text{nat. } \boxed{X = V_0 \vee \underline{X \in V_1}}^{\uparrow} \rightarrow X \in \lfloor SupL \rfloor)$$

where the wave-front has moved outwards. Matching both the object and meta parts of the wave rule with those of the conjecture allows us to select a rewrite rule which moves exactly the symbols we want moved, in order to match with our induction hypothesis.

Rules which move the unwanted parts of expressions into sinks are useful because then the universal quantification in the hypothesis can be used to allow the substitution necessary for a successful match.

Examples of all of the above will be given in the following sections.

3 The Methods

3.1 Overview

The methods used to guide a proof are specific to Whelk or have been adapted from the Oyster/CLAM system. They roughly fall into three categories:

1. Simplifications

2. Induction and Rippling

3. Proof Critics

Proof critics are actions triggered by the proof planner when the rippling gets blocked.

In the current state of our system, the methods are tried in the order shown above. A future extension will take advantage of the best-first planner [Manning *et al* 93] to modify the order according to the state of the proof.

The correctness of those methods relies on the correctness of the available operations at Whelk's level. Whelk only allows operations that are correct in the logic it uses.

3.2 Simplifications

The chosen simplifications are very simple, and are only given here for completeness. They constitute a very natural way to simplify expressions. Moreover, it is easy to find a measure of complexity which decreases with the application of a simplification step, thus avoiding infinite loops. Those simplifications are not to be confused with the simplifications Whelk performs at the extracted program level, to eliminate all true and false symbols from the rough generated program [Wiggins 92]. All the simplifications given here are already fully implemented.

3.2.1 Base cases

Some proof plans for base cases have been designed, which complete small parts of the proof tree. They are patterns which occur very frequently in proofs, and mainly deal with the decidability operator. For instance, $\partial(\text{axiom})$, $\partial(\neg\text{axiom})$, $\partial(X = Y)$, once recognized, will be proved and will not generate any search. In those expressions, axiom represents (the instantiation of) an axiom in Whelk's knowledge base. Axioms can also be detected in more complex expressions (see below).

3.2.2 Axiom Identification

The conjecture to be proved is scanned to determine if it contains the instantiation of an axiom that Whelk knows or of its negation. For example, the expression $\text{member}(X, [X|Y])$ is always $true$, and an expression containing it can thus be simplified by the usual rules; the expression $\text{member}(X, [])$ is always $false$, and the enclosing expression can also be simplified. The corresponding axioms, in the knowledge base of Whelk, are

$$\forall H{:}nat.\ \forall T{:}lnat. \qquad \text{member}(H, [H|T]) \tag{7}$$

$$\forall X{:}nat. \qquad \neg\text{member}(X, []) \tag{8}$$

3.2.3 Symbol Elimination

In some cases, variables or function calls can be eliminated: for instance,

$$\exists X{:}nat.\ X = 0 \wedge p(X) \quad \text{can be replaced by} \quad p(0)$$
$$\text{length}([]) \qquad\qquad\qquad\qquad\qquad\qquad 0$$
$$\text{app}([], L) \qquad\qquad\qquad\qquad\qquad\qquad L$$

eliminating the existentially quantified variable X or the functions length and app.

3.3 Induction and Rippling

Those methods, including recursion analysis, induction, rippling, fertilization [Bundy et al 93], ... are very close to those used in functional style and, as such, easy to adapt to the relational style. But they have a more limited use in a relational context than in their original context, mainly because of the lack of function nesting (more on this in [Åhs 93]), and the most interesting part is the addition of proof critics [Ireland 92] to improve their range of action (see next section).

The key heuristic used in a functional context is rippling, a tactic for manipulating the induction conclusion to enable the induction hypothesis to be used in the proof. We can illustrate the basic version of rippling, *rippling-out*, by an example from [Bundy et al 93], a simple proof of the associativity of $+$

$$\forall X{:}nat.\ \forall Y{:}nat.\ \forall Z{:}nat.\ X + (Y + Z) = (X + Y) + Z \tag{9}$$

by successor induction on X. We have to prove:

$$X + (Y + Z) = (X + Y) + Z \tag{10}$$

$$\vdash \boxed{s(\underline{X})}^{\uparrow} + (Y + Z) = (\boxed{s(\underline{X})}^{\uparrow} + Y) + Z \tag{11}$$

The rewriting rule (wave-rule) we will need is

$$\boxed{s(\underline{U})}^\uparrow + V \Rightarrow \boxed{s(\underline{U+V})}^\uparrow \tag{12}$$

Initially, the wave-fronts are functions which immediately dominate the induction variable (in this case, the successor function). The role of rippling-out is to move them outwards, using the available wave-rules. In this case, two applications of rippling-out (using wave-rule (12)) to (11) will successively give:

$$\boxed{s(\underline{X})}^\uparrow + (Y+Z) = (\boxed{s(\underline{X})}^\uparrow + Y) + Z$$

$$\boxed{s(X+(Y+Z))}^\uparrow = \boxed{s(\underline{X+Y})}^\uparrow + Z \tag{13}$$

$$\boxed{s(X+(Y+Z))}^\uparrow = \boxed{s(\underline{(X+Y)+Z})}^\uparrow \tag{14}$$

We have now reached a point where the induction hypothesis (10) can be used (fertilization), to give:

$$\boxed{s(\underline{(X+Y)+Z})}^\uparrow = \boxed{s(\underline{(X+Y)+Z})}^\uparrow \tag{15}$$

3.4 Proof Critics

We now reach the most original contribution of this paper: we have developed two new methods, which both try to fill the gap between existing methods and the Whelk system. They are in the form of proof critics [Ireland 92]: it means that those methods are only applied when the rippling process is blocked. The first one allows the splitting of the proof in two subproofs, and the second one allows the introduction of auxiliary variables in the synthesised program.

3.4.1 Splitting in Cases

This proof critic is related to the way the decidability operator is treated. This operator can only be removed from the current conjecture if we can prove that, given the hypotheses, what is inside its scope is always true or always false. Let's take an example: we will synthesize a predicate that holds if both its arguments (naturals) are equal (it's useless, as the equality predicate is available in the target language, but the proof scheme is interesting). Following the general form of a conjecture (1), $\vdash \forall \overline{a}:\overline{\tau}. \; \partial S(\overline{a})$, we have to prove:

$$\vdash \forall X{:}nat. \; \forall Y{:}nat. \; \partial(X=Y) \tag{16}$$

The first step in this proof is to move the universal quantifiers from the conjecture to the hypotheses, giving (remember, new hypotheses are marked with a star on their left)

$$
\begin{aligned}
\star \quad & X{:}nat, \; Y{:}nat \\
& \vdash \partial(X=Y)
\end{aligned}
\tag{17}
$$

Now, we are blocked by the decidability operator. And we can only remove it if we know that either $X = Y$, always, or $\neg X = Y$, always. The solution to that problem, in Whelk, is to import an axiom which splits the problem in two. Here, we use the axiom[1]

$$\forall X{:}nat. \ \forall Y{:}nat. \ X = Y \lor \neg X = Y \tag{18}$$

which is instantiated to our variables and added to the hypotheses list:

$$
\begin{aligned}
& X{:}nat, \ Y{:}nat, \\
\star \quad & X = Y \lor \neg X = Y \\
& \vdash \partial(X = Y)
\end{aligned} \tag{19}
$$

and allows us to split in cases:

$$
\begin{aligned}
& X{:}nat, \ Y{:}nat, \\
\star \quad & X = Y \\
& \vdash \partial(X = Y)
\end{aligned} \tag{20}
\qquad
\begin{aligned}
& X{:}nat, \ Y{:}nat, \\
\star \quad & \neg X = Y \\
& \vdash \partial(X = Y)
\end{aligned} \tag{21}
$$

The program synthesized so far is

$$
\begin{aligned}
equal(X, Y) &\leftrightarrow \\
& X = Y \land \dots \\
\lor \ & \neg X = Y \land \dots
\end{aligned}
$$

Now, we can say that in the first case (20), given the hypotheses, what is inside the scope of the decidability operator is always true, and in the second case (21), always false. That ends the proof. The synthesized program, before simplification, is

$$
\begin{aligned}
equal(X, Y) &\leftrightarrow \\
& X = Y \land true \\
\lor \ & \neg X = Y \land false
\end{aligned}
$$

and after simplification,

$$
\begin{aligned}
equal(X, Y) &\leftrightarrow \\
& X = Y
\end{aligned}
$$

It is important to notice here that the splitting in cases generates two subproofs, each subproof corresponding to one case. This operation produces a disjunction in the synthesised program, but the disjunction may not appear in the simplified program if one or both of the disjunctive parts is always false.

The idea of a case splitting had already been explored, notably in [Constable et al 86], where it was called "unroll". The main problem with this method is to avoid applying it too readily: with a proof critic rather than a usual method, a case splitting is applied only when it is needed, that is, when rippling is blocked and the system can more adequately choose a variable on which to split. A similar technique, with some differences in the choice of the variable,

---

[1] The logic used is constructive, so the excluded middle does not apply and $X = Y \lor \neg X = Y$ is not a tautology.

has been independently used by I. Kraan[2] in her synthesis system (no published reference).

So far, we have shown that case splitting is necessary to treat the decidability operator. But when do we have to use it, and which axiom do we have to choose to produce a "useful" case splitting? In the case we treated above, those questions do not arise, as the expression $\partial(X = Y)$ is actually recognized as a base case (section 3.2). In the non-base cases, the proof critic is triggered by a blocked rippling, with a wave front moving outwards. The wave front must be the argument of a predicate or a function, as in $p(X, \boxed{[V_0|V_1]}^\uparrow)$. The basic idea is to force the rewriting of that predicate or function, by splitting in cases. The system will search for a rewriting rule involving the other arguments[3] of the predicate or function, for instance something like

$$\forall L{:}lnat. \qquad p(0, L) \tag{22}$$
$$\forall X{:}nat. \ \forall L{:}lnat. \qquad \neg X = 0 \to (p(X, L) \leftrightarrow q(L)) \tag{23}$$

which involves the first argument of our predicate. The splitting in cases, with each case corresponding to one rewriting rule, is thus:

$$\star \qquad X = 0 \vee \neg X = 0 \tag{24}$$

The wave rules can help to determine when such a split is possible. Note that the search for the argument on which to split is a recursive process: if we had $p(f(X, Y), \boxed{[V_0|V_1]}^\uparrow)$ to rewrite, we should analyze p first, select its first argument, and then analyze f to select one of its arguments, and so on.

This proof critic has one of its most important uses with the equality predicate: if an expression such as $X = \boxed{\boxed{[Hd|Tl]}}^\uparrow$ appears in the conjecture, the corresponding rewriting rule is

$$\forall H_1{:}nat. \ \forall T_1{:}lnat. \ \forall H_2{:}nat. \ \forall T_2{:}lnat.$$
$$[H_1|T_1] = [H_2|T_2] \leftrightarrow H_1 = H_2 \wedge T_1 = T_2 \tag{25}$$

and we will thus split with

$$\star \qquad X = [] \vee (\exists V_0. \ \exists V_1. \ X = [V_0|V_1]) \tag{26}$$

In the first case, when we replace X by $[]$, what is in the scope of the decidability operator becomes impossible, and a *false* program fragment is generated. In the second case, we can use our rewriting rule.

3.4.2 Auxiliary Variable Introduction

A major difference between functional and relational programming is the need for auxiliary structures to hold intermediate results. For instance, $X = f(g(Y))$, in a functional style, will usually be translated $p_g(Y, Z) \wedge p_f(Z, X)$, with Z as intermediate result.

---

[2] Dept. of AI, University of Edinburgh
[3] We do not want to rewrite the wave front, this is mainly managed by the rippling method.

Those intermediate structures are existentially quantified variables, and can only arise in two ways in Whelk: either they must be introduced by an induction, or there must be a hypothesis with an existentially quantified variable, and the use of this variable will generate the existentially quantified variable in the synthesised program.

But how can we introduce such a hypothesis? There are two possibilities to have a totally new hypothesis[4] introduced in the proof: an axiom can be imported from the knowledge base of Whelk, or the cut rule can be used to introduce a free hypothesis. In the second case, the hypothesis introduced has to be proven in a subproof.

The use of an axiom is of course limited to the existing axioms, but is very frequently used. For instance, when the splitting in cases uses

$$\star \qquad X = [] \vee (\exists V_0. \exists V_1. X = [V_0|V_1]) \qquad (27)$$

in the second case the variables V_0 and V_1 are automatically introduced, and the access to the head and the tail of a list is a common operation in logic programming.

In more sophisticated operations, though, the cut rule is needed. This leads to the problem of the subproof that must be done. The creation of new hypotheses must be carefully designed to avoid a complexity explosion in the resulting problems. One problem which is not too complex to deal with is the problem of a blocked wave front moving inwards, towards a sink. A sink is a variable which is universally quantified in the induction hypothesis (section 2.3). For instance, in

$$\forall SubL. \partial(\forall X. X \in SubL \rightarrow X \in V_1) \qquad (28)$$

$$\vdash \partial(\forall X. \boxed{X \in \lfloor SubL \rfloor \wedge \neg X = V_0}^{\downarrow} \rightarrow X \in V_1) \qquad (29)$$

SubL is a sink. The hypothesis holds for every value of SubL. Perhaps, for an unknown value of this variable, the mismatching parts between the conjecture and the hypothesis will be equivalent. That is, we make the hypothesis that

$$\star \qquad \exists AuxL. \forall X. X \in AuxL \leftrightarrow (X \in SubL \wedge \neg X = V_0) \qquad (30)$$

If we can prove (constructively) this hypothesis, the corresponding program fragment will in fact produce a witness such that the hypothesis holds, and the rest of the proof will be straightforward: the new hypothesis is used to transform the conjecture, to give:

$$\forall SubL. \partial(\forall X. X \in SubL \rightarrow X \in V_1)$$

$$\vdash \partial(\forall X. X \in \lfloor AuxL \rfloor \rightarrow X \in V_1) \qquad (31)$$

and the induction hypothesis can now be used to terminate that proof (fertilization).

More generally, we use the cut rule to introduce the hypothesis that the mismatching parts are equivalent for some value of the sink. This has the effect of concentrating the problem on the mismatching parts, as we are no more concerned with the other parts of the conjecture.

---

[4] That is, not derived from the existing hypotheses (e.g. by the splitting of a disjunction).

Due to the lack of space, we can not develop here a complete proof using this proof critic, but it has been proved useful in a synthesis of the **subset**/2 predicate.

4 Application: The delete Predicate Synthesis

We will now give an example of the application of those methods to a simple problem: the synthesis of the **delete** predicate (this proof was done by hand in [Bundy *et al* 90a]). To simplify the reading, the type information used in Whelk will be omitted in the equations, and the hypothesis list will not always be fully rewritten. This should not cause any misunderstanding.

We start, as explained in section 2.1, with the synthesis conjecture:

$$\vdash \forall Old. \ \forall X. \ \forall New.$$
$$\partial(\exists L_1. \ \exists L_2. \ Old = app(L_1, [X|L_2]) \wedge New = app(L_1, L_2)) \tag{32}$$

and we will synthesise the **delete** predicate, where **delete**(Old, X, New) holds iff the list New is the list Old with one occurrence of X deleted.

No possible simplification is detected, so an induction will be tried. To determine the induction parameter, recursion analysis [Boyer & Moore 79] is used. This process will identify a variable on which a proof by induction is likely to succeed, based on the available rewriting rules. At this point, both Old and New are possible candidates, but only the first case will be developed here.

The induction on Old gives us two subconjectures:

Base Case

$$\vdash \forall X. \ \forall New.$$
$$\partial(\exists L_1. \ \exists L_2. \ [] = app(L_1, [X|L_2]) \wedge New = app(L_1, L_2)) \tag{33}$$

Step Case

$\star$ $\quad V_0$:nat, V_1:lnat,

$\star$ $\quad \forall X. \ \forall New.$
$$\partial(\exists L_1. \ \exists L_2. \ V_1 = app(L_1, [X|L_2]) \wedge New = app(L_1, L_2)) \tag{34}$$
$$\vdash \forall X. \ \forall New.$$
$$\partial(\exists L_1. \ \exists L_2. \ \boxed{[V_0|V_1]}^{\uparrow} = app(L_1, [X|L_2])$$
$$\wedge New = app(L_1, L_2)) \tag{35}$$

and at this point, the generated program fragment looks like

$$\texttt{delete}(Old, X, New) \leftrightarrow$$
$$Old = [] \wedge \ldots$$
$$\vee \ Old = [V_0|V_1] \wedge \ldots$$

each "..." corresponding to the fragment generated by one subconjecture's proof. In the base case (33), the axiom

$$\forall L{:}lnat.\ \forall H{:}nat.\ \forall T{:}lnat.\ \neg app(L, [H|T]) = []\tag{36}$$

is identified[5], and the first "..." is thus easily replaced by $false$, giving after simplification[6]

$$\begin{aligned}\texttt{delete}(Old, X, New) &\leftrightarrow\\ Old &= [V_0|V_1] \wedge \ldots\end{aligned}$$

If we come back to the step case (35), we can note that the rippling process is immediately blocked. The case splitting proof critic is triggered, which performs the following steps:

1. The wave front is identified as an argument of the equality predicate.

2. The other argument, $app(L_1, [X|L_2])$, is selected to force the rewriting

3. That argument is identified as a function. One of the function's arguments must be chosen to force the splitting.

4. From

$$\forall L. \qquad app([], L) = L\tag{37}$$
$$\forall Hd.\ \forall Tl.\ \forall L. \qquad app([Hd|Tl], L) = [Hd|app(Tl, L)]\tag{38}$$

the first argument of app, L_1, is selected, producing the splitting:

$$\star \qquad L_1 = [] \ \vee\ (\exists V_2.\ \exists V_3.\ L_1 = [V_2|V_3])\tag{39}$$

This gives the two subconjectures

$$\vdash \partial(\exists L_2.\ \boxed{[V_0|\underline{V_1}]}^{\uparrow} = app([], [X|L_2]) \wedge New = app([], L_2))\tag{40}$$

$$\vdash \partial(\exists V_2.\ \exists V_3.\ \exists L_2.\ \boxed{[V_0|\underline{V_1}]}^{\uparrow} = app(\boxed{[V_2|\underline{V_3}]}^{\uparrow}, [X|L_2])$$
$$\wedge New = app(\boxed{[V_2|\underline{V_3}]}^{\uparrow}, L_2))\tag{41}$$

Note the appearance of new wave fronts in the second case. Fortunately, they will be immediately rewritten.

The effect on the program synthesised so far is the introduction of a disjunction:

$$\begin{aligned}\texttt{delete}(Old, X, New) &\leftrightarrow\\ Old &= [V_0|V_1] \wedge (\ldots \vee \ldots)\end{aligned}$$

---

[5]Whelk knows the symmetry property of the equality relation

[6]In Whelk, the program simplification process is only applied when the proof is complete and a Prolog or Gödel program is extracted. Here, we will apply it as soon as possible to simplify the reading.

The first subconjecture (40) is easy to treat: after a rewriting and simplification, we get

$$\vdash \partial(\exists L_2.\ [V_0|V_1] = [X|L_2] \wedge New = L_2) \tag{42}$$

and with a simplification by elimination of L_2, we get

$$\vdash \partial([V_0|V_1] = [X|New]) \tag{43}$$

which is a base case of our proof system. We can then partially improve our program:

$$\mathtt{delete}(Old, X, New) \leftrightarrow$$
$$Old = [V_0|V_1]$$
$$\wedge\ ([V_0|V_1] = [X|New] \vee \ldots)$$

The second subconjecture (41), after a rewriting and rippling, becomes:

$$\vdash \partial(\exists V_2.\ \exists V_3.\ \exists L_2.\ \boxed{[V_0|\underline{V_1}]}^{\uparrow} = \boxed{[V_2|\underline{app(V_3, [X|L_2])}]}^{\uparrow}$$
$$\wedge\ New = \boxed{[V_2|\underline{app(V_3, L_2)}]}^{\uparrow}) \tag{44}$$

A further rippling, thanks to the case splitting, is now possible to give:

$$\vdash \partial(\exists V_2.\ \exists V_3.\ \exists L_2.\ \boxed{V_0 = V_2 \wedge \underline{V_1 = app(V_3, [X|L_2])}}^{\uparrow}$$
$$\wedge\ New = \boxed{[V_2|\underline{app(V_3, L_2)}]}^{\uparrow}) \tag{45}$$

With a simplification by elimination of V_2, we get (the induction hypothesis has been reminded)

$$\forall X.\ \forall New.\ \partial(\exists L_1.\ \exists L_2.\ V_1 = app(L_1, [X|L_2]) \wedge New = app(L_1, L_2)) \tag{46}$$

$$\vdash \partial(\exists V_3.\ \exists L_2.\ V_1 = app(V_3, [X|L_2]) \wedge New = \boxed{[V_0|\underline{app(V_3, L_2)}]}^{\uparrow}) \tag{47}$$

The rippling is blocked, and the case splitting is once again triggered. The wave front is an argument of the equality predicate, and we can split on the other argument:

$$\star \qquad New = [] \vee (\exists V_4.\ \exists V_5.\ New = [V_4|V_5]) \tag{48}$$

In the first case ($New = []$), the expression $[] = [V_0|app(V_3, L_2)]$ is simplified as $false$ (axiom identification, see section 3.2) and after further simplification of the conjecture, the corresponding program fragment is generated as $false$. So we have, before simplification of that program fragment:

$$\mathtt{delete}(Old, X, New) \leftrightarrow$$
$$Old = [V_0|V_1]$$
$$\wedge\ ([V_0|V_1] = [X|New] \vee New = [] \wedge false \vee New = [V_4|V_5] \wedge \ldots)$$

We are then left with

$$\forall X. \ \forall New. \ \partial(\exists L_1. \ \exists L_2. \ V_1 = app(L_1, [X|L_2]) \land New = app(L_1, L_2)) \quad (49)$$

$$\vdash \partial(\exists V_3. \ \exists L_2. \ V_1 = app(V_3, [X|L_2]) \land \boxed{[V_4|\underline{V_5}]}^{\uparrow} = \boxed{[V_0|\underline{app(V_3, L_2)}]}^{\uparrow}) \quad (50)$$

to prove. We can first use the rewriting allowed by the case splitting to have

$$\vdash \partial(\exists V_3. \ \exists L_2. \ V_1 = app(V_3, [X|L_2]) \land \boxed{V_4 = V_0 \land \underline{V_5 = app(V_3, L_2)}}^{\uparrow}) \quad (51)$$

and a further rippling will give

$$\vdash \partial(V_4 = V_0)$$
$$\land \ \partial(\exists V_3. \ \exists L_2. \ V_1 = app(V_3, [X|L_2]) \land V_5 = app(V_3, L_2)) \quad (52)$$

The conjecture can now be split in two, the first subconjecture

$$\vdash \partial(V_4 = V_0) \quad (53)$$

being solved by the base case method (section 3.2.1), and the second one

$$\vdash \partial(\exists V_3. \ \exists L_2. \ V_1 = app(V_3, [X|L_2]) \land V_5 = app(V_3, L_2)) \quad (54)$$

being an instantiation of the induction hypothesis. The final synthesised program, after Whelk's simplifications, is then

$$\begin{aligned}
&\texttt{delete}(Old, X, New) \leftrightarrow \\
&\quad Old = [V_0|V_1] \\
&\quad \land \ (\ [V_0|V_1] = [X|New] \\
&\quad \quad \lor \ New = [V_4|V_5] \land V_4 = V_0 \land \texttt{delete}(V_1, X, V_5))
\end{aligned}$$

5 Conclusion

The methods we have developed — the simplifications and the proof critics — together with the methods adapted from existing functional ones — induction, rippling, etc — are able to guide significant parts of proofs in Whelk. They are by no means complete, or able to discover "eureka steps" needed in a proof — they do not incorporate enough knowledge and complexity to make some of the clever design decisions — but they encapsulate and isolate small pieces of expertise. More precisely, once fully incorporated in the CLAM proof planner, they should be able to free the Whelk user from most of the routine part of a proof (and even some more), but should let the user make the important design decisions. The example chosen here, the delete predicate synthesis, is typical of the complexity that can be fully automatically managed by those methods.

What has to be done now is the integration of those methods with the CLAMproof planner (the interface between CLAM and Whelk was not yet available at the time of this work). Of course, this set of methods will be extended with more powerful methods. A last aspect to be considered is a better control of the structure of the resulting program, for instance by taking into account available mode information.

80

References

[Åhs 93]   T. Åhs. Relational rippling (working title), 1993. Ph.L. Thesis, Computing Science Department, Uppsala University, Sweden.

[Boyer & Moore 79]   R.S. Boyer and J.S. Moore. *A Computational Logic*. Academic Press, 1979. ACM monograph series.

[Bundy 88]   A. Bundy. The use of explicit plans to guide inductive proofs. In R. Lusk and R. Overbeek, editors, *9th Conference on Automated Deduction*, pages 111–120. Springer-Verlag, 1988. Longer version available from Edinburgh as DAI Research Paper No. 349.

[Bundy *et al* 90a]   A. Bundy, A. Smaill, and G. A. Wiggins. The synthesis of logic programs from inductive proofs. In J. Lloyd, editor, *Computational Logic*, pages 135–149. Springer-Verlag, 1990. Esprit Basic Research Series. Also available from Edinburgh as DAI Research Paper 501.

[Bundy *et al* 90b]   A. Bundy, F. van Harmelen, C. Horn, and A. Smaill. The Oyster-Clam system. In M.E. Stickel, editor, *10th International Conference on Automated Deduction*, pages 647–648. Springer-Verlag, 1990. Lecture Notes in Artificial Intelligence No. 449. Also available from Edinburgh as DAI Research Paper 507.

[Bundy *et al* 93]   A. Bundy, A. Stevens, F. van Harmelen, A. Ireland, and A. Smaill. Rippling: A heuristic for guiding inductive proofs. *Artificial Intelligence*, 62:185–253, 1993. Also available from Edinburgh as DAI Research Paper No. 567.

[Constable *et al* 86]   R.L. Constable, S.F. Allen, H.M. Bromley, *et al.* *Implementing Mathematics with the Nuprl Proof Development System*. Prentice Hall, 1986.

[Ireland 92]   A. Ireland. The Use of Planning Critics in Mechanizing Inductive Proofs. In A. Voronkov, editor, *International Conference on Logic Programming and Automated Reasoning – LPAR 92, St. Petersburg*, Lecture Notes in Artificial Intelligence No. 624, pages 178–189. Springer-Verlag, 1992. Also available from Edinburgh as DAI Research Paper 592.

[Manning *et al* 93]   A. Manning, A. Ireland, and A. Bundy. Increasing the versatility of heuristic based theorem provers. In A. Voronkov, editor, *International Conference on Logic Programming and Automated Reasoning – LPAR 93, St. Petersburg*, number 698 in Lecture Notes in Artificial Intelligence, pages pp 194–204. Springer-Verlag, 1993.

[Wiggins 92]   G. A. Wiggins. Synthesis and transformation of logic programs in the Whelk proof development system. In K. R. Apt, editor, *Proceedings of JICSLP-92*, pages 351–368. M.I.T. Press, Cambridge, MA, 1992.

[Wiggins *et al* 91]   G. A. Wiggins, A. Bundy, I. Kraan, and J. Hesketh. Synthesis and transformation of logic programs through constructive, inductive proof. In K-K. Lau and T. Clement, editors, *Proceedings of LoPSTr-91*, pages 27–45. Springer Verlag, 1991. Workshops in Computing Series.

Combining Prolog Programs in a Techniques Editing System (Abstract)

María Vargas-Vera

Department of Artificial Intelligence, University of Edinburgh
Edinburgh, Scotland, Great Britain
email: mariav@aisb.ed.ac.uk

Dave Robertson

Department of Artificial Intelligence, University of Edinburgh
Edinburgh, Scotland, Great Britain
email: dr@aisb.ed.ac.uk

Robert Inder

Human Communication Research Center, University of Edinburgh
Edinburgh, Scotland, Great Britain
email: robert@cogsci.ed.ac.uk

Kirschenbaum *et al.* proposed in [KLS89] the *stepwise enhancement* methodology for constructing logic programs. This methodology encourages software reuse and standardisation and tools embodying it are easily implemented. Based upon this methodology, we have developed [VVVR93] a system to construct modular large-scale Prolog programs using a techniques editing system and program combination. This integrated environment allows users to:

1. build Prolog programs by means of a *Prolog Techniques Editor* (PTE);

2. combine the programs devised using the Prolog Techniques Editor into more complex ones by using the *Composition* system.

The PTE offers a set of control flows and programming techniques and guides users through a series of interactions, at the end of which a program is obtained and tested. If the behaviour of the final program differs from the intended one, the user may backtrack to previous decision points and examine different alternatives.

The composition system uses information supplied by the PTE regarding the flow of control (*program history*) of each program in order to reduce user interaction and obtain efficient combined programs. The primary component of the composition system is the *selection procedure*. The selection procedure automatically selects a composition method according to the features of the two programs we want to combine, determined by the flow of control and the techniques used in their construction. For instance, two programs can be combined using the *meta-composition* method if they have the following features in common:

- *the skeleton employed*: both programs should be constructed using the same skeleton;

- *number of clauses*: both programs should have the same number of clauses as the original skeleton;

- *data structures*: programs should make use of the same data structure; and

- *pattern*: the pattern used to recurse up or down the data structure should be the same in both programs.

These features give rise to a number of different classes of programs. Our system, however, is not restricted to combining programs of the same class: programs of different classes can also be combined in a limited range of cases. Different combining methods can be used depending on the features of the programs, the composition system automatically choosing the most appropriate one.

The composition system allows the reuse of software and the development of optimised complex programs which can be repeatedly combined, producing more complex programs. We aim at more sophisticated programs which are difficult to combine using conventional program transformations. This is achieved by employing information supplied by the PTE (the *program history*) regarding the flow of control of each program to be combined. Although progress was made in the problem of combining arbitrary programs, it is still the case that not all pairs of programs can be combined in a single tail recursive program: only pairs of programs sharing certain structural features may be combined in a single program. Therefore we supply a classification hierarchy which allows appropriate combinations to be identified according to these features.

We have also developed a mathematical framework which guarantees the soundness of the composition process at three different levels. The first group of properties guarantees that the equivalence of programs is preserved after applying each combining method. The combined program is equivalent to the initial pair of programs because it is constructed by applying transformational operations. (Proofs that the unfold and fold operations preserve equivalence in programs are in [TS84]). The second group of properties guarantees that the type of the combined program is one of the types in our classification. This information helps in the selection of each method at different stages of the combination process and also in assigning the type to the combined program. Finally, in the third group, we define properties at the user level. This set of properties is of particular importance in the definition of the join specification; for instance, the commutativity of the operands of the join specification. One result of this is that by having this mathematical framework it is possible to guarantee that the composition process is sound [VV93].

Our conclusion is that, by using a small amount of knowledge about the program, called the program history, and with little user interaction, we can produce efficient combined programs. The described system has been implemented using SICStus Prolog (version 2.1.1) running under Unix on a Sun workstation.

For future work, programs developed using conventional editors could be incorporated into this environment by having their components (skeletons and techniques) identified and their history extracted. One plausible approach is to analyse the program and find out which class (of our classification) it belongs to. This is presently being investigated.

Acknowledgements

We would like to give acknowledgements to Edward Carter and Jeremy Crowe for their useful comments on this paper and also to the anonymous LoPSTr-93 referees for their constructive criticisms.

References

[KLS89]   Marc Kirschenbaum, Arun Lakhotia, and Leon S. Sterling. Skeletons and Techniques for Prolog Programming. Tr 89-170, Case Western Reserve University, 1989.

[TS84]   Hisao Tamaki and Taisuke Sato. Unfold/Fold Transformation of Logic Programs. In *Proceedings of the Second International Conference on Logic Programming*, pages 127–138, Sweden, 1984.

[VV93]   Maria Vargas-Vera. *Guidance during Program Composition in a Prolog Techniques Editor*. PhD thesis, Department of Artificial Intelligence, Edinburgh University, 1993. In preparation.

[VVVR93] Maria Vargas-Vera, Wamberto Vasconcelos, and Dave Robertson. Building Large-Scale Prolog Programs using a Techniques Editing System. Technical Report 635, Department of Artificial Intelligence, University of Edinburgh, 1993.

Designing Prolog Programming Techniques

Wamberto Weber Vasconcelos*

wamb@aisb.ed.ac.uk

Department of Artificial Intelligence, University of Edinburgh

80 South Bridge, Edinburgh EH1 1HN

Scotland — Great Britain

Abstract

We propose a medium in which expert programmers can design, test and organise Prolog programming techniques. The proposed approach employs simple single-argument program fragments and their combinations in order to represent techniques. The devised techniques can be made available to other programmers, by means of techniques-based editors.

1 Introduction

Due to the simplicity and compactness of the syntax of Prolog, commonly occurring patterns in programs can be detected automatically [Loo88, Bow92] or manually and used in a variety of ways, *e.g.* the detection of bugs [Loo88], the construction of (similar) programs [GH91, KLS89], the automatic explanation of programs [Gab92] and teaching purposes (automatic or human tutoring) [BBD+91, Rob91].

These patterns are loosely named *techniques* [Bow92, Brn91, BBD+91] and, together with knowledge of *when* and *where* to use them, provide a useful account of the body of knowledge necessary for the systematic development of correct Prolog programs. Such work is motivated by the prospect of transferring the largely informal and error-prone task of writing a program into that of finding a technique (or a set of techniques) which solves a given problem.

Current attempts to describe Prolog techniques remain largely informal or have limited coverage. Techniques have been depicted by means of examples (with an informal explanation in some natural language) showing instances of their successful applications [O'K90, BBD+91, KLS89, SS86, SK91]. If these techniques are to be put to use in tutoring systems or techniques editors, it is necessary to bridge the gap between their informal definition and a representation that can be used by a computer.

In this paper we propose an (albeit constrained) medium comprised by a notation, a suggested way to use this notation and a tool embodying it, in which expert programmers can express their knowledge and make it accessible

---

*On leave from State University of Ceará, Ceará, Brazil; sponsored by Brazilian National Research Council (CNPq), under grant no. 201340/91-7.

to others. We incorporate the stepwise enhancement method of Kirschenbaum *et al.* [KLS89] in our attempt to formalise programming techniques. Our ultimate goal is to provide an automated tool with which expert programmers could formally express, organise and test their programming knowledge and make it available to other users (novices or other expert programmers) by means of techniques-based editors.

In the following section a brief account of the stepwise refinement method is given and key concepts such as skeletons, techniques and additions are explained. In the third section we introduce the proposed representation for techniques and how a tool, the Prolog Techniques Meta-Editor, embodies it and makes it available to expert programmers. Finally, some conclusions are drawn and directions for future research are discussed.

2 Stepwise Enhancement using Skeletons and Techniques

In [KLS89], Wirth's *stepwise refinement method* is elegantly adapted to the context of Prolog programming. This adaptation uses a set of syntactic entities, called *skeletons*, describing the flow of control of a Prolog program, and a set of syntactic transformations, called *techniques*, to be applied to these skeletons. These techniques convey the programming practices (*e.g.* adding parameters and binding them properly) carried out by experienced programmers upon very simple programs processing input data (*e.g.* traversing a list) in a straightforward way.

This approach advocates the development of programs by means of stepwise enhancements in which programmers first isolate the flow of control needed to solve the problem. Then they choose from amongst the skeletons the one which best suits their needs. After the skeleton selection, the programmer customises it to obtain the final program. This customisation process is achieved by applying techniques to skeletons yielding *enhancements* (*i.e.*, skeletons enhanced with extra arguments, goals and/or clauses). The enhancements can be re-used, allowing one to repeat the process of application of techniques until the final program is obtained. If appropriate sets of skeletons and techniques are provided, the task of writing a program (largely informal and error-prone) could be transferred to that of finding a skeleton and a sequence of techniques.

2.1 Skeletons

Skeletons are basic syntactic constructs depicting the flow of control of a Prolog program [KLS89, Vas92]. They are presented in [KLS89] as basic Prolog programs themselves processing input data in a simple way, and are used to build more complex (and more useful) programs by establishing a flow of control which will be followed while computations are carried out. For instance, the list decomposition skeleton below

```
s([]).
s([X|Xs]):- s(Xs).
```

is found in programs traversing a list, as in the first argument of **reverse**:

```
reverse([],R,R).
reverse([X|Xs],R0,R):-
        reverse(Xs,[X|R0],R).
```

Skeletons do not perform any other computations apart from obtaining new values from an input and recursively iterating this process; terminating conditions (if any) may also be depicted. Techniques, explained below, are required for extra computations carried out as the flow of control of the skeleton is followed.

2.2   Techniques

Techniques are presented in [KLS89] as a mapping from a skeleton to a complete program using the same flow of control. The techniques act upon skeletons, adding arguments to goals, adding goals to clauses or clauses to a skeleton. Skeletons and techniques can be used to construct programs, with the skeleton controlling the manner in which the data is processed, and the techniques determining what is to be done with it, as the execution of the program progresses.

In this work we suggest a formalisation for a large and useful subclass of programming techniques, *viz.*, those techniques described by the arguments and subgoals (and their inter-relationships) added to existing skeletons. The approach advocated consists of isolating the arguments and subgoals comprising a technique and representing them by means of a sequence of single-argument programs along with an appropriate way to merge them and bind their variables. These single-argument programs are named *additions*.

Collecting values and building data structures with them, or counting the number of iterations of a loop are two examples of interesting computations that may be performed, once the flow of control is established by a skeleton. For instance, technique *count-down*, counting the number of times a loop is performed can be represented as:

```
t(...Count,Total):-
        ⋮
        Total = Count.
t(...Count,Total):-
        ⋮
        Count1 is Count + 1,
        t(...Count1,Total).
```

If it is applied to the skeleton above, it yields:

```
s([],Count,Total):-
        Total = Count.
s([X|Xs],Count,Total):-
        Count1 is Count + 1,
        s(Xs,Count1,Total).
```

Technique *count-down* can be seen as the appropriate merging of additions q and r:

```
q(Count):-                          r(Total):-
      Var = Count.                        Total = Var.
q(Count):-                          r(Total):-
      Count1 is Count + 1,                r(Total).
      q(Count1).
```

Addition q uses its argument in input mode, adding one unit at each recursive iteration and binding its final value to Var in the base-case clause. Addition r passes its argument down the recursive call, and in the base-case has a Var bound to it. These two additions are merged together and the Var variables are unified, giving rise to technique *count-down*.

3 Designing Skeletons, Additions and Techniques

The stepwise enhancement approach has been put to use in [Rob91], by means of a *Prolog Techniques Editor* (PTE). This knowledge-based software development tool provides its users with a set of skeletons and applicable techniques and guides the user through a series of interactions at the end of which a program is obtained and tested. If the resulting behaviour differs from the intended one, the user may backtrack to previous decision points and examine different alternatives.

During the preparation of the skeletons and techniques which will be offered to the users of the PTE, much ingenuity and labour is required, for no formalisation or methodology has been proposed as an aid. After studying patterns frequently found in programs and acclaimed techniques informally described in Prolog textbooks and papers, the PTE developer chooses a number of skeletons and techniques and manually encodes them in a way that the PTE can use. Later expansions of the PTE by adding, removing or altering skeletons and techniques may involve much work.

An interactive system, the *Prolog Techniques Meta-Editor* (or Meta-Editor, for short), aimed at *expert* programmers, with which one can create and manage a library of skeletons and programming techniques is proposed here. Such a tool is aimed at helping expert programmers to devise and test new skeletons and additions, and define relationships (the programming techniques) between them. Figure 1 below shows the relationship between a PTE and the herewith proposed Prolog Techniques Meta-Editor. The expert programmer prepares and tests skeletons, additions and techniques by means of the Meta-Editor. These constructs are stored in a *library* of programming practices and supplied to the users of the Prolog Techniques Editor. The PTE can be seen as a generic system which could take an arbitrary body of programming knowledge (for example, list-processing programming techniques or programming techniques for novices) and offer it to its users. The Meta-Editor uses ideas of the Recursive Techniques Editor [BGB91] and adapts them to the systematic program development advocated by Kirschenbaum *et al* [KLS89]. The Meta-Editor provides a repertoire of commands similar to that of the Recursive Techniques Editor but aimed at enabling expert programmers to define and manage a library of programming techniques.

Skeletons, additions and techniques are an attempt at representing the com-

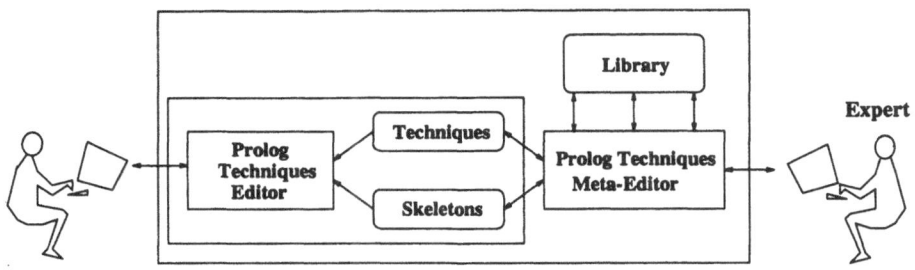

Figure 1: Prolog Techniques Editor and Prolog Techniques Meta-Editor

mon programming practices programmers make use of when devising Prolog programs. In this work, the issue of whether every conceivable programming practice can be devised (completeness) is not a main concern. The usability of the approach, measured by the usefulness of the programming practices that can be devised is, however, an important point. The proposed formalism allows re-using components and devising more complex entities in an incremental manner, also defining natural hierarchies of components. These are advantages which might help the users of the Meta-Editor.

3.1 Designing Skeletons

The proposed Meta-Editor offers its users a repertoire of basic commands through which an initial skeleton consisting of a single general clause of the form below can be gradually customised:

$$s(X) :- $$
$$\quad test(X),$$
$$\quad obtain(X, \vec{Y}, \vec{Z}), \quad \langle offer(\vec{Y}) \rangle$$
$$\quad \overrightarrow{s(Z)} \ .$$

$\vec{Y}$ and $\vec{Z}$ are (possibly empty) vectors of variables and $\overrightarrow{s(Z)}$ is a (possibly empty) vector of recursive calls, one for each variable $Z_i \in \vec{Z}$. In the clause above, a *test* is carried out using X, then a computation *obtain* is performed also using X obtaining the vectors $\vec{Y}$ of *Y-values* and $\vec{Z}$ of *Z-values*. Finally, a vector of recursive calls follows, one for each of the Z-values.

The $\vec{Y}$ stands for the values obtained from X to be used within the clause. The annotation $\langle offer(\vec{Y}) \rangle$, as shall be seen, is useful when relating additions to skeletons, listing the values offered within each clause. The $\vec{Z}$ stands for the values obtained from X to be used in the recursive call(s). In order to enforce the establishment of a flow of control, it is required that at least one recursive clause, *i.e.*, a non-empty vector of Z-values, must exist in a skeleton. The subgoal *test(X)* stands for a call to a clause of form

$$test(X) :- test_1(X), \ldots, test_t(X)$$

where each $test_i(X)$ can be a constant-dependent test (a test which depends on a constant C, *e.g.*, $X = C, X > C$, etc.), a system single-argument test (a test provided by the system which depends solely on X, *e.g.* atom(X), call(X), etc.) or a user-defined test (predicates which are not covered by the previous cases).

The subgoal $obtain(X, \vec{Y}, \vec{Z})$ can be specialised into a sequence of computations in terms of X, assigning values to $\vec{Y}$ and $\vec{Z}$. Each of these computations can be in the form of data structures decomposition (*e.g.*, list or binary tree decomposition), arithmetic calculations in terms of X (*e.g.* adding or subtracting a constant value from X) or auxiliary procedures (calls of system or user-defined predicates or retrieval of facts in the data-base).

Skeletons are devised by having the cardinality of $\vec{Y}$ and $\vec{Z}$ specified and the subgoals *test* and *obtain* of each clause defined and unfolded into the skeleton. It is, however, useful to consider more abstract forms of skeletons and hence we allow vectors and predicates to be left unspecified. Unspecified vectors and subgoals stand for *all* their possible instances.

A standard session would initially have the expert programmer defining the number of clauses of the skeleton. After that, the user would go through each clause and would define the number of components of the $\vec{Y}$ and $\vec{Z}$ vectors; these may as well be left unspecified. The predicates *test* and *obtain* are then specified and unfolded into the clause(s); here it may also be the case that some (or all) of these predicates are left unspecified. The Meta-Editor also offers the possibility of re-using previously edited components and further customising them, providing guidance in the definition of the predicates *test* and *obtain*: a

list	*visit-graph*	*meta-interpreter*

s(X):-
  X = [],
  Y1 = X. ⟨*offer*(Y1)⟩
s(X):-
  X = [Y1|Z1], ⟨*offer*(Y1)⟩
  s(Z1).
	s(X):-
	  X = end,
	  Y1 = X.⟨*offer*(Y1)⟩
	s(X):-
	  edge(X,Z1),
	  Y1 = X,⟨*offer*(Y1)⟩
	  s(Z1).
		s(X):-
		  X = true,
		  Y1 = X.⟨*offer*(Y1)⟩
		s(X):-
		  sys(X), call(X),
		  Y1 = X.⟨*offer*(Y1)⟩
		s(X):-
		  clause(X,Z1),
		  s(Z1).
		s(X):-
		  X = (Z1,Z2),
		  s(Z1),
		  s(Z2).

Figure 2: Some skeletons devised using the Meta-Editor.

number of appropriate stereotyped clauses are offered for each of them. Useful flows of control, such as those shown in Figure 2, can be devised using the initial template and the following commands:

1. *Y- and Z-Values*: specifies the actual number of elements of $\vec{Y}$ and $\vec{Z}$. In the case of Z-Values, the number and arguments of the recursive calls are appropriately adjusted.

2. *Copy*: copies a clause n times.

3. *Fundamental*: inserts a copy of the initial (fundamental) template anywhere in the skeleton.

4. *Remove*: removes a clause (in order to avoid meaningless skeletons, at least one recursive clause has to be left).

5. *Define test and obtain*: *test* and *obtain* are defined and unfolded into the clause. Cliché definitions are offered to the users who customises them to suit their needs (*e.g.* defining the functor of a data structure decomposition).

3.2 Designing Additions

Techniques are comprised of the combination of additions, *i.e.* single-argument program fragments combined together performing computations as the skeleton defines the flow of control. The Meta-Editor encourages the methodical development of simple additions — the building blocks of a technique — which can be subsequently combined into more complex program fragments.

In order to help expert programmers devise additions, the Meta-Editor offers an initial generic template comprised of a single clause and commands for its customisation, in a similar way to the devising of skeletons. However, additions have different initial clauses depending on their intended use mode (input or output). An *input mode addition* (or input addition) has the following initial template:

$$a(X) :- \qquad\qquad\qquad \langle required(\vec{R})\rangle$$
$$prepare(X, \vec{R}, \vec{Y}, \vec{Z}), \quad \langle offer(\vec{Y})\rangle$$
$$\overrightarrow{a(Z)} \ .$$

In this clause, the (possibly empty) $\vec{R}$ vector of *R-values*, together with the input value X, is used to *prepare* the vectors $\vec{Y}$ and $\vec{Z}$. The R-values are variable symbols which should be linked to offered values of other additions or skeletons, giving rise to more complex computations. An *output mode addition* (or output addition) has the following initial template:

$$a(X) :-$$
$$\overrightarrow{a(Z)}, \qquad\qquad\qquad \langle required(\vec{R})\rangle$$
$$prepare(\vec{R}, \vec{Z}, \vec{Y}, X). \quad \langle offer(\vec{Y})\rangle$$

The ordering of subgoals in the template of the output addition reflects the fact that the argument in the head goal and in the recursive call(s) are initially free variables: it is necessary that the recursive call(s) come first in the clause, binding the vector $\vec{Z}$. Only after the recursive subgoals are executed is that the computation *prepare*, assigning values to $\vec{Y}$ and X, is carried out.

Different templates are necessary because of the strict left-to-right evaluation of Prolog: different orderings of subgoals may produce different results. The two templates are an attempt to enable different orderings of the subgoals to be devised. The template for input additions may also be specialised in an *interleaved* version in which each recursive call has its own *prepare* subgoal. For instance, if we take $\vec{Z} = (Z_1, Z_2)$ we have the following interleaved version of an input addition:

$$a(X) :- \qquad\qquad\qquad \langle required(\vec{R})\rangle$$
$$prepare_1(X, \vec{R}, \vec{Y}, Z_1), \quad \langle offer(\vec{Y})\rangle$$
$$a(Z_1), \qquad\qquad\qquad \langle required(\vec{S})\rangle$$
$$prepare_2(X, \vec{S}, \vec{W}, Z_2), \quad \langle offer(\vec{W})\rangle$$
$$a(Z_2).$$

The subgoal $prepare(\vec{A}, \vec{B}, \vec{C}, \vec{D})$, as the *obtain* subgoal of skeletons, can be specialised into a sequence of computations in terms of $\vec{A}$ and $\vec{B}$, assigning values to $\vec{C}$ and $\vec{D}$, in the form of data structures compositions, arithmetic calculations and calls to auxiliary procedures.

The editing of additions is carried out in a similar way to that of skeletons. Depending on whether the user wishes to edit an addition to be used in input or output mode, one of the templates above is initially shown. A typical session would have the expert programmer initially specifying the number of clauses of the addition and then (s)he going through each clause defining $\vec{R}, \vec{Y}$ and $\vec{Z}$ (or leaving them unspecified and hence treated generically). The *prepare* predicates would then be specified and unfolded into the appropriate clauses. A repertoire of commands similar to that of the skeleton editing is available for devising additions. Some examples of useful additions are shown in Figure 3.

carry-value-up (-)	build-list-up (-)	build-list-down (+)

a(X):- ⟨required(R1)⟩
   X = R1.
a(X):-
   Z1 = X,
     a(Z1).
	a(X):- ⟨required($\vec{R}$)⟩
	   Y1 = [$\vec{R}$], ⟨offer(Y1)⟩
	   X = Y1.
	a(X):-
	   a(Z1), ⟨required($\vec{R}$)⟩
	   X = [$\vec{R}$|Z1].
		a(X):- ⟨required($\vec{R}$)⟩
		   Y1 = [$\vec{R}$|X]. ⟨offer(Y1)⟩
		a(X):- ⟨required($\vec{R}$)⟩
		   Z1 = [$\vec{R}$|X],
		     a(Z1).

Figure 3: Additions devised through the Meta-Editor: the *(+)* and *(-)* indicate that the addition is to be used in input and output mode, respectively.

3.3   Design of Techniques

After additions have been devised, the Meta-Editor offers the possibility of combining them and linking (Definition 3.5 below) their offered and required values. This provides the integration between different additions comprising a technique.

An addition depicts the adjustments to be carried out on each clause of skeletons (or programs) and also works as a pattern describing those skeletons (or programs) to which it is applicable. In order to preserve the declarative meaning of each skeleton and addition, the combination of additions with other additions and their application to skeletons is only possible if their clauses are *compatible* as formalised by Definition 3.2 below.

The combination process is carried out by having the user of the Meta-Editor firstly choosing compatible additions which are then appropriately combined together (Definition 3.3 below). After this, the Meta-Editor guides the user through the definition of links between variables within the combined addition. For instance, additions *build-list-down* and *carry-value-up* shown in Figure 3 can be combined as:

```
a(A1,B1):-
    A2 = [C⃗|A1],    ⟨offer(A2),required(B2)⟩
    B1 = B2.
a(A1,B1):-
    A2 = [C⃗|A1],
    B2 = B1,
    a(A2,B2).
```

The variable names are changed to avoid accidental bindings between them. Also, annotations which are useless for that particular combination (such as $\langle required(\vec{C})\rangle$ in the example above where no values are offered by *carry-value-up*) are suppressed. After the combined addition is shown, the user may wish to link the offered and required variables within each clause — in the current example, the user may authorise the link B2 with A2 in the first clause, obtaining the following *linked combination* (the annotation $\langle required(\vec{C})\rangle$ is also shown for future combinations):

```
a(A1,B1):-              ⟨required(C⃗)⟩
    A2 = [C⃗|A1],    ⟨offer(A2)⟩
    B1 = A2.
a(A1,B1):-              ⟨required(C⃗)⟩
    A2 = [C⃗|A1],
    B2 = B1,
    a(A2,B2).
```

Linked combinations may subsequently have their remaining required variables linked to offered values of skeletons, giving rise to a programming technique. The linked combination shown previously can be used to define, for instance, a technique building a list with the nodes of a graph obtained by skeleton *visit-graph* (Figure 2):

```
a(X,A1,B1):-
    X = end,
    Y1 = X,
    A2 = [Y1|A1],    ⟨offer(A2)⟩
    B1 = A2.
a(X,A1,B1):-
    edge(X,Z1),
    Y1 = X,
    A2 = [Y1|A1],
    B2 = B1,
    a(Z1,A2,B2).
```

The technique itself is underlined, but for clarity it is shown applied to the skeleton. The required vector $\vec{C}$ was linked to Y1 in both base-case and recursive clauses of the skeleton. A technique is fully defined when there are no more required values to be linked.

A programming technique can be further combined with other (combined) additions and/or techniques; however, the combination of techniques is only allowed if they share the same skeleton. Once a technique is defined for a skeleton, it is automatically defined for any of its specialisations (if the skeleton has unspecified parts).

The compatibility between two clauses is related to the number of recursive calls: only those clauses with the same number of recursive calls are permitted to be combined. A clause with a vector of recursive calls may be combined with another clause by having its vector of recursive calls first specialised to the same number of recursive calls of the other clause:

Definition 3.1 Clauses c_1 and c_2 are *compatible*, $comp_c(c_1, c_2)$, *iff*:

1. c_1 and c_2 have the same number (possibly zero) of recursive calls, or

2. c_1 or c_2 has an unspecified number of recursive calls (a vector).

The compatibility of each clause in a fragment (skeleton or addition) F_l with another clause in F_r is a necessary and sufficient condition to have them combined together:

Definition 3.2 Program fragment F_l is *compatible* with F_r, $comp_f(F_l, F_r)$, *iff* for every clause l of F_l there is exactly one clause r in F_r such that $comp_c(l, r)$.

It is worth noticing that F_r may have other clauses which are not compatible with any clause of F_l, however F_l is still compatible with F_r, but F_r is not compatible with F_l, *i.e.*, the compatibility of program fragments is not symmetric.

The combination of two compatible clauses is performed by pairing off the recursive calls and producing for each pair a combined recursive call with the arguments of the original calls. When combining clauses a distinction should be made between the left- and right-hand side clauses, because the non-recursive subgoals are slotted in the combined version according to the order of the original clauses, the left-hand side subgoals (in their original relative ordering) coming before the right-hand side ones (also in their original ordering). In the definition below $\vec{A}$ stands for a (possibly empty) sequence of arguments and $\vec{S}$ stands for a (possibly empty) sequence of non-recursive subgoals:

Definition 3.3 The *combination between two compatible clauses* $c_i, i = l, r$, of form

$$p(\vec{A^i}) :- \vec{S^i}\, p(\vec{A_0^i})\, \vec{S_0^i} \cdots p(\vec{A_m^i})\, \vec{S_m^i}$$

is $\dot{c} = c_l \cdot c_r$, of form

$$p(\vec{A^l}, \vec{A^r}) :- \vec{S^l}\, \vec{S^r}\, p(\vec{A_0^l}, \vec{A_0^r})\, \vec{S_0^l}\, \vec{S_0^r} \cdots p(\vec{A_m^l}, \vec{A_m^r})\, \vec{S_m^l}\, \vec{S_m^r}$$

If both clauses have unspecified vectors of recursive calls, then their vectors of recursive calls should be considered as a single recursive call and combined as such. If only one of the clauses has a vector of recursive calls, then this clause has its vector first customised to the number of recursive calls of the other clause and then they are combined as in the definition above. Whenever clauses are combined, variables will not get accidentally bound by virtue of their sharing the same name.

In the combination of program fragments one must also make the distinction between left- and right-hand side components because their combination is made up of individual combinations of each clause of the left-hand side fragment with one clause of the right-hand side program fragment:

Definition 3.4 The *combination between compatible program fragments* $F_l = l_1, \ldots, l_m$ and $F_r = r_1, \ldots, r_n$, is $\dot{C} = F_l \cdot F_r = \dot{c}_1, \ldots, \dot{c}_m$, $\dot{c}_i = l_i \cdot r_j$, $comp_c(l_i, r_j)$.

One can see that the combination $\dot{C}$ of program fragments F_l and F_r is still compatible with both F_l and F_r, $comp_f(\dot{C}, F_l)$ and $comp_f(\dot{C}, F_r)$.

The required values $\vec{R}$ of each clause (if they exist) should be assigned a value of some offered value $Y_i \in \vec{Y}$, after a combination takes place. This provides the integration between the components of a programming technique:

Definition 3.5 The *links* L between a clause c with required values $\vec{R}$ and a compatible clause c', with offered values $\vec{Y}$, is a finite set of pairs A/B where A is either the vector $\vec{R}$ or one of its elements $R_i \in \vec{R}$ and B is either the vector $\vec{Y}$ or one of its elements $Y_j \in \vec{Y}$ or a constant. We shall use c/L to denote clause c after its required values R, $R/Y \in \mathsf{L}$, are replaced by Y, and $\mathcal{L}$ is used to refer to a set of links $\mathcal{L} = \{\mathsf{L}_1, \ldots, \mathsf{L}_n\}$ between two program fragments.

When a link is created between a vector and a particular set of offered values (or a vector of offered values), the vector of required values is properly substituted for the set of offered variables (or the vector of offered values) within the clause. When a vector of offered values is linked to a set of required values, then the clause of the offered values is customised by having the vector of values appropriately substituted for a specific set of offered values with its cardinality the same as that of the required values.

The links are supplied by expert programmers and convey the knowledge used to integrate the independent additions comprising a programming technique. Each required value of a vector in an addition (or a combination of additions) should appear exactly once in the set L of links. The set of links can be provided in a generic way if vectors of values are found. To prevent experts from linking required values twice, once a variable $R \in \vec{R}$ is used, it is removed from the annotation *required*.

Definition 3.6 The *linked combination between compatible program fragments* $F_l = l_1, \ldots, l_m$, and $F_r = r_1, \ldots, r_n$, with sets of links $\mathsf{L}_1, \ldots, \mathsf{L}_n$ (between r_i and l_j) is $\widehat{C} = \hat{c}_1, \ldots, \hat{c}_m$, $\hat{c}_i = l_i \cdot r_j/\mathsf{L}_j$, $comp_c(l_i, r_j)$.

Although the definitions above allow all sorts of combinations between compatible program fragments, not all of them make sense according to our adopted approach. Skeletons, for instance, are not allowed to be combined with other skeletons since they dictate the flow of control of a program and this must be unique. Some meaningless or wrong combinations/links between additions can also be ruled out on syntactic grounds:

1. *Non-empty links between additions* – Additions are only allowed to be combined and stored if the set of links between them is not empty. If they do not share values, *i.e.* their set of links is empty, then they are not integrated and it is meaningless to combine them[1].

---

[1] Techniques, however, may have empty links between the skeleton and the addition(s) because an addition might simply use the flow of control of the skeleton, *e.g.* a technique which counts the number of times a loop is performed.

2. *Missing required or offered values* – In order to have two additions linked, there must be at least one offered value in one addition and at least one required value in the other one (in compatible clauses).

3. *Incompatible types of required and offered values* – If the computation(s) of an addition make(s) use of the built-in predicate **is** it can be inferred that its required and/or offered values are *numeric*. Required numeric values can only be linked to offered numeric values – attempts to combine additions with incompatible values are prevented.

4. *Incompatible ordering of required and offered values* – The links between required numeric values and offered numeric values (or vice-versa) are only permitted if in the combined clause the *offer* annotation comes before the *required* annotation. The reason for this constraint is that the required numeric values need to be instantiated, *i.e.* linked to offered values, before the computation (using predicate **is**) is executed.

These cases capture some potential problems that may occur while the expert programmer is devising techniques. The Meta-Editor can offer support to its users by spotting these cases and rejecting the faulty combination. The envisaged setting is one in which "clusters" of properly combined and linked additions are offered to programmers who may test them on skeletons. These clusters are the *programming techniques*:

Definition 3.7 A *programming technique* T is the triple $\mathsf{T} = \langle \mathsf{S}, \widehat{\mathsf{A}}, \mathcal{L} \rangle$ where S is a skeleton, $\widehat{\mathsf{A}}$ is a linked combination of additions compatible with S, $comp_f(\mathsf{S}, \widehat{\mathsf{A}})$, and $\mathcal{L}$ is a (possibly empty) set of links between the clauses of $\widehat{\mathsf{A}}$ and S.

Programming techniques are devised with a particular skeleton (or class of skeletons) S in mind and sometimes there must be links between the skeleton and the combined addition so that offered values of the former can be linked with required values of the latter. It is worth noticing that once a technique is defined for a generic skeleton, then the technique is automatically defined for future specialisations of the skeleton.

Example: Given output addition *build-list-down* (Figure 3) and the following generic skeleton *single-recursion*:

```
s(X):-
      test(X),
      obtain(X, Y).        ⟨offer(Y)⟩
s(X):-
      test(X),
      obtain(X, Y, Z1),    ⟨offer(Y)⟩
      s(Z1).
```

then we can define the technique $\mathsf{T} = \langle \textit{single-recursion}, \textit{build-list-down}, \mathcal{L} \rangle$, where $\mathcal{L} = \{\mathsf{L}_1, \mathsf{L}_2\}$, $\mathsf{L}_i = \{\vec{R}/\vec{Y}\}$, $i = 1, 2$, which builds a list with values provided by the skeleton. This definition is such that any further specialisations of the skeleton *single-recursion* (through specifying subgoals *test*, *obtain* and the cardinality of $\vec{Y}$) can be enhanced with it.

The combination of additions is carried out by specifying the left- and right-hand side components: only compatible additions are permitted to be combined. The combination process relies entirely on the expert programmer's expertise and in the current stage, the Meta-Editor simply rules out, on syntactic grounds, those additions that are not compatible. An incremental procedure takes place during the preparation of combinations: initially two basic compatible additions are chosen by the expert and combined/linked. The resulting combined/linked addition may be subsequently combined/linked with other additions or other (previously prepared) combined/linked additions.

The Meta-Editor supplies the user with the set of existing input and output additions and combined additions and the user informs which of them will play the role of the left-hand side program fragment in the combination process. After the left-hand side component is chosen, the user is offered those compatible input and output additions and compatible combinations and chooses one to play the role of the right-hand side program fragment. The Meta-Editor then displays their combination (with their variable names changed to avoid clashes) and, if there are any *required* annotations, the user may link them to offered values within the same clause. Combined additions may also be edited and further customised.

After a combined addition is defined, the user may define sets of techniques which make use of it by providing links between the combination and different skeletons. If the final combined addition is such that there are no more *required* annotations, then a technique is automatically defined with the most generic compatible skeleton as part of it. If the combined addition has *required* values to be linked, then the user must inform the skeleton and the links between the skeleton and the combined addition in order to define a technique.

4   Conclusions and Directions of Research

Existing attempts to describe Prolog techniques are largely informal, these normally being depicted by means of examples and an explanation in a natural language. In this paper, we have adopted the stepwise enhancement approach advocated in [KLS89] and suggested a simple and methodical way of formalising the notion of Prolog programming techniques and skeletons. A tool, the Prolog Techniques Meta-Editor, embedding the proposed approach, which assists expert programmers in devising their techniques was also presented.

The proposed approach uses simple one-argument program fragments (the skeletons and additions) expressed in a notation much similar to Prolog itself, and a small repertoire of commands to customise them. The way program fragments are represented encourages a methodical design in which more specific instances are gradually prepared. The devised program fragments can be incrementally combined into more sophisticated constructs giving rise to the programming techniques. The skeletons and techniques are then offered to users of a Prolog Techniques Editor. The components of a technique can be re-used to define other techniques and techniques can also be used to define other more complex techniques.

The notation used to formalise skeletons enables the expert programmer to concentrate on a single value (whether a complex data structure or a simple atom) and the different ways this value is used to obtain new values. The manner of formalising techniques encourages expert programmers to focus on the relationships between different arguments. The program (or class of programs) the technique is aimed at is specified by having the expert programmer providing a skeleton: the technique can be applied only to programs built from that skeleton.

The formalisation employed naturally defines a hierarchy of program fragments in which the topmost nodes are the initial templates offered to expert programmers; their offspring are more specialised forms of them and the leaf nodes are fully specified program fragments. The library of the Meta-Editor could be managed according to this hierarchical view. For instance, the skeleton *single-recursion* shown previously can be seen as a more generic form of skeletons *list* and *visit-graph* presented in Figure 2 — any technique devised for the former is automatically defined for the latter ones. A facility ("browser") to guide the expert programmer through an existing hierarchy of program fragments should be made available as one the services to manage the library of programming practices of the Meta-Editor.

In theory, given an appropriate set of skeletons and techniques every Prolog program can be devised. However, the size of such set and the complexity of its components greatly impair its use. If the programs built using the Prolog Techniques Editor are allowed to be further combined then the set of skeletons and techniques can be kept small and a large number of programs (more complex ones) can still be produced [VVRV93].

The formalism presented in this paper does not support the construction of every conceivable programming technique, and hence not every Prolog program may be developed in this approach. "Bad" programming practices (*e.g.* having a test after a sequence of subgoals which are not related to it – tests should be performed as early as possible so as to save computational effort) should not be able to be devised, and those programs incorporating them should not have their construction supported. However, by dropping some of the restrictions in the definitions given above, removing the concepts of skeletons and techniques and regarding only the additions (with tests) and their combinations as the building blocks of programs, a richer class of programming practices, and hence programs, can be devised.

Additions and techniques that change the flow of control were avoided. These can change the behaviour of the skeleton and their combination may require more careful analysis. Moreover, some techniques, making use of higher-level information such as the number of recursive clauses of the skeleton (for instance *collect* [KLS89]) or adding clauses (initialisation calls) were not addressed. They are material for future research.

The automatic acquisition of skeletons and techniques from a given program is a problem currently under investigation. A program would be supplied with the use mode of the arguments of each subgoal and would be decomposed into its program fragments which would then be matched against the existing library of programming practices. The closest match plus the necessary adjustments to transform it into the extracted program fragment would conveniently incorporate new components to the existing library.

Acknowledgements: Thanks are due to D. Robertson, J. Hesketh, A. Bowles and M. Vargas-Vera for invaluable discussions, to S. Simpson and I. Frank for the proof-reading and to the anonymous LoPSTr '93 referees for the constructive criticisms.

References

[BBD+91] P. Brna, P. Bundy, T. Dodd, C. K. Eisenstadt, M. Looi, H. Pain, D. Robertson, B. Smith, and M. Van Someren. Prolog Programming Techniques. *Instructional Science*, 20(2):111–133, 1991.

[BGB91] A. Bundy, G. Grosse, and P. Brna. A Prolog Techniques Recursive Editor. *Instructional Science*, 20(2):135–172, 1991.

[Bow92] A. W Bowles. *Detecting Prolog Programming Techniques Using Abstract Interpretation*. PhD thesis, Department of Artificial Intelligence, University of Edinburgh, 1992.

[Brn91] P. Brna. Teaching Prolog Techniques. Research Paper 530, Department of Artificial Intelligence, University of Edinburgh, 1991.

[Gab92] D. S. Gabriel. TX: a Prolog Explanation System. Msc dissertation, Department of Artificial Intelligence, University of Edinburgh, 1992.

[GH91] T. S. Gegg-Harrison. Learning Prolog in a Schema-Based Environment. *Instructional Science*, 20:173–192, 1991.

[KLS89] M. Kirschenbaum, A. Lakhotia, and L. Sterling. Skeletons and Techniques for Prolog Programming. Technical Report 89-170, Case Western Reserve University, Ohio, U.S.A., 1989.

[Loo88] C.-K. Looi. *Automatic Program Analysis in a Prolog Intelligent Teaching System*. PhD thesis, Department of Artificial Intelligence, University of Edinburgh, 1988.

[O'K90] R. A. O'Keefe. *The Craft of Prolog*. MIT Press, 1990.

[Rob91] D. Robertson. A Simple Prolog Techniques Editor for Novice Users. In *3rd Annual Conference on Logic Programming*, Edinburgh, Scotland, April 1991. Springer-Verlag.

[SK91] L. Sterling and M. Kirschenbaum. Applying Techniques to Skeletons. Technical Report 91-179, Center for Automation and Intelligent Systems Research, Case Western Reserve University, Ohio, U.S.A., 1991.

[SS86] L. Sterling and E. Shapiro. *The Art of Prolog: Advanced Programming Techniques*. MIT Press, 1986.

[Vas92] W. W. Vasconcelos. Formalising the Knowledge of a Prolog Techniques Editor. In *9th Brazilian Symposium on Artificial Intelligence*, Rio de Janeiro, Brazil, October 1992.

[VVRV93] M. Vargas-Vera, D. Robertson, and W. W. Vasconcelos. Building Large-Scale Prolog Programs using a Techniques Editing System. Research Paper 635, Department of Artificial Intelligence, University of Edinburgh, 1993. To be presented as a poster in the International Logic Programming Symposium, Vancouver, British Columbia, Canada, Oct., 1993.

Interactive Program Derivation Using Program Schemata and Incrementally Generated Strategies

Anna-Lena Johansson

Computing Science Department, Uppsala University,
Uppsala, SWEDEN

Abstract

In this article we will study the problem of ascertaining of the correctness of a program by formally deriving the program from its formal specification and concentrate on the introduction of recursion into logic programs. We will also discuss an interactive system using program schemata and generated derivation strategies to aid a user in the process performing the synthesis task.

1 Program Derivation and Program Schemata

1.1 Schemata for Programs

In the area of logic programming we can use a program schema to describe a family of programs. The concept of a program schema is not a new idea. Schemata have been used as a means of description, as a guide for writing programs, in tutoring systems, and as a design strategy for program construction. In this paper we will use program schemata to aid the derivation of Horn-clause programs from first order predicate logic specifications.

Let us now see how we can capture families of recursive programs by program schemata. The justification for the program schema is a stepwise induction schema constructed from a well-founded induction schema, a definition of a set, and an ordering relation over the set, i.e. a well-founded set[0].

The set of lists can be described by the following definition that states that the empty list, [], is a list and a constructed list, [U|Y], is a list when Y is a list.

$$\forall X \, (\text{list}(X) \leftrightarrow X = [] \lor \exists U \exists Y \, (X = [U|Y] \, \& \, \text{list}(Y)))$$

The set of lists can be ordered by stating that a list Y immediately precedes the list X, $Y \prec X$, when Y is the tail of the list X.

$$\forall X \forall Y \, (\text{list}(X) \, \& \, \text{list}(Y) \rightarrow (Y \prec X \leftrightarrow \exists U \, X = [U|Y]))$$

---

[0]In this paper we will exemplify with program schemas over the set of lists although the described work is not restricted to this set.

The induction schema for stepwise induction on lists tells us that the property F can be proved for all lists by proving F for the empty list [] and proving it for the constructed list [U|Y] provided it holds for the tail of the list Y.

$$F([]) \text{ \& } \forall U \forall Y \text{ (list(Y)} \rightarrow (F(Y) \rightarrow F([U|Y]))) \rightarrow \forall Z \text{ (list(Z)} \rightarrow F(Z))$$

Correspondingly, program schema for a property defined recursively over the set of lists will state that the property is true for the empty list, [], and that the property is true for a constructed list, represented as $[U^*|Y^*]$, if the property is true for Y^*[1].

$$P([])$$
$$P([U^*|Y^*]) \leftarrow P(Y^*)$$

The schema for the same well-founded set but with the statement to be proved being a relation $P(X^*,V,Z)$[2], where the variable names V and Z represents the arguments that are unchanged and the arguments that are changed in the recursion, respectively. The schema needs an additional relation R_1 to establish the relation between the additional arguments in the base case. An additional relation R_2 is needed in the step clause to establish the relation between the antecedent and the consequence.

$$P([],V,Z) \leftarrow R_1(V,Z)$$
$$P([U^*|Y^*],V,Z) \leftarrow P(Y^*,V,Z1) \text{ \& } R_2(U^*,Y^*,V,Z1,Z)$$

The general form of a program schema irrespective of the actual well-founded set, but partitioning the set into two types of elements: minimal $0_0, 0_1, ..., 0_r$ and non-minimal can be formulated with r+1 clauses for the minimal elements and one clause for the non-minimal element.

1.2 Program Derivation Method

Assume a specification of a relation P and a program schema with the unknown relations R_1, R_2 .... To turn the program schema into a program the program derivation method has to find relations ρ_1, ρ_2 .... The derivations ascertain, in fact, that we can, using the induction schema corresponding to the program schema, prove that the program for the relation P with the unknown relations R_1, R_2 ... instantiated with the relations ρ_1, ρ_2 ... follows from the specification of the relation P.

$$\text{Spec P } \vdash \text{ (P([],V,Z)} \leftarrow \rho_1(V,Z))$$
$$\text{\& (P([U^*|Y^*],V,Z)} \leftarrow P(Y^*,V,Z1) \text{ \& } \rho_2(U^*,Y^*,V,Z1,Z))$$

The process of obtaining the program has two steps:
- instantiating the relation P in the program schema with the program relation and
- instantiating the unknown relations in the program schema.

The instantiation of the schema with the program relation is a straightforward substitution of the program relation name for P. The relations ρ_1 and ρ_2 are found

---

[1]We will use the convention that variable names ?* are used as variable names for the induction arguments.

[2]The induction is not restricted to the first argument. Schemas can also be constructed for the patterns $P(V,Z,X^*)$ and $P(V,X^*,Z)$, among others.

by a derivation process which starts with a program schema instantiated with the program relation. For each clause of the program schema, the antecedent and the consequence of the implication are expanded and compaired in order to identify a sufficient relation ρ to make the consequence imply the antecedent.

Let us illustrate the proposed methodology for finding the unknown relations R_1 and R_2 by a simple example. The different stages in the process of finding the unknown relation are illustrated in a table with four columns, see below. The conclusion of the clause is shown in the first column, the condition in the third column and the fourth column holds a justification of how the current row is obtained from the previous.

The starting point for a derivation is a program clause including an unknown relation that is needed to make the condition part imply the conclusion part in the clause. The clause is developed by equivalence transformations until we can identify two parts in the conclusion: one or more instances of the induction hypothesis and a remainder. This remainder has to be implied by the unknown relation in the condition part. The formula R is a formula that implies the parts of the conclusion that is not implied by the induction hypothesis P in the condition part.

The problem example is to synthesise a program for a subset-relation. The relation is specified between two sets; a set X is a subset of another set Y iff every element on the set X is also an element on the set Y.

Specification:

$\forall X \forall Y \; (subset(X,Y) \leftrightarrow \forall V \; (on(V,X) \rightarrow on(V,Y)))$

In the program that we want to derive we have chosen to represent the sets by simple lists. The specification places a condition on the elements of the first set that forces an inspection of every element on this set. The inspection of every element on the first set can be made by recursively going through the list that represents the set. Consequently, the first argument is chosen as induction argument in a program schema.

Program Schema for program relation:

$subset([],Y) \leftarrow R_1(Y)$

$subset([U*|Y*],Y) \leftarrow subset(Y*,Y) \, \& \, R_2(U*,Y*,Y)$

The derivation of the base clause in the program schema is a sequence of:

- **Unfold (steps 1 - 3),**

	Conclusion		Conditions	Justification
1	$subset([],Y)$	$\leftarrow$	$R_1(Y)$	
	⋮		⋮	
3	$\forall V \; (false \rightarrow on(V,Y))$	$\leftarrow$	$R_1(Y)$	unfold

- **Simplify (steps 4 - 5),**

	⋮		⋮	
5	true	$\leftarrow$	$R_1(Y)$	simplify $\rightarrow$, simplify $\forall$

- **Comparison between conclusions and conditions (step 6)**

6	true	$\leftarrow$	true	compare

The derived definition of the relation $R_1(Y)$: $\forall Y \ (R_1(Y) \leftrightarrow true)$.

The derivation of the step clause in the program schema is a sequence of:

- **Unfold (steps 1 - 3),**

	Conclusion		Conditions	Just
1	subset([U*|Y*],Y)	←	subset(Y*,Y) & R_2(U*,Y*,Y)	
	⋮		⋮	
3	$\forall V \ (V - U^* \lor on(V,Y^*) \to$ on(V,Y))	←	$\forall V \ (on(V,Y^*) \to on(V,Y))$ & R_2(U*,Y*,Y)	unfold

- **Distribute (steps 4 - 5),**

	⋮		⋮	
5	$\forall V \ (V - U^* \to on(V,Y))$ & $\forall V \ (on(V,Y^*) \to on(V,Y))$	←	$\forall V \ (on(V,Y^*) \to on(V,Y))$ & R_2(U*,Y*,Y)	dist $\lor$ over $\to$, dist & over $\forall$

- **Simplify (step 6)**

6	on(U*,Y) & $\forall V \ (on(V,Y^*) \to on(V,Y))$	←	$\forall V \ (on(V,Y^*) \to on(V,Y))$ & R_2(U*,Y*,Y)	simp

- **Comparison (step 7 - 9)**

7	$\forall V \ (on(V,Y^*) \to on(V,Y))$	←	$\forall V \ (on(V,Y^*) \to on(V,Y))$ & on(U*,Y) & R_2*(U*,Y*,Y)	To R
8	true	←	$\forall V \ (on(V,Y^*) \to on(V,Y))$ & on(U*,Y) & R_2*(U*,Y*,Y)	CA
9	true	←	$\forall V \ (on(V,Y^*) \to on(V,Y))$ & on(U*,Y)	comp

The derived definition of the relation R_2(U*,Y*,Y):

$\forall U \forall Y \forall Z \ (R_2(U,Y,Z) \leftrightarrow on(U,Z))$

Program for program relation:

subset([],Y) ←
subset([U*\|Y*],Y) ← subset(Y*,Y) & on(U*,Y)

The developing process will end when a comparison discovers that every formula in the conclusion part is implied by the condition part. As conjunctures in the conclusion can be successively eliminated, it is usually the case that the conclusion part will be reduced to the logical constant true at the end of the process.

1.3   Rules in the Derivation

In the derivation two types of rules are used: equivalence transformations and rules for comparison between the conclusion part and the condition part of a clause.

The equivalence transformations are used for unfolding, simplification, and distribution. Let us take a closer look at the rules for comparison between conclusion and condition part. We have already mentioned a rule for absorbing a formula in the conclusion part. Apart from this rule we use two rules for adding information to the unknown relation R. These rules are called 'To R' and 'CS'.

To R:

Let $C_1, ..., C_i, ..., C_n$ be formulas in the conjunctive conclusion and let the antecedent be separated into the known conditions H and the currently unknown condition R. Let C_i be a formula that is not implied by H. Let R be a conjunction $C_i \& R^*$.

$$\frac{C_1 \& ... \& C_i \& ... \& C_n \leftarrow H \& R \quad R \leftrightarrow C_i \& R^*}{C_1 \& ... \& C_i \& ... \& C_n \leftarrow H \& C_i \& R^*}$$

After the application of the 'To R'-rule C_i is implied by R. We have made the assumption that R has the definition: $R \leftrightarrow C_i \& R^*$. The currently unknown condition has changed to R^*.

CS (Condition Strengthening)

Let C be the conclusion and let the antecedent be separated into a condition H and an unknown condition R_A. R_A is a formula constructed from a specified occurrence of A using only the operators & and $\vee$, and R_B results from R_A by replacing this occurrence of A by B.

$$\frac{C \leftarrow H \& R_A \quad B \rightarrow A}{C \leftarrow H \& R_B}$$

The 'To R' and 'CS' rules are both used to developed the unknown relation; by the use of the rules we get more information about the definiens of the unknown relation. There is a difference of how the rules affect the relation between the conclusion and the condition in the clause. The 'To R' rule has the effect that a formula that is identical to a formula in the conclusion is added to the condition. Suppose, on the one hand, that the 'To R' rule is the only rule used to instantiate the unknown relation then it must be the case that the conclusion and the condition are equivalent and we have derived an unknown relation enforces an equivalence. Suppose, on the other hand, that we also use the 'CS' rule then the condition implies the conclusion but the conclusion does not necessarily imply the condition. Thus we have no direct equivalence between the conclusion and the condition but we can describe the new formula as a conditional equivalence taking the introduced strengthening formula as the condition. Let C be the conclusion and let the antecedent be separated into two conditions H and A. Furthermore, assume that the conclusion and the antecedent are equivalent. The strengthening of A to B ($B \rightarrow A$) can be described as a new equivalence between the conclusion and the antecedent with the formula A replaced by the formula B, under the condition B.

$$\frac{C \leftrightarrow H \& A \quad B \rightarrow A}{(C \leftrightarrow H \& B) \leftarrow B}$$

Even the result of an application of the rule 'To R' can described as an conditional equivalence letting the truthvalue true be the condition. Thus we can say that each table derivation ends in a conditional equivalence. A conditional equivalence is derived for each minimal element and each non-minimal element in the well-founded set. The use of the program schema

$P([],V,Z) \leftarrow R_1(V,Z)$

$P([U|Y],V,Z) \leftarrow P(Y,V,Z1) \& R_2(U,Y,V,Z1,Z)$

results in conditonal equivalences where the instantiation, ρ, of the unknown relation can be divided into two parts: ρ_{1a} and ρ_{1b}. The subformula ρ_{1a} has been obtained by the use of the 'To R' rule and ρ_{1b} has been obtained by the use of the 'CS' rule.

Conditional equivalences:

$\rho_{1b}(V,Z) \rightarrow (P([],V,Z) \leftrightarrow \rho_{1a}(V,Z) \& \rho_{1b}(V,Z))$

$\rho_{2b}(U,Y,V,Z1,Z) \rightarrow$
$\quad (P([U|Y],V,Z) \leftrightarrow P(Y,V,Z1) \& \rho_{2a}(U,Y,V,Z1,Z) \& \rho_{2b}(U,Y,V,Z1,Z))$

where $\rho_{1b}(V,Z)$ and $\rho_{2b}(U,Y,V,Z1,Z)$ can be identical to true, and

$(\rho_1(V,Z) \leftrightarrow \rho_{1a}(V,Z) \& \rho_{1b}(V,Z))$

$(\rho_2(U,Y,V,Z1,Z) \leftrightarrow \rho_{2a}(U,Y,V,Z1,Z) \& \rho_{2b}(U,Y,V,Z1,Z))$

The derived equivalences can be used as clause development rules in later derivations. Let us call the above descriptions for equivalence programs for P. The program is made up of the if-parts of the equivalence.

Program for relation P:

$P([],V,Z) \leftarrow \rho_{1a}(V,Z) \& \rho_{1b}(V,Z)$

$P([U|Y],V,Z) \leftarrow P(Y,V,Z1) \& \rho_{2a}(U,Y,V,Z1,Z) \& \rho_{2b}(U,Y,V,Z1,Z)$

When the relations ρ_{1b} and ρ_{2b} are identical to true, the equivalences describing the relation P can be transformed into an equivalent recursive definition of the relation P. Furthermore, this recursive specification of P has been shown by induction in the table derivations to be equivalent to the non-recursive specification of P using the induction schema corresponding to the program schema. Thus we have a correct and complete program.

Recursive specification of P:

$(P(X,V,Z) \leftrightarrow$
$\quad X = [] \& \rho_{1a}(V,Z) \vee \exists U \exists Y \exists Z1 (X = [U|Y] \& P(Y,V,Z1) \& \rho_{2a}(U,Y,V,Z1,Z)))$

On the other hand, when the relations ρ_{1b} and ρ_{2b} are not identical to true then the set of consequences of the equivalence program with restrictions for P is a subset of the set of consequences of the specification of the relation P. The program is correct but not complete with respect to the specification. However, let us study the non-recursive specification of P and describe its form with the following formula (see [5]):

Non-recursive specification of P:

$(P(X,V,Z) \leftrightarrow P_a(X,V,Z) \& P_b(X,V,Z))$, where the formula P_a can be equal to true

The semantics of the restrictions on the equivalence program is that there is a relation P_c that implies the relation P_b and that a specification of a relation P' equal to the specification of the relation P but with the relation P_c substituted for the relation P_b is equivalent to the equivalence program.

$P_c(X,V,Z) \rightarrow P_b(X,V,Z)$

Non-recursive specification of P':
$(P'(X,V,Z) \leftrightarrow P_a(X,V,Z) \& P_c(X,V,Z)))$,
where the formula P_a can be equal to true

The set of consequences of the equivalence program with restrictions for P is equal to the set of consequences of the specification of the relation P'. The program is both correct and complete with respect to the specification P'. Then we also have a recursive definition of the relation P' which can be shown to be equivalent to the non-recursive specification of P' and to the equivalence program for P when taking away the restrictions.

Recursive specification of P':
$(P'(X,V,Z) \leftrightarrow$
$X - [] \& \rho_1(V,Z) \vee \exists U \exists Y \exists Z1 (X - [U|Y] \& P(Y,V,Z1) \& \rho_2(U,Y,V,Z1,Z))))$

2   The Incremental Generation of Strategies

2.1   The Construction of a Derivation

A system supporting the program derivation using the described methodology is being implemented using the LPA MacProlog System [6]. The system is designed for interactive use.

The synthesis system is not intended as an automatic theorem proving program nevertheless some facilities for automatic theorem proving can be of considerable assistence to the user, by essentially performing the inference steps belonging to the strategies unfold, simplify and distribute. Thus leaving the creativity and innovations to the comparison steps assisted by the advisory rules in the system and the user. The strategy for deriving an unknown relation is presented as the iteration of equivalence transformations: unfold, distribute, and simplify followed by relation development inferences that compare conclusion and condition.

The problem of deriving the unknown relations for in a program schema, with two clauses, can be refined into the problem of deriving R1 and the problem of deriving R2. The user is presented with the a list of the subproblems and can select one of them with a pointing-device.

- **Derive Unknown Relations**
    - **Derive R1**
    - **Derive R2**

Let us elaborate on the strategy for base clauses and step clauses separately. The derivation of a base clause, on the one hand, typically starts with the sequence: unfold, simplify, and compare.

- **Derive R1**
    - **Unfold - R1**
    - **Simplify - R1**
    - **Compare - R1**

This sequence applies when the minimal element in the well-founded set also is the base element in a data structure such as the empty list or the empty tree.

Unfolding a relation taking the base element of a data structure as argument usually introduces a logical constant (true or false) in the conclusion thus leaving the field open for simplifications. This is not the case when the minimal element is not the base element of a data structure for example, taking the set of all list containing certain element as the well-founded set and therefore the sequence unfold, and compare is generated in these cases. The strategy sequences that follows the first sequence depends on the previous comparison step. Does the comparison step introduce identities that contain terms to unfold, and the terms become first level arguments[3] to formulas in the conclusion, the step is naturally followed by an unfold (and in relevant cases by a simplification), and a comparison. In other cases a new comparison step follows.

- **Derive R1**
  - **Unfold - R1**
  - **Simplify - R1**
  - **Compare - R1**
  - **Derive R1***
    - **Compare - R1***
    - **Derive R1****

The derivation of a step clause, on the other hand, typically starts with the sequence: unfold, distribute, simplify, and compare. Here the clause development inference distribute is included. Distribution is used to bring out a subformula that is hidden inside logical connectives to be compared with a similar formula that is a hypothesis in the condition part of the clause. Just like for a base clause the strategy sequences that follows the initial sequence depends on the comparison step. If the comparison step introduces an unfold term in the conclusion part then the sequence will be: unfold, distribute, simplify, and compare. If the comparison step does not introduce an unfold term and there are formulas in the conclusion where distribute can be applied then the sequence will be: distribute, simplify, and compare. In the other cases the sequence will be: compare.

The derivation is brought to its end when the conclusion part has been emptied. This situation appears when each of the conclusions have been taken away as already implied by the condition part.

2.2 Example Derivation

Let us continue by studying the generation of strategies in a derivation of the unknown relation in a step clause. We take a relation union(X,Y,Z) where X is a structure containing all elements of Y and Z and no more.

Specification:
$\forall X \forall Y \forall Z$ (union(X,Y,Z) $\leftrightarrow$ $\forall$S (on(S,Y) $\lor$ on(S,Z) $\leftrightarrow$ on(S,X)))

Now, let us derive a program from this specification. We have chosen to derive a program for a list data structure that is successively decomposed into the head and the tail of the list. The union-relation has three arguments. We have chosen the second argument of the relation as induction argument and consequently the first and the third argument are auxiliary arguments.

---

[3]An example of an first level argument is the term nil in the formula "ot(nil)". In the formula "ot(t(nil,U,nil))" the term nil is not a first level argument.

Program Schema for the program relation:

union(X,[],Z) ← R₁(X,Z)

union(X,[U*|Y*],Z) ← union(V,Y*,W) & R₂(U*,Y*,V,W,X,Z)

When starting the derivation of the unknown relation R₂ the derivation sequence: unfold, distribute, (simplify,) compare is generated. The initial unfold of a step clause will always introduce new formulas where the induction hypotheses have to be brought out by distribution.

• **Derive R2**

• **Unfold - R2**

Conclusion		Conditions	Justif.
union(X,[U*|Y*],Z)	←	union(V,Y*,W) & R₂(U*,Y*,V,W,X,Z)	instant PS
⋮		⋮	
∀S (S = U* ∨ on(S,Y*) ∨ on(S,Z)) ↔ on(S,X))	←	∀S (on(S,Y*) ∨ on(S,W) ↔ on(S,V)) & R₂(U*,Y*,V,W,X,Z)	unfold, unfold

The situation after the initial unfolding is depicted in Figure 2. Viewing the equivalence formula in the conclusion part as a combination of two implications: ∀S (S = U* ∨ on(S,Y*) ∨ on(S,Z) → on(S,X)) and ∀S (on(S,X) → S = U* ∨ on(S,Y*) ∨ on(S,Z)), we have the choice of bringing out on(S,Y*) from a antecedent or from a consequence of an implication. We will choose bring out the formula from the antecedent since there is a chance that the identity also present in the antecedent can reduce the remainder to an interesting formula.

• **Distribute (bring out on(S,Y*)) - R2**

⋮		⋮	
∀S (S = U* → on(S,X)) & ∀S (on(S,Y*) ∨ on(S,Z) → on(S,X)) & ∀S (on(S,X) → S = U* ∨ on(S,Y*) ∨ on(S,Z))	←	∀S (on(S,Y*) ∨ on(S,W) ↔ on(S,V)) & R₂(U*,Y*,V,W,X,Z)	distrib → over ∨, distrib ∀ over &

Simplification can be applied to the first subformula in the conclusion, reducing it to the atomic formula on(U*,X).

• **Simplify - R2**

on(U*,X) & ∀S (on(S,Y*) ∨ on(S,Z) → on(S,X)) & ∀S (on(S,X) → S = U* ∨ on(S,Y*) ∨ on(S,Z))	←	∀S (on(S,Y*) ∨ on(S,W) ↔ on(S,V)) & R₂(U*,Y*,V,W,X,Z)	simp

When it comes to the comparison we notice that the atomic formula on(U*,X) has no target formula in the condition part; we will take it to be a partial instantiation of the relation R₂. The condition that the element U* is to be present on the list X is strengthened to the condition that U* is to be the first element of this list and that the corresponding variable V will denote the tail, X = [U*|V].

- **Compare - R2**

$\forall S$ (on(S,Y*) ∨ on(S,Z) → on(S,[U*|V])) & $\forall S$ (on(S, [U*|V]) → S - U* ∨ on(S,Y*) ∨ on(S,Z))	←	$\forall S$ (on(S,Y*) ∨ on(S,W) ↔ on(S,V)) & X - [U*|V] & R₂*(U*,Y*,V,W,X,Z)	to R

Introducing the of the term [U*\|V] having the same form as the induction conclusion term motives a strategy containing the derivation sequence: unfold, distribute, (simplify,) compare.

- **Unfold - R2***

$\forall S$ (on(S,Y*) ∨ on(S,Z) → S - U* ∨ on(S,V)) & $\forall S$ (S - U* ∨ on(S,V) → S - U* ∨ on(S,Y*) ∨ on(S,Z))	←	$\forall S$ (on(S,Y*) ∨ on(S,W) ↔ on(S,V)) & X - [U*|V] & R₂*(U*,Y*,V,W,X,Z)	unfold

Again, there are two possibilities for distribution. We will chose to bring out on(S,V) from the second implication with the same motivation as the first set of distributions.

- **Distribute (bring out on(S,V)) - R2***

⋮		⋮	
$\forall S$ (on(S,Y*) ∨ on(S,Z) → S - U* ∨ on(S,V)) & $\forall S$ (S - U* → S - U* ∨ on(S,Y*) ∨ on(S,Z)) & $\forall S$ ((on(S,V) → S - U*) ∨ (on(S,V) → on(S,Y*) ∨ on(S,Z)))	←	$\forall S$ (on(S,Y*) ∨ on(S,W) ↔ on(S,V)) & X - [U*|V] & R₂*(U*,Y*,V,W,X,Z)	distrib → over ∨, distrib → over ∨, distrib $\forall$ over &

The sequence of distributions comes to a stop when trying to distribute $\forall$ over ∨. Simplification is applicable and reduces the second subformula in the above conlusion conjunct to the truthvalue true.

- **Simplify - R2***

⋮		⋮	
$\forall S$ (on(S,Y*) ∨ on(S,Z) → S - U* ∨ on(S,V)) & $\forall S$ ((on(S,V) → S - U*) ∨ (on(S,V) → on(S,Y*) ∨ on(S,Z)))	←	$\forall S$ (on(S,Y*) ∨ on(S,W) ↔ on(S,V)) & X - [U*|V] & R₂*(U*,Y*,V,W,X,Z)	simplify

Compairing the conclusion with the conditions we can notice that it is possible to make the equivalence in the conditions imply the second subformula in the conjunct by adding the strengthening formula Z - W.

- **Compare - R2***

$\forall S$ (on(S,Y*) ∨ on(S,W) → S - U* ∨ on(S,V))	←	$\forall S$ (on(S,Y*) ∨ on(S,W) ↔ on(S,V)) & X - [U*|V] & Z - W & R₂**(U*,Y*,V,W,X,Z)	CS

After the comparison step it is time to generate a new derivation sequence. The comparison step did not introduce a new unfold term consequently no unfold sequence is necessary. Instead the derivation sequence: distribute, (simplify,), compare, is motivated by the fact that there still are remaining distributions to be done to bring out the formula on(S,V).

• Distribute (bring out on(S,V)) - R2**

⋮		⋮	
$\forall S$ ((on(S,Y*) $\vee$ on(S,W) $\rightarrow$ S - U*) $\vee$ (on(S,Y*) $\vee$ on(S,W) $\rightarrow$ on(S,V)))	$\leftarrow$	$\forall S$ (on(S,Y*) $\vee$ on(S,W) $\leftrightarrow$ on(S,V)) & X - [U*|V] & Z - W & R$_2$**(U*,Y*,V,W,X,Z)	distrib

Simplification is not possible and the comparison will result in the absorption of the remaining conclusion formula by the equivalence in the condition part.

• Compare - R2**

true	$\leftarrow$	$\forall S$ (on(S,Y*) $\vee$ on(S,W) $\leftrightarrow$ on(S,V)) & X - [U*|V] & Z - W & R$_2$**(U*,Y*,V,W,X,Z)	absorb
true	$\leftarrow$	$\forall S$ (on(S,Y*) $\vee$ on(S,W) $\leftrightarrow$ on(S,V)) & X - [U*|V] & Z - W	

The relation R$_2$ is defined by the conjunction X - [U*|V] & Z - W:

$$\forall U \forall V \forall W \forall X \forall Z \ (R_2(U^*,Y^*,V,W,X,Z) \leftrightarrow X - [U^*|V] \ \& \ Z - W)$$

The derived user-defined rule:

$$\forall U \forall Y \forall V \forall W \forall X \forall Z \ (X - [U|V] \rightarrow$$
$$(union(X, [U|Y],Z) \leftrightarrow union(V,Y,W) \ \& \ Z - W \ \& \ X - [U|V]))$$

The instantiated program description clause:

$$union(X,[U|Y],Z) \leftarrow union(V,Y,W) \ \& \ Z - W \ \& \ X - [U|V]$$

3   Related Work and Further Work

First among the related work the program development system KIDS should be mentioned. KIDS covers among others the divide-and-conquer synthesis strategy [12]. The program is specified by an input-output specification and the design strategy uses a functional program scheme. The program schema divides into two cases depending on whether or not the input is primitive. The non-primitive input is decomposed into two parts where one is handled recursively and the other by an unknown function; the results are composed into the output. This approach uses a program schema that is functional whereas ours is relational. Furthermore, our approach for finding the unknown relation has similarities with Smith's method of deriving preconditions.

Lau & Prestwich [10, 11] describes an interactive approach to deriving recursive program clauses starting from user-provided meta-goal in the form of an incomplete implication. During the synthesis process definitions are restricted to be in either conjunctive, disjunctive, existential, or universal form. The synthesis of the recursive program clauses is performed according to a pre-programmed strategy taking the form of the definitions into account. The synthesis is not supported by an induction schema (given externally or internally) and the synthesis of the non-recursive program clauses are not included in the presentation of the approach. The exact interaction with the user during the derivation is not described.

The Dream group at Edinburgh have two approaches to the synthesis of logic programs, both supporting the proofs-as-programs approach. In the first approach [8, 9], an application of the proof planner CLAM [2], a verification conjecture, $\forall$args (prog(args) $\leftrightarrow$ spec(args)), is proved classically and a second-order metavariable in the conjecture will be instantiated to a program during the proof planning process. The program is given an initial structure, for example (i = [] & B(j) $\lor$ $\exists h \exists t$ (i = [h|t] & C(h,t,j))) where B and C are schemavariables. The second approach using the proof development system Whelk [14] uses a first order typed constructive logic with equality and the system contains a set of program construction rules. A specification conjecture $\forall$args δS(args) is proved such that $\forall$args* (S(args) $\leftrightarrow$ P(args)). In comparison to the above approaches the approach described in this paper does not require equivalence between specification and program it enforces only that the specification imply the program, this means that correctness is ascertained but not necessarily completeness. The interaction with the user is not described sufficiently to make a comparison possible.

The approach described in this paper is primarily user-oriented. The use of a table for showing the inference steps makes it possible for the user to always have current status of the conclusion and the target formulas in the condition in view. The system supports the derivation by presenting incrementally generated strategies for the derivation. The strategies are given as a support and it is possible for the user to change or abondone if the user feels cramped by them.

In this paper we have described a method for program derivation using a schema approach and incrementally generated derivation strategies. The method is being implemented in an interactive system. A possible use for the system is as a tutorial aid in courses on programming and formal reasoning. This usage puts strong demands on the user-interface of the system. A program derivation makes use of different knowledge such as well-founded sets, specifictions, schemata, rules and the user has to be presented with knowledge about the status of derivation, the status of the program under development and much more [1], [7], [13]. The system has not as yet been tested by students.

The derivation of a program includes many difficult choices. One of them is the choice of a well-founded set for the program schema. We have chosen to let the user make this important choice. The importance of the well-founded set for the understanding of the program has as result that we cannot be satisfied with a derivation of a program description for a well-founded set that has the appropriate well-founded set as a subset.

References

1. Barstow, D. et al, Interactive programming environments, McGraw-Hill, New York, 1984.
2. Bundy , A., van Harmelen, F., Horn, C. & Smaill, A. , The Oyster-Clam system, In M.E. Stickel (eds), 10th International Conference on Automated Deduction, pages 647-648. Springer-Verlag, 1990. Lecture Notes in Artificial Intelligence No 449, 1990.

112

3. Bundy, A., Stevens, A., van Harmelen, F., Ireland, A., Smaill, A.: Rippling: A Heuristic for Guiding Inductive Proofs, DAI Research Paper No. 567, Dept. of AI, University of Edinburgh, 1992.

4. Deville, Y. & Burnay, J. Generalisation and Program Schemata, Proceedings of the North American Conference on Logic Programming 1989, E.L. Lusk, R.A. Overbeek (eds.), MIT Press, October 1989, pp. 409-425, 1989.

5. Edman, A. & Tärnlund, S-Å. Mechanization of an Oracle in a Debugging System, Proceedings IJCAI-83, Karlsruhe, West Germany, 1983.

6. Johns, N. MacProlog 4.0 Reference Manual, Logic Programming Associates Ltd, Studio 4, Royal Victoria Patriotic Building, Trinity Road, London SW17 3SX, England, 1991.

7. Jones, C. B. & Jones, K. D. & Lindsay, P. A. & Moore, R. mural, A Formal Development Support System, Springer-Verlag, London, 1991.

8. Kraan, I. & Basin, D. & Bundy, A. Logic Program Synthesis via Proof Planning, In K-K. Lau, (Eds), Proceedings of LOPSTR'92 (pp. 1-14), Workshops in Computing Series, Springer-Verlag, 1992.

9. Kraan, I. & Basin, D. & Bundy, A. Middle-Out Reasoning for Logic Program Synthesis, Proceedings

10. Lau, K-K. & Prestwich, S. D. Top-down synthesis of recursive logic procedures from first-order logic specifications, In D.H.D. Warren and P. Szeredi (eds), Proc 7th Int. Conf. on Logic Programming, MIT Press, 1990.

11. Lau, K-K. & Prestwich, S. D. Synthesis of a Family of Recursive Sorting Procedures, In V. Saraswat and K. Ueda (eds), Proc. 1991 Int. Logic Programming Symp., MIT Press 1991.

12. Smith, D. R. Top-Down Synthesis of Divide-and-Conquer Algorithms, Artificial Intelligence, Volume 27, pp. 43-96, 1985.

13. Théry, L. & Bertot, Y. & Kahn, G. Real Theorem Provers Deserve Real User-Interfaces, Research Report no 1684, INRIA, Sophia Antipolis, France, 1992.

14. Wiggins, G.A., Synthesis and transformation of logic programs in the Whelk proof development system, in K. R. Apt (Eds) Proceedings of JICSLP-92, 1992.

The Power of Partial Evaluation *

D.A. de Waal

Department of Computer Science

University of Bristol

Bristol

United Kingdom

andre@uk.ac.bristol.compsci

Abstract

In this paper we show how to perform effective specialisation of a clausal theorem prover for first order logic, using only partial evaluation and a well-designed reimplementation of the theorem prover. We take the clausal theorem prover given by Poole and Goebel in [17], and show that partial evaluation of this prover (written as a meta-program) with respect to some object theory, does not give the required specialisation. We then give a version of this meta-program that is amenable to specialisation and show that partial evaluation of this program with respect to some object theory can give results comparable to the results obtained by a special purpose analysis.

1   Introduction

In this paper we show how to perform effective specialisation of a clausal theorem prover [17] for first order logic, using only partial evaluation [8] [13] [2] [15] and a well-designed reimplementation of the theorem prover. We show that a special analysis phase is unnecessary to achieve the deletion of the negative ancestor check (see Section 2) where appropriate.

The motivation for this work is the following problem: *we try to specialise a meta-program with respect to some object program, but we do not get the specialisation results we expect.*

There are at least three possible solutions that need investigation:

1. Develop a problem specific analysis method that can be used to get the required specialisation. This was done by Poole and Goebel in [17].

2. Extend current analysis and transformation techniques. This route was developed by de Waal and Gallagher in [5] [6].

3. Rewrite the meta-program such that it becomes amenable to program specialisation. This is the subject of this paper.

The aim therefore is to show how partial evaluation of a well-designed meta-program with respect to some object theory can produce results comparable

---

*Work supported by ESPRIT Project PRINCE (5246)

to that obtained by a special purpose static analysis applied to a more naive version of the meta-program and object theory.

We take the clausal theorem prover given by Poole and Goebel in [17], and show that partial evaluation of this prover (written as a meta-program) with respect to some object theory, does not give any specialisation except for the elimination of the overhead incurred by the meta-program and some local optimisation [9] [10]. The deletion of the overhead incurred by the meta-program is the least that is to be expected from any partial evaluation of a meta-program with respect to some object theory. We then give a version of the meta-program that is amenable to specialisation and show that partial evaluation of this program with respect to some object theory can give results comparable to the results obtained by the special purpose analysis developed in [17].

In keeping with current thinking that a partial evaluator should be an integral part of a logic programming system that supports meta-programming, we feel that it will be very useful if the partial evaluator could perform the optimisations achieved by Poole and Goebel simultaneously with the deletion of the overhead caused by the meta-interpreter.

The fact that the result of partial evaluation depends directly on the way the meta-program is written, is not encouraging at all. However, this comparison between two apparently very similar programs that give notable different specialisation results, may suggest some emergence of a methodology for the writing of meta-programs amenable to program specialisation.

In the next section the Poole-Goebel clausal theorem prover is described. In Section 3 we discuss the limitations of partial evaluation of the prover with respect to some definite [14] object theory. In Section 4 the prover is rewritten into a more amenable form and partially evaluated with respect to the object theory of Section 3. The revised prover is given in Section 4. Partial evaluation of this prover is then discussed. A more interesting example is then developed in Section 5. Section 6 contains a comparison between the method developed in the paper and the method of Poole and Goebel. Broader issues related to partial evaluation and meta-programming in general are discussed in Section 7.

2 Clausal Theorem Prover

Consider the following clausal theorem prover in Prolog, described by Poole and Goebel in [17]. This theorem prover is based on the model elimination proof procedure by Loveland [16].

$neg(X, Y)$ is true if X is the negation of Y with X and Y both in their simplest form. *clause* is not the normal Prolog *clause*. *clause*(X, Y) is true if $X \leftarrow Y$ is a contrapositive of an arbitrary clause of the form $a_1 \vee \ldots \vee a_n \leftarrow b_1 \wedge \ldots \wedge b_m$ and X is a literal. *member*(X, Y) is true if X is a member of the list Y.

The negative ancestor check corresponds to ancestor resolution and with input resolution constitute a complete inference system for the first-order predicate calculus.

```
% prove(G,A) is true if and only if  Clauses ⊨ A ⊃ G
prove(G, A) ← member(G, A).              % Negative ancestor check
prove(G, A) ← clause(G, B),              % Input resolution
      neg(G, GN),
      proveall(B, [GN|A]).

proveall([ ], _ ).
proveall([G|R], A) ← prove(G, A),
      proveall(R, A).

member(X, [X| _ ]).
member(X, [ _ |Xs ]) ←
      member(X, Xs).
```

Program 1: Clausal theorem prover

It is not the purpose of this paper to describe in detail the problems with the above procedure when used as a full first order clausal theorem prover in Prolog. However, it is worth noting that if this procedure is to be executed using current Prolog technology, the depth first search strategy of most Prolog systems makes the procedure incomplete. Furthermore, the occur check is also missing from most Prolog implementations and this may make the procedure unsound.

The first problem can fairly easily be rectified, by augmenting Program 1 with a "manual" iterative deepening procedure where the above procedure is then run with successively larger depth bounds as specified by the user. Such a "manual" iterative deepening procedure will be incorporated into the revised program given in Section 4.

The second problem may also be overcome by using the sound unification provided as an option by Prolog systems such as Prolog by BIM [3]. It is also very likely that new logic programming languages such as Gödel will have the occur check implemented in the near future [12].

3 Partial Evaluation of the Theorem Prover

¿From the analysis in [17] it is known that for any definite object theory the negative ancestor check is redundant. We will now show that this is not achievable through partial evaluation of the prover given in Program 1 with respect to the following naive reverse program (a definite theory):

```
reverse([ ], [ ]).
reverse([X|Xs], Z) ←
      reverse(Xs, Y),
      append(Y, [X], Z).

append([ ], X, X).
append([X|Xs], Y, [X|Zs]) ←
      append(Xs, Y, Zs).
```

Object Theory 1: Naive reverse

The result of partially evaluating the prover given in Program 1 with respect to the above object theory with top-level goal $prove(reverse(\_ , \_), [\,])$ is given in Program 2. All the partially evaluated programs given in this paper were generated automatically by the program specialisation system SP, which is currently being developed at the University of Bristol [9].

$prove(reverse(X0, X1), [X2|X3]) \leftarrow$
    $member\_1(reverse(X0, X1), X2, X3).$
$prove(reverse([\,], [\,]), X0).$
$prove(reverse([X0|X1], X2), X3) \leftarrow$
    $prove\_2(X1, X4, X0, X2, X3),$
    $prove\_3(X4, X0, X2, X1, X3).$

$member\_1(X0, X0, X1).$
$member\_1(X0, X1, [X2|X3]) \leftarrow$
    $member\_1(X0, X2, X3).$

$prove\_2(X0, X1, X2, X3, [X4|X5]) \leftarrow$
    $member\_1(reverse(X0, X1), X4, X5).$
$prove\_2([\,], [\,], X0, X1, X2).$
$prove\_2([X0|X1], X2, X3, X4, X5) \leftarrow$
    $prove\_2(X1, X6, X0, X2, [not(reverse([X3, X0|X1], X4))|X5]),$
    $prove\_3(X6, X0, X2, X1, [not(reverse([X3, X0|X1], X4))|X5]).$

$prove\_3(X0, X1, X2, X3, [X4|X5]) \leftarrow$
    $member\_1(append(X0, [X1], X2), X4, X5).$
$prove\_3([\,], X0, [X0], X1, X2).$
$prove\_3([X0|X1], X2, [X0|X3], X4, X5) \leftarrow$
    $prove\_4(X1, X2, X3, X0, reverse([X2|X4], [X0|X3]), X5).$

$prove\_4(X0, X1, X2, X3, X4, [X5|X6]) \leftarrow$
    $member\_1(append(X0, [X1], X2), X5, X6).$
$prove\_4([\,], X0, [X0], X1, X2, X3).$
$prove\_4([X0|X1], X2, [X0|X3], X4, X5, X6) \leftarrow$
    $prove\_4(X1, X2, X3, X0, append([X4, X0|X1], [X2],$
        $[X4, X0|X3]), [not(X5)|X6]).$

Program 2: Program 1 partially evaluated with respect
to Object Theory 1

Most of the overheads of the meta-program have been eliminated. All that remain are the specialised *prove* procedures for *reverse* and *append* and a general member procedure, *member_1*.

Note that the negative ancestor check stays intact, although it is not needed. Partial evaluation was unable to delete the negative ancestor check because it is unable to detect that all calls to *member_1* will fail finitely (all ancestor lists will be of finite length). The negative ancestor list will only contain instances of *not(reverse)* and *not(append)* and the first argument of all calls to *member_1* will never contain a negated atom. Because partial evaluation has to terminate (to be of any use), partial evaluation can not evaluate all possible ancestor checks. It therefore has to generalise at some stage to terminate and to guarantee that a successful branch has not been pruned from the search tree.

Although it might seem unreasonable at this stage to expect partial evaluation to do any more than what was achieved in Program 2, we feel that a special analysis phase is unnecessary to achieve the deletion of the negative ancestor check.

We will now show that the negative ancestor check can be deleted by rewriting the clausal theorem prover and partially evaluating the improved prover with respect to naive reverse.

4 Amenable Clausal Theorem Prover

The "problem" with the prover given in Program 1 is that the occurrence (and absence) of all instances of negated ancestor literals are kept in one list. It is therefore impossible to distinguish between the absence of a negated ancestor literal in the ancestor list and the generalisation introduced by partial evaluation for termination purposes. If we had a finite number of ancestor lists, but with only occurrences of one literal in each list, partial evaluation might be able to make use of the empty list indicating the absence of certain literals from the ancestor list. As the negative ancestor check can only succeed when there is at least one literal in the ancestor list, an empty list would indicate failure of the ancestor check for this specific literal.

$$solve(G, A, D) \leftarrow predicate(G), prove(G, A, D).$$

$$prove(G, A, D) \leftarrow D > 0, memberl(G, A).$$
$$prove(G, A, D) \leftarrow D > 1, D1 \ is \ D - 1,$$
$$clause((G : -B)),$$
$$neg(G, GN),$$
$$addanc(GN, A, GNA),$$
$$proveall(B, GNA, D1).$$

$$proveall([\ ], \_, \_).$$
$$proveall([G|R], A, D) \leftarrow prove(G, A, D),$$
$$proveall(R, A, D).$$

$$memberl(G, [[A|As]|\_]) \leftarrow bound(G, A),$$
$$member(G, As).$$
$$memberl(G, [[A|\_]|B]) \leftarrow$$
$$memberl(G, B).$$

$$addanc(G, [[A|As]|Bs], [[A, G|As]|Bs]) \leftarrow bound(G, A).$$
$$addanc(G, [[A|As]|B], [[A|As]|C]) \leftarrow$$
$$addanc(G, B, C).$$

Program 3: Clausal theorem prover amenable to partial evaluation

The idea of having a finite number of ancestor lists is not new. The ancestor list has been implemented in this way in the Prolog Technology Theorem Prover

[18]. However, there it was done for efficiency reasons and not with the aim of deleting ancestor checks through the use of partial evaluation. This also confirms that our amenable clausal theorem prover is a reasonable program that we might expected from a competent programmer.

Consider the theorem prover given in Program 3 amenable to partial evaluation with the "manual" iterative deepening procedure described in Section 1.

$solve(G, A, D)$ is true if and only if $Clauses \models A \supset G$ with maximum depth of search $\leq D$. $memberl(X, Y)$ is true if X is a member of one of the lists that constitutes Y. $addanc(X, Y, Z)$ is true if X can be added to one of the lists constituting Y to give resulting list Z. $bound(X, Y)$ is true if the predicate symbol appearing in X matches one of the predicate symbols in Y.

Partial evaluation of Program 3 with respect to Object Theory 1 with an unbounded depth bound and top-level goal $solve(reverse(\_ , \_), [[reverse], [append], [not(reverse)], [not(append)]], \_)$ gives the following partially evaluated program.

$$solve(reverse(X0, X1), [[reverse], [append], [not(reverse)],$$
$$[not(append)]], X2) \leftarrow$$
$$prove\_1(X0, X1, [\ ], X2).$$

$$prove\_1([\ ], [\ ], X0, X1) \leftarrow X1 > 1, X2 \ is \ X1 - 1.$$
$$prove\_1([X0|X1], X2, X3, X4) \leftarrow X4 > 1, X5 \ is \ X4 - 1,$$
$$prove\_1(X1, X6, [not(reverse([X0|X1], X2))|X3], X5),$$
$$prove\_2(X6, X0, X2, X1, X2, X3, [\ ], X5).$$

$$prove\_2([\ ], X0, [X0], X1, X2, X3, X4, X5) \leftarrow X5 > 1, X6 \ is \ X5 - 1.$$
$$prove\_2([X0|X1], X2, [X0|X3], X4, X5, X6, X7, X8) \leftarrow$$
$$X8 > 1, X9 \ is \ X8 - 1,$$
$$prove\_2(X1, X2, X3, X4, X5, X6, [not(append([X0|X1], [X2],$$
$$[X0|X3]))|X7], X9).$$

Program 4: Program 3 partially evaluated with respect
to Object Theory 1

This program includes most of the optimisations discussed in [17]. All the unnecessary contrapositives have been deleted. The negative ancestor check has been eliminated. However, the redundant ancestor list is still being built although it is never used. In this example it is much more efficiently handled than was previously the case and partial evaluation has further optimised it. This program is a considerable simplification of the partially evaluated program given in Program 2.

5 Example

In this section we consider the following prime number theorem from [4]. This example shows that partial evaluation can selectively delete redundant negative ancestor checks where appropriate and does not just reproduce the well known result in automatic theorem proving that the negative ancestor check is not needed for definite programs.

% If a is prime and $a = b^2/c^2$ then a divides b.
% $d(X, Y) \equiv X$ divides Y, $m(X, Y, Z) \equiv X * Y = Z$, $p(X) \equiv X$ prime.
1. $p(a)$
2. $m(a, s(c), s(b))$
3. $m(X, X, s(X))$
4. $\neg m(X, Y, Z) \lor m(Y, X, Z)$
5. $\neg m(X, Y, Z) \lor d(X, Z)$
6. $\neg p(X) \lor \neg m(Y, Z, U) \lor \neg d(X, U) \lor d(X, Y) \lor d(X, Z)$
7. $\neg d(a, b)$

Object Theory 2: A prime number theorem

Partial evaluation of the prover given in Program 3 with respect to Object Theory 2 and top-level goal $(d(\_,\_), [[p], [m], [d], [not(p)], [not(m)], [not(d)]], \_)$ gives the following partially evaluated program.

$solve(d(X0, X1), [[p], [m], [d], [not(p)], [not(m)], [not(d)]], X2) \leftarrow$
  $prove\_1(X0, X1, [\,], X2).$

$prove\_1(X0, X1, X2, X3) \leftarrow X3 > 1, X4 \text{ is } X3 - 1,$
  $prove\_2(X0, X5, X1, [\,], [\,], X0, X1, X2, X4).$
$prove\_1(a, X0, X1, X2) \leftarrow X2 > 1, X3 \text{ is } X2 - 1,$
  $X3 > 1, X4 \text{ is } X3 - 1,$
  $prove\_2(X5, X0, X6, [\,], [\,], a, X0, X1, X3),$
  $prove\_1(a, X6, [not(d(a, X0))|X1], X3),$
  $prove\_5(a, X5, [\,], X0, X1, X3).$
$prove\_1(a, X0, X1, X2) \leftarrow X2 > 1, X3 \text{ is } X2 - 1,$
  $X3 > 1, X4 \text{ is } X3 - 1,$
  $prove\_2(X0, X5, X6, [\,], [\,], a, X0, X1, X3),$
  $prove\_1(a, X6, [not(d(a, X0))|X1], X3),$
  $prove\_5(a, X5, [\,], X0, X1, X3).$

$prove\_2(a, s(c), s(b), X0, X1, X2, X3, X4, X5) \leftarrow X5 > 1, X6 \text{ is } X5 - 1.$
$prove\_2(X0, X0, s(X0), X1, X2, X3, X4, X5, X6) \leftarrow X6 > 1, X7 \text{ is } X6 - 1.$
$prove\_2(X0, X1, X2, X3, X4, X5, X6, X7, X8) \leftarrow X8 > 1, X9 \text{ is } X8 - 1,$
  $prove\_2(X1, X0, X2, X3, [not(m(X0, X1, X2))|X4], X5, X6, X7, X9).$

$prove\_5(X0, X1, X2, X3, X4, X5) \leftarrow X5 > 0,$
  $member\_1(X0, X1, [not(d(X0, X3))|X4]).$
$prove\_5(a, X0, X1, X2, X3, X4) \leftarrow X4 > 1, X5 \text{ is } X4 - 1,$
  $X5 > 1, X6 \text{ is } X5 - 1,$
  $prove\_2(X7, X8, X0, [d(a, X0)|X1], [\,], a, X2, X3, X5),$
  $prove\_5(a, X7, [d(a, X0)|X1], X2, X3, X5),$
  $prove\_5(a, X8, [d(a, X0)|X1], X2, X3, X5).$

$member\_1(X0, X1, [not(d(X0, X1))|X2]).$
$member\_1(X0, X1, [X2|X3]) \leftarrow$
  $member\_1(X0, X1, X3).$

Program 4: Program 3 partially evaluated with respect
    to Object Theory 2

The only ancestor check remaining is the check for $not(d(\_, \_))$. Note also that for this example the redundant building of the negative ancestor list that we experienced with the naive reverse example has nearly been completely eliminated (note the many [ ]'s appearing in the negative ancestor list arguments). However, this is very much dependent on the object theory being used and needs further investigation. The above program is very efficient and finds a proof to the prime number theorem in a few milliseconds.

6 Comparison

In [17] a static analysis on signed predicate symbols was done to determine unnecessary negative ancestor checks and redundant contrapositives of clauses in the object theory.

The revised prover used the fact that there are only a finite number of different predicate symbols in any first order theory to optimise the handling of the negative ancestor list. This enabled partial evaluation to detect that the ancestor check will never succeed for certain predicates in the object theory. The improved prover can be seen as having the static analysis partially built into it. However, we need partial evaluation to fully exploit this optimisation. Without partial evaluation we still get a useful decrease in the time it takes to prove large theorems, but the resulting program still contains many redundant operations.

In [17] the following set of clauses was analysed.

1. $a \leftarrow b \wedge c;$
2. $a \vee b \leftarrow d;$
3. $c \vee e \leftarrow f;$
4. $\neg g \leftarrow e;$
5. $g \leftarrow c;$
6. $g;$
7. $f \leftarrow h;$
8. $h;$
9. $d;$

Object Theory 3: Set of clauses from [17]

Their analyses showed that negative ancestor checks may still be necessary for a, $\neg a$, b and $\neg b$. Partial evaluation of the revised prover given in Program 3 with respect Object Theory 2 has negative ancestor checks remaining for $\neg a$ and f. For this specific example our method is at least as precise as their static analysis.

It also shows that both methods give only approximations of the negative ancestor checks that really need to be done as $\neg a$ is the only literal in common given by the two methods.

7 Discussion

Criticism against the writing of "vanilla" type interpreters (such as the prover given in Program 1) has been expressed in [12]. If these criticism is taken seriously, it might seem that trying to analyse and partially evaluate these kind of interpreters are futile and that the method developed in [17] and the method described in this paper are not general but specific to this style of writing meta-programs.

This is not the case as both methods can be directly transferred from the non-ground representation (vanilla type interpreters) to the ground-representation as used in [12] [11]. It is easy to see that the Poole-Goebel analysis is independent of the representation used to implement the object theory. For the method developed in this paper it might be argued that partial evaluation of the ground representation is not as "easy" as shown here, because a ground unification algorithm has to be specialised and substitutions have to be handled explicitly.

Experiments so far with a ground representation similar to the one used in [7], have shown that specialisation of unification is not crucial to this method. All the optimisations achieved in this paper can be achieved for the ground representation by ignoring all arguments to predicates in the object theory. As Poole-Goebel have indicated, their analysis is an analysis of signed predicate symbols. The same can be said for the method developed in this paper. However, efficient specialisation of unification may make this method even more powerful and precise.

Although we rewrote a specific theorem prover in this paper, this does not preclude generalisation of this rewriting method to other meta-programs. Good specialisation results can also be expected by applying this method to meta-programs where:

- the meta-program collects some "history" and makes decisions based on this information and

- there is a finite number of predicate names in the object theory.

The crucial idea is the identification of some property of the object theory that may be exploited by the meta-program to achieve useful specialisation through partial evaluation. Optimisations that were previously only possible with specialised analysis techniques may now be possible with partial evaluation.

In [1] Amtoft reviews program transformations and sets up a multilevel transition semantics in which it is expressed. He identifies "strong" transformations and a non-optimal execution strategy for the original untransformed program which may lead to an order of magnitude reduction in execution time in the transformed program.

It seems that the partial evaluation of a meta-program rewritten using the method described in this paper is an instance of such a "strong" transformation. For example, the reduction in execution time using Program 3 and Object Theory 1 may be made arbitrary large by adding redundant predicates to the object theory. Before partial evaluation, each time the negative ancestor check needs to be done, the negative ancestor list has to be traversed to find the relevant sublist that has to be checked. In the worst case, the relevant sublist will be the last in the list. Partial evaluation will eliminate the redundant traversal of the ancestor list (see Programs 3 and 4 for concrete examples of how this is done) and this may lead to an arbitrary reduction in execution time by changing the number of redundant predicates.

In [19] van Harmelen discusses the limitations of partial evaluation. He concludes that partial evaluation is in principle a powerful technique, but is rather restricted in its use for optimising meta-interpreters and gives the lack of static information that can be derived from the program code as a possible reason. We can only partly agree with the above statement, as we have used such static information in this paper to optimise the Poole-Goebel theorem prover. Furthermore, we believe that partial evaluation extended with abstract interpretation provides a very powerful specialisation technique for the specialisation of proof procedures written as meta-interpreters [5].

8   Future Work

Future work will centre around answering the following three questions:

1. Should we try and extend current analysis and transformation methods so that the specialisation results will be independent of the data structures chosen by the user to implement his program?

2. Should we work on methodology to provide "guidelines" for the writing of programs that can be specialised by current techniques?

3. Should we write "general" programs where the data structures are not "hard wired" into the program as proposed by Jan Komorowski and then only choose appropriate data structures (that will give good specialisation results) during the specialisation phase?

Acknowledgements

I would like to thank John Gallagher for the clarification of various issues that came up during discussions that led to the writing of this paper as well as the constructive comments of anonymous referees and LOPSTR'93 participants.

References

[1] T. Amtoft Hansen. Properties of unfolding-based meta-level systems. In *Symposium on Partial Evaluation and Semantics-Based Program Manipulation*, pages 243–254, ACM Press, 1991.

[2] K. Benkerimi and J.W. Lloyd. A partial evaluation procedure for logic programs. In S.K. Debray and M. Hermenegildo, editors, *Proceedings of the North American Conference on Logic Programming*, Austin, pages 343–358, MIT Press, 1990.

[3] BIM. Prolog by BIM Reference Manual, Release 3.1. 1991.

[4] C. Chang and R.C.-T Lee. *Symbolic Logic and Mechanical Theorem Proving*. Academic Press, 1973.

[5] D.A. de Waal and J. Gallagher. *The Applicability of Logic Program Analysis and Transformation to Theorem Proving.* Technical Report, University of Bristol, September 1993.

[6] D.A. de Waal and J. Gallagher. *Logic Program Specialisation with Deletion of Useless Clauses.* Technical Report, University of Bristol, September 1993. (To appear as a poster at ILPS'93).

[7] F. Defoort. *De Grondrepresentatie in Prolog en in Gödel.* Master's thesis, Katholieke Universiteit Leuven, 1991.

[8] Y. Futamura. Partial evaluation of computation process - an approach to a compiler-compiler. *Systems, Computers, Controls,* 2(5):45–50, 1971.

[9] J. Gallagher. *A System for Specialising Logic programs.* Technical Report TR-91-32, University of Bristol, November 1991.

[10] J. Gallagher and M. Bruynooghe. Some low-level source transformations for logic programs. In *Proceedings of Meta90 Workshop on Meta Programming in Logic,* Leuven, Belgium, April 1990.

[11] C.A. Gurr. Specialising the ground representation in the logic programming language Gödel. In Y. Deville, editor, *Logic Program Synthesis and Transformation,* Springer-Verlag, 1994.

[12] P.M. Hill and J.W. Lloyd. *The Gödel Programming Language.* Technical Report CSTR-92-27, University of Bristol, October 1992.

[13] H.J. Komorowski. *A Specification of an Abstract Prolog Machine and its Application to Partial Evaluation.* Technical Report LSST 69, Linköping University, 1981.

[14] J.W. Lloyd. *Foundations of Logic Programming: 2nd Edition.* Springer-Verlag, 1987.

[15] J.W. Lloyd and J.C. Shepherdson. Partial Evaluation in Logic Programming. *Journal of Logic Programming,* 11(3 & 4):217–242, 1991.

[16] D.W. Loveland. *Automated theorem proving: a logical basis.* North-Holland, 1978.

[17] D.L. Poole and R. Goebel. Gracefully adding negation and disjunction to Prolog. In E. Shapiro, editor, *Third International Conference on Logic Programming,* pages 635–641, Lecture Notes in Computer Science, Springer-Verlag, 1986.

[18] M.E. Stickel. A Prolog Technology Theorem Prover. In *International Symposium on Logic Programming,* Atlantic City, NJ, pages 211–217, Feb. 6-9 1984.

[19] F. van Harmelen. The limitations of partial evaluation. In J. Dassow and J. Kelemen, editors, *5th International Meeting of Young Computer Scientists,* pages 170–187, Lecture Notes in Computer Science, Springer-Verlag, 1988.

Specialising the Ground Representation in the Logic Programming Language Gödel

C.A.Gurr

Department of Computer Science, University of Bristol

Bristol, U.K.

Abstract

Meta-programs form a class of logic programs of major importance. In the past it has proved very difficult to provide a declarative semantics for meta-programs in languages such as Prolog. These problems have been identified as largely being caused by the fact that Prolog fails to handle the necessary representation requirements adequately. The ground representation is receiving increasing recognition as being necessary to adequately represent meta-programs. However, the expense it incurs has largely precluded its use to date.

The logic programming language Gödel is a declarative successor to Prolog. Gödel provides considerable support for meta-programming, in the form of a ground representation. Using this representation, Gödel meta-programs have the advantage of having a declarative semantics and can be optimised by program specialisation, to execute in a time comparable to equivalent Prolog meta-programs which use a non-ground representation.

Keywords: Partial evaluation, meta-programming, ground representation.

1 Introduction.

The Prolog language, and variants of it, are fraught with problems caused by their non-logical features, and this means that it is not possible to provide a declarative semantics for most, practical, Prolog programs. This applies most strongly to meta-programs in Prolog, where Prolog's declarative problems are compounded by the fact that the non-ground representation is used to represent terms, formulas and programs, despite the fact that, with such a representation, no declarative semantics can be provided for the Prolog features such as **var**, **nonvar**, **assert** and **retract**. The use of a ground representation ([2, 8, 7]) is receiving increasing recognition as being essential for declarative meta-programming, although, until now, the expense that is incurred by the use of such a representation has largely precluded its use.

The logic programming language Gödel [9] has been developed with the intention that it be "a declarative successor to Prolog". Gödel directly addresses the semantic problems of Prolog, providing declarative replacements for the non-logical features of Prolog (such as unsafe negation, Prolog's **setof**, unification without occur-checking, and inadequate facilities for meta-programming).

Gödel provides a ground representation for meta-programming which enables users to write meta-programs that:

- Have a declarative semantics.

- Are clearly readable and straightforward to write.

- Are potentially comparable, in execution time, to Prolog meta-programs which use the non-ground representation.

Gödel's ground representation is presented to the user via an abstract data type, thus avoiding the need for the user to have knowledge of its implementation, and therefore not confusing the user with a profusion of constant and function symbols. In addition to this, the development of large meta-programming applications such as interpreters, theorem provers, partial evaluators and debuggers, in Gödel, have influenced the development of Gödel's ground representation, so that a natural and clearly readable style of meta-programming with the ground representation is now emerging. This is exemplified by the comparison between the 'naive' Gödel meta-interpreter in figure 4, where unification and resolution are handled explicitly in the code, and the more natural meta-interpreter of figure 3, where resolution is handled implicitly by the Gödel system predicate **Resolve**, discussed in more detail in section 4.1. Henceforth we shall refer to meta-programs which use a ground representation as 'ground' meta-programs and meta-programs which use a non-ground representation as 'non-ground' meta-programs.

Using a ground representation means that unification, particularly the binding of variables (i.e. substitutions), must be handled explicitly by the meta-program. Programmers are unable to rely upon the underlying system to perform unification for them. This can cause considerable execution overheads in meta-programs. However, through program specialisation the speed of Gödel meta-programs can be optimised so as to remove these overheads, producing specialised versions of unification that may be comparable in execution time to the implicit unification of the underlying system. Certain other specialisations, described below, may also be performed on ground meta-programs. Performing the above specialisations can therefore produce ground Gödel meta-programs that have the potential of executing in a time comparable to equivalent non-ground Prolog meta-programs.

The program specialisation technique that we use is partial evaluation[1], a specialisation technique that has been shown to have great potential, particularly in Functional and Logic Programming. It was first explicitly introduced into Computer Science by Futamura [5] and into Logic Programming by Komorowski [10]. Partial evaluation was put on a firm theoretical basis in [14]. While partial evaluation is capable of removing the majority of the overheads associated with the ground representation, to date attention has focused mainly on the elimination of overheads in non-ground Prolog meta-programs, in Prolog interpreters [6, 12, 16, 17, 18], for example, and, more generally, in [11, 13, 19, 20].

The desire to specialise Gödel meta-programs has prompted the development of a declarative partial evaluator, $SAGE^2$, written in Gödel, that is capable of partially evaluating any program in the Gödel language. Using $SAGE$ we have been able to specialise Gödel meta-programs, including $SAGE$ itself, to produce residual programs that execute in a significantly reduced time.

---

[1] Also referred to, in this context, as partial deduction.
[2] Self-Applicable Gödel partial Evaluator.

The layout of this paper is as follows. In the following section we describe Gödel's meta-programming facilities in more detail. In the third and fourth sections we describe how the ground representation and ground unification, respectively, may be specialised. Finally, we present some results and conclusions, and discuss directions of future research.

2   The Ground Representation in Gödel.

The main facilities provided by the Gödel language are types, modules, control (in the form of control declarations, constraint solving, and a pruning operator), meta-programming and input/output. This means that Gödel, being a rich and expressive language, has a complex syntax. As Gödel's ground representation is intended to be sufficient to represent Gödel programs, as well as arbitrary theories, it must allow for the construction of terms of sufficient complexity to describe arbitrary formulas and Gödel's types, modules, control, meta-programming and input/output facilities. The current implementation of the ground representation [3] requires some 75 constants and function symbols to construct the terms necessary to adequately represent the entire Gödel language. If all of these symbols were visible in Gödel meta-programs, it would be necessary for the user to be familiar with the entire representation and competent in the manipulation of all these symbols, before he/she would be competent in the writing of meta-programs. To avoid confronting the user with such complexity unnecessarily, in Gödel, the representations of object level expressions and programs are treated as abstract data types. This also has the added advantage that meta-programs are independent of any specific implementation of the ground representation.

Example Figure 1 gives the Gödel code for finding the variables in an object level term. The predicates **Variable**, **ConstantTerm** and **FunctionTerm** are provided by Gödel. The first argument to such predicates are, respectively, the representations of object level variables, constants, and terms with a function at the top level.

The ground representation is an extremely powerful tool for meta-programming. However, it has the disadvantage of considerably increasing computation time. For example, consider an interpreter that computes the answer for some object program and query, using SLDNF-resolution. In the current implementation of Gödel, such an interpreter will run at 100-200 times slower than executing the program and query directly.

There are two major contributory factors to the expense of the ground representation in Gödel. The first is a direct result of supporting the ground representation as an abstract data type. The second, and potentially more serious, factor is that, when using the ground representation, the process of unification must be performed explicitly. However, the expense incurred by both of these factors has been overcome by partially evaluating meta-programs with respect to particular object programs, using the partial evaluator *SAGE*, that is itself written in Gödel. We discuss the above two factors, and their solutions, in more detail in the following two sections.

```
VarsInTerm(term,vars) <-
  VarsInTerm1(term,[],vars).

VarsInTerm1(term,vars,[term|vars]) <-
  Variable(term).
VarsInTerm1(term,vars,vars) <-
  ConstantTerm(term,name).
VarsInTerm1(term,vars,vars1) <-
  FunctionTerm(term,name,args) &
  VarsInTerm2(args,vars,vars1).

VarsInTerm2([],vars,vars).
VarsInTerm2([term|rest],vars,vars1) <-
  VarsInTerm1(term,vars,vars2) &
  VarsInTerm2(rest,vars2,vars1).
```

Figure 1: Gödel code for **VarsInTerm**.

3 Specialising the Representation of Gödel.

The major disadvantage to supporting the ground representation as an abstract data type is that we pay a price for not making visible those constants and function symbols used by the ground representation. Consider the predicate **VarsInTerm1** in figure 1, which has three statements in its definition. In each statement the first argument (which is the key argument) in the head of the statement is a variable. As such, no implementation of Gödel would be capable of differentiating between the three statements at the time of procedure entry. Thus a choicepoint would need to be created, and the execution time of the above code is increased by the time taken to create this choicepoint, and also by any necessary backtracking. The use of choicepoints will also inhibit garbage collection. As meta-programs using the ground representation often process some very large terms (for example, the *representation* of *SAGE* is a Gödel term of approximately 1MByte in size), garbage collection is very important. Any impairment to the efficiency of garbage collection will, potentially, cause a serious increase in the memory-usage of a meta-program. We need, therefore, to prevent the creation of these superfluous choicepoints.

Ideally we would like to be able to perform some form of indexing upon the first arguments to **VarsInTerm1**. If the constants and function symbols used in Gödel's representation were accessible to the user, rather than hidden by the abstract data type, we would be able to use these symbols in the definition of **VarsInTerms1** and thus could perform first argument indexing upon this predicate. Such indexing would prevent the need for the creation of choicepoints and all the attendant expense. In our experience, meta-programs which are written without access to the symbols in the ground representation currently run up to three times slower than equivalent programs that do have access to the ground representation. Fortunately, through program specialisation, it is possible for a meta-program written without access to the symbols in the ground representation, to achieve the efficiency of one that has.

```
VarsInTerm1(Var(v,n),vars,[Var(v,n)|vars]).
VarsInTerm1(CTerm(name),vars,vars).
VarsInTerm1(Term(name,args),vars,vars1) <-
    VarsInTerm2(args,vars,vars1).
```

Figure 2: Specialised code for `VarsInTerm1(term,vars,vars1)`.

In Gödel's representation, variables are represented by a term `Var(v,n)`, where `v` is a string and `n` an integer (this representation for variables is described in more detail below); constant terms are represented by a term `CTerm(name)`, where `name` is a Gödel term representing the name of this constant; function terms are represented by a term `Term(name,args)`, where `name` is the representation of the name of this function term and `args` is the list of representations of its arguments.

We may specialise the Gödel code in figure 1, even without further knowledge of the values of any arguments. The first atom in the body of each statement in the definition of `VarsInTerm1` may be unfolded. The result of this will be to make visible the relevant function symbols in Gödel's ground representation. Figure 2 illustrates the specialised code for `VarsInTerm1`. As the relevant function symbols representing variables, constant and function terms now appear in the first argument of the heads of the statements defining `VarsInTerm1`, the Gödel system may perform first argument indexing to differentiate between the three statements. Consequently, when a call is made to `VarsInTerm1`, with the first argument instantiated, no choicepoints are created, and no backtracking is necessary at any point in the computation. When such specialisations are performed upon an entire meta-program, the resulting gains in efficiency are considerable.

The *SAGE* partial evaluator is capable of performing an automatic specialisation of the code in figure 1. The residual code will leave the definitions of the predicates `VarsInTerm` and `VarsInTerm2` unchanged, and replace the definition of `VarsInTerm1` with the code in figure 2.

4   Specialising Resolution in the Ground Representation.

The greatest expense incurred by the use of the ground representation occurs in the manipulation of substitutions. When any variable binding is made, this must be explicitly recorded. Thus any unification, and similarly the composition and application of substitutions, must be performed explicitly. This produces significant overheads in the manipulation of the representations of terms and formulas. In this section we discuss how this expense may be greatly reduced, potentially leading to a specialised form of unification that is comparable to the WAM code [1, 21] for the object program. The need to specialise an explicit unification algorithm for efficiency has also been investigated in [4, 11]. Specialising meta-interpreters for propositional logic to produce WAM-like code has been investigated in [15].

```
Solve(program, goal, v, v, subst, subst) <-
  EmptyFormula(goal).
Solve(program, goal, v_in, v_out, subst_in, subst_out) <-
  And(left, right, goal) &
  Solve(program, left, v_in, new_v, subst_in, new_subst) &
  Solve(program, right, new_v, v_out, new_subst, subst_out).
Solve(program, goal, v_in, v_out, subst_in, subst_out) <-
  Atom(goal) &
  StatementMatchAtom(program, module, goal, statement) &
  Resolve(goal, statement, v_in, new_v, subst_in, new_subst, new_goal) &
  Solve(program, new_goal, new_v, v_out, new_subst, subst_out).
```

Figure 3: A Simple Gödel Meta-Interpreter

In meta-programming the main manipulations of substitutions occur during resolution or unfolding, where we must unify an atom in some goal with a statement in the object program. Figure 3 gives the main part of a very simple Gödel meta-interpreter for definite programs. It is in the third statement of this program that we see the Gödel predicate **Resolve** being used to resolve an atom in the current goal with respect to a statement selected from the object program. The remaining predicates in Figures 3 and 4 are provided by Gödel, and the following comments are adapted from the definition of Gödel [9]:

```
EmptyFormula(
      formula).     % Representation of the empty formula.

And(
      left ,        % Representation of a formula W.
      right ,       % Representation of a formula V.
      and).         % Representation of the formula  W & V.

IsImpliedBy(
      left ,        % Representation of a formula W.
      right ,       % Representation of a formula V.
      isimpliedby). % Representation of the formula  W <- V.

StatementMatchAtom(
      program ,     % Representation of a program.
      module ,      % Name of a module in this program.
      atom ,        % Representation of an atom in the language of
                    % this program.
      statement).   % Representation of a statement in this module
                    % whose proposition or predicate in the head is
                    % the same as the proposition or predicate in this
                    % atom.

ApplySubstToFormula(
      formula ,     % Representation of a formula.
```

```
        subst ,          % Representation of a term substitution.
        formula1).       % Representation of the formula obtained by
                         % applying this substitution to this formula.

RenameFormulas(
        formulas ,       % List of representations of formulas.
        formulas1 ,      % List of representations of formulas.
        formulas2).      % List of representations of the formulas obtained
                         % by renaming the free variables of the formulas in
                         % the second argument by a specific, unique term
                         % substitution such that they become distinct from
                         % the free variables in the formulas in the first
                         % argument.

ComposeTermSubsts(
        subst1 ,         % Representation of a term substitution.
        subst2 ,         % Representation of a term substitution.
        subst3).         % Representation of the substitution obtained by
                         % composing these two substitutions (in the order
                         % that they appear as arguments).
```

The implementation of **Resolve** must handle the following operations:

- Renaming the statement to ensure that the variables in the renamed statement are different from all other variables in the current goal.

- Applying the current answer substitution to the atom to ensure that any variables bound in the current answer substitution are correctly instantiated.

- Unifying the atom with the head of the renamed statement.

- Composing the mgu of the atom and the head of the statement with the current answer substitution to return the new answer substitution.

Each of these four operations is potentially very expensive when we are dealing with the explicit representation of substitutions, therefore it is vital that **Resolve** be implemented as efficiently as possible.

By contrast to the use of **Resolve**, as in the interpreter of Figure 3, consider the somewhat naive (although still declarative) interpreter of Figure 4. The third statement in the interpreter performs the same task as that of the third statement in the interpreter of Figure 3. However this naive interpreter is arguably more obtuse than that of Figure 3, as the manipulation of formulas and substitutions is here being performed explicitly. There would appear to be two very strong arguments for avoiding this style of meta-programming. The first is that it is more arduous for a programmer, requiring as it does explicit and sophisticated manipulation of formulas and substitutions. The second is not immediately apparent, but it is that the implementation of the interpreter of Figure 4 would be noticeably less efficient than that of Figure 3. Furthermore, the interpreter of Figure 3 may be specialised with respect to an object program in order to remove the majority of the expense of the ground representation, as we shall describe below. With the inherent inefficiencies of

```
Demo(program, goal, subst, subst) <-
  EmptyFormula(goal).
Demo(program, goal, subst_in, subst_out) <-
  And(left, right, goal) &
  Demo(program, left, v_in, new_v, subst_in, new_subst) &
  Demo(program, right, new_v, v_out, new_subst, subst_out).
Demo(program,goal,subst_in,subst_out) <-
  Atom(goal) &
  StatementMatchAtom(program, module, goal, statement) &
  RenameFormulas([goal], [statement], [statement1]) &
  IsImpliedBy(head, body, statement1) &
  ApplySubstToFormula(goal, subst_in, goal1) &
  UnifyAtoms(goal1, head, mgu) &
  ComposeTermSubsts(subst_in, mgu, new_subst) &
  Demo(program, body, new_subst, subst_out).
```

Figure 4: A Naive Gödel Meta-Interpreter

the interpreter of Figure 4 however, with its repeated explicit manipulation of the representations of the atom, statement and current substitution, it is far from clear that any specialisation could specialise the resolution process to the same extent.

4.1 Specialising Resolve

When we specialise a meta-program such as the interpreter in Figure 3 to a known object program, the statements in the object program will be known. Therefore we may specialise **Resolve** with respect to each statement in the object program. Specialising a call to **Resolve** with respect to a known statement will remove the vast majority of the expense of the ground representation. To see how this is achieved we must look more carefully at the implementation of **Resolve**.

The atom **Resolve(atom,st,v,v1,s,s1,body)** is called to perform the resolution of the atom **atom** with the statement **st**. The integers **v** and **v1** are used to rename the statement with **v** being the integer value used in renaming before the resolution step is performed and **v1** being the corresponding value after the resolution step has been performed. The representations of term substitutions **s** and **s1** represent respectively the answer substitution before and after the resolution step. The last argument, **body**, is the representation of the body of the renamed statement.

4.1.1 Variable Renaming

In a call to **Resolve**, all variables in the statements are renamed as they are encountered. This saves us from having to perform more than one pass over the statements during resolution. Any variable encountered, which could potentially appear in the new goal, is replaced by a variable with a name that does not occur elsewhere in the current computation. Variables in a statement

```
P(x,y,z,F(x,u)) <-
  Q(x,x1) &
  P(x1,y,z,u).
```

Figure 5: A Gödel Statement

fall into one of three categories, depending on where they are first encountered. These are:

1. The variable appears in an argument position in the head of the statement. This variable will be bound to the term in the atom's matching argument position and thus does not need to be renamed.

2. The variable appears as a subterm of a term in the head of the statement. This variable may need to be renamed, but this cannot be determined until the matching term in the atom is known.

3. The variable appears only in the body of the statement. This variable must be renamed.

For example, in the statement in Figure 5 the variables **x**, **y** and **z** are variables of the first type, variable **u** is of the second type and variable **x1** is of the third type. Thus while variable **x1** will certainly require renaming and variable **u** *may* require renaming, the remaining variables need not be renamed. To see how renaming is achieved we must look more closely at how variables are represented in Gödel.

When represented (by the term **Var(name,N)**), Gödel variables have names of the form **name_N**, where **name** is the *root* of the name of the variable (a string) and the non-negative integer **N** is called the *index* of the variable. To specialise renaming at all times we record **Max**, the highest integer index occurring in a variable in the current computation, and a new variable will be given the name **v_Max1**, where **Max1** is the increment of **Max**. In addition, new names are given only to variables that are guaranteed to occur in the resolvent. In this way the creation of new variables is kept to a minimum. A call to **Resolve** takes the increment of the current value of **Max** as its third argument and returns as its fourth argument the increment of the value of **Max** after all renaming has been performed. Thus specialising the renaming of the statement in Figure 5 of this statement would create the terms **Var("v",max+1)** and (assuming that the variable u also required renaming) **Var("v",max+2)**, where **max** is the current highest variable index.

4.1.2 Applying the Current Substitution

Before we attempt to unify the atom with the head of the statement we must consider the possibility that certain variables in the atom will have become bound in the current substitution. Such bindings must be taken into consideration and yet to apply the current substitution to all the terms in the atom is an unnecessary expense. To reduce this expense we must consider the terms in the head of the statement, these terms will each be one of:

1. A variable. Unless this is a repeated variable then the unification of this variable with the matching term in the atom will always succeed. Thus we do not need to apply the current substitution to the matching term in the atom.

2. A constant. We must apply the current substitution to the matching term in the atom before attempting to unify it with this constant.

3. A term with a function at the top level. We must test whether the matching term in the atom is bound in the current substitution to either a variable or to a term with a matching function at the top level. If the term in the atom is bound to a term with a matching function at the top level then we will compare this term's arguments with the arguments of the term in the statement.

Note that in the third case, even though we must test whether the matching term in the atom is a term with a function at the top level, we do not necessarily need to apply the current substitution to the arguments of this term. In the statement in Figure 5 for example, if the fourth argument of an atom we wished to resolve with this statement were bound to some term $F(\mathcal{T}_1, \mathcal{T}_2)$, we would not need to apply the current substitution to the term $\mathcal{T}_2$ in order to unify it with the matching variable u in the term $F(\mathbf{x}, \mathbf{u})$.

4.1.3 Head Unification in Resolve

The third operation to be performed in the resolution of an atom with a statement is the unification of the atom and the head of the statement. The unification algorithm employed enforces occur-checking for safeness. Although occur-checking is potentially very expensive, this expense may be greatly reduced by enforcing occur-checking for repeated variables in the head of the statement only.

After renaming, all variables in the statement are guaranteed not to appear elsewhere in either the current goal or the current substitution. This means that any bindings for variables in the head of the statement may be applied to the body of the statement and then discarded. Consequently only that part of the mgu of the atom and the renamed head of the statement that records the bindings of variables in the atom will need to be composed with the current substitution in order to produce the new substitution.

For example, when unifying an atom with the statement in Figure 5, the bindings for the variables $\mathbf{x}$, $\mathbf{y}$ and $\mathbf{z}$ in the statement are recorded separately from any potential bindings for variables in the atom. These bindings may then be applied to the body of the statement, replacing the variables $\mathbf{x}$, $\mathbf{y}$ and $\mathbf{z}$ by the terms to which they have been bound. There will only be one potential occur-check during the unification of an atom with the head of this statement and that will be if the fourth argument of the atom is a term $F(\mathcal{T}_1, \mathcal{T}_2)$. In this case the first argument of this function term will be unified with the first argument of the atom and an occur-check will be performed for this unification step alone.

4.1.4   Composition of the Mgu with the Current Substitution

Having performed the unification of an atom with the head of a statement we must in theory combine the mgu of this unification with the current substitution. In reality it is more efficient for any bindings made to variables in the atom to be composed with the current substitution immediately. In order to achieve these compositions we have a set of predicates, each of which performs one specific unification operation. The predicates which unify arguments of the head of the statement with the matching arguments of the atom are as follows:

UnifyTerms(term1,term2,subst,subst1) attempts to unify the atom's two terms **term1** and **term2**. **UnifyTerms** is the only one of these specific argument unification operations which enforces occur-checking and is used to unify repeated variables in the head of the statement. In this and the two subsequent atoms, **subst** is the current substitution and **subst1** is this substitution after the relevant unification step.

GetConstant(term,constant,subst,subst1) attempts to unify the atom's term **term** with the constant **constant**.

GetFunction(term,function,mode,subst,subst1) attempts to unify the atom's term **term** with a term **function** with a function at the top level. If **term** is bound in the current substitution to a variable then **mode** is set to **Write** and **function** will subsequently be instantiated to a renamed version of the term to which this variable is to be bound. If **term** is bound in the current substitution to a term with a matching function at the top level then **mode** is set to **Read**.

If an argument in the head of the statement is a term with a function at the top level, then there are two cases in which a call to **GetFunction** will succeed. In the first case the atom's matching argument is a variable and we must construct a renamed version of the term in the head of the statement and then bind this variable to it. In the second case the atom's matching argument is a term with a matching function at the top level and we must unify the arguments of this term with the corresponding arguments in the statement's term.

For example, the term $F(x,u)$ appears in the head of a statement in Figure 5. Thus we make a call to **GetFunction** which will succeed with **mode** set to **Write** if the atom's fourth argument is bound to a variable in the current substitution and will succeed with **mode** set to **Read** if the atom's fourth argument is bound in the current substitution to some term $F(\mathcal{T}_1,\mathcal{T}_2)$.

The following predicates perform the unification operations necessary for processing the arguments of function terms in the head of the statement, either renaming variables when in **Write** mode or unifying these arguments with the arguments of the matching function term in the atom when in **Read** mode.

UnifyVariable(mode,term,var,ind,ind1) in **Write** mode will instantiate **var** to the new variable **Var("v",ind)** and **ind1 = ind+1**. In **Read** mode, **var** is instantiated to the atom's term **term** and **ind1 = ind**.

UnifyValue(mode,term,term1,subst,subst1) in **Write** mode will instantiate **term1** to **term**. In **Read** mode this call will unify (with occur-checking) the atom's two terms **term** and **term1**. In this and the two subsequent atoms, **subst** is the current substitution and **subst1** is this substitution after the relevant unification step.

UnifyConstant(**mode,term,constant,subst,subst1**) in **Write** mode will instantiate **term** to the constant **constant**. In **Read** mode this call attempts to unify the atom's term **term** with the constant **constant**.

UnifyFunction(**mode,term,function,mode1,subst,subst1**)   in   **Write** mode will instantiate **term** to the term **function** and **mode1** is set to **Write**. In **Read** mode this call attempts to unify the atom's term **term** with a term **function** with a function at the top level. If **term** is bound in the current substitution to a variable then **mode1** is set to **Write** and **function** will subsequently be instantiated to a renamed version of the term to which this variable is to be bound (as for **GetFunction**). If **term** is bound in the current substitution to a term with a matching function at the top level then **mode** is set to **Read**.

Example Figure 6 illustrates the result of specialising **Resolve** with respect to the statement in Figure 5. In the second argument in the head of this specialised statement, the term **statement** denotes the representation of the statement in Figure 5, which we have omitted for the sake of brevity. The residual calls in the body of the specialised call to **Resolve** unify the atom's fourth argument with a term with a function named **F** at the top level and two arguments. If the atom's fourth argument is bound to a variable in **subst_in** then **mode** is set to **Write** by the call to **GetFunction**, which also binds this variable, in **new_subst**, to a new term with this function at the top level. The subsequent calls to **UnifyValue** and **UnifyVariable** will then instantiate the arguments of this new function term to the atom's first argument, **arg1**, and a new variable, **var**. They will also set **subst_out = new_subst** and **v1 = v+1**. If the atom's fourth argument is bound in **subst_in** to a term with a matching function symbol at the top level then **mode** is set to **Read** and **new_subst = subst_in**. The call to **UnifyValue** then unifies, with occur-checking, the atom's first argument, **arg1**, with the first argument, **sub1**, of this function term. If successful, this unification will return the new substitution **subst_out**. The call to **UnifyVariable** then instantiates **var** to the second argument, **sub2**, of the atom's function term and sets **v1 = v**.

A more complex example of the specialised code for **Resolve** is given in Figure 7. Here, by specialising **Resolve** to the statement P(x,x,A,F(y,F(x,A))) <- Q(y) we may see an example of a call to each of the seven predicates described above.

The above seven predicates we refer to as the *WAM-like predicates*, as they are analogous to emulators for the WAM instructions GetValue (in the case of **UnifyTerms**), GetConstant, GetFunction, UnifyValue, UnifyVariable and UnifyConstant, after which they are named. Note that a subtle difference in the manner in which the WAM implements the unification of nested function terms and the manner in which **Resolve** implements it means that the WAM does not have an equivalent to the **UnifyFunction** instruction.

Specialising the interpreter in Figure 3 with respect to an object program, we would replace the code for **Resolve** by its specialisation. This would consist of, for each statement in the object program, one statement that performed the

```
Resolve(
  Atom(P', [arg1, arg2, arg3, arg4]),
  statement,
  v, v1+1 ,
  subst_in, subst_out,
  Atom(Q', [arg1, Var("v", v1)]) &'
   Atom(P', [Var("v", v1), arg2, arg3, var])
      ) <-
    GetFunction(arg4, F'([sub1, sub2]), mode, subst_in, new_subst) &
    UnifyValue(mode, arg1, sub1, new_subst, subst_out) &
    UnifyVariable(mode, sub2, var, v, v1).
```

Figure 6: Specialised code for **Resolve**

```
Statement:  P(x, x, A, F(y, F(x, A))) <- Q(y).
Specialised call to Resolve:

Resolve(
  Atom(P', [arg1, arg2, arg3, arg4]),
  statement,
  v, v1,
  subst_in, subst_out,
  Atom(Q', [var])
      ) <-
    UnifyTerms(arg1, arg2, subst_in, s1) &
    GetConstant(arg3, A', s1, s2) &
    GetFunction(arg4, F'([sub1, sub2]), mode, s2, s3) &
    UnifyVariable(mode, sub1, var, v, v1) &
    UnifyFunction(mode, sub2, F'([sub21, sub22]), mode1, s3, s4) &
    UnifyValue(mode1, arg1, sub21, s4, s5) &
    UnifyConstant(mode1, sub22, A', s5, subst_out).
```

Figure 7: More specialised code for **Resolve**

resolution of some (unknown) atom with the particular object statement. The residual code in these specialised versions of **Resolve** would be a conjunction of atoms with WAM-like predicates. These predicates are analogous to instructions in the WAM and substitutions may be represented in a format analogous to that of the WAM's heap (global stack). As such, these operations could be implemented by Gödel at a very low level, leading to a computation time for the specialised form of a meta-program, such as that in Figure 3, comparable to that of the object program itself.

The Gödel code for **Resolve**, discussed here, is in fact the code that forms the heart of *SAGE*'s unfolding process. As such, it was designed with the intention that it should be both efficient and able to be specialised in order to produce highly optimised residual code. Thus the above example of specialising **Resolve** illustrates a part of the self-application of *SAGE*. It also highlights our main aim in the definition of **Resolve**, which was, in a declarative meta-programming style, to produce an implementation of resolution for the ground representation that was both efficient and capable of producing yet more efficient code upon specialisation. From this code has been developed Gödel's current implementation of substitutions and unification, so that the code for **Resolve** can also be utilised by other meta-programs and specialised by *SAGE* in order to remove the overheads of the ground representation, while retaining the power of meta-programming.

5   Results.

Example Program	Runtime		Speedup
	Original	Specialised	
Model Elimination (1)	22.56s	029.s	77.79
Model Elimination (2)	26.19s	0.35s	74.83
Demo: Transpose(8x8)	2.94s	0.14s	21.00
Demo: Transpose(8x16)	5.80s	0.23s	25.21
Demo: Fib(10)	11.68s	0.13s	89.85
Demo: Fib(15)	118.34s	1.13s	104.73
Demo: Fib(17)	347.85s	2.84s	122.48
Coroutine: BmSort(7)	2.98s	0.14s	21.29
Coroutine: BmSort(13)	14.08s	0.52s	27.08
Coroutine: EightQueens	5.12s	0.21s	24.38

The above table gives the speedups seen in specialised meta-programs, as a factor of the runtime of the original versus the specialised program. The example meta-programs are implemented using our efficient meta-programming techniques, as in the interpreter of figure 3, and are specialised with respect to particular object programs/theories to produce specialised ground meta-programs. The example programs are, respectively, a theorem prover, provided by André de Waal, based on the model elimination method and specialised with respect to two theories; an SLDNF interpreter specialised with respect to a program performing matrix transposition and a program to compute Fibonacci numbers; and a coroutining interpreter specialised with respect to a list sorting program that uses the 'British Museum' sorting algorithm and a program that solves the eight queens problem. An analysis of these results shows that a factor of approximately 3 times speedup is obtained by introducing better indexing and that the rest of the speedup is almost entirely due to specialising calls to **Resolve**.

With a lower-level implementation of both the WAM-like predicates mentioned above and the representations of substitutions, these results may be improved yet further, as the expense of emulating these WAM-like instructions in Gödel is removed. This will lead to an execution time for specialised versions of **Resolve** that will be comparable to the WAM code for the object statements themselves. Such improvements will be most noticeable in the specialised code for statements such as those in the matrix transposition program. Thus such an implementation would cause the greatest speedups to the above example of interpreting the matrix transposition program, bringing the results for this example into line with those of the other examples.

All of the specialisations described in this paper are performed automatically by *SAGE*. This means that users, without knowledge of the specific implementation of Gödel's ground representation, may write declarative ground Gödel meta-programs and, without further intervention on the part of the user, such programs can be specialised to produce equivalent programs which will potentially execute in a time comparable to similar Prolog non-ground meta-programs.

6 Conclusions.

The ground representation, provided by Gödel as an abstract data type, leads to clear and easily readable programs. In addition, Gödel's ground representation aids the user by internally handling the majority of any necessary manipulation of substitutions, when using the Gödel predicates **UnifyTerms**, **UnifyAtoms** and **Resolve**. These predicates deal with almost all of the unification and composition and application of substitutions necessary in meta-programming, thus leading to clearer, simpler, meta-programs (e.g. figure 3, as opposed to figure 4).

Having written a Gödel meta-program, an *automatic* specialisation may be performed by *SAGE*. Thus, without any further involvement on the part of the user, the overheads imposed by using an abstract data type may be removed. At the same time, specialising the meta-program with respect to an object program, a version of the meta-program is produced that, while still declarative, will execute in a significantly improved time. With a suitable implementation of Gödel's representation of substitutions, and the relevant primitive operations upon them, such a meta-program would execute in a time comparable to an equivalent Prolog meta-program which utilised Prolog's (non-declarative) non-ground representation.

We claim that the above results demonstrate that the ground representation is not only an essential tool for declarative meta-programming, but also that it is a practical one, as, through program specialisation, we may remove the expense incurred by its use. Using the ground representation in this way, many of the potential applications of meta-programming that have so far proved impossible in Prolog, such as effective self-applicable partial evaluators, now seem eminently achievable.

7 Acknowledgements.

I would like to thank firstly my supervisor, John Lloyd, and also Tony Bowers, John Gallagher and André de Waal, for advice and stimulating discussions concerning the realisation and implementation of a self-applicable partial evaluator. This work was supported by an SERC studentship award.

References

[1] H Ait-Kaci. *Warren's Abstract Machine: A Tutorial Reconstruction.* MIT Press, Cambridge, MA, 1991.

[2] K A Bowen and R A Kowalski. Amalgamating language and metalanguage in logic programming. In K L Clark and S-A Tarnlund, editors, *Logic Programming*, pages 153–172, 1982.

[3] A F Bowers. Representing Gödel object programs in Gödel. Technical Report CSTR-92-31, Department of Computer Science, University of Bristol, November 1992.

[4] D.A. de Waal and J. Gallagher. Specialisation of a unification algorithm. In T. Clement and K.-K. Lau, editors, *Logic Program Synthesis and Transformation*, Manchester 1991, pages 205–221. Workshops in Computing, Springer-Verlag, 1992.

[5] Y Futamura. Partial evaluation of computation process - an approach to a compiler-compiler. *Systems, Computers, Controls*, 2(5):45–50, 1971.

[6] J Gallagher. Transforming logic programs by specialising interpreters. In *ECAI-86*, pages 109–122, Brighton, 1986.

[7] P M Hill and J W Lloyd. Meta-programming for dynamic knowledge bases. Technical Report CS-88-18, Department of Computer Science, University of Bristol, 1988.

[8] P M Hill and J W Lloyd. Analysis of meta-programs. In H D Abramson and M H Rogers, editors, *Meta-Programming in Logic Programming, Proceedings of the Meta88 Workshop, June 1988*. MIT Press, 1989.

[9] P M Hill and J W Lloyd. The Gödel Programming Language. Technical Report CSTR-92-27, Department of Computer Science, University of Bristol, 1992. Revised May 1993. To be published by MIT Press.

[10] H J Komorowski. A specification of an abstract prolog machine and its application to partial evaluation. Technical Report LSST 69, Linkoping University, 1981.

[11] P Kursawe. How to invent a prolog machine. *New Generation Computing*, 5:97–114, 1987.

[12] A Lakhotia and L Sterling. How to control unfolding when specialising interpreters. *New Generation Computing*, 8:61–70, 1990.

[13] G Levi and G Sardu. Partial evaluation of metaprograms in a "multiple worlds" logic. *New Generation Computing*, 6:227–248, 1988.

[14] J W Lloyd and J C Shepherdson. Partial evaluation in logic programming. *Journal of Logic Programming*, 11:217–242, 1991.

[15] U Nilsson. Towards a methodology for the design of abstract machines for logic programming languages. *Journal of Logic Programming*, 16(1&2):163–189, May 1993.

[16] S Owen. Issues in the partial evaluation of meta-interpreters. In H D Abramson and M H Rogers, editors, *Meta-Programming in Logic Programming, Proceedings of the Meta88 Workshop, June 1988*, pages 319–340. MIT Press, 1989.

[17] S Safra and E Shapiro. Meta interpreters for real. In H J Kugler, editor, *Information Processing 86*, pages 271–278. North-Holland, 1986.

[18] L S Sterling and R D Beer. Meta-interpreters for expert system construction. *Journal of Logic Programming*, 6:163–178, 1989.

[19] A Takeuchi and K Furukawa. Partial evaluation of Prolog programs and its application to meta-programming. In H J Kugler, editor, *Information Processing 86*, pages 415–420, Dublin, 1986. North Holland.

[20] R Venken. A Prolog meta-interpreter for partial evaluation and its application to source to source transformation and query optimisation. In *ECAI-84: Advances in Artificial Intelligence*, pages 91–100, Pisa, 1984. North-Holland.

[21] D H D Warren. An abstract prolog instruction set. Technical Note 309, SRI International, 1983.

Synthesis of Programs from Unfold/Fold Proofs

Maurizio Proietti
IASI-CNR
Viale Manzoni 30
00185 Roma, Italy
proietti@iasi.rm.cnr.it

Alberto Pettorossi
Electronics Department
University of Rome II
00133 Roma, Italy
adp@iasi.rm.cnr.it

Abstract

We address some issues related to the use of equivalence formulas for transforming and synthesizing logic programs.

In the first part of the paper we describe a program transformation method based on the *unfold/fold rules* which can be used for proving that a given first order equivalence formula of the form: $\forall X$ ($\exists Y$ F(X,Y) $\leftrightarrow$ $\exists Z$ G(X,Z)), where F and G are conjunctions of atoms, is true in the least Herbrand model of a given program. Equivalence formulas of that form can be used to perform *goal replacement* steps, which allow us to transform clauses by replacing goals by equivalent ones while preserving the least Herbrand model. We provide some simple conditions ensuring total correctness of the goal replacement steps.

In the second part of the paper we show how the unfold/fold proof method described in the first part can be applied for solving synthesis problems which can be formulated as follows. Let us consider a program P and an equivalence formula of the form: $\forall X$ ($\exists Y$ F(X,Y) $\leftrightarrow$ $\exists Z$ (H(X,Z), newp(X,Z))), where F and H contain predicates defined in P and newp is a predicate symbol *not* occurring in P. We want to synthesize a set of clauses, say Eureka, such that the above equivalence formula is true in the least Herbrand model of P $\cup$ Eureka.

1 Introduction

Unfold/fold rules were originally introduced as basic transformations for improving programs while preserving their semantics [7, 22]. They can also be applied in several areas of program development, such as program analysis, synthesis, specialization, and verification. In particular, in [15] one may find a method based on unfold/fold rules which can be used for proving the equivalence of functional expressions. This method can also be adapted to the case of logic programs (see, for instance, [4]).

In Section 2 we follow the approach of [15] and we show how it can be applied to prove in the least Herbrand model of a given program P, the validity of an

This work has been partially supported by the 'Progetto Finalizzato Sistemi Informatici e Calcolo Parallelo' of the CNR Italy under grant n. 89.00026.69, MURST 40%, and Esprit Project Compulog II.

equivalence formula of the form: $\forall X\ (\exists Y\ F(X,Y) \leftrightarrow \exists Z\ G(X,Z))$, where F and G are conjunctions of atoms.

The validity of the formula $\forall X\ (\exists Y\ F(X,Y) \leftrightarrow \exists Z\ G(X,Z))$ in the least Herbrand model of P can in turn be used for performing program transformations. Indeed, if we replace $F(X,Y)$ by $G(X,Z)$ in a clause C_1 of P, then we get a new clause C_2 which is true in the least Herbrand model of P (provided that suitable conditions on the variables Y and Z hold). Thus, the least Herbrand model of the program $Q = (P - \{C_1\}) \cup \{C_2\}$ is contained in the least Herbrand model of P, that is, the replacement of $F(X,Y)$ by $G(X,Z)$ is *partially correct*.

Notice that the unfold/fold proof method cannot be applied for proving that an equivalence formula is a logical consequence of a program P (i.e. it is true in every model of P) because in general the unfold/fold rules do not preserve the set of all models of P.

In Section 3 we give some simple conditions which ensure the *total correctness* of the replacement of $F(X,Y)$ by $G(X,Z)$, that is, the *equality* of the least Herbrand models of P and Q. In our approach these conditions can be formulated in terms of the existence of suitable unfold/fold transformations which preserve the least Herbrand model semantics.

In Section 4 we present a method which allows us to synthesize programs from specifications using unfold/fold proofs. The basic idea is related to the *proofs as programs* paradigm [1, 19]: the constructive proof of a property can be used for synthesizing a program which satisfies that property. This principle has been applied also in the area of logic program synthesis [6, 9]. In this paper we consider specifications expressed by equivalence formulas of the following form: $\forall X\ (\exists Y\ F(X,Y) \leftrightarrow \exists Z\ (H(X,Z), newp(X,Z)))$, where F and H contain predicates defined in a given program P and newp is a predicate symbol *not* occurring in P. We are required to find a set of clauses, say Eureka, defining the predicate newp, such that the validity of a given equivalence formula in the least Herbrand model of P $\cup$ Eureka can be proved by using the unfold/fold proof method.

We finally show through a couple of examples given in Sections 4 and 5 that program specialization and difference-list introduction can be viewed as applications of our synthesis method.

2 The Unfold/Fold Proof Method

In this paper we consider definite logic programs and we assume that their semantics is defined in terms of the least Herbrand model. Given a program P its least Herbrand model is denoted by $M(P)$.

The transformation rules we consider are the *unfolding*, *folding*, and *goal replacement* as defined in [11, 22]. These transformation rules (collectively called *unfold/fold* rules) preserve the least Herbrand model semantics in the sense that if program P is transformed into program Q using the rules then $M(P) = M(Q)$.

Suppose that, given a program P, we want to prove that $\forall X\ (\exists Y\ F(X,Y) \leftrightarrow \exists Z\ G(X,Z))$ is true in $M(P)$, that is:

$$M(P) \models \forall X \ (\exists Y \ F(X,Y) \leftrightarrow \exists Z \ G(X,Z))$$

where $F(X,Y)$ and $G(X,Z)$ are *conjunctions* of atoms, and X, Y, Z denote pairwise disjoint vectors of variables.

We proceed (similarly to what has been suggested in [15] for the functional case) by introducing two new clauses:

C_1. goal1(X) ← F(X,Y)
C_2. goal2(X) ← G(X,Z)

where goal1 and goal2 are predicate symbols not occurring in P. We then look for two sets of clauses S_1 and S_2 such that: i) $P \cup S_1$ and $P \cup S_2$ can be derived by unfold/fold transformations from $P \cup \{C_1\}$ and $P \cup \{C_2\}$, respectively, ii) the head of each clause in S_1 and S_2 has predicate symbol goal1 and goal2, respectively, and iii) S_2 can be obtained from S_1 by substituting the predicate symbol goal2 for goal1 and by variable renaming. This derivation has been represented in Fig. 1, where, as in the following figures, 'replace' stands for one or more applications of the goal replacement rule.

Notice that if we find such sets S_1 and S_2 then it is the case that the predicate goal1 does not occur in S_2 and similarly, the predicate goal2 does not occur in S_1.

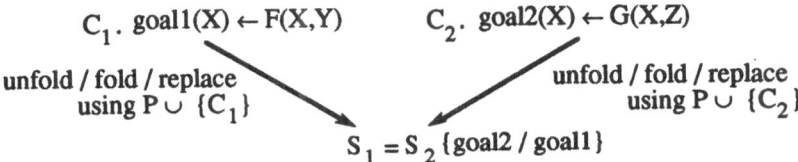

Figure 1. Unfold/fold proof of $M(P) \models \forall X \ (\exists Y \ F(X,Y) \leftrightarrow \exists Z \ G(X,Z))$.

Theorem. The unfold/fold proof method is sound w.r.t. the least Herbrand model semantics.

Proof. We assume that all our programs are written using symbols taken from a fixed language L and we may consider the Herbrand universe HU associated with L. The least Herbrand model of P is defined as the least model of P with universe HU. Thus, HU is common to all programs derived during the transformation process. The unfold/fold transformation rules preserve this notion of least Herbrand model semantics.

Since S_2 is equal to S_1 modulo the substitution of goal2 for goal1 and variable renaming, we have that for every term $t \in$ HU:

$$M(P \cup S_1) \models goal1(t) \quad \text{iff} \quad M(P \cup S_2) \models goal2(t).$$

In $P \cup \{C_1\}$ the predicate goal1 is defined by clause C_1 only, and in $P \cup \{C_2\}$ goal2 is defined by clause C_2 only. Thus, we have that the following properties hold for every term $t \in$ HU:

$$M(P \cup \{C_1\}) \models goal1(t) \quad \text{iff} \quad M(P \cup \{C_1\}) \models \exists Y \ F(t,Y)$$
$$M(P \cup \{C_2\}) \models goal2(t) \quad \text{iff} \quad M(P \cup \{C_2\}) \models \exists Z \ G(t,Z)).$$

From the assumption that our transformations preserve the least Herbrand model it follows that $M(P \cup S_1) = M(P \cup \{C_1\})$ and $M(P \cup S_2) = M(P \cup \{C_2\})$. Thus, we have that for every term $t \in$ HU:

$$M(P \cup \{C_1\}) \models \exists Y\ F(t,Y) \quad \text{iff} \quad M(P \cup \{C_2\}) \models \exists Z\ G(t,Z)).$$

Now, since the predicate symbols occurring in $F(t,Y)$ and $G(t,Z)$ do not depend on goal1 and goal2, we can replace both $M(P \cup \{C_1\})$ and $M(P \cup \{C_2\})$ by $M(P)$ and we conclude that for every term $t \in HU$:

$$M(P) \models \exists Y\ F(t,Y) \quad \text{iff} \quad M(P) \models \exists Z\ G(t,Z)).$$

By observing that the universe of $M(P)$ is HU we immediately get the desired equivalence

$$M(P) \models \forall X\ (\exists Y\ F(X,Y) \leftrightarrow \exists Z\ G(X,Z)).\qquad\blacksquare$$

The following example shows an application of the unfold/fold proof method.

Example 1. Let us consider the following program [5]:

$$Fst(P): \quad p(X) \leftarrow r(X1),\ s(X1,X)$$
$$s(X,X) \leftarrow$$
$$s(X,Y) \leftarrow q(X,Z),\ s(Z,Y)$$

and let us assume that we want to prove the following property:

Eq1. $M(Fst(P)) \models \forall X,Y\ (\exists Z\ (q(X,Z),\ s(Z,Y)) \leftrightarrow \exists W\ (s(X,W),\ q(W,Y))).$

We apply the unfold/fold proof method and we introduce the following two clauses:

$$C_1.\quad goal1(X,Y) \leftarrow q(X,Z),\ s(Z,Y)$$
$$C_2.\quad goal2(X,Y) \leftarrow s(X,W),\ q(W,Y).$$

By unfolding the atoms with predicate s and then folding, clauses C_1 and C_2 can be transformed into the following two sets of clauses S_1 and S_2, respectively:

$$S_1:\quad goal1(X,Y) \leftarrow q(X,Y)$$
$$goal1(X,Y) \leftarrow q(X,Z),\ goal1(Z,Y)$$

$$S_2:\quad goal2(X,Y) \leftarrow q(X,Y)$$
$$goal2(X,Y) \leftarrow q(X,Z1),\ goal2(Z1,Y).$$

The transformation is illustrated in Fig. 2. S_1 and S_2 are the same set of clauses modulo predicate and variable renaming. Therefore, property Eq1 holds. $\blacksquare$

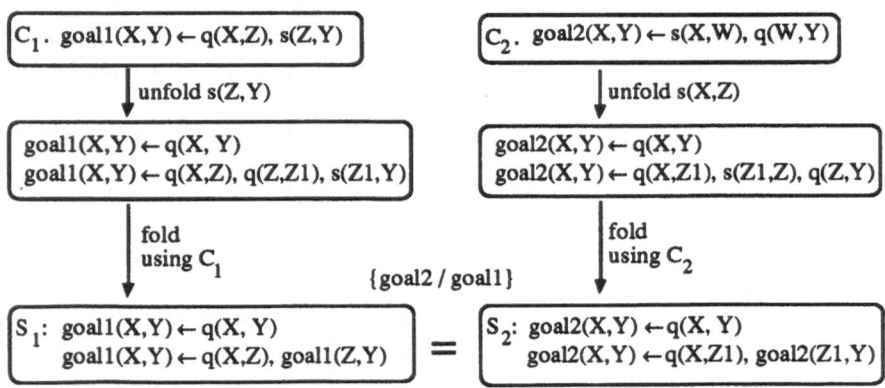

Figure 2. Unfold/fold proof of
$M(Fst(P)) \models \forall X,Y\ (\exists Z\ (q(X,Z),\ s(Z,Y)) \leftrightarrow \exists W\ (s(X,W),\ q(W,Y))).$

3 Unfold/Fold Proofs and Goal Replacement

One of the main reasons for considering equivalence formulas is that they can be used to justify the goal replacement rule [3, 11, 18, 22] as we now explain. Let P be a program and C be a clause in P of the form: H ← M, F(X,Y), N, where M, F(X,Y), and N are conjunctions of atoms, and X, Y are disjoint vectors of variables.

If we replace F(X,Y) by the conjunction G(X,Z) and the following conditions hold:

1) no variable in {Y, Z} occurs in {H, M, N}, and
2) $M(P) \models \forall X\ (\exists Y\ F(X,Y) \leftrightarrow \exists Z\ G(X,Z))$.

then the resulting clause H ← M, G(X,Z), N, call it D, is true in M(P).

Therefore, the transformation of P into Q = (P − {C}) ∪ {D} is partially correct, that is, $M(Q) \subseteq M(P)$. However, it may happen that $M(Q) \neq M(P)$, as it is shown by the following example.

Example 2. Let us consider the program

$$P:\ p \leftarrow q \qquad\qquad q \leftarrow$$

We have that $M(P) \models q \leftrightarrow p$. By replacing q by p in p ← q we get:

$$Q:\ p \leftarrow p \qquad\qquad q \leftarrow$$

and $M(Q) = \{q\} \neq \{p,q\} = M(P)$. ∎

A condition for the goal replacement rule to be totally correct, is its *reversibility*. The replacement of F(X,Y) by G(X,Z) is said to be *reversible* iff in addition to conditions 1) and 2) above, we have:

3) $M(Q) \models \forall X\ (\exists Y\ F(X,Y) \leftrightarrow \exists Z\ G(X,Z))$.

Indeed, the replacement of G(X,Z) by F(X,Y) in Q yields P, and by 1) and 3) this replacement is partially correct, that is, $M(P) \subseteq M(Q)$.

Notice that also condition 3) can be shown by using our unfold/fold method. As an example of the use of our correctness criterion for goal replacement we now look at a transformation taken from [5].

Example 3. (*Simulating Bottom-up Evaluation*) In [5] it is proved that for any given definition of the predicates r and q the following two programs P and Fst(P) are equivalent w.r.t. the least Herbrand model semantics, that is, M(P) = M(Fst(P))):

P :	p(X) ← r(X)	s(X,X) ←
	p(X) ← p(Y), q(Y,X)	s(X,Y) ← s(X,W), q(W,Y)

Fst(P) :	p(X) ← r(X1), s(X1,X)	s(X,X) ←
		s(X,Y) ← q(X,Z), s(Z,Y).

If we use Fst(P), instead of P, for evaluating a goal: ← p(x) we get the effect of "simulating a forward-reasoning (bottom-up) computation within the framework of an overall backward-reasoning (top-down) execution strategy" [5, p. 125]. We will now prove the same equivalence using the unfold/fold method.

Since the equivalence formula $\forall X,Y$ $(\exists Z$ $(q(X,Z), s(Z,Y)) \leftrightarrow \exists W$ $(s(X,W), q(W,Y)))$ is true in $M(Fst(P))$ (see Example 1), we may apply the goal replacement rule and transform $Fst(P)$ into the following program:

R : $p(X) \leftarrow r(X1), s(X1,X)$ $s(X,X) \leftarrow$

$s(X,Y) \leftarrow s(X,W), q(W,Y).$

In order to prove that the goal replacement is totally correct, that is, $M(R)$ is equal to $M(Fst(P))$, it suffices to prove that the goal replacement is reversible, that is, $\forall X,Y$ $(\exists Z$ $(q(X,Z), s(Z,Y)) \leftrightarrow \exists W$ $(s(X,W), q(W,Y)))$ is true in $M(R)$.

This can be done by applying again the unfold/fold proof method as follows. We consider again clauses C_1 and C_2 of Example 1:

C_1. $goal1(X,Y) \leftarrow q(X,Z), s(Z,Y)$
C_2. $goal2(X,Y) \leftarrow s(X,W), q(W,Y)$

and we show that, by using the clauses in R, C_1 and C_2 can be transformed into the following two sets of clauses S_3 and S_4, respectively (see Fig. 3):

S_3: $goal1(X, Y) \leftarrow q(X, Y)$
$goal1(X, Y) \leftarrow goal1(X, Z1), q(Z1,Y)$

S_4: $goal2(X, Y) \leftarrow q(X, Y)$
$goal2(X, Y) \leftarrow goal2(X, Z), q(Z, Y)$

which are equal modulo predicate and variable renaming.

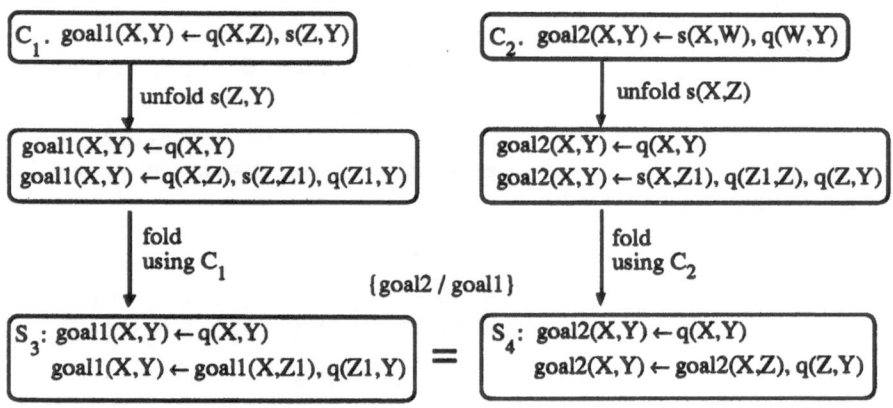

Figure 3. Unfold/fold proof of
$M(R) \models \forall X,Y$ $(\exists Z$ $(q(X,Z), s(Z,Y)) \leftrightarrow \exists W$ $(s(X,W), q(W,Y)))$.

Now we may complete the equivalence proof of P and $Fst(P)$ by transforming the definition of p in R into the one in P (see Fig. 4).   ■

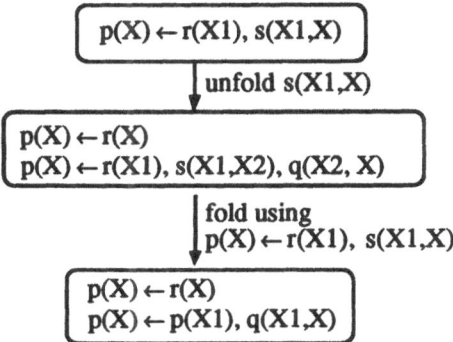

Figure 4. Transformation of R into P.

4 Synthesis of Programs from Unfold/Fold Proofs: A General Strategy and Its Application for Specializing Programs

In this section we use the unfold/fold proof technique for the synthesis of logic programs from specifications. We assume that a specification is given as an equivalence formula of the form: $\forall X\ (\exists Y\ F(X,Y) \leftrightarrow \exists Z\ (H(X,Z), newp(X,Z)))$, where F and H contain predicates defined in a given program P and newp is a predicate symbol *not* occurring in P. As usual, X, Y and Z are pairwise disjoint vectors of variables. We are required to find a set of clauses, say Eureka, such that the given equivalence formula is true in the least Herbrand model of $P \cup$ Eureka.

The synthesis of the set Eureka can be viewed as an instance of an *abduction problem* [13] where φ is the 'observed formula' and Eureka is a set of 'abductive explanations' to be added to the theory P for justifying φ.

As a first example of a specification by an equivalence formula we now consider the *program specialization* problem. Given a program P, a predicate p(X) defined in P, and a set I of input values, we want to specialize p to I by producing a new predicate pI(X), together with a set Eureka of clauses defining pI(X), such that p(X) is equivalent to pI(X) for all X in I.

We assume that I is described by a predicate defined in P, say input(X), such that X belongs to I iff input(X) is true in the least Herbrand model of P. Thus, we may define the problem of specializing p to I as follows: find a set Eureka of clauses such that

$$M(P \cup \text{Eureka}) \models \forall X\ (\text{input}(X), p(X) \leftrightarrow \text{input}(X), pI(X)).$$

Obviously, one such a pI is p itself. However, in the following example we will show that our synthesis method is powerful enough to produce a non-trivial solution which is more efficient than p.

Example 4. (*Specializing Append with Type Checks*) Let us consider the following program for concatenating lists:

Append : append([],Ys,Ys) ← list(Ys)
  append([X|Xs],Ys,[X|Zs]) ← list(Xs), list(Ys), list(Zs),
                                     append(Xs,Ys,Zs)

  list([]) ←
  list([X|Xs]) ← list(Xs).

Our specialization problem is similar to the one of [10]. We suppose that the user query is of the form:

Q : ← list(Xs), list(Ys), list(Zs), append(Xs,Ys,Zs).

and we would like to specialize our predicate append to the class of queries which are instances of Q. In other words, we would like to define a new predicate, say appendlist(Xs,Ys,Zs), and find a set Eureka of clauses such that:

M(Append∪Eureka) ⊨
  ∀Xs,Ys,Zs (list(Xs), list(Ys), list(Zs), append(Xs,Ys,Zs) ↔
                  list(Xs), list(Ys), list(Zs), appendlist(Xs,Ys,Zs)).

Thus, in this case input(Xs,Ys,Zs) is list(Xs), list(Ys), list(Zs). ∎

We will propose a general synthesis method which allows us to find the set Eureka of clauses such that the given equivalence formula can be proved by using the unfold/fold proof method we presented in Section 2. Our method consists of five phases (see also Fig. 5).

(1) We first introduce the following two clauses:

  C_1. goal1(X) ← F(X,Y)
  C_2. goal2(X) ← H(X,Z), newp(X,Z)

where goal1 and goal2 are predicate symbols not occurring in P.

(2) We use the unfold/fold transformation rules starting from clause C_1 to produce a new set S_1 of clauses such that P ∪ {C_1} is equivalent to P ∪ S_1. The head of each clause of S_1 has predicate goal1, and no other clause in P has goal1 as head predicate.

(3) We get a set S_2 of clauses from the set S_1 by replacing the predicate symbol goal1 by goal2.

(4) We eliminate the occurrences of goal2 from the bodies of the clauses in S_2 by performing some unfolding steps using clause C_2. We then possibly perform some goal replacement steps, thereby getting a new set of clauses, say T_2.

(5) Finally, we look for a set Eureka of clauses which allows us to derive P ∪ Eureka ∪ T_2 from P ∪ Eureka ∪ {C_2}. ∎

Notice that, when the set Eureka found during Phase (5) is derived, the diagram of Fig. 5 is an instance of Fig. 1, because we may go from T_2 to S_2 by replace and folding steps. More formally, we have that for the set Eureka specified at Phase (5), the following property holds:

Eq2. M(P ∪ Eureka) ⊨ ∀X (∃Y F(X,Y) ↔ ∃Z (H(X,Z), newp(X,Z))).

Indeed, by (2) $P \cup$ Eureka $\cup \{C_1\}$ can be transformed into $P \cup$ Eureka $\cup S_1$. By (5) $P \cup$ Eureka $\cup T_2$ can be derived from $P \cup$ Eureka $\cup \{C_2\}$, and by (4) $P \cup$ Eureka $\cup S_2$ can be derived from $P \cup$ Eureka $\cup T_2$ by some replace and folding steps using C_2. Thus, i) $P \cup$ Eureka $\cup \{C_1\}$ can be transformed into $P \cup$ Eureka $\cup S_1$, ii) $P \cup$ Eureka $\cup \{C_2\}$ can be transformed into $P \cup$ Eureka $\cup S_2$, and iii) by (3) S_1 differs from S_2 only for the name of the predicates. In other words, we have an unfold/fold proof of Eq2.

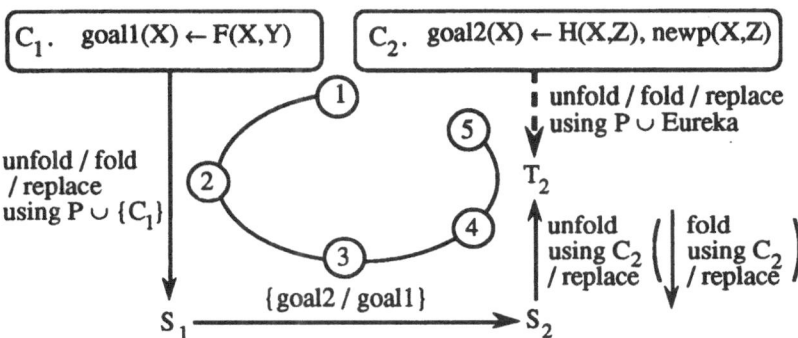

Figure 5. Synthesis from unfold/fold proofs and its five phases.

Example 5. (Specializing Append with Type Checks Continued) In order to find the set Eureka of clauses for appendlist(Xs,Ys,Zs), we apply our synthesis method as follows:

(1) We introduce two clauses:
    C_1. goal1(Xs,Ys,Zs) ← list(Xs), list(Ys), list(Zs), append(Xs,Ys,Zs)
    C_2. goal2(Xs,Ys,Zs) ← list(Xs), list(Ys), list(Zs), appendlist(Xs,Ys,Zs).

(2) We perform unfolding, folding, and goal replacement steps starting from clause C_1 and we produce the following set of clauses:
    S_1: goal1([],Ys,Ys) ← list(Ys)
    goal1([X|Xs],Ys,[X|Zs]) ← goal1(Xs,Ys,Zs).

(3) We replace the predicate symbol goal1 by goal2 and we get the following set of clauses:
    S_2: goal2([],Ys,Ys) ← list(Ys)
    goal2([X|Xs],Ys,[X|Zs]) ← goal2(Xs,Ys,Zs).

(4) We perform unfolding steps using clause C_2 and we get the set T_2 made out of the following two clauses:
    D_1. goal2([],Ys,Ys) ← list(Ys)
    D_2. goal2([X|Xs],Ys,[X|Zs]) ← list(Xs), list(Ys), list(Zs),
                                        appendlist(Xs,Ys,Zs).

(5) We are now left with the problem of finding the set Eureka of clauses which allows us to derive $P \cup$ Eureka $\cup T_2$ from $P \cup$ Eureka $\cup \{C_2\}$.
    In what follows we will see how this problem can be solved. ∎

Phase (5) is the most complex one, and in general, no algorithm can be given for finding the set Eureka. We now specify a strategy which has been successful in the derivation of the Eureka set in the cases we have looked at. We will see this strategy in action in Examples 6 and 7 below.

Our strategy is made out of three steps (see Fig. 6). The first step is motivated by the fact that in order to derive the clauses of T_2 from C_2, we may perform an unfolding step which is driven by the need of deriving the heads of the clauses of T_2 from the head of C_2.

Notice also that the unfolding of a clause, say C, w.r.t. an atom in its body of can be performed by i) instantiating the variables in the head of C, thereby getting a clause D, and then ii) performing an unfolding step which does not instantiate the variables in the head of D.

As an example, let us consider the unfolding of a clause C of the form: $h(X) \leftarrow b(X,u)$ using clause $b(t,Y) \leftarrow d(Y)$. This unfolding can be performed by first instantiating the variables in $h(X)$, thereby getting the clause D: $h(t) \leftarrow b(t,u)$, and then unfolding D, thereby getting $h(t) \leftarrow d(u)$. This unfolding step does not requires further instantiation of the variables in $h(t)$ when unifying $b(t,Y)$ and $b(t,u)$.

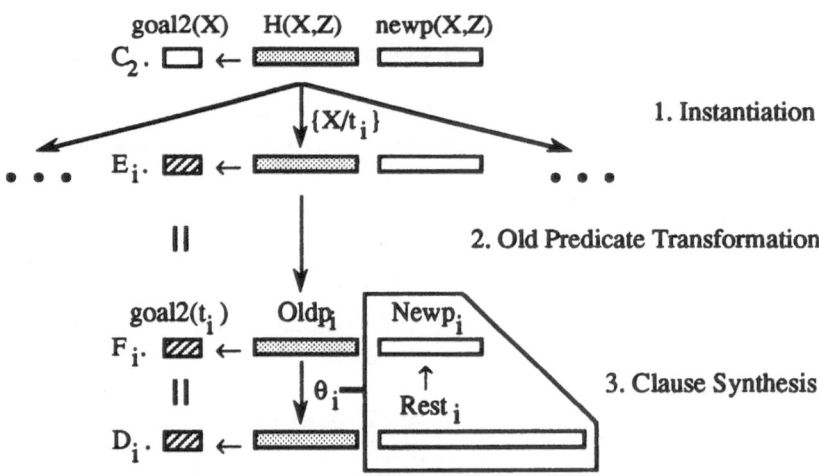

Figure 6. Strategy for synthesis of the set Eureka of clauses.

Step 1. (*Instantiation*) In this step we derive a multiset S_E of instances of C_2 such that the heads of the clauses in S_E are equal to the heads of the clauses in T_2. By definition, C_2 is of the form:

$$goal2(X) \leftarrow H(X,Z), newp(X,Z).$$

Let T_2 be $\{D_i \mid i = 1,...,n\}$, where D_i is of the form:

$D_i.$ $goal2(t_i) \leftarrow Body_i$

and each D_i has no variables in common with C_2. We produce the multiset $S_E = \{E_i \mid i = 1,...,n\}$ of clauses by applying to clause C_2 the substitution $\{X/t_i\}$ for $i = 1,...,n$.

Thus, for $i = 1,...,n$ we have: $E_i = C_2\{X/t_i\} = goal2(t_i) \leftarrow H(t_i,Z), newp(t_i,Z)$.

Step 2. (*Old Predicate Transformation*) Starting from each clause E_i, we repeatedly apply unfold/fold transformations which do not involve the predicates goal2 and newp. In particular, folding steps using C_2 are not allowed. Unfolding steps are allowed only if they produce exactly one clause whose head is equal (modulo variable renaming) to the one of E_i. Notice that by complying with these restrictions each derived clause will contain exactly one occurrence of the predicate newp. We stop this transformation process beginning from each E_i when we get (possibly by variable renaming) a clause of the form:

$\quad$ F_i. $\quad$ $goal2(t_i) \leftarrow Oldp_i, Newp_i$

where $Newp_i = newp(...)$ and there exists an idempotent substitution θ_i satisfying the following conditions:

$\quad$ a) $\quad Body_i = Oldp_i \theta_i, Rest_i$,
$\quad$ b) $\quad t_i \theta_i = t_i$,
$\quad$ c) $\quad A_i \cap B_i \subseteq L_i$, and
$\quad$ d) $\quad B_i \cap L_i \subseteq A_i \cap L_i$

where A_i stands for $vars(Newp_i)$, B_i stands for $vars(Rest_i) \cup vars(\theta_i)$, and L_i stands for $vars(goal2(t_i), Oldp_i)$, where $vars(G)$ denotes the set of variables occurring in a goal G and $vars(\theta_i)$ denotes the set of variables occurring in the non-identical bindings of θ_i.

Step 3. (*Clause Synthesis*) For each clause F_i and substitution θ_i derived at Step 2 we consider the clause:

$\quad$ N_i. $\quad$ $Newp_i \theta_i \leftarrow Rest_i$

and we take Eureka to be the set $\{N_i \mid i = 1,...,n\}$.

Conditions a), b), c), and d) ensure that by unfolding clause F_i w.r.t. $Newp_i$ using N_i we get (a variant of) D_i. We do not show here the detailed proof of the fact that T_2 can indeed be derived from C_2 by means of unfold/fold transformations using clauses of $P \cup$ Eureka, when Eureka has been constructed according to Steps 1, 2, and 3 above.

Example 6. (*Specializing Append with Type Checks Continued*)
Step 1. By instantiation, from C_2 of Phase (1) of Example 5, we get:

$\quad$ E_1. $\quad$ $goal2([],Ys,Ys) \leftarrow list([]), list(Ys), list(Ys), appendlist([],Ys,Ys)$
$\quad$ E_2. $\quad$ $goal2([X|Xs],Ys,[X|Zs]) \leftarrow list([X|Xs]), list(Ys), list([X|Zs]),$
$\quad\quad\quad\quad\quad\quad\quad\quad\quad\quad\quad\quad\quad\quad\quad$ $appendlist([X|Xs],Ys,[X|Zs])$.

The heads of clauses E_1 and E_2 are equal to those of clauses D_1 and D_2 in T_2 of Example 5, respectively.

Step 2. By unfolding clauses E_1 and E_2 w.r.t. list atoms and deleting duplicate atoms (this is an instance of goal replacement) we get the two clauses:

$\quad$ F_1. $\quad$ $goal2([],Ys,Ys) \leftarrow list(Ys), appendlist([],Ys,Ys)$
$\quad$ F_2. $\quad$ $goal2([X|Xs],Ys,[X|Zs]) \leftarrow list(Xs), list(Ys), list(Zs),$
$\quad\quad\quad\quad\quad\quad\quad\quad\quad\quad\quad\quad\quad\quad\quad$ $appendlist([X|Xs],Ys,[X|Zs])$.

We have that:
- both θ_1 and θ_2 are the identity substitution,
- $Oldp_1 = Oldp_1 \ \theta_1 = list(Ys)$ and $Oldp_2 = Oldp_2 \ \theta_2 = list(Xs), list(Ys), list(Zs)$,
- $Newp_1 = appendlist([],Ys,Ys)$ and $Newp_2 = appendlist([X|Xs],Ys,[X|Zs])$,
- $Rest_1$ is the empty goal and $Rest_2$ is $appendlist(Xs,Ys,Zs)$.

Step 3. The set Eureka is made out the following two clauses:

N_1. $appendlist([],Ys,Ys) \leftarrow$
N_2. $appendlist([X|Xs],Ys,[X|Zs]) \leftarrow appendlist(Xs,Ys,Zs)$.

When we execute appendlist, instead of append, no list type check is performed. Indeed, those checks are not necessary if we know in advance that the input arguments of append are lists. ∎

5 Synthesis of Programs that Use Difference-lists

Difference-lists are data structures which are sometimes used, instead of lists, for implementing algorithms that manipulate sequences of elements. The advantage of using difference-lists is that the concatenation of two sequences represented as difference-lists can often be performed in constant time, while if we use the standard append program, it takes linear time w.r.t. the length of the first list.

A difference-list can be thought of as a pair of lists, denoted by L\R, such that there exists a third list X for which append(X,R,L) is true [8]. In that case we say that X is *represented* by the difference-list L\R. Obviously, a single list can be represented by many difference-lists.

Programs that use lists are often simpler to write and understand than the equivalent ones which make use of difference-lists. Thus, one may be interested in providing general techniques for the automatic transformation of programs which use lists, into programs which use difference-lists. Several such techniques have been proposed in the literature [12, 23, 24].

We will show that through our synthesis method we can perform the desired transformation for introducing difference-lists. Our method is very general and it can be used also to perform other changes of data representations.

The problem of transforming programs which use difference-lists, instead of lists, can be formulated as follows. Let p(X,Y) be a predicate defined in a program P where Y is a list. We want to synthesize a new predicate, say diff_p(X,L\R), where L\R is a difference-list, together with an additional set of clauses, say Eureka, defining diff_p. We also want diff_p(X,L\R) to be equivalent to p(X,Y) when L\R is a difference-list representing Y.

Thus, the relationship between p(X,Y) and diff_p(X,L\R) can be expressed by the following specification:

$$M(P \cup Eureka) \models$$
$$\forall X,Y \ ((list(Y), p(X,Y)) \leftrightarrow \exists L,R \ (diff\_list(Y,L\backslash R), diff\_p(X,L\backslash R)))$$

where diff_list(Y,L\R) holds iff L\R is a difference-list representing Y.

By definition of difference-lists the atom diff_list(Y,L\R) is equivalent to append(Y,R,L). Thus, the above specification can also be written as follows:

M(P ∪ Eureka) ⊨
 $\forall$X,Y ((list(Y), p(X,Y)) ↔ $\exists$L,R (append(Y,R,L), diff_p(X,L\R))).

In the following example taken from [21, p. 253], we consider a simple program which uses difference-lists, and we show how it can be derived by our synthesis method.

Example 7. (Implementing Queues by Difference-lists) Let us consider the following program Queue defining a predicate queue(S) which holds iff S is a sequence of enqueue and dequeue operations represented as a list of terms of the form enqueue(X) and dequeue(X).

Queue : queue(S) ← queue2(S,[])
    queue2([enqueue(X)|Xs],Q) ← append(Q,[X],Q1), queue2(Xs,Q1)
    queue2([dequeue(X)|Xs],[X|Q]) ← queue2(Xs,Q)
    queue2([],Q) ←

Queues are represented as lists. The second argument of queue2 is a queue which is initially empty (represented as []), and it is updated according to the sequence of enqueue and dequeue operations specified by the value of the first argument. Since the concatenation between lists which is performed in the case of an enqueue operation is expensive, we would like to represent the second argument of queue2 as a difference-list.

Thus, we look for a predicate diff_queue2(S,L\R) defined by a set Eureka of clauses such that:
Eq3. M(Queue ∪ Eureka) ⊨$\forall$S,Q ((list(Q), queue2(S,Q)) ↔
                $\exists$L,R (append(Q,R,L), diff_queue2(S,L\R))).
    The predicates list and append are defined as usual (see Examples 4 and 5).

The synthesis of Eureka can be performed by routine application of our five-phase method.

(1) We introduce two clauses:
    C_1. goal1(S,Q) ← list(Q), queue2(S,Q)
    C_2. goal2(S,Q) ← append(Q,R,L), diff_queue2(S,L\R).

(2) By unfolding, goal replacement, and folding steps we transform clause C_1 into the following set of clauses:
    S_1: goal1([enqueue(X)|Xs], Q) ← append(Q,[X],QX), goal1(Xs,QX)
      goal1([dequeue(X)|Xs], [X|Q]) ← goal1(Xs,Q)
      goal1([],Q) ← append(Q,R,L).

The goal replacement steps are based on the following properties which can be proved by our unfold/fold method:
M(Queue ∪ {C_1}) ⊨$\forall$Q (list(Q) ↔ $\exists$R,L append(Q,R,L)) and
M(Queue ∪ {C_1}) ⊨$\forall$X,Q,QX (list(Q), append(Q,[X],QX) ↔
                list(QX), append(Q,[X],QX)).

(3) By replacing the predicate symbol goal1 by goal2 we get the following set of clauses:

S_2: goal2([enqueue(X)|Xs], Q) ← append(Q,[X],QX), goal2(Xs,QX)
  goal2([dequeue(X)|Xs], [X|Q]) ← goal2(Xs,Q)
  goal2([],Q) ← append(Q,R,L).

(4) By unfolding using clause C_2 and applying the associativity law of append we get the set T_2 made out of the following three clauses:

D_1. goal2([enqueue(X)|Xs], Q) ← append(Q,[X|R],L),
              diff_queue2(Xs,L\R)

D_2. goal2([dequeue(X)|Xs], [X|Q]) ← append(Q,R,L),
              diff_queue2(Xs,L\R)

D_3. goal2([],Q) ← append(Q,R,L).

(5) The set Eureka can now be synthesized by the following three steps:

Step 1. (*Instantiation*) By instantiation from C_2 we get:

E_1. goal2([enqueue(X)|Xs], Q) ← append(Q,R,L),
              diff_queue2([enqueue(X)|Xs],L\R)

E_2. goal2([dequeue(X)|Xs], [X|Q]) ← append([X|Q],R,L),
              diff_queue2([dequeue(X)|Xs],L\R)

E_3. goal2([],Q) ← append(Q,R,L), diff_queue2([],L\R).

Step 2. (*Old Predicate Transformation*) By unfolding clause E_2 we get (by rewriting clauses E_1 and E_3, renamed as F_1 and F_3, respectively):

F_1. goal2([enqueue(X)|Xs], Q) ← append(Q,R1,L),
              diff_queue2([enqueue(X)|Xs],L\R1)

F_2. goal2([dequeue(X)|Xs], [X|Q]) ← append(Q,R,L),
              diff_queue2([dequeue(X)|Xs],[X|L]\R)

F_3. goal2([],Q) ← append(Q,R,L), diff_queue2([],L\R).

We have that:

- θ_1 is {R1/[X|R]), while θ_2 and θ_3 are both the identity substitution,
- $Oldp_1 = Oldp_2 = Oldp_3$ = append(Q,R,L),
- $Newp_1$ = diff_queue2([enqueue(X)|Xs],L\R),
  $Newp_2$ = diff_queue2([dequeue(X)|Xs],[X|L]\R), and
  $Newp_3$ = diff_queue2([],L\R),
- $Rest_1$ = diff_queue2(Xs,L\R), $Rest_2$ = diff_queue2(Xs,L\R), and $Rest_3$ is the empty goal.

Step 3. (*Clause Synthesis*) The set Eureka is made out the following clauses:

  diff_queue2([enqueue(X)|Xs], L\[X|R]) ← diff_queue2(Xs,L\R)
  diff_queue2([dequeue(X)|Xs], [X|L]\R) ← diff_queue2(Xs,L\R)
  diff_queue2([],L\R) ←

Notice that, by Eq3, for Y=[] the following property holds:

  M(Queue ∪ Eureka) |= ∀X (queue2(X,[]) ↔ ∃R diff_queue2(X,R\R)).

Thus, we can express the predicate queue in terms of diff_queue2 as follows:

  queue(S) ← diff_queue2(S,R\R).

This clause, together with the clauses of the set Eureka (see Step 3), is analogous to the program presented in [21]. ∎

6 Related Work and Conclusions

We have presented some methods based on unfold/fold transformations, which can be used for proving properties of programs, and for performing program synthesis, transformation, and specialization.

In particular, we have described a method for synthesizing programs from unfold/fold proofs of program properties. Although our method makes use of unfold/fold transformations, we feel that it falls into the category of *synthesis methods* because the initial specification is not in Horn clause form, but it is assumed to be a more general formula of the form:

$$\forall X \; (\exists Y \; F(X,Y) \leftrightarrow \exists Z \; (H(X,Z), newp(X,Z)))$$ (†)

where G and H are conjunctions of atoms and newp is the predicate for which we would like to synthesize a program.

Thus, our starting point is similar to the one of the synthesis methods considered in [6, 9], but our method uses different techniques. In particular, our initial specification is similar to the one considered in [16], where the synthesis conjecture is of the form:

$$\forall X \; (spec(X) \leftrightarrow prog(X))$$

where prog(X) has an unspecified definition.

The method we propose is very general and it is widely applicable. It extends the standard techniques which are currently available in the framework of unfold/fold program transformation. An informal argument to support this claim can be given as follows.

By using the unfold/fold rules as defined in [22], a new predicate, say newp, can be defined in terms of already defined predicates in an *explicit* way only, in the sense that one may add to the current program P a clause C of the form:

$$newp(X,Z) \leftarrow F(X,Y)$$

where F is a conjunction of atoms whose predicates occur in P. Thus, in the least Herbrand model of $P \cup \{C\}$ the new predicate newp is specified by:

$$\forall X \; (\exists Y \; F(X,Y) \leftrightarrow \exists Z \; newp(X,Z))$$

which is less general formula than the ones we have considered in this paper. Indeed, we allow for an *implicit definition* of the new predicate newp as indicated by the formula (†) above.

Implicit definitions are also considered in [14] where some modifications of the unfolding and folding rules are introduced to deal with generalized definitions of the form:

$$(H(X,Z) \wedge newp(X,Z)) \leftarrow F(X,Y).$$

In our method we do not need to introduce extra or modified rules. Moreover, in [14] the form of allowed derivations is very restricted, while in our case, the unfold/fold proofs may be of any general form.

The reader may also verify that the two synthesis examples we have presented, that is, program specialization and introduction of difference-lists, cannot be derived in a natural way by using the unfold/fold transformations of [22]. Some modified versions of the rules should be used instead, like, for instance, the unfold/fold rules with *constraints* introduced by [2] for specializing logic programs, or the *inverse definition* and the *data structure mapping* introduced by [23].

We would like to stress the point that the program specialization method proposed here as an application of our synthesis method, is strictly more general than the usual partial evaluation methods [17]. Indeed, we are able to specialize our initial program w.r.t. a set of input values which can be described by *any* predicate, while in [17] the set of input values can only be a set of instances of a given tuple of terms.

More formally, by using our method one can solve problems specified by the formula:
$$\forall X \ ((input(X), p(X)) \leftrightarrow (input(X), pI(X)))$$
where input(X) is any predicate and pI(X) is the specialized version of p(X) for each X satisfying input(X). On the other hand, the methods based on [17] can only solve problems specified by:
$$\forall Y \ (p(t(Y)) \leftrightarrow pI(t(Y)))$$
which can be viewed as an instance of the above specification where input(X) is the equality X=t.

Notice that the methods we presented can also be extended to the case where we consider other semantics functions different from the least Herbrand model, and other transformation rules.

A final remark concerns the mechanization of our synthesis method. As usual in the case of general purpose synthesis and transformation techniques, special strategies are needed in order to deal with particular cases and ensure the derivation of efficient programs. In our case we have at our disposal various strategies, such as the ones described in [20], and we can apply them for guiding the application of the unfold/fold transformation rules.

Acknowledgements

We would like to thank the participants in the LoPSTr '93 Workshop in Louvain-la-Neuve (Belgium) and the referees who stimulated us with interesting suggestions and comments.

References

1. Bates JL, Constable RL. Proofs as programs. ACM Toplas 1985; 7:113–136
2. Bossi A, Cocco N, Dulli S. A method for specializing logic programs. ACM

Toplas 1990; 12:253-302
3. Bossi A, Cocco N, Etalle S. Transforming normal programs by replacement. In: Pettorossi A (ed) Meta-programming in logic, Proceedings of the Third International Workshop. Springer-Verlag, Berlin, 1992, pp 265–279 (Lecture notes in computer science no. 649)
4. Boulanger D, Bruynooghe M. Deriving fold/unfold transformations of logic programs using extended OLDT-based abstract interpretation. Technical report, CW no. 163, Catholic University of Leuven, Belgium, 1992
5. Brough DR, Hogger CJ. Grammar-related transformations of logic programs. New Generation Computing 1991; 9:115–134
6. Bundy A, Smaill A, Wiggins G. The synthesis of logic programs from inductive proofs. In: Lloyd JW (ed) Computational logic, Symposium Proceedings, Brussels, November 1990. Springer-Verlag, Berlin, 1990, pp 135–149
7. Burstall RM, Darlington J. A transformation system for developing recursive programs. Journal of the ACM 1977; 24:44–67
8. Clark KL, Tärnlund S-Å. A first order theory of data and programs. In: Proceedings Information Processing 77. North Holland, 1977, pp 939–944
9. Fribourg L. Extracting logic programs from proofs that use extended Prolog execution and induction. In: Warren HD, Szeredi P (eds) Proceedings Seventh International Conference on Logic Programming, Jerusalem, Israel, June 18–20, 1990. The MIT Press, 1990, pp 685–699
10. Gallagher J, de Waal DA. Deletion of redundant unary type predicates from logic programs. In: Lau K-K, Clement T (eds) Logic program synthesis and transformation", Proceedings of LoPSTr '92, Manchester 1992. Springer-Verlag, London, 1993, pp 151–167 (Workshops in Computing)
11. Gardner PA, Shepherdson JC. Unfold/fold transformations of logic programs. In: Lassez J-L, Plotkin G (eds) Computational logic, Essays in honor of Alan Robinson. The MIT Press, 1991, 565–583
12. Hansson Å, Tärnlund S-Å. Program transformation by data structure mapping. In: Clark KL, Tärnlund S-Å (eds) Logic programming. Academic Press, 1982, pp 117–122
13. Kakas AC, Kowalski RA, Toni F. Abductive logic programming. Journal of Logic and Computation 1992; 2:719–770
14. Kanamori T, Maeji M. Derivation of logic programs from implicit definition. Technical report, TR-178, ICOT, Tokyo, Japan, 1986
15. Kott L. The McCarthy's recursion induction principle: "oldy" but "goody". Calcolo 1982; 19:59–69
16. Kraan I, Basin D, Bundy A. Logic program synthesis via proof planning. In: Lau K-K, Clement T (eds) Logic program synthesis and transformation, Proceedings of LoPSTr '92, Manchester 1992. Springer-Verlag, London, 1993, pp 1–14 (Workshops in Computing)
17. Lloyd JW, Shepherdson JC. Partial evaluation in logic programming. Journal of Logic Programming 1991; 11:217–242
18. Maher MJ. Correctness of a logic program transformation system. IBM Research Report RC 13496, T.J. Watson Research Center, 1987

19. Manna Z, Waldinger R. A deductive approach to program synthesis. ACM Toplas, 1980; 2:90–121
20. Proietti M, Pettorossi A. The loop absorption and the generalization strategies for the development of logic programs and partial deduction. Journal of Logic Programming 1993; 16:123–161
21. Sterling L, Shapiro E. The art of Prolog. The MIT Press, 1986
22. Tamaki H, Sato T. Unfold/fold transformation of logic programs. In: Tärnlund S-Å (ed) Proceedings 2nd International Conference on Logic Programming. Uppsala, Sweden, 1984, pp 243–251
23. Zhang J. An automatic d-list transformation algorithm for Prolog programs. Technical report, Department of Computer Science, University College of Swansea, U.K., 1987
24. Zhang J, Grant PW. An automatic difference-list transformation algorithm for Prolog. In: Kodratoff Y (ed) Proceedings 1988 European Conference on Artificial Intelligence, ECAI 88. Pitman, 1988, pp 320–325

Some Further Issues in Finite Unfolding (Abstract)

Bern Martens *

Departement Computerwetenschappen, Katholieke Universiteit Leuven
Heverlee, Belgium
e-mail : bern@cs.kuleuven.ac.be

Danny De Schreye †

Departement Computerwetenschappen, Katholieke Universiteit Leuven
Heverlee, Belgium
e-mail : dannyd@cs.kuleuven.ac.be

Partial deduction (or evaluation) is an important issue in the research on logic programming. An essential ingredient in any partial deduction method is a good unfolding strategy. Indeed, finite, possibly incomplete, SLD-trees have to be built to serve as a basis for synthesising specialised clauses. It is essential that *finite* SLD-trees are constructed, and yet they should be non-trivial if we want the partial deduction to bring us any substantial gain. In previous work, we have shown how a general framework for devising terminating unfolding strategies can be based on well-founded measures ([1]) and we have demonstrated its use as a basic ingredient for partial deduction ([4]). Experiments with a prototype implementation show satisfactory behaviour for large classes of programs ([2]). However, in some cases, the generated SLD-trees, although finite, can sensibly be further expanded. This abstract briefly indicates some of the main issues. A full technical treatment with a particular stress on the development of completely automatic algorithms can be found in [3].

The basic framework in [1] essentially associates with (nearly) each goal in an SLD-tree an element (its weight) in a well-founded set. A literal in a goal is unfolded if the resulting weight is smaller than the one associated with the closest relevant ancestor goal in the same derivation. A proper instantiation of this "relevance" notion then guarantees the construction of finite SLD-trees. Concrete automatic algorithms in [1] and [4] are based on counting functor symbols in (a subset of) the selected literal's arguments. The resulting number is compared with the weight of the closest selected ancestor literal containing the same (recursive) predicate symbol.

A first refinement pertains to the concrete way of assigning weights to goals. Instead of working with one single subset of arguments per predicate, we can consider *partitions of the complete set of argument positions*. When we impose a priority order among sets in the partition, counting functors in each set results in a weight that is a tuple of natural numbers, rather than just a single number. This can be shown to offer extra unfolding possibilities.

---

*Partly supported by ESPRIT BRA COMPULOG II and partly by GOA "Non-Standard Applications of Abstract Interpretation", Belgium

†Research Associate of the Belgian National Fund for Scientific Research

Particularly interesting is the opportunity to take yet a further step. Indeed, the basic idea of introducing *lexicographical priorities* among different argument sets can be extended to allow *the simultaneous consideration of more than one literal in a goal*. This is relevant in the context of a *co-routining* computation rule. Consider the following prototypical example:

$produce([], []) \leftarrow$
$produce([X|Xs], [X|Ys]) \leftarrow produce(Xs, Ys)$
$consume([]) \leftarrow$
$consume([X|Xs]) \leftarrow consume(Xs)$

Maximal unfolding, guided by a co-routining computation rule and consuming all information in a query like

$\leftarrow produce([1, 2|Xs], Y), consume(Y)$

is possible when the first component of a weight in $I\!N^2$ is determined by the first argument of *produce* and the second by the argument of *consume*.

Also important is the fact that the same technique allows to cope with another problem. Indeed, using the techniques in [1], we can often not process *instantiations produced by unfoldings of other literals (situated further to the right) in the goal*. Considering arguments of several literals and using lexicographical priorities largely eliminates this difficulty.

Next, structure based weights, as discussed above, are obviously not a good basis to control unfolding of datalog (i.e. functor-free) (sub-)programs. We have therefore extended the basic framework to allow *a combination with the well-known "variant" check*. The core idea is that a goal can be unfolded, even when its weight is equal to the one associated with its relevant ancestor, if their selected literals are not variants of each other. Under the right circumstances, such refined unfolding rules can still be shown to terminate. For precise technical details, we refer to [3]. Experimental results in [2] show very satisfactory behaviour of the combined rule.

Finally, obtaining good automatic unfolding methods for *meta interpreters* is a subject of current research. In particular, we investigate techniques for focusing on subarguments and gathering useful supporting information through off-line analysis. Again, more details can be found in [3].

References

[1] M. Bruynooghe, D. De Schreye, and B. Martens. A general criterion for avoiding infinite unfolding during partial deduction. *New Generation Computing*, 11(1):47–79, 1992.

[2] T. Horváth. Experiments in partial deduction. Master's thesis, Departement Computerwetenschappen, K.U.Leuven, Leuven, Belgium, July 1993. In English.

[3] B. Martens and D. De Schreye. Advanced techniques in finite unfolding. Technical Report CW180, Departement Computerwetenschappen, K.U.Leuven, Belgium, October 1993.

[4] B. Martens, D. De Schreye, and T. Horváth. Sound and complete partial deduction with unfolding based on well-founded measures. To Appear in *Theoretical Computer Science*.

A Transformation Based on the Equality between Terms

Ulrich Neumerkel

Institut für Computersprachen, Technische Universität Wien

ulrich@mips.complang.tuwien.ac.at

Abstract

We present a new transformation of Prolog programs preserving operational equivalence. Our transformation — EBC (equality based continuation) transformation — relies on the introduction of equations between
terms. These equations are used to introduce alternative and more efficient representations of terms. When applied to binary Prolog programs,
EBC is able to perform the following optimizations by mere source to
source transformations: removal of existential variables in programs using difference lists and accumulators, reduction of the number of occur-
checks, interprocedural register allocation when executed on the WAM,
linearization of recursions, optimization of continuation-like user data
structures.

1   Introduction

The limitations of fold/unfold transformations.   Currently, most program transformation schemes for Prolog programs and logic programs are based
on the framework of fold/unfold transformations as defined by [24] or [16]. This
framework is an adaption of fold/unfold transformations originally developed
within functional languages [6]. Fold/unfold transformations introduce equal-
ities between logic programs expressed at the level of 'control structures', i.e.,
predicates, clauses and goals. Transformations within fold/unfold are therefore
able to improve or specialize a program on the level of the control structures.
They allow a programmer to write more generic and reusable programs and
specialize them thereafter, in particular, with the strategy of partial evaluation.

However, the 'data structures' of logic programs, i.e., terms play only a sec-
ondary role in these transformations. Fold/unfold transformation do not define
directly any transformation rules for terms[1]. By reasoning on the goal level,
current fold/unfold transformations are unable to transform a given dynamic
data structure in another different dynamic data structure. E.g., a program
manipulating lists can only be transformed into a program that either contains
no corresponding lists at all or that contains (parts of) that very lists, e.g., in
the form of a difference-list. Similarly, redundancies between goals cannot be
removed in many cases because a goal can only be absorbed or transformed to

---

[1]Note that the fold/unfold framework is in principle able to describe any transformation
desired because the rules for goal replacement (Chapter 3 [24]) allow to replace a goal by
any 'equivalent' one. However, no transformations capable to transform data structures are
known from the literature.

a different goal. For example, it is impossible to remove all existential variables attached to the difference list in programs corresponding to grammar rules.

Our transformation overcomes the deficiencies of fold/unfold transformations currently in use by using equivalences between terms instead. When our transformation is applied to binary Prolog we are able to improve programs on the goal level as well since goals are encoded as terms.

Binary Prolog. Binary Prolog [25] corresponds to the notion of continuation passing style (CPS) [26] in functional programming languages. When encoding Prolog with the help of binary Prolog using Tarau's transformation [25] Prolog's AND-control is encoded with terms. These new terms are called continuations corresponding to closures in functional programming languages [1]. There are several advantages of using binary Prolog: First, binary Prolog is simpler to implement. Second, binary programs are better amenable to source to source transformations, in particular, our EBC-transformation.

EBC-transformations. In order to change the representation of a program we introduce alternative representations of terms. Conceptually, the syntactic unification of Prolog is extended by new equations that do not alter the behavior of unification. In general we therefore need to introduce new function symbols. The new equations are describing alternative and hopefully more efficient representations of terms. Our approach of extending unification is quite different from other approaches like CLP. In EBC we are transforming ordinary Prolog programs without any extension while CLP provides extensions to unification visible to the user. We are restricting the additional equations to cases that can be implemented with syntactic unification only. In particular we are restricting ourselves to terms that serve as continuations. In this case the extended unification can be implemented with syntactic unification.

Contents. We start our presentation by giving a detailed example in Sect. 2. This example shows how difference lists and in particular grammar rules can profit from our optimization. In Sect. 3 we present the general framework of EBC-transformation underlining the basic notion of *conservative extension* to unification. The optimization of context arguments is discussed in Sect. 4. General strategies for EBC are discussed in Sect. 5. We present all equational schemes developed so far. Finally, related work can be found in Sect. 6.

2 Transformation of difference lists

This section shows how EBC treats typical programs with difference lists. Such programs are a source of inefficiency in current Prolog implementations when compared to their procedural counterparts.

Notation. <u>subcontinuations</u> are underlined and **changed parts** are bold. Equations introduced are written A $\doteq$ B to avoid confusion with Prolog's =/2 and $\doteq$ used in unification theory. We do not distinguish between function and predicate symbols in binary programs. Symbols in an equation refer to both.

2.1 A first example

We present an informal derivation in seven steps of a simple program containing an existential variable within a difference lists. The formal transformation rules are described in Section 3. The predicate expr/3 describes the relation between a difference list containing terminal symbols and the corresponding abstract syntax tree. Fold/unfold frameworks are unable to remove Xs1[2].

```
expr(t(T)) ⟶                   expr(t(T), [t(T)|Xs],Xs).
   [t(T)].                     expr(node(TL,TR), [op|Xs0],Xs) ←
expr(node(TL,TR)) ⟶               expr(TL, Xs0,Xs1),
   [op],                          expr(TR, Xs1,Xs).
   expr(TL),
   expr(TR).
```

1st step: binary form. First the program is transformed into binary form with Tarau's transformation [25]. A new argument is added to represent the continuation in an explicit manner. The goals after the first goal in the body are encoded as function symbols placed in the continuation argument of the first goal. Facts are transformed into rules, that call the remaining continuation, denoted as the meta-call Cont.

```
expr(t(T), [t(T)|Xs],Xs, Cont) ←
   Cont.
expr(node(TL,TR), [op|Xs0],Xs, Cont) ←
   expr(TL, Xs0,Xs1, expr(TR, Xs1,Xs, Cont)).
```

2nd step: separation of an output argument. The equation below introduces two new structures expr1/3 and rest/2. These two new function symbols serve as an alternative (and hopefully more efficient) representation for the old function symbol expr/4. By and large, the equation is compiled into the program as follows. In the body of the clauses the equation is used to replace the old function symbol. For every clause containing the expr/4 in the head, we add a new alternative clause. In our example, the program is duplicated.

```
expr(T, Xs0,Xs, Cont) = expr1(T, Xs0, rest(Xs, Cont)).

expr(t(T), [t(T)|Xs], Xs, Cont) ←
   Cont.
expr(node(TL,TR), [op|Xs0],Xs, Cont) ←
   expr1(TL, Xs0, rest(Xs1, expr1(TR, Xs1, rest(Xs, Cont))))).

expr1(t(T), [t(T)|Xs], rest(Xs, Cont)) ←
   Cont.
expr1(node(TL,TR), [op|Xs0], rest(Xs, Cont)) ←
   expr1(TL, Xs0, rest(Xs1, expr1(TR, Xs1, rest(Xs, Cont))))).
```

3rd step: folding of the redundant definition. The definition of expr/4 is expressed with the help of expr1/3. This step serves only to redo the duplication of code. For a practical transformation system it is indeed easier to combine step 2 and 3 to a single transformation step.

---

[2]To be more precise, the strategy presented by Proietti and Pettorossi [21] is able to remove the existential variable, but introduces a new, different existential variable.

```
expr(T, Xs0,Xs, Cont) ←
    expr1(T, Xs0, rest(Xs, Cont)).

expr1(t(T), [t(T)|Xs], rest(Xs, Cont)) ←
    Cont.
expr1(node(TL,TR), [op|Xs0], rest(Xs, Cont)) ←
    expr1(TL, Xs0, rest(Xs1, expr1(TR, Xs1, rest(Xs, Cont)) )).
```

4th step: simplification of the continuation. The structure rest(Xs,Cont) is redundant in the rule. It does not contribute anything to the computation. This can be seen from the equation above: rest(Xs,Cont) will always occur where expr1/3 occurs. It is therefore safe to generalize the second clause in expr1/3. This generalization does not require a global analysis of the program.

```
expr(T, Xs0,Xs, Cont) ←
    expr1(T, Xs0, rest(Xs, Cont)).

expr1(t(T), [t(T)|Xs], rest(Xs, Cont)) ←
    Cont.
expr1(node(TL,TR), [op|Xs0], RestXsCont) ←
    expr1(TL, Xs0, rest(Xs1, expr1(TR, Xs1, RestXsCont))).
```

5th step: definition of a separate predicate to execute the continuation. To make the continuations in expr1/3 more uniform we define a new predicate demo_rest/2 that deals with the continuation rest/2. Again, as step 3, this step serves only to keep the program compact. When transforming several predicates this step helps to keep the program compact. For every predicate a single clause is added for demo_rest/2. Without this step, step 6 would expand every fact of the original program to several rules.

```
expr(T, Xs0,Xs, Cont) ←
    expr1(T, Xs0, rest(Xs, Cont)).

expr1(t(T), [t(T)|Xs], RestXsCont) ←
    demo_rest(RestXsCont, Xs).
expr1(node(TL,TR), [op|Xs0], RestXsCont) ←
    expr1(TL, Xs0, rest(Xs1, expr1(TR, Xs1, RestXsCont))).

demo_rest(rest(Xs, Cont), Xs) ←
    Cont.
```

6th step: compaction of the continuation. The existential variable Xs1 occurs only in rest/2 and expr1/3. A new structure rest_expr1/3 is introduced to combine both. Xs1 is therefore reduced to a void variable. demo_rest/2 contains new clause in order to read the new representation rest_expr1/3.

```
rest(Xs1, expr1(TR, Xs1, RestXsCont)) = rest_expr1(TR, Xs1, RestXsCont).

expr(T, Xs0,Xs, Cont) ←
    expr1(T, Xs0, rest(Xs, Cont)).

expr1(t(T), [t(T)|Xs], RestXsCont) ←
    demo_rest(RestXsCont, Xs).
expr1(node(TL,TR), [op|Xs0], RestXsCont) ←
    expr1(TL, Xs0, rest_expr1(TR, _Xs1, RestXsCont)).

demo_rest(rest(Xs, Cont), Xs) ←
    Cont.
demo_rest(rest_expr1(TR, Xs, RestXsCont), Xs) ←
    expr1(TR, Xs, RestXsCont).
```

7th step: elimination of the void existential variable. Since Xs1 is now a void variable we reduce it completely with the equation below. Note, that this equation does not preserve equivalence between general terms. It has to be ensured that it is applied (as in this example) only to void variables and that the corresponding simplified structure rest_expr2/2 is read only once. In the case of continuations this is trivially true. In a transformation system it is useful to combine step 6 and 7.

rest_expr1(TR, _Xs1, RestXsCont) $\doteq$ rest_expr2(TR, RestXsCont).

expr(T, Xs0,Xs, Cont) ←
    expr1(T, Xs0, rest(Xs, Cont)).

expr1(t(T), [t(T)|Xs], RestXsCont) ←
    demo_rest(RestXsCont, Xs).
expr1(node(TL,TR), [op|Xs0], RestXsCont) ←
    expr1(TL, Xs0, **rest_expr2(TR, RestXsCont)**).

demo_rest(rest(Xs, Cont), Xs) ←
    Cont.
demo_rest(**rest_expr2(TR, RestXsCont)**, Xs) ←
    expr1(TR, Xs, RestXsCont).

2.2 Arbitrary grammar rules

The transformation above is easily extended to optimize arbitrary translated DCG-clauses, or as a further generalization EDCGs [22].

- For every binary predicate $p/n + 2$ an equation is added to split the rest list from the other arguments (as in step 2): $p(a_1,...a_n,$ Xs0, Xs, Cont) $\doteq$ $p\prime(a_1,...a_n,$ Xs0, rest(Xs, Cont)). It is important to note that all equations must contain *the same* function symbol rest/2.

- The definition of the interface rule as in step 3 can be avoided if all calls to phrase/3 are known statically.

- Simplification as in step 4.

- The definition of demo_rest/2 is the same as above. I.e., there is only a single auxiliary predicate introduced, independent of the number of different predicates.

- For every function symbol $p\prime/n + 1$ introduced above, a new equation is added: rest(Xs, $p\prime(a_1,...a_n,$ Xs, XsCont)) $\doteq$ rest_$p\prime(a_1,...a_n,$ XsCont).

To summarize, every grammar rule is translated to a single new clause, a single auxiliary predicate is defined, that serves as the 'meta-call' within the grammar.

2.3 Optimizations performed

The final program in our example above shows most of the optimizations performed by EBC on general grammar rules. All these optimizations can be observed on existing Prolog systems based on the WAM.

1. It contains a smaller continuation. Instead of five memory cells only three are used. I.e., all memory used to represent the difference list is saved.

2. The program analyses the first 2551 phrases 67% faster with BinProlog 1.39 and 30% faster with the compiler SICStus Prolog 2.1. SICStus Prolog uses an environment stack for the original program, but still the transformed version is faster though using the heap. Both systems were measured on SPARCstation ELC, CPU 33MHz Cypress, 8Mb RAM.

3. The number of argument registers is reduced by one, therefore reducing the size of choice points.

4. All trail checks related to passing the difference list further on are omitted.

5. In the case, that occur-checks are desired, all occur-checks related to the difference list in the original program are eliminated up to a single occur-check for every solution of the goal :- expr(T, Xs0, Xs). For the goal $\leftarrow$ expr(T, Xs, []) *no* occur-check has to be executed for handling the difference list. Note, that one of the arguments against the occur-check is that it reduces Prolog's efficiency in handling difference lists.

   Joachim Beer's extension to the WAM [3, 4] designed to reduce the number of trails and occur-checks should be seen as a rather complementary approach to occur-check reduction since his machine cannot handle difference lists in the same manner. In particular, in the program quicksort/3 as defined in [4], page 54, we are able to remove all of the 50 necessary occur-checks, while Beer's machine still performs 49.

2.4 Application to DCGs and similar formalisms

The example above presented a typical case occurring in many programs. By using difference lists a state is propagated further. In the case of DCGs the state is the string to be analyzed or generated. With the help of EBC-transformations these states do not require space within the continuation as long as all predicates share the difference list. The following table shows the gain in space consumption of our transformation for generalized DCGs (like EDCGs [22]) that are also capable of including 'external predicates' (e.g. for symbol table lookup) within the grammar. These generalized DCGs posses n implicit states. The gain for 'ordinary' DCGs, where only a single simple state is present, is given with $n = 1$. Our transformation has an additional initialization cost for implementing the entry predicate phrase. However, all continuations within the grammar are either reduced in size or equal (when using external predicates heavily). In particular, in the usual case (case 5), the size of the continuation is reduced considerably.

The additional states in an EDCG can be used for tasks currently implemented with side effects or manual transformations. E.g.: a) error recovery b) line counting c) indentation checks d) safe left recursions. With the help of our transformation, the cost for such additional arguments is very small, comparable to the cost of global variables in procedural languages.

	situation	gain
1 orig. EBC	$\leftarrow \mathrm{phrase}(g, x_1, \ldots, x_n, y_1, \ldots, y_n\ ).$ 0 $(2+n)$	$-(2+n)$
2 orig. EBC	$\leftarrow \mathrm{phrase}(g, x_1, \ldots, x_n, [], \ldots, []).$ 0 (2)	-2
3 orig. EBC	$\leftarrow \ldots, \mathrm{phrase}(g, x_1, \ldots, x_n, y_1, \ldots, y_n).$ $(2 + n_g + 2n)$ $(2 + n_g + n) + (2 + n)$	-2
4 orig. EBC	$\leftarrow \ldots, \mathrm{phrase}(g, x_1, \ldots, x_n, [], \ldots, []).$ $(2 + n_g + 2n)$ $(2 + n_g + n) + (2)$	$n-2$
5 orig. EBC	$\ldots \longrightarrow \ldots, g, \ldots$ $(2 + n_g + 2n)$ $(2 + n_g)$	$2n$
6 orig. EBC	$\ldots \longrightarrow \{\ldots\}.$ $(2 + 2n)$ $(2 + n)$	n
7 orig. EBC	$\ldots \longrightarrow \{\ldots\}, g, \ldots$ $(2 + n_g + 2n)$ $(2 + n_g + n)$	n
8 orig. EBC	$\ldots \longrightarrow \ldots, g, \{\ldots\}.$ $(2 + n_g + 2n) + (2 + 2n)$ $(2 + n_g) + (2 + n) + (2 + n)$	$2n-2$
9 orig. EBC	$\ldots \longrightarrow \ldots, g, \{\ldots\}, h, \ldots$ $(2 + n_g + 2n) + (2 + n_h + 2n)$ $(2 + n_g) + (2 + n) + (2 + n_h + n)$	$2n-2$

3 EBC-transformation

EBC-transformations transform a given binary program into an equivalent one. We do not consider currently non-binary programs. The transformation formalism is divided into three parts: The equations providing alternative representations. The compilation of these equations into the program. The simplification of the compiled programs.

In the sequel we make no distinction between predicate symbols and function symbols. A binary program can be represented by a single binary predicate, encoding all predicate symbols with function symbols. We use the word continuation for the head and the (single) goal of a binary clause. If a continuation is a function symbol it contains (beside others) a single argument that is used to hold further subcontinuations. Usually this argument is the last one. We denote by T_{old}, the set of terms constructed from the function symbols F_{old} that are present in the original program and some variables. $T_{new} \supset T_{old}$ denotes the corresponding set of the new program. θ and σ are substitutions.

3.1 Conservative extension

We define a *conservative extension to syntactic unification* as a set E of equations of the form '$x \dot{=} y$' with $x, y \in T_{new}$ such that for all terms s and $t \in T_{old}$:
$$\exists \theta . s\theta = t\theta \quad \text{iff} \quad \exists \rho . s\rho =_E t\rho \ [3]$$

---

[3] $=_E$ means equality modulo the equations E.

As long as the equations in E contain only terms in T_{old} such an extension is considered trivial. No alternative representations could be constructed.

Our notion of conservative extension can be seen as a restriction to the notion of consistency in rewrite systems and algebraic specifications [10]. A set of equations E is consistent if for all *ground* terms the condition above holds. I.e., consistency is a necessary but not sufficient condition to qualify E as a conservative extension. The following example gives an equation that qualifies as consistent but not as a conservative extension.

$$F_{old} = \{f, g, c\}, \quad F_{new} = \{h\}, \quad E = \{f(X) \dot{=} g(h(X))\}$$

The equation E is consistent with respect to F_{old}. On the other hand, E is not a conservative extension since there is no substitution θ for $f(c) = g(X)\theta$ but there is a $\rho = \{Y \mapsto h(c)\}$ with $f(c)\rho =_E g(Y)\rho$.

3.2 Compilation of equations

We are interested to implement the equational unification above with the help of syntactic unification. Since we want to keep the overhead for compiling equations as low as possible we are only compiling equations over terms that are never variables at runtime. To avoid any dataflow analysis we restrict ourselves to the continuation generated by the transformation from Prolog to binary Prolog. The compilation is divided into the compilation of goals and heads.

Compilation of goals. In the goal of a clause continuations are simply written. I.e., no unification takes place. We are therefore free to replace any subcontinuation that matches a given equation by the other side of the equation. Let r be a subcontinuation, and $s \dot{=} t$ an equation. The subcontinuation r can be replaced by $t\theta$ if $r = s\theta$. Remark that we are allowed to use the equations in every direction desired.

As a special case, equations $s \dot{=} t$ with $\text{VAR}(s) \subset \text{VAR}(t)$ are allowed to eliminate void variables. In this case, all void variables in the equation must match void variables in the subcontinuation.

Compilation of heads. The head of a clause reads and unifies continuations. It must therefore be able to deal with all alternative representations of a term. For every clause C we create for every rewriting yielding a different head a new clause C_i. All resulting clauses C_i must not be unifiable with one another. Usually, only a single transformation step is required for every combination of a clause and an equation. The rewriting of clauses must not necessarily terminate. This is in particular the case when recursive equations are used. If a clause can be rewritten for the second time the term to be rewritten is separated into a new auxiliary predicate. In this manner, simple infinite rewritings can be compiled into recursive predicates.

3.3 Simplification of clauses

In most of the interesting applications of EBC investigated so far a simplification step is required after the compilation of equations. In this step redundancies in the program are removed that have been made explicit by the introduced equations. The conditions for simplification depend only on the equations E compiled in the previous step and the clause to be simplified. No global analysis is required to validate the simplification step.

The original clause $C_o = H_o \leftarrow B_o$ was compiled into $C = H \leftarrow B$, besides possibly other clauses. Simplification is carried out by generalizing a binary clause $C = H \leftarrow B$ to a clause $C_g = H_g \leftarrow B_g$ under the following conditions:

1. $C = C_g\theta$, and $\mathrm{dom}(\theta) \subseteq \mathrm{VAR}(B_g)$. I.e., only those generalizations of the head are allowed, that are covered by generalizations in the body.

2. For every clause $H \leftarrow B$ and its generalization(s) $H_g \leftarrow B_g$ the following condition must hold for all $i, j \geq 1$:

$$\mathrm{Old}(P_i(H) \leftarrow P_j(G)) = \mathrm{Old}(P_i(H_g) \leftarrow P_j(G_g))$$

$\mathrm{Old}(H \leftarrow B)$ is the set of rules $H_o \leftarrow G_o$ constructed with T_{old} that are unifiable with $H \leftarrow B$.

$P_i(L)$ is a projection of the continuation L that substitutes the i-th sub-continuation of L by a new free variable $Cont_i$. $P_1(L) = Cont_1$, i.e., the whole term is substituted. $P_2(L)$ substitutes the first subcontinuation by $Cont_2$ etc.

This condition ensures that during execution the bindings at the outer continuations will be identical to the original program. This means that built-in predicates, read and write statements, cuts etc. may be used in the programs to be transformed at any place[4].

Examples. Given the equation p(E, Cont) = q(E, r(E, Cont)), the clause p(E, Cont) ← q(E, r(E, Cont)) can be generalized to p(E, Cont) ← q(E, r(_E, Cont)). However, it is not allowed to generalize to p(E, Cont) ← q(_E, r(E, Cont)).

Note, that simplification is driven heavily by the redundancy exposed in the equations E:

```
p(X,X, Cont) ←
    q(X,X, Cont).

p(A,B, Cont) = p1(r(A,B, Cont)).
q(A,B, Cont) = q1(r(A,B, Cont)).

p1(r(A,A, Cont)) ←
    q1(r(A,A, Cont)).
```

The following generalization is invalid, since Old(p1(ABCont) ← p1(ABCont)) contains the clause p(X,Y, Cont) ← q(X,Y, Cont) while Old(p1(r(A,A, Cont)) ← q1(r(A,A, Cont)) does not contain this clause.

```
p1(ABCont) ← % violates Cond. 2
    q1(ABCont).
```

However, the same generalization is valid, under a different set of equations:

---

[4] Cuts are represented in binary Prolog with an auxiliary variable used for labeling.

p(A,A, Cont) $\rightleftharpoons$ p2(r(A,A, Cont)).
q(A,A, Cont) $\rightleftharpoons$ q2(r(A,A, Cont)).

p2(r(A,A, Cont)) ←
   q2(r(A,A, Cont)).

p2(ABCont) ← % valid
   q2(ABCont).

4   Transformation of context arguments

The application of the generalization rules is demonstrated by the following program that uses the built-in predicate var/1 that is sensible to bindings. While the goal var/1 is part of the body, we will still write it as a separate goal to ease reading.

equalnodes(nil, _El).   equalnodes(nil, _El, Cont) ←
equalnodes(node(El,L,R), El) ←   Cont.
   var(El),   equalnodes(node(El,L,R), El, Cont) ←
   equalnodes(L, El),   var(El),
   equalnodes(R, El).   equalnodes(L, El, equalnodes(R, El, Cont)).

The continuation contains the redundant variable El. We make this redundancy more explicit by duplicating the occurrences of El.

equalnodes(T, El, Cont) $\rightleftharpoons$ equalnodes1(T, El, rest(El, Cont)).

equalnodes(T, El, Cont) ←
   equalnodes1(T, El, rest(El, Cont)).

equalnodes1(nil, El, **rest(El, Cont)**) ←
   Cont.
equalnodes1(node(El,L,R), El, **rest(El, Cont)**) ←
   var(El),
   equalnodes1(L, El, **rest(El,** equalnodes1(R, El, **rest(El, Cont)**))).

In the following step several variables are renamed.

equalnodes(T, El, Cont) ←
   equalnodes1(T, El, rest(**_El**, Cont)).

equalnodes1(nil, El, rest(El, Cont)) ←
   Cont.
equalnodes1(node(El,L,R), El, rest(**El2**, Cont)) ←
   var(El),
   equalnodes1(L, El, rest(**El1**, equalnodes1(R, **El1**, rest(**El2**, Cont)))).

Note that the e.g.,following generalizations are invalid:

% wrong example
equalnodes(T, El, Cont) ←
   equalnodes1(T, _El, rest(El, Cont)). % violates Cond. 2

equalnodes1(nil, _El1, rest(_El2, Cont)) ← % violates Cond. 1
   Cont.
equalnodes1(node(El,L,R), El2, rest(El1, Cont)) ←
   var(El),
   equalnodes1(L, El2, rest(El1, equalnodes1(R, El1, rest(El, Cont)))).
% El2 and El violate Cond. 2

The redundant subcontinuation is removed in the clause equalnodes1/3.

```
equalnodes(T, El, Cont) ←
    equalnodes1(T, El, rest(_El, Cont)).

equalnodes1(nil, El, rest(El, Cont)) ←
    Cont.
equalnodes1(node(El,L,R), El, ElCont) ←
    var(El),
    equalnodes1(L, El, rest(El1, equalnodes1(R, El1, ElCont) )).
```

The subsequent steps are similar to our first example expr/4. We omit the intermediary steps, only showing the result and the equations used.

```
rest(El, equalnodes(R, El, ElCont)) = rest_equalnodes(R, ElCont).
rest(_El, Cont) = rest1(Cont).

equalnodes(T, El, Cont) ←
    equalnodes1(T, El, rest1(Cont)).

equalnodes1(nil, El, ElCont) ←
    restel(ElCont, El).
equalnodes1(node(El,L,R), El, ElCont) ←
    var(El),
    equalnodes1(L, El, rest_equalnodes1(R, ElCont)).

restel(rest1(Cont),_El) ←
    Cont.
restel(rest_equalnodes(R, ElCont),El) ←
    equalnodes(R, El, ElCont).
```

The final program does no more contain the variable El in its continuation. Furthermore, El resides always in the second argument. Executed on the WAM, the variable El can be considered as being allocated 'globally', (i.e.: interprocedurally) in the second argument register.

5 Strategies and schemes of equations

For a transformation system to be of practical use, strategies avoiding the very large search space have to be developed. There are several sources that contribute to the search space of EBC-transformations: a) the choice of an appropriate scheme of equations b) the effective instantiation of the scheme c) the choice of simplifications.

The development of schemes of conservative equations seems to be an inherent manual operation. The methods developed within the context of rewrite systems and algebraic specification might be adaptable to automate this process. However, a scheme of equations often determines a particular optimization. E.g. optimization of difference lists, context arguments. It seems that a practical transformation system might only choose from given schemes of equations; similar to a compiler for an imperative programming language that comprises several optimization passes like common subexpression elimination, global or even interprocedural register allocation etc. Below, we present the equational schemes and their use in optimization.

The effective instantiation of an equation scheme is often 'driven' by the subsequent simplification. Since the conditions for simplification are closely related to the equations used, we can on the other hand take the simplifications as a condition for the application of a certain equation. For example, in predicate expr/4 the equation expr(T, Xs0,Xs, $\underline{Cont}$) = expr1(T, Xs0, $\underline{rest(Xs, Cont)}$) was the only choice possible to allow a subsequent simplification of the continuation rest(Xs, Cont). If we would have tried expr(T, Xs0,Xs, <u>Cont</u>) = **expr2**(T, Xs, <u>rest(Xs0,Cont)</u>). instead, no simplification of rest(Xs, Cont) would have been possible. The search for an appropriate equation can therefore be pruned by the subsequent simplification. It seems therefore appropriate to associate to every equation specialized simplification operations thus avoiding the search space within simplification.

For the sake of simplicity, we present concrete equations for the encountered schemes, the arguments of function symbols might be appropriately increased.

Output argument splitting. An argument Out is only passed further from the head to the last goal in a clause. Typically, the second argument of a difference list or an accumulator is an output argument.

old1(Args,Out,Cont) = new1(Args,new(Out, Cont))
old2(Args,Out,Cont) = new2(Args,new(Out, Cont))
...

Simplification: removal of new(B, Cont)

Forced output argument splitting. A context argument Ctx is passed around, by duplicating its occurrences it can be treated as an output argument above.

old1(Args, Ctx, Cont) = new1(Args, Ctx, new(Ctx, Cont))
old2(Args, Ctx, Cont) = new2(Args, Ctx, new(Ctx, Cont))
...

Simplification: renaming of duplicated variables, removal of new(Ctx, Cont).

Compacting continuations. Two continuations that share some arguments, or variables are folded into a new one. The new structure contains the union Args12 of both arguments.

old1(Args1, old2(Args2, Cont)) = new(Args12, Cont).

No simplification required. However, most occurrences of old1/2 should have been replaced. Note that Args1 and Args2 may contain function symbols oldf/1 that are not continuations themselves. e.g.:

old1(A, old2(oldf(A), Cont)) = new(A, Cont).

Recursive context introduction. Used to split recursive programs into several iterations.

old1(A, old2(B, Cont)) = old1(A, new(A, old2(B, Cont))).

Simplification: renaming of duplicated variables.

Merging/splitting user continuations. In a program a recursive data structure is used in a 'continuation like' manner. By the following equations, such data structures can be merged with the system continuation. No analysis is required to ensure that a user data structure is 'continuation like'. For, if it is not, not all occurrences can be merged with the system continuation. Typical examples for this scheme merge a list with the continuation; or split recursive parts of a continuation in order to implement them with a counter. See [20] for an exemplary use.

old1(oldc,old2(Cont)) $\doteq$ newc(Cont).
old1(oldf(F), Cont) $\doteq$ newf(old1(F,Cont)).

Condition of application: all occurrences of oldc/0 and oldf/1 should have been replaced.

6   Related work

Source-to-source transformations. Sato and Tamaki's CPS-conversion [23] separates input and output arguments, yielding binary programs. However, their method has to rely on a previous analysis. Otherwise, they do not preserve finite failure and infinite loops. The derived program perm/2 in [23] loops for ← perm(_,const) while the original fails. Further, as observed by Tarau [25], clause indexing is not preserved.

Particular strategies within fold/unfold have been investigated. Proietti and Pettorossi present a fold/unfold-strategy [21] to remove existential variables. Such variables cannot be removed by EBC and vice versa. A fold/unfold-strategy to remove unnecessary structures is presented by Gallagher and Bruynooghe [9]. Demoen [7] considers transformations for binary programs that are explicable within the framework of fold/unfold-transformations. I.e., folding of goals in order to 'build up continuations incrementally' (Sect. 1), partial evaluation (Sect. 2.1); void variable elimination in the body (Sect. 2.3), register move optimization (Sect. 2.5).

Low-level optimizations. Beer [4] optimizes uninitialized variables. Meyer uses destructive assignments in environments [17]. Compile time garbage collection [14, 18, 11] might yield similar results for difference lists. However, no published results on programs like DCGs are known to the author.

Other formalisms. The compilation of unification in EBC-transformations is related to narrowing ([2] 6.1.3). Grammars in λ-Prolog [15] do not need any auxiliary variables. Thus λ-Prolog is an interesting formalism for further transformations. In functional languages CPS-transformations have been originally investigated [26]. We have so far not found transformations corresponding to EBC in functional languages. The reasons for this seems to be the absence of the logical variable. The close relation of Attribute Grammars and logic programs [8] suggests that optimizations for AGs [13, 12] can be applied to Prolog; as investigated by Bouquard [5] comparing WAM and FNC-2.

7 Further work

The further development of strategies seems to be most promising since EBC-transformations are able to obtain programs that are very close to their counterparts in procedural programming languages. Although our transformation rules are equivalence preserving they are not completely invertible. In particular, the simplification of continuations cannot be inverted. This means, that for certain transformations, we have to 'invent' the desired program and then derive from the invented program the original program. Further research is required to improve the transformation rules.

The precise relation between fold/unfold for logic programs and EBC is not yet clear to the author. It seems, however, that fold/unfold does not cover EBC-transformations. For example, the existential variable in expr/4 has resisted the author's attempts for removal within fold/unfold.

Our transformation circumvents the environment stack of the classic WAM. However, WAM compilation can be easily adopted compiling the continuations back into stack frames. Registers would be valid beyond the 'proceed barrier'.

Acknowledgements. I thank Gernot Salzer for many comments on EBC-transformations. The three anonymous referees provided many appreciated comments.

References

[1] A. Appel. *Compiling with Continuations.* Cambridge University Press, 1992. ISBN 0-521-41695-7.

[2] F. Baader and J. Siekmann. Unification theory. In D. Gabbay, C. Hogger, and J. Robinson, editors, *Handbook of Logic in Artificial Intelligence and Logic Programming.* Oxford University Press, Oxford, UK, 1993. To appear.

[3] J. Beer. The occur-check problem revisited. *The Journal of Logic Programming,* 5(3):243–262, September 1988.

[4] J. Beer. *Concepts, Design, and Performance Analysis of a Parallel Prolog Machine,* volume 404 of *Lecture Notes in Computer Science.* Springer-Verlag, 1989.

[5] J.-L. Bouquard. *Etude des rapports entre Grammaire Attribuées et Programmation Logique: Application au test d'occurrence et à l'analyse statique.* PhD thesis, Université d'Orleans, 1992.

[6] R. Burstall and J. Darlington. A transformation system for developing recursive programs. *Journal of the ACM,* 24:44–67, 1977.

[7] B. Demoen. On the transformation of a Prolog program to a more efficient binary program. Technical Report 130, K.U.Leuven Department of Computer Science, revised version LOPSTR92, 1992.

[8] P. Deransart and J. Maluszynski. Relating logic programs and attribute grammars. *Journal of Logic Programming,* 2(2):119–155, 1985.

[9] J. Gallager and M. Bruynooghe. Some low-level source transformations for logic programs. In M. Bruynooghe, editor, *Proceedings of the Second Workshop on Meta-programming in Logic,* pages 229–244. K.U. Leuven, Department of Computer Science, Apr. 1990.

[10] J. V. Guttag and J. J. Horning. The algebraic specification of abstract data types. *Acta Informatica,* 10:27–52, 1978.

[11] G. Hamilton and S. Jones. Compile-time garbage collection by necessity analysis. In S. P. Jones, G. Hutton, and C. Holst, editors, *Functional Programming, Glasgow 1990,* pages 66–70. Springer-Verlag, London, 1991.

[12] C. Julié and D. Parigot. Space optimization in the FNC-2 attribute grammar system. In P. Deransart and M. Jourdan, editors, *Attribute Grammars and their Applications (WAGA)*, volume 461 of *Lecture Notes in Computer Science*, pages 29–45. Springer-Verlag, Sept. 1990.

[13] U. Kastens and M. Schmidt. Lifetime analysis for procedure parameters. In B. Robinet and R. Wilhelm, editors, *Proceedings of the 1st European Symposium on Programming (ESOP '86)*, volume 213 of *Lecture Notes in Computer Science*, pages 53–69. Springer-Verlag, Mar. 1986.

[14] F. Kluźniak. Compile time garbage collection for Ground Prolog. In R. A. Kowalski and K. A. Bowen, editors, *Proceedings of the Fifth International Conference and Symposium on Logic Programming*, pages 1490–1505, Seatle, 1988. ALP, IEEE, The MIT Press.

[15] S. Le Huitouze, P. Louvet, and O. Ridoux. Logic grammars and λ-Prolog. In D. Warren, editor, *Proceedings of the Tenth International Conference on Logic Programming*, pages 64–79, Budapest, Hungary, 1993. The MIT Press.

[16] J. Lloyd and J. Shepherdson. Partial evaluation in logic programming. *Journal of Logic Programming*, 11:217–242, 1991.

[17] M. Meier. Recursion vs. iteration in Prolog. In K. Furukawa, editor, *Proceedings of the Eighth International Conference on Logic Programming*, pages 157–169, Paris, France, 1991. The MIT Press.

[18] A. Mulkers, W. Winsborough, and M. Bruynooghe. Analysis of shared data structures for compile-time garbage. In D. H. D. Warren and P. Szeredi, editors, *Proceedings of the Seventh International Conference on Logic Programming*, pages 747–762, Jerusalem, 1990. The MIT Press.

[19] U. Neumerkel. Specialization of Prolog programs with partially static goals and binarization, Dissertation. Bericht TR 1851-1992-12, Institut für Computersprachen, Technische Universität Wien, 1992.

[20] U. Neumerkel. Une transformation de programme basée sur la notion d'équations entre termes. In *Secondes journées francophones sur la programmation en logique (JFPL'93)*, Nîmes-Avingnon, France, 1993.

[21] M. Proietti and A. Pettorossi. Unfolding-definition-folding in this order, for avoiding unnecessary variables in logic programs. In J. Małuszyński and M. Wirsing, editors, *Programming Languages Implementation and Logic Programming*, volume 528 of *Lecture Notes in Computer Science*, pages 347–358, Passau, Germany, Aug. 1991. Springer-Verlag.

[22] P. V. Roy. A useful extension to Prolog's Definite Clause Grammar notation. *SIGPLAN notices*, 24(11):132–134, Nov. 1989.

[23] T. Sato and H. Tamaki. Existential continuation. *New Generation Computing*, 6(4):421–438, 1989.

[24] H. Tamaki and T. Sato. Unfold/fold transformation of logic programs. In S.-Å. Tärnlund, editor, *Second International Logic Programming Conference*, pages 127–138, Uppsala, 1984.

[25] P. Tarau and M. Boyer. Elementary logic programs. In P. Deransart and J. Małuszyński, editors, *Programming Languages Implementation and Logic Programming*, volume 456 of *Lecture Notes in Computer Science*, pages 159–173, Linköping, Sweden, Aug. 1990. Springer-Verlag.

[26] M. Wand. Continuation-based program transformation strategies. *Journal of the Association for Computing Machinery*, 27(1):164–180, 1980.

Automatic Exploitation of Non-Determinate Independent And-Parallelism in the Basic Andorra Model*

M. Olmedilla
F. Bueno
M. Hermenegildo
Facultad de Informática
Universidad Politécnica de Madrid (UPM)
28660, Boadilla del Monte, Madrid — SPAIN

Abstract

The Andorra Principle states that determinate goals can (and should) be run before other goals, possibly in parallel. This principle has been applied in a framework called the basic Andorra model, which allows (dependent) and–parallelism among determinate goals as well as or–parallelism. We show that it is possible to extend this model in order to also allow and–parallelism among independent, nondeterminate goals, thus supporting full independent and–parallelism, without greatly modifying the underlying implementation machinery. We propose to realize such an extension by making each (nondeterminate) independent goal determinate using a special all–solutions built–in predicate. We also show that this can be achieved automatically by compile–time translation from source Prolog programs by proposing a transformation that fulfills this objective. Finally, we provide some implementation results.

1 Introduction and Motivation

The "Andorra Principle" [SCWY91b] is a control rule for logic programs which states that "determinate" goals should execute ahead of non–determinate goals (possibly in parallel). A goal is determinate if only one clause in the predicate definition will match with it [SCWY91b]. The execution of determinate goals ahead of time has the advantage of maintaining execution within a unique branch of computation and thus postponing the complexity which is inherent to non–deterministic execution (i.e. creation of choice–points and backtracking). Furthermore, the execution of determinate goals ahead of time can reduce the search space of other goals, and even make them become also determinate. The "basic Andorra model" [SCWY91b] is a framework based on the Andorra Principle which allows the and–parallel execution of *determinate* goals within each branch of the execution tree (i.e. determinate, or deterministic "stream and–parallelism"), as well as or–parallel execution of different branches of the tree.

---

*The research presented in this paper has been supported in part by ESPRIT project 2471 "PEPMA" and by CICYT project TIC90-1105-CE.

It has been implemented in the Andorra–I system [SCWY91b, SCWY91a], which subsumes standard Prolog, including side–effects and most standard built–ins, the cut pruning operator, and also the commit pruning operator, as in committed–choice languages.

A similar approach is that of "Parallel NU–Prolog" (PNU–Prolog) [Nai88] in which determinate goals can also be executed ahead of time albeit under control of the programmer through explicit delay declarations. The corresponding framework supports or–parallelism and determinate dependent and–parallelism in a similar way to the basic Andorra model.

The above models have in common that they prevent the and–parallel execution of goals which are not (or, perhaps quite importantly in practice, cannot be determined to be) determinate. It is true in general that parallel execution of non–determinate goals can actually result in slow–down. However, it has also been shown that there are several identifiable classes of non–determinate goals whose and–parallel execution is advantageous, in particular goals which are (strictly or non–strictly) independent [DeG84, HR89, HR90]. The execution of independent goals in parallel has the very desirable properties of improving or, in the worst case, preserving the program efficiency. This is the basis for a large number of proposals and systems which exploit such "Independent And–Parallelism", either by itself or in combination with or–parallelism.

One way to combine independent and–parallelism with that exploited by the basic Andorra model is to extend the model itself, giving rise to a new model. Examples are the Extended Andorra Model (EAM) [War90, HJ90] and the IDIOM model [GSCYH91]. However, this requires in principle a new (and probably complex) implementation. We present an alternative which can simplify the process by making use of an existing implementation of the basic Andorra model, Andorra–I. Our technique is based on an automatic transformation of Prolog programs into programs that can be run in a slightly enhanced version of the Andorra–I system while at the same time exploiting parallelism among non–determinate independent goals, in addition to the forms of parallelism already present in the basic Andorra model. The technique is based on the use of determinate built–ins to encapsulate independent goals in order to allow their parallel execution in Andorra–I. This technique is related to the transformation proposed for supporting and–parallelism within or–parallelism in [CDO88], although it serves a quite different purpose. Here, our aim is to exploit the and–parallelism capability of the target system. This aim resembles that of [Ued87], where a transformation for the optimization of exhaustive search programs was proposed. Our transformation can be regarded also as such an optimization, although our technique can be seen as opposite to the one proposed there. It is much closer to a transformation proposed in the context of PNU–Prolog [Nai88], both in style and spirit. However, our transformation is automatic and deals also automatically with the issue of preserving the search space by encapsulating only independent goals. It also incorporates many optimizations.

We introduce our proposal in the next section and in Section 3 we present in detail the transformation on which it is based. A number of optimizations to it are discussed in Section 4. The implementation of an algorithm for its automation is presented in Section 5. Some characteristic examples of the transformation and the corresponding optimizations are given in Section 6. Section 7 presents and discusses some implementation results. Section 8 concludes.

2 Towards Independent And–Parallelism in Andorra–I

The control rule in the basic Andorra model and Andorra–I allows goals to be *reduced* in parallel provided these reductions are determinate. By a reduction we mean the replacement of a goal in the resolvent by the body of a clause against which it matches. A reduction is determinate if there is only one such matching clause. On the other hand, in the context of independent and–parallelism two goals in a resolvent can be run in parallel provided they are independent, for a given notion of independence. Note that the whole execution trees associated which each goal, including all their alternatives, are allowed to proceed in parallel without any further check.

In order to support independent and–parallelism in Andorra–I we have to bridge the two main differences between the models which are apparent from the discussion above. First, non–determinate goals will not be reduced in parallel in Andorra–I even if they are independent. We would like to somehow detect such independent goals and ensure that they are reduced in parallel by Andorra–I. Furthermore, we do not only want to have a single reduction of each of those goals proceed in parallel, but rather guarantee that the whole execution tree under each of those goals proceeds in parallel with the rest of the computation.

One way to solve the first problem above, i.e. allow the parallel reduction of non–determinate independent goals in Andorra–I, is to make them appear determinate to the implementation. This can be done by encapsulating such goals using Prolog's "all–solutions" built–in predicates (such as bagof/3 or findall/3). Such built–in predicates collect the solutions for a predicate and are thus considered, or can be made, determinate under some circumstances (by appropriate existential quantification of variables). In that case the reduction of the goal against its (several) matching clauses and the creation of the corresponding choice–point will be performed by the system as a single, determinate step which can proceed in parallel with other determinate steps. However, if there are other choice–points in the execution of the descendants of the original independent goals they will still be unnecessarily sequentialized, i.e. the second problem above is not yet solved. To solve this problem independent goals have to be "marked" in such a way that their complete execution is ensured. In other Andorra languages, such as the Andorra kernel language [JH91], this can be achieved via encapsulation of partial computations in (deep) *guards*, and this technique has actually been exploited to ensure parallel execution of independent goals by (automatic) program transformation [BH92]. In fact this could also be achieved within the Andorra–I language by at least two means: the first one would be to also encapsulate in all–solutions predicates (specialized versions of) all the non–determinate goals called in the execution trees of the independent goals. Alternatively, it can be assumed that the above mentioned all–solutions predicates are implemented in such a way that their subcomputation is also "encapsulated": in Andorra–I this means to consider a separate resolvent for this computation, which will be executed by a separate abstract machine.

We will assume for simplicity the latter solution. For those literals which are known to be independent, a transformation will be performed at compile–time encapsulating each of them in a bagof/3 or findall/3 literal in such a way that it becomes determinate. At execution–time, the corresponding goals will be found to be determinate, and, therefore, executed in parallel and to completion in the way mentioned above. The only remaining problem is to collect and combine all the solutions generated by the independent goals, which will be done by adding appropriate calls to the member/2 predicate. The complete transformation and some possible optimizations are explained in the rest of the paper. For the sake of simplicity and also for historical reasons, we will be using the bagof/3 predicate in the discussion, which we will refer to simply as "bagof." Minor differences which appear when using the findall/3 built–in (which, being more primitive, can be more efficient than bagof) are also discussed.

3   Transformation

3.1   Detection of independence

The first step in the transformation will deal with the matter of detecting goals which are independent, under some definition of independence (see [HR89, HR90]). For example, under the classical notion of *strict* independence, goals or terms are independent if they do not have variables in common. Program variables are then independent if they are always bound at execution time to independent terms, and program atoms are independent if all their variables are.

A number of algorithms have already been proposed for detecting independent atoms at compile–time: they take as input a Prolog program, generate a series of sufficient conditions for the independent and–parallel execution of some goals [DeG84, Her86, HR89, HR90], possibly using compile–time analysis to simplify such conditions [CDD85, MH89, MH91, JL89], and transform the program into another program which exploits the parallelism while possibly performing some additional run–time analysis [DeG87, MH90, JL88]. Such a transformation assumes a target language capable of expressing parallelism. Herein we will assume for concreteness that this language is &–Prolog [HG90]. Therefore, we assume as the starting point in our transformation that the original Prolog program has been translated to an &–Prolog program in which the correct exploitation of available independent and–parallelism has been made explicit. We also assume that such parallelism is expressed via the parallel conjunction operator "&" and if–then–else constructs, where the conditions in such constructs are sufficient for independence of the literals affected by & in the body of the conditionals. Such conditions include for example checks on the groundness and independence of variables appearing in such literals. As an example, consider the clause:

```
q(X,Y,Z) :- p(X,Y), p(X,Z).
```

which might be transformed as

```
q(X,Y,Z) :- ground(X), indep(Y,Z) -> p(X,Y) & p(X,Z)
            ; p(X,Y), p(X,Z).
```

and which can be read as "if X is ground and Y and Z are independent, then run p(X,Y) and p(X,Z) in parallel, otherwise run them sequentially."

3.2 Encapsulation in all–solutions predicates

Given the program annotated with such conditionals the second step of the transformation will be to replace each of the literals connected by "&" in the "then" part of the conditional with a call to bagof in which the corresponding literal is the second argument and a tuple containing the literal variables is the first argument of the call to bagof. Provided the bagof call is determinate the corresponding goal will be scheduled in parallel in Andorra–I, achieving the desired effect. The semantics of the bagof built–in predicate in Andorra–I has to support that of the corresponding standard Prolog construct. Thus, the goal `bagof(Term,Goal,List)` is true if `List` includes all solutions (abstraction made of their ordering) for the term `Term` for which the corresponding instance of `Goal` is true. Note that if `Term` includes all the variables of `Goal` the bagof goal will be considered determinate and proceed in parallel. On the other hand, if `Goal` contains uninstantiated variables not included in `Term` the bagof goal will not be determinate and will then wait for such variables to become instantiated. However, this can be avoided if these variables are existentially quantified in `Goal`: their instantiation will not be considered relevant and the bagof goal will not wait for their values and proceed in parallel. Thus, appropriate existential quantification of variables is also part of the transformation process.

One issue that arises when using an all–solutions predicate to encapsulate goals is that this forces computation of all solutions for this particular goal. The possible disadvantage of this is that unnecessary (speculative) computation may be performed if only one solution is desired at the top level or the all–solutions predicate is in the scope of a cut. However, if we assume that in Andorra–I, as in other systems which exploit or–parallelism, the case where the program is queried for all solutions is frequent, the problem is alleviated. Furthermore, encapsulation of goals in an all–solutions predicate can actually also save much work if, as in our transformation, only independent goals are encapsulated, since the recomputation of these goals done by Prolog and Andorra–I while performing the join is avoided: in the transformed program the join is performed simply by picking up the solutions from the lists of results using the member/2 predicates, avoiding any recomputation.

A final issue is that overhead may also be introduced if the transformation (unnecessarily) encapsulates goals that are found to be independent but which are completely deterministic (not just the first reduction, but the entire tree) and the Andorra–I system can detect it. In any case this situation can be improved using a determinacy analysis and avoiding encapsulation of independent goals which can be found to be deterministic by Andorra–I.

3.3 Gathering the solutions

In addition to the "bagof encapsulation" mentioned above, the solutions for each one of the goals need to be gathered and combined forming the Cartesian product (i.e. a "join" operation of the solutions for the "forked" parallel goals must be performed). To do this, advantage can be taken of backtracking, present in Andorra–I as in Prolog: since all solutions for each goal are collected in a list structure, they can be retrieved using a member/2 predicate for each encapsulated literal. All solutions will then be traversed by backtracking in a standard Andorra–I computation.

More precisely, in an Andorra–I computation two distinct phases are performed [SCWY91a]: in the determinate phase determinate goals are evaluated (in and–parallel); when this ends, the nondeterminate phase selects a goal for reduction and creates a choice–point, branches of which can be explored in or–parallel. If no particular control is specified, the goal reduced is the leftmost goal, as in Prolog. In the presence of failure, the failing branch is abandoned, and execution proceeds with the rest of the branches. Backtracking is performed for this purpose, if needed. No backtracking is needed through determinate goals. In this framework, the bagofs constructed as explained above will be executed in the determinate phase, provided that the conditions for independence succeed, giving all solutions for their variables, which will afterwards be traversed by the member/2 goals in the nondeterminate phase, through backtracking. Note, however, that the execution of the calls to bagof can themselves create determinate and non–determinate phases since they start an Andorra–I subcomputation.

Following the guidelines above, the previous example would be transformed as follows:

```
ground(X), indep(Y,Z)
   -> bagof((X,Y),p(X,Y),P1),
      bagof((X,Z),p(X,Z),P2),
      member((X,Y),P1),
      member((X,Z),P2)
   ; p(X,Y), p(X,Z).
```

Since *all* variables in the original literals have been included in the term that captures the solutions, the first argument of the bagofs, the bagofs are guaranteed to be determinate. However, as we will show in the following section, optimizations can be applied which reduce the number of variables (and thus the amount of copying) and then, as mentioned above, existential quantification of the remaining variables has to be considered.

Note that the original variables X, Y and Z have been used in the member/2 predicates; this poses no new problems if we assume that after the execution of bagof these variables are not further instantiated, as is normally the case. Another issue is whether these variables are "touched" (bindings made to them, which may later be retracted during backtracking) during the execution of the goals in the bagof calls. In many simple implementations of bagof these variables are in fact instantiated during execution. In that case, and depending on the type of notion of independence being used, some form of isolation of environments may be necessary to prevent non–determinate goals running in parallel from affecting each other. This can be easily done by performing a run–time renaming of variables before the bagof (or including such operation in the bagof itself) but obviously at some cost. Such operations can simply be bypassed in the case of strictly independent goals (since there are no shared variables) and greatly reduced through compile–time analysis in the case of non–strictly independent goals [CH93]. Both of these important cases are covered and taken care of automatically by the annotation phase.

3.4 Sequentialization

The final steps in the transformation deal with some additional issues having to do with the characteristics of pruning in Andorra–I, the interaction between the two types of and–parallelism present after the transformation, and the way this affects the validity of the information from global analysis possibly used in the transformation process. Regarding pruning operators fortunately most of the problems are dealt with by the Andorra–I preprocessor [SCWY91b]. Andorra–I has inherited from the committed–choice languages the concept of a *guard*. The body of a clause may be separated into a guard part and a body part by a guard operator, which can be either one of the two pruning operators: cut (!) or commit (|). As commit is not included in standard Prolog programs, we will only consider the complications arising from the use of cut. One simple problem is for example the fact that in Andorra–I only one cut is allowed per clause. The transformation overcomes this by folding the original clause, creating a new predicate defined by a single clause with a body containing the literals from the original body which appeared after the first cut. Then this new clause can be recursively transformed in the same way.

Regarding the binding environment of the conditions on the conditionals, such conditions will be evaluated in Andorra–I in the same context as in Prolog only if they are executed when leftmost and no goals to their right have been executed ahead of time. Otherwise, there is no guarantee that their evaluation will be as in Prolog: it can be the case that they fail where they will succeed in Prolog or vice versa. To avoid this, some extra sequentialization needs to be added to the transformed program. On the other hand, it can be argued that the sequentialization is not necessary (unless global analysis is used, as discussed below) and can be omitted: the amount of (independent–and) parallelism gained in this case may be different from that obtained running the original program with independent and–parallelism only (both less and more).

Nonetheless, if evaluation of the conditions is to be preserved, first, and to guarantee execution only when leftmost, the parallel expressions should be sequentialized to their left using for example the sequentialization operator '::' of Andorra–I. In addition, and as discussed to some extent elsewhere [GSCYH91, BH92], goals to the right of the parallel conditionals themselves which execute ahead of time could also vary the state of instantiation of the variables involved in the conditions. This case will only affect indep/2 checks (i.e. not ground/1 checks since if a variable is ground under the Prolog execution, it will remain ground no matter how many other goals are run before the check in Andorra–I), thus sequentialization to the left is sufficient to guarantee the evaluation of ground/1 checks. In order to also preserve that of indep/2 checks, the parallel expressions should also be sequentialized to their right. This may further restrict the parallelism available. However, it can be avoided in Andorra–I if the determinate phase selects determinate goals in a left–to–right order. In this case, checks for ground/1 and indep/2 (in a conditional parallel expression) or the bagof/3 goals themselves (in unconditional expressions) would be selected before other determinate goals to their right. This is true for the body of the clause where the expression appears, but calls to the procedure including this clause do still need to be sequentialized.

On the other hand, and as mentioned before, the annotation algorithms which encode the independent and–parallelism (as well as the Andorra–I preprocessor) make several optimizations based on a global analysis of the program performed assuming the Prolog semantics; thus, information on the state of instantiation of variables will be inferred assuming a Prolog execution. For the transformation to be correct, such optimizations must be guaranteed to be valid. One possibility is to change the analyzers to cover non–standard schedulings (e.g. [MdlBH92]), but if traditional analyzers are to be used, the execution in Andorra–I should resemble that of Prolog at least at the point just before the and–parallel expressions (whether conditional or not) and thus these expressions should be executed only when leftmost. Sequentialization to the left is then mandatory. Sequentialization to the right can then be used to preserve the correctness of eliminating indep/2 checks in the optimizations, or alternatively this particular type of optimizations can be inhibited. Clearly, as such sequentialization is intended to preserve the semantics on which the analysis is based, it can be avoided if programs are translated without the aid of global analysis and only local analysis–based optimizations are performed.

4   Some optimizations to the transformation

As mentioned above, a number of optimizations are possible during the transformation. First, there is no need to include in the tuple for the first argument of the calls to bagof variables whose values are known, i.e. variables which are ground at run–time. This is the case of variable X in the example in Section 3.3: because the calls to bagof are only executed when the condition for independence succeeds, at the point of their execution it is known that the variable X is bound to a ground term. Therefore, it can be omitted from the tuple, which can reduce the size of the solution list (i.e. P1, P2). This optimization is applicable in general to every variable which can be known at compile–time to be ground at execution–time. This information can in principle be obtained by a local analysis based on the inspection of the conditions of the conditionals to detect which variables are ground, as in that example, or by a global analysis of the program which can infer such variable groundness. However, as mentioned before, the annotation algorithms already take advantage of such a global analysis to reduce the number of checks in the conditionals. In those cases a check known through global analysis to always be true at run–time will be removed from the conditionals and therefore will possibly not be seen by the transformation. Therefore, it is best to provide the transformation with direct access to the information inferred by the global analyzer in order to perform the optimizations in the best possible way with for the information available.

To ensure that the above optimization is correct in every case, the fact that all variables of a given literal may be known to be ground has to be taken into account. In this case it may appear that the encapsulation in bagof could be omitted. However, note that there is no guarantee that the unencapsulated goal would be determinate and thus parallelism may be lost. Therefore it is preferable to still wrap the goal in a bagof call and select any one of the variables in the literal to be included in the first argument of the call to bagof. On the other hand, since the list of solutions for such a goal would have only one element, there is no reason to include the member/2 literal and it can be safely omitted.

Second, a literal may include anonymous variables as arguments, i.e. variables whose values are not relevant for execution of the body of the clause in which they appear. As before, there is no need to include these variables in the tuple in the first argument of the call to bagof. Instead, they can be existentially quantified so that their values are ignored, but the call to bagof remains determinate. Note also that variables which are guaranteed not to be used in the computation after the execution of the bagof also fall in this category. Note also that if the anonymous variables are explicitly identified in the program using '_' then this optimization requires a renaming of these variables so that they can be referred to in the existential quantification as well as in the literal. Alternatively, the (slightly less common) findall/3 built-in can be used to avoid existential quantification of variables. This built-in can be faster although it can also generate more spurious solutions than bagof (and thus more backtracking) in the transformed programs.

Continuing with the example above, assume that p/2 has an additional argument which is not relevant in the computation:[1]

```
q(X,Y,Z) :- ground(X), indep(Y,Z) -> p(X,Y,_) & p(X,Z,_)
                                    ; p(X,Y,_),  p(X,Z,_).
```

The transformation including the optimizations described above would lead to:

```
ground(X), indep(Y,Z)
    -> bagof(Y,A1^p(X,Y,A1),P1),
       bagof(Z,A2^p(X,Z,A2),P2),
       member(Y,P1),
       member(Z,P2)
    ; p(X,Y,_), p(X,Z,_).
```

Another possible optimization is to eliminate the call to member/2 for literals which can be determined to produce at most one solution. Also, predicates which are found to be deterministic do not need to be transformed. Finally, a possible optimization concerns built-in predicates. Many of them are themselves determinate, and thus it makes no sense to encapsulate them in a call to bagof. For the rest, the main consideration on whether to encapsulate them is one of granularity: only goals with a reasonable execution size should be parallelized, otherwise the extra work needed for running in parallel would overcome the advantage obtained from parallel execution. This implies that many built-ins should not be parallelized. However, these issues are generally already taken into account in the process of annotating the parallelism.

5   Implementation of the transformation

We now describe an implementation approach for the proposed transformation, which we have actually followed, resulting in an automatic translator. It is based on the general outline of the transformation given in section 3, where global analysis (possibly based on abstract interpretation) is optional:

1. Annotate literals to encode in (independent-and) parallelism. Optimizations on conditions apply. Considerations on granularity also apply. Local and global analysis is used.

---

[1]Note that checks of independence among anonymous variables may be eliminated by the annotator even if only local analysis is performed.

2. For each literal in a parallel conjunction the correspondent calls to bagof and member predicates are constructed. Optimizations for these apply. Local and global analysis is used again.

3. Other issues such as cuts and necessary sequentializations are considered.

In the implementation, advantage has been taken of the tools already developed in the context of &–Prolog. The transformation is tightly integrated with these tools, in the way shown in figure 1. As mentioned above, annotators for parallelism are available that already provide the first step in the transformation [MH90]. The annotation process is aided by a number of global analyzers, based on abstract interpretation [CC77], which are part of the &–Prolog compiler as well, namely the "modes" analyzer [HWD92], the "sharing" analyzer [MH92], the "sharing+freeness" analyzer [MH91], as well as the "ASub" analyzer [Son86, CDY91] and combinations of the above [CMB$^+$93]. In addition, the native global analyzer of the Andorra–I system [SCWY91b], itself based on some of the ideas of the &–Prolog analyzers, has also been incorporated as another analysis tool to the system presented in the figure. The source Prolog program is first preprocessed and analyzed, and then annotated for parallelism. The information produced during the analysis phase is made available for the following steps.

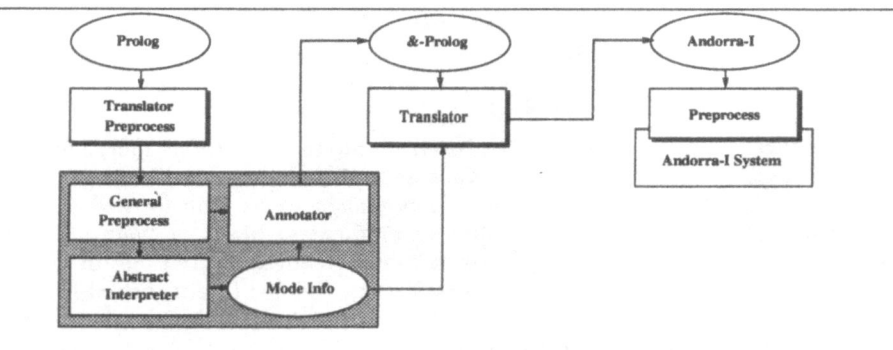

Figure 1: Overview of the full translator implementation.

Parallelized goals are then encapsulated in calls to bagof (and/or findall) following the techniques presented in the previous sections. During such encapsulation information from global analysis is used to simplify these calls, as described in section 3. The algorithm used during this step is as follows:

1. For each predicate,

   • unfold multiple cut occurrences,
   • perform 2 for each (resulting) clause,
   • iterate.

2. For each non–transformed conditional or CGE in its body,

   • perform 3 with the above construct,

- sequentialize to its left and right (depending on the style of transformation desired — see section 3), propagating the sequentialization upwards through the call graph,
- iterate.

3. For each parallel literal in the conditional or CGE,

   - obtain the set of anonymous variables in the literal (A),
   - obtain the set V of all variables in the literal (not including the anonymous variables),
   - rename the variables in A apart in the literal,
   - perform local analysis and access global analysis information obtaining the ground variables for the literal, subtract them from V giving V',
   - existentially quantify the variables in A,
   - create a tuple with variables in V',
   - replace the literal with the corresponding bagof/3 and member/2 calls,
   - iterate.

The resulting (Prolog) program is then passed on to the Andorra–I preprocessor which then will deal with preserving Prolog semantics for any side-effects, cuts, etc.

Finally, the definitions for the new predicates ground/1, indep/2 and member/2, for which calls are added to the original program in the translation process, would need to be included in the transformed program. However this step is not needed in practice if these are already system built–ins.

6 Examples

This section illustrates the behaviour of the implementation of the proposed transformation, as described in the previous section. This will be done by presenting the translated output for a number of benchmark programs, which hopefully illustrate a number of the issues involved in the translation and which have been previously discussed.

We begin with a slightly modified version of the "query" program by D.H.D. Warren [War77], which performs a query to a database consisting of a number of facts (not shown for brevity):

```
query([C1,D1,C2,D2]) :-
        pop(C1,P1), area(C1,A1), D1 is (P1*100)/A1,
        pop(C2,P2), area(C2,A2), D2 is (P2*100)/A2,
        check(D1,D2).

check(D1,D2):-
        D1 > D2,
        T1 is 20*D1,
        T2 is 21*D2,
        T1 < T2.
```

For the intended query mode — where the argument to query/1 is always free — `pop(C1,P1)`, `area(C1,A1)` and `pop(C2,P2)`, `area(C2,A2)` are highly nondeterminate and independent, and thus eligible for and–parallel execution. This is automatically captured by our translator, which gives as output the following translated version:

```
query([C1,D1,C2,D2]) :-
        bagof((C2,P2,A2),'query/1/1/$cge/1'(A2,P2,C2),L_bagof_1),
        bagof((C1,P1,A1),'query/1/1/$cge/2'(A1,P1,C1),L_bagof_2),
        member((C2,P2,A2),L_bagof_1),
        member((C1,P1,A1),L_bagof_2),
        D1 is P1*100/A1,
        D2 is P2*100/A2,
        check(D1,D2).

'query/1/1/$cge/1'(A2,P2,C2) :- pop(C2,P2), area(C2,A2).

'query/1/1/$cge/2'(A1,P1,C1) :- pop(C1,P1), area(C1,A1).

member(X,[X|_]).
member(X,[_|T]) :- member(X,T).
```

Although not strictly necessary, new predicates are created for the independent conjunctions and these encapsulated in bagofs. Note that is/2 goals have not been parallelized due to granularity considerations. However, they have been (safely) reordered to allow for and–parallelism between the bagof calls.

The next example is the safe/1 predicate in a well known program for solving the N-Queens problem, written in a manner such that negation is avoided:

```
safe([Q|Qs]):- safe(Qs), attacking(Q, Qs, A), A=no.
safe([]).

attacking(Q, Qs, yes):- attack(Q, Qs), !.
attacking(_, _,  no).
```

In the standard query mode for this program safe/1 is called with a ground argument. Then, the determinate recursive call is independent of the nondeterminate goal for attacking/3 in the body of the first clause for safe/1. We thus have a case of encapsulation of goals with ground variables. The result of the transformation is as follows:

```
safe([Q|Qs]) :-
        bagof(Qs,safe(Qs),L_bagof_1),
        bagof(A,attacking(Q,Qs,A),L_bagof_2),
        member(A,L_bagof_2),
        A=no.
safe([]).
```

Note that the member/2 goal for the first bagof has been omitted, as it is unnecessary. Also, gathering of solutions for the ground variables in the second bagof has been omitted. In fact the first bagof itself can be omitted, recalling that the safe/1 goal is determinate; this is not done automatically yet[2] but the optimization is performed if this information is provided through a compiler directive. Also the member/2 goal of the second bagof can be omitted, if it can be proved that attacking/3 gives only one solution — as is the case; this would require and additional type of analysis, detecting "single solution" goals.[3] Again, the optimization is performed if the information is available.

On the contrary, in the following example although both member/2 goals can be omitted, none of the corresponding bagofs can, as the encapsulated goals are in fact nondeterminate. In this example the common/3 predicate is true if a given list is a sublist of two other given lists. We declare an intended use where it is used to check this property for three ground lists:

```
common(L,L1,L2):-              sublist([],[]).
        sublist(L,L1),          sublist([X|L],[X|L1]):- sublist(L,L1).
        sublist(L,L2).          sublist(L,[_|L1]):- sublist(L,L1).
```

Since all the variables in the subgoals are ground, the translator selects any of them to put in the call to bagof (alternatively, a new variable would serve the same purpose). The output program is as follows:

```
common(L,L1,L2) :-
        bagof(L1,sublist(L,L1),L_bagof_1),
        bagof(L2,sublist(L,L2),L_bagof_2).
```

	sequential	parallel	independent
qsort(50)	659	434	261
qsort(10)	81	54	54
qsort(2)	11	8	15
common(50)	103	90	52
tak(14)	5931	4745	277
deriv	28	28	18
deriv–det	28	8	18
query	229	5	17
query–all	1301	5	53
projgeom(4)	1444	130	148
projgeom(4)–all	52099	164	191

Table 1: Full parallel Andorra–I.

7   Results and Discussion

We have tested the proposed transformation on a number of programs in order to assess its effectiveness. We have used as test–bed meta–interpreters for

---

[2] A determinacy analyzer is available within the &–Prolog compiler but it has not been yet interfaced with the current implementation of the transformation.

[3] Such an analysis is part of the granularity analysis currently being performed in the &–Prolog compiler, but it has not yet been interfaced with the transformation.

	prolog	andorra–I		
		sequential	parallel	independent
query–det	235	231	230	278
query–det–all	1327	1303	1302	1395
projgeom(4)	2042	1444	1199	1115
projgeom(4)–all	78586	52099	44056	43027

Table 2: Determinate and–parallel only Andorra–I.

Prolog and Andorra–I which count inferences made during the computation: actually reduced heads count as an inference, but a head unification that fails is not counted as such. Tables 1 and 2 provide the results in terms of such inferences, for the three cases of Andorra–I executing the original program sequentially, Andorra–I executing the original program in parallel, and Andorra–I executing the transformed program in parallel (now also exploiting independent and–parallelism).

The programs benchmarked fall into three categories: deterministic programs (which give only one solution in a deterministic computation, i.e. no backtracking is performed), programs which give only one solution but allow for backtracking and search (although "spurious"), and programs which are non–deterministic in their own right (i.e. they provide many solutions). For the first category, we used the well–known quick–sort program, which has been tested with three lists of different length, and the "common" program, presented in section 6. Among the "spurious" backtracking programs we have used a puzzle written by Takeuchi which has only two clauses and both are applicable (at least w.r.t. just head unification), but only one gives the solution; the program is highly recursive. A version of the symbolic differentiation "deriv" is also included in this class: it has a clause which is always applicable and only fails after entering it. A determinate version of this program (which does not include that clause) has been also included as a reference point in the discussion. A good practical example of this second category (although not included for brevity) is a classical "clause by clause" compiler, where the process of compiling each clause is non–deterministic (involving some search during register allocation, for example) but giving only one solution, and all clauses can be compiled in parallel. The database query of section 6 falls into the third category of programs. Two versions are considered, one with no determinate goals at all and another one with the pop/2 plus area/2 goals folded into a one–clause predicate (recall the example in section 6). Five solutions to the query are possible. The "projgeom" program (originally by William Older), also in this class, builds up a perfect difference set of order $n = 4$, in our case, which determines a finite cyclic projective geometry with $n(n+1)+1$ points. There are ten solutions, and extensive search is performed. In these cases, the results when asking only for the first solution and when asking for all solutions are given. Also in the case of this third category of programs, results for allowing only and–parallelism (i.e. disallowing or–parallelism) are given (Table 2). Our Andorra–I meta–interpreter allows selectively turning on or off or–parallelism and determinate and–parallelism in order to separately identify the contribution of each of them to the speedups. Discussion of the results follows.

In the first category of programs the transformation behaves satisfactorily. In these cases, no or–parallelism is exploited, just determinate and–parallelism. Nonetheless, since the exploitation of determinism is limited in one or another direction, the parallelism Andorra–I can take advantage of is also limited. On the other hand, the bagof encapsulation allows exploitation of opportunities for parallelism in every case. The parallelism in qsort is limited because the qsort goals only become determinate after the list splitting has at least produced the constructor of the list. Furthermore, most of the times this makes *only one* qsort literal become determinate. On the other hand, bagof encapsulation makes *both* qsort goals not only be reduced but also executed in parallel. Parallelism in the untransformed common program is also limited because in this case whether a literal is determinate or not depends on the particular values its arguments get instantiated to — i.e. not only simply on whether they get instantiated, as in qsort. It should be noted, however, that these results are quite sensitive to the level of determinacy detection assumed for the Andorra–I execution.

The interpretation of these results advises using compile–time analysis to guide the transformation in the sense of performing it whenever it can be determined that the literals involved are scarcely determinate during the computation. In addition, as the different tests on qsort show, other analyses such as those determining granularity can also be helpful for guiding the transformation. We have already pointed out the meaningfulness of such an analysis in the task of automatic parallelization, and this result provides further arguments in the same direction.

The effectiveness of the transformation is much more relevant in the second category of programs. In these cases no determinate and–parallelism is exploited and the or–parallelism is almost irrelevant. What happens in fact is that alternative branches in the computation are opened which do not lead to a solution. The solution is obtained in one and only one branch. The gain w.r.t. the sequential computation is negligible (or even none, as in deriv[4]) and due to an or–process finding the solution in the correct branch without having to wait for the previous branches to fail for backtracking, which is what happens in the sequential computation. The gain when introducing independent and–parallelism is clear. In the case of tak, for example, three sub–computations out of the four recursive goals in the body of one of the clauses are run in and–parallel.

In the third category, although the results are still quite adequate with respect to the sequential execution, some slow–down is obtained with respect to the standard Andorra–I parallel execution. This is due to the overhead in the execution of the member predicates (note that their inferences are being counted). We believe that this could be greatly alleviated if a built–in version of this predicate is used, optimized for the particular query mode and purpose for which it is used in our transformation. It is also worth noting that in the case of projgeom, as well as in the tak and qsort examples discussed before, a sequentialization of literals has been done in order to force the computation to warrant that the independence conditions generated in the analysis phase of the transformation are valid. This sequentialization prevents any determin-

---

[4]To illustrate the point of the role of determinate and–parallelism a determinate version of deriv has been included. This one effectively exploits this parallelism and it can be seen that in this case the overhead introduced by the member goals of the corresponding bagofs is significant.

ism from being exploited in the transformed program: despite this, the loss in performance for this is comparatively small. The little relevance of the determinate phase of the computation in this case is also exemplified by the results shown in table 2, corresponding to the exploitation of and–parallelism (and no or–parallelism) which offers quite different results.

8 Conclusions

We have presented a transformation which allows the exploitation of general independent and–parallelism in a system like Andorra–I, already supporting determinate dependent and–parallelism and or–parallelism, and which can be automatically performed at compile–time. We believe that this can, at least in principle, be done without fundamental modifications to the implementation of the underlying execution model. We argue that this provides a path for extension of the model which, while having limitations, might be simpler and easier than others previously proposed. Our initial results from an implementation of the transformation are encouraging. Exploitation of independent and–parallelism by these means in addition — or sometimes even in place of — determinate and–parallelism appears profitable in a number of cases. However, we have also found that the extra overhead introduced by the traversal of the solution lists in the calls to member/2 can be significant. As a solution, and as a proposal for future work, we plan on evaluating better, deterministic implementations of such predicates which are specialized for the purposes for which they are used in the transformation. Also an interesting alternative is to implement an *incremental* bagof/findall which will "serve" the solutions as soon as they are computed, thus making the use of member/2 unnecessary. Finally, since our experiments have been run using a completely automated transformation tool, some of the optimizations proposed were not performed, since not all the analyzers that would be required to perform such optimizations were available or yet interfaced with our tool. In particular, no analysis of determinism or of the number of solutions was performed. We also plan further exploration of the improvements which can be obtained using such information.

9 Acknowledgements

The authors would like to thank Vitor Santos-Costa, from U. of Bristol, for many useful discussions on Andorra–I, during which the original idea for this work arose. Also to Maria Jose García de la Banda and the members of the CLIP group at U.P.M. for their help on earlier drafts of this report and during the implementation of the translator herein presented.

References

[BH92]   F. Bueno and M. Hermenegildo.   An Automatic Translation Scheme from Prolog to the Andorra Kernel Language. In **International Conference on Fifth Generation Computer Systems**, 759–769. Institute for New Generation Computer Technology (ICOT), June 1992.

[CC77]   P. Cousot and R. Cousot. Abstract Interpretation: A Unified
            Lattice Model for Static Analysis of Programs by Construction or
            Approximation of Fixpoints. In **Acm Symp. on Principles of
            Programming Languages**, 238–252. ACM, 1977.

[CDD85]   J.-H. Chang, A. M. Despain, and D. Degroot. And-Parallelism of
            Logic Programs Based on Static Data Dependency Analysis. In
            Compcon Spring '85, 218–225, February 1985.

[CDO88]   M. Carlsson, K. Danhof, and R. Overbeek. A Simplified Approach
            to the Implementation of And-Parallelism in an Or-Parallel En-
            vironment. In **International Conference and Symposium
            on Logic Programming**, 1565–1577. University of Washington,
            MIT Press, August 1988.

[CDY91]   M. Codish, D. Dams, and E. Yardeni. Derivation and Safety of
            an Abstract Unification Algorithm for Groundness and Aliasing
            Analysis. In **International Conference on Logic Program-
            ming**, 79–96. MIT Press, June 1991.

[CH93]   D. Cabeza and M. Hermenegildo. Towards Extracting Non-strict
            Independent And-parallelism Using Sharing and Freeness Infor-
            mation. Technical report CLIP5/92.1. U. of Madrid (UPM), Fac-
            ultad Informática UPM, 28660-Boadilla del Monte, Madrid-Spain,
            August 1993.

[CMB$^+$93] M. Codish, A. Mulkers, M. Bruynooghe, M.J.García de la Banda,
            and M. Hermenegildo. Improving Abstract Interpretations by
            Combining Domains. In **ACM SIGPLAN Symposium on
            Partial Evaluation and Semantics Based Program Manip-
            ulation**, 194–206. ACM, June 1993.

[DeG84]   D. DeGroot. Restricted AND-Parallelism. In **International
            Conference on Fifth Generation Computer Systems**, 471–
            478. ICOT, November 1984.

[DeG87]   D. DeGroot. A Technique for Compiling Execution Graph Ex-
            pressions for Restricted AND-parallelism in Logic Programs. In
            International Supercomputing Conference, 80–89. Springer
            Verlag, 1987.

[GSCYH91]   G. Gupta, V. Santos-Costa, R. Yang, and M. Hermenegildo. ID-
            IOM: Integrating Dependent and-, Independent and-, and Or-
            parallelism. In **International Logic Programming Sympo-
            sium**, 152–166. MIT Press, October 1991.

[Her86]   M. V. Hermenegildo. **An Abstract Machine Based Execution
            Model for Computer Architecture Design and Efficient
            Implementation of Logic Programs in Parallel**. PhD thesis,
            U. of Texas at Austin, August 1986.

[HG90]   M. Hermenegildo and K. Greene. &-Prolog and its Performance: Exploiting Independent And-Parallelism. In **International Conference on Logic Programming**, 253–268. MIT Press, June 1990.

[HJ90]   S. Haridi and S. Janson. Kernel Andorra Prolog and its Computation Model. In **International Conference on Logic Programming**, 31–46. MIT Press, June 1990.

[HR89]   M. Hermenegildo and F. Rossi. On the Correctness and Efficiency of Independent And-Parallelism in Logic Programs. In **North American Conference on Logic Programming**, 369–390. MIT Press, October 1989.

[HR90]   M. Hermenegildo and F. Rossi. Non-Strict Independent And-Parallelism. In **International Conference on Logic Programming**, 237–252. MIT Press, June 1990.

[HWD92]   M. Hermenegildo, R. Warren, and S. Debray. Global Flow Analysis as a Practical Compilation Tool. **Journal of Logic Programming**, 13(4):349–367, August 1992.

[JH91]   S. Janson and S. Haridi. Programming Paradigms of the Andorra Kernel Language. In **International Logic Programming Symposium**, 167–183. MIT Press, 1991.

[JL88]   D. Jacobs and A. Langen. Compilation of Logic Programs for Restricted And-Parallelism. In **European Symposium on Programming**, 284–297, 1988.

[JL89]   D. Jacobs and A. Langen. Accurate and Efficient Approximation of Variable Aliasing in Logic Programs. In **North American Conference on Logic Programming**, 154-165. MIT Press, October 1989.

[MdlBH92] K. Marriott, M. Garcia de la Banda, and M. Hermenegildo. Analyzing Logic Programs with Dynamic Scheduling. Technical Report CLIP6/93.1, U. of Madrid (UPM), Facultad Informática UPM, 28660-Boadilla del Monte, Madrid-Spain, October 1992. To appear in **Principles of Programming Languages** 1993.

[MH89]   K. Muthukumar and M. Hermenegildo. Determination of Variable Dependence Information at Compile-Time Through Abstract Interpretation. In **North American Conference on Logic Programming**, 166–189. MIT Press, October 1989.

[MH90]   K. Muthukumar and M. Hermenegildo. The CDG, UDG, and MEL Methods for Automatic Compile-time Parallelization of Logic Programs for Independent And-parallelism. In **International Conference on Logic Programming**, 221–237. MIT Press, June 1990.

[MH91]   K. Muthukumar and M. Hermenegildo. Combined Determination of Sharing and Freeness of Program Variables Through Abstract Interpretation. In **International Conference on Logic Programming**, 49–63. MIT Press, June 1991.

[MH92]   K. Muthukumar and M. Hermenegildo. Compile-time Derivation of Variable Dependency Using Abstract Interpretation. **Journal of Logic Programming**, 13(2 and 3):315–347, July 1992.

[Nai88]   L. Naish. Parallelizing NU-Prolog. In **International Conference and Symposium on Logic Programming**, 1546–1564. University of Washington, MIT Press, August 1988.

[SCWY91a] V. Santos-Costa, D.H.D. Warren, and R. Yang. The Andorra-I Engine: A Parallel Implementation of the Basic Andorra Model. In **International Conference on Logic Programming**, 825–839. MIT Press, June 1991.

[SCWY91b] V. Santos-Costa, D.H.D. Warren, and R. Yang. The Andorra-I Preprocessor: Supporting Full Prolog on the Basic Andorra Model. In **International Conference on Logic Programming**, 443–456. MIT Press, June 1991.

[Son86]   H. Sondergaard. An application of abstract interpretation of logic programs: occur check reduction. In **European Symposium on Programming, LNCS 123**, 327–338. Springer-Verlag, 1986.

[Ued87]   K. Ueda. Making Exhaustive Search Programs Deterministic. **New Generation Computing**, 5(1):29–44, 1987.

[War77]   D. H. D. Warren. **Applied Logic—Its Use and Implementation as Programming Tool**. PhD thesis, University of Edinburgh, 1977. Also available as SRI Technical Note 290.

[War90]   D. H. D. Warren. The Extended Andorra Model with Implicit Control. In Sverker Jansson, editor, **Parallel Logic Programming Workshop**. SICS, Box 1263, S-163 13 Spanga, SWEDEN, June 1990.

Memoing with Abstract Answers and Delphi Lemmas

Paul Tarau

Département d'Informatique, Université de Moncton

Moncton, Canada

Koen De Bosschere

Vakgroep Elektronica en Informatiesystemen, Universiteit Gent

Gent, Belgium

Abstract

Abstract answers are most general computed answers of logic programs. For each derivation leading to a computed answer there is a unique abstract answer obtained by replicating the steps of the derivation, except the first one. After describing a meta-interpreter returning abstract answers we derive a class of program transformations that compute them more efficiently. Abstract answers are ideal lemmas as their 'hit rate' is much higher than in the case of naive memoing. Experimental evidence to this claim is presented by showing an order of magnitude speed-up for the naive reverse benchmark through an automatic program transformation using abstract answers as lemmas. To ensure tight control on the amount of memoing a simple but very effective technique is introduced: Delphi lemmas are abstract answers memoized only by acquiescence of an oracle. We show that random oracles perform surprisingly well as Delphi lemmas tend naturally to cover the 'hot spots' of the program.

Keywords: abstract and conditional answers, program transformations, memoing, lemmas

1   Introduction

Memoing techniques have been an important research topic in logic programming and deductive databases (see [16], [12]). Various practical tools for memoing exist from programmer defined assert based mechanisms (see [11]) and extension tables as in SB-Prolog to dedicated interpreters like [17]. However, they all share the following basic ideas:

- atoms obtained in the course of resolution are memoized as such;

- there is no mechanism to improve the 'hit rate' of the lemmas;

- a fixed memoing algorithm is used;

- memoing is seen as a tool but not as a resource.

Without minimizing the merits of the memoing facilities we mentioned before (which support execution of left-recursive rules and ensure termination of Datalog programs [16]) we have noticed that very often the existing memoing facilities are simply not 'smarter than programmers' who therefore tend to code their lemmas directly with **assert** and **retract** or by carrying around clumsy and difficult to index data structures. This is especially true with theorem provers that suffer in terms of performances and readability from the absence of a practical higher level memoing mechanism provided by the underlying Prolog system.

This paper tries to solve these problems in a simple but radical way. First, instead of memoing actual instances of answers created during the resolution process, we will replace them with their more general instances, such that while preserving soundness we can ensure the best possible future reuse. We show that the overhead can be compiled away by using program transformations. We consider memoing as a possibly expensive resource that is not a priori better than recomputation. To ensure tight control on memoing, we abolish the predictability of *what* is memoized and *when*, by delegating it to an oracle external to the resolution process. Due to statistical properties of execution traces this will be surprisingly better with a random oracle[1] than with naive fixed algorithm memoing approaches, especially when we have the possibility to control the amount of copying involved in the memoing process.

2 Resolution revisited

Although classical texts on SLD and SLDNF resolution (see [9] and [1]) do explain well the basic logical mechanisms behind Prolog engines one aspect is neglected in all but some partial evaluation oriented papers like [10] and [6][2]: the resolvent is seen as an conjunction of literals instead of being seen as a logical implication. For instance, in the case of SLD-resolution, starting from a goal :-G hides the fact that we are actually looking for a computed answer starting from the tautologically true clause G:-G. Even worse, resolution is seen as a 'refutation' procedure although everyone uses it intuitively as a constructive entailment process where we simply unfold clauses of a program until a fact A:-true is eventually reached.

Without going into the details of such a reconstruction we now define the *composition* operator $\oplus$ that combines clauses by unfolding the leftmost body-goal of the first argument with the second clause.

Definition 1 *Let* $A_0:-A_1,A_2,\ldots,A_n$ *and* $B_0:-B_1,\ldots,B_m$ *be two clauses (suppose* $n > 0, m \geq 0$). *We define*

$$(A_0:-A_1,A_2,\ldots,A_n) \oplus (B_0:-B_1,\ldots,B_m) = (A_0:-B_1,\ldots,B_m,A_2,\ldots,A_n)\theta$$

with $\theta = mgu(A_1,B_0)$. *If the atoms* A_1 *and* B_0 *do not unify, the result of the composition is denoted as* $\perp$.

Furthermore, as usual, we consider $A_0:-true,A_2,\ldots,A_n$ *to be equivalent to* $A_0:-A_2,\ldots,A_n$, *and for any clause* C, $\perp\oplus$ C = C $\oplus \perp = \perp$. *We suppose (when necessary) that at least one operand has been renamed to a variant with fresh variables.*

---

[1]This random oracle has however a 'tunable' probability.

[2]In this paper a definition of most general resultants is given.

Let us call this Prolog-like inference rule LF-SLD resolution (LF for 'left-first'). Note that by working on the program P' obtained from P by replacing each clause with the set of clauses obtained by all possible permutations of atoms occurring in the clause's body every SLD-derivation on P can be mapped to an LF-SLD derivation on P'. Extension of this inference mechanism to SLDNF-resolution is easy. Note also that clause composition is an associative operation and therefore a sequence of such compositions is a well defined concept.

Definition 2 *An LF-SLD derivation is a sequence of clauses $C_1, \ldots, C_n$ such that the result of their composition $C_1 \oplus \ldots \oplus C_n$ is different from $\bot$.*

Let P be a definite program and let G be an atomic definite goal. We can then construct the clause G:-G. which is a logical tautology. Derivations starting with G:-G are of special interest as they can be used to produce computed answers for G and P.

3 Abstract and conditional answers

As clause composition is an associative operation it makes sense to remove the first step from a derivation G:-G and then compose the clause G':-G' obtained from another goal G' with the rest of it.

Definition 3 *A derivation starting with G:-G for an atomic goal G and terminating with a fact of the form A:-true is called a standard LF-SLD derivation. A derivation starting with a clause of the program instead of G:-G is called an abstract LF-SLD derivation and a derivation not terminated by a fact is called a conditional LF-SLD derivation. A (standard, abstract, conditional) answer is the result of the composition of the clauses occurring in a (standard, abstract, conditional) LF-SLD derivation. By combining them we can talk about abstract conditional answers.*

Abstract answers are composed exclusively from clauses of the program P, that 'shadow' more specific standard answers obtained starting from G:-G and using it as a 'path-finder' for a derivation. Conditional answers are very useful in partial evaluation[3] (see [4]), type inference (see [15]) and in expressing partial computations similar to those occurring in higher order functional programs (see [3]).

Example 1 *Let us consider the program:*

(C_1) plus(0,Y,Y):-true.
(C_2) plus(s(X),Y,s(Z)):-plus(X,Y,Z).

and G:-G =

     plus(s(0),s(0),R):-plus(s(0),s(0),R).

We obtain, as the result of $(G:-G) \oplus C_2$, the conditional answer

---

[3]Introduced in logic programming by [8]; also known as partial deduction.

```
plus(s(0),s(0),s(Z1)):-plus(0,s(0),Z1).
```

Then, by composing with (C_1), the expression (G:-G)$\oplus C_2 \oplus C_1$ *is equal to the standard answer:*

```
plus(s(0),s(0),s(s(0))):-true.
```

The corresponding abstract answer ($C_2 \oplus C_1$), *obtained by omitting the first composition*

```
plus(s(0),A,s(A)):-true.
```

contains the useful generalization that 'the successor of 0 *plus* A *is the successor of* A *'.*

Note that working with clause compositions ensures that each step of a derivation corresponds to a logical consequence of the program. This incremental logical soundness contrasts with standard SLD-derivation where only the (final) computed answer has this property.

Theorem 1 *If S is a (standard, abstract, conditional) answer of P, then S is a logical consequence of P.*

This theorem is a consequence of more general results of [4], [7] or [2]. A short direct proof in the case of binary logic programs is given in [13].

In the examples that follow, we often use S instead of S:-**true** for efficiency and readability.

4   A meta-interpreter for abstract answers

The following code (working on *definite programs*) is obtained from the 'vanilla' meta-interpreter but its extension to more sophisticated meta-interpreters dealing with *cut*, negation and system predicates can be done with well-known meta-interpretation techniques.

```
% demo(G,AbsG) is true if AbsG is an abstract answer of P
% the clauses of P being given by "clause/3"

demo(true,true):-!.
demo((A,B),(AbsA,AbsB)):-!,demo(A,AbsA),demo(B,AbsB).
demo(H,AbsH):-
     clause(H,B,Ref),
     demo(B,AbsB),
     instance(Ref,(AbsH:-AbsB)).
```

The interpreter uses two system predicates available on most Prolog systems **clause/3** which returns a database reference **Ref** and **instance/2** which returns a new copy of the clause referred to by **Ref**.

Example 2 *If P =*

```
app([],Ys,Ys).
app([A|Xs],Ys,[A|Zs]):-app(Xs,Ys,Zs).

nrev([],[]).
nrev([X|Xs],R) :- nrev(Xs,T), app(T,[X],R).
```

and

```
G  = nrev([a,b,c],X)
```

we obtain in the query

```
?- G=nrev([1,2,3],X),demo(G,Abstract).
```

the following abstract answer

```
Abstract = nrev([A,B,C],[C,B,A]).
```

5   Computing abstract answers with a program transformation

We can obtain the same result without meta-interpretation by constructing a transformed program. We will define a general program-transformation scheme and then study three of its instances.

Definition 4 *Let $ABS(\phi, P)$ be the program obtained by replacing each clause $A_0:-A_1,\ldots,A_n$ of the program P by $\phi(A_0,A_0') :- \phi(A_1,A_1'),\ldots, \phi(A_n,A_n')$, where $A_0':-A_1',\ldots,A_n'$ is a variant of $A_0 :- A_1,\ldots,A_n$ with no shared variables between them.*

Using the program transformation $ABS(\phi, P)$ is not only an order of magnitude more efficient than meta-interpretation of P, but also conserves the operational meaning of programs containing *cut* or system predicates. We will now present three possible instances of the transformation ϕ.

5.1   Naive

As a first attempt, let us define $\phi(a(X_1,\ldots,X_n),a(Y_1,\ldots,Y_n))$ as the atom $p(a(X_1,\ldots,X_n),a(Y_1,\ldots,Y_n))$, where $p/2$ is a new predicate symbol.

Example 3 $ABS(naive, P) =$

```
p(append([],Ys,Ys),append([],Ys1,Ys1)).
p(append([A|Xs],Ys,[A|Zs]),append([A1|Xs1],Ys1,[A1|Zs1])):-
   p(append(Xs,Ys,Zs),append(Xs1,Ys1,Zs1)).

p(nrev([],[]),nrev([],[])).
p(nrev([X|Xs],R),nrev([X1|Xs1],R1)):-
   p(nrev(Xs,T),nrev(Xs1,T1)),
   p(append(T,[X],R),append(T1,[X1],R1)).
```

The query

```
?- p(nrev([a,b,c],_),Abstract).
```

returns the abstract answer:

```
Abstract = nrev([A,B,C],[C,B,A]).
```

5.2   Indexed

We can define $\phi(a(X_1,\ldots,X_n),a(Y_1,\ldots,Y_n))$ as $a(X_1,\ldots,X_n,a(Y_1,\ldots,Y_n))$
to preserve indexing on the first argument of the original program.

Example 4 *ABS(indexed, P)* =

```
append([],Ys,Ys,append([],Ys1,Ys1)).
append([A|Xs],Ys,[A|Zs],append([A1|Xs1],Ys1,[A1|Zs1])):-
  append(Xs,Ys,Zs,append(Xs1,Ys1,Zs1)).

nrev([],[],nrev([],[])).
nrev([X|Xs],R,nrev([X1|Xs1],R1)):-
  nrev(Xs,T,nrev(Xs1,T1)),
  append(T,[X],R,append(T1,[X1],R1)).
```

The query

```
?- nrev([a,b,c],_,Abstract).
```

returns the abstract answer:

```
Abstract = nrev([A,B,C],[C,B,A]).
```

5.3   Flat

Finally, by defining the transformation $\phi(a(X_1,\ldots,X_n),a(Y_1,\ldots,Y_n))$ as being simply $a(X_1,\ldots,X_n,Y_1,\ldots,Y_n)$ we can avoid the construction of useless structures.

Example 5 *ABS(flat, P)* =

```
append([],Ys,Ys,[],Ys1,Ys1).
append([A|Xs],Ys,[A|Zs],[A1|Xs1],Ys1,[A1|Zs1]):-
  append(Xs,Ys,Zs,Xs1,Ys1,Zs1).

nrev([],[],[],[]).
nrev([X|Xs],R,[X1|Xs1],R1):-
  nrev(Xs,T,Xs1,T1),
  append(T,[X],R,T1,[X1],R1).
```

The query

```
?- nrev([a,b,c],_,X,Y), Abstract=nrev(X,Y).
```

returns the abstract answer:

```
Abstract = nrev([A,B,C],[C,B,A]).
```

Theorem 2 *The* naive, indexed *and* flat *transformations compute abstract answers together with standard answers within a constant factor from computing only the standard answers for P. Moreover, the transformed program generates precisely the same standard answers as the original program while computing the abstract answers too. For a program P and a goal G there exists a unique abstract answer for every standard answer. Conversely, every abstract answer is also a standard answer.*

Proof. This follows immediately from the fact that terms involved in the computation of standard answers are always more specific than those used to compute abstract answers, for each derivation step. Therefore the computational effort spent for an abstract solution is at most as large as the effort spent in the computation of the standard solution.

Note also that, in principle, computation of the abstract solution can be carried out by a parallel thread as no interference occurs between the two sequences of unifications.

The execution speeds are shown in table 1. It follows that the program transformation is much faster than the meta-interpreter and that the overhead of the computation of an abstract answer using our best transformation flat is limited to 57 % w.r.t. direct execution of naive reverse.

version	runtime (μs)	relative time w.r.t nrev
original nrev	105	1.00
demo	3174	30.22
naive	374	3.56
index	208	1.98
flat	165	1.57

Table 1: Execution speeds for the program transformations on a Sparcstation ELC with Sicstus Prolog 2.1 compact code.

6   Abstract answers as lemmas

Abstract answers are good candidates for reusable lemmas. By accumulating an abstract answer S:-true, the equivalent of the search for an entire LF-SLD-refutation can be replaced with the composition of the clause G:-G for a given atomic goal G and a memoized abstract answer S:-true. In the same way, a partial computation can be concentrated as an abstract conditional answer.

Remark the non-trivial nature of lemmas obtained from abstract or abstract conditional answers as they replace possibly infinite sets of standard answers.

Compared to memoing of standard answers, memoing of abstract or abstract conditional answers is more appropriate as the generality of the saved computation allows a better hit rate. Moreover, soundness is ensured as they are logical consequences of the program.

The computational overhead of this kind of lemma generation is minimized as the computation of abstract answers can be 'compiled' through the program transformation $P \rightarrow ABS(\phi, P)$.

However, as it is also the case with usual lemma generation, the actual gain in efficiency depends on indexing of dynamic code and programmer defined 'pragmas' specifying what is worth to be memoized.

On the practical side, suppose we want count the number of LIPS using a large number of iterations of the well known nrev/2 predicate. By using random values in the list to reverse we can prevent a clever Prolog system from using the memoing of something like nrev([12,13,1,5,9],[9,5,1,13,12]) as an answer to nrev([1,2,3,4,5],X). By using memoing of the abstract answer nrev([A,B,C,D,E],[E,D,C,B,A]), the only way to ensure fairness of the benchmark is to have lists of random content and random length at each iteration. We can go even further. As nrev/2 is a recursive predicate we can use as lemmas nrev([A$_1$,...,A$_n$],[A$_n$,...,A$_1$]) for each n. Obviously, this makes nrev/2 linear[4] with respect to n and practically invalidates its use as a Prolog benchmark.

6.1   Naive abstract lemmas

Let P be the nrev/2 program. Starting from $ABS(\phi, P)$, we can write a Prolog program that asserts as lemmas the abstract answers computed by $ABS(\phi, P)$ and that uses them to speed up the computation of the answers. We will compare the performances with the original nrev/2 program.

This is the easiest way to use abstract answers as lemmas. However performances suffer due to creation of lemmas that eventually force a sequential search. Empirical tests confirm however a small speed-up with naive abstract lemmas, at least in the case of the nrev/2 predicate.

6.2   Length-indexed abstract lemmas

An easy way to overcome this is by using the parameter that uniquely determines the appropriate lemma as a key. In the case of a program like naive reverse this is the length of the list[5]. This ensures constant time access to the only relevant lemma and is enough to achieve $O(N)$ performances on the benchmark. Note that such size-related parameters can be found relatively easily. However this step cannot be automated in the general case. On the other hand, indexing methods like switching trees or switching graphs can be used 'automatically' if provided by the underlying Prolog implementation.

6.3   Delphi lemmas

Delphi lemmas are intended to reduce the time and the space spent for relatively useless lemmas. The basic idea is that lemmas are only really useful for the hot spots of the execution trace of the program.

---

[4]Constant in terms of LIPS but linear in terms of real work due to the unification of two lists of size n

[5]We refer the reader to the program listed in section 6.4 for the details of this transformation.

Suppose we consult an oracle before each decision to generate a lemma. A very smart (say human) oracle can decide for the naive reverse program for a list of length 100 iterated 50 times that the only lemma that is really worth to be generated is

```
nrev([A1,...,A100], [A100,...,A1]).
```

This ensures a hit for each call and no search. How can we get close to this automatically? A surprisingly simple answer is to use a random oracle with a sufficiently low probability of answering **yes**. This means that the probability of generating lemmas will only be high for the hot spots of the program. In practice, the probability should be a parameter allowing the programmer to empirically fine-tune lemma generation. Here is the code (Sicstus Prolog 2.1):

```
:- ensure_loaded(library(random)).

nrev_lemma(Xs,Ys,Xs1,Ys1):-
    nrev_fact(Xs,Ys,Xs1,Ys1), !.
nrev_lemma(Xs,Ys,Xs1,Ys1):-
    nrev(Xs,Ys,Xs1,Ys1),
    make_nrev_lemma(Xs1,Ys1).

make_nrev_lemma(Xs1,Ys1):-random(X), X>0.04,!.
make_nrev_lemma(Xs1,Ys1):-
    copy_term(Xs1+Ys1,Xs2+Ys2),
    asserta(nrev_fact(Xs1,Ys1,Xs2,Ys2)).

app([],Ys,Ys,[],Ys1,Ys1).
app([A|Xs],Ys,[A|Zs],[A1|Xs1],Ys1,[A1|Zs1]):-
    app(Xs,Ys,Zs,Xs1,Ys1,Zs1).

nrev([],[],[],[]).
nrev([X|Xs],R,[X1|Xs1],R1):-
    nrev_lemma(Xs,T,Xs1,T1),
    app(T,[X],R,T1,[X1],R1).

nrev(Xs,Ys=nrev(Xs1,Ys1)):-
    nrev(Xs,Ys,Xs1,Ys1).
```

The execution speed of the nrev/2 programs using Delphi lemmas w.r.t. the probability is depicted in figure 1.

Remark that obtaining a variant with Delphi lemmas from a program P is a fully automatic operation if for instance the programmer declares something like:

```
:- delphi(nrev/2, 0.04).
```

specifying the predicates to be memoized and the probability of lemma generation for each of them.

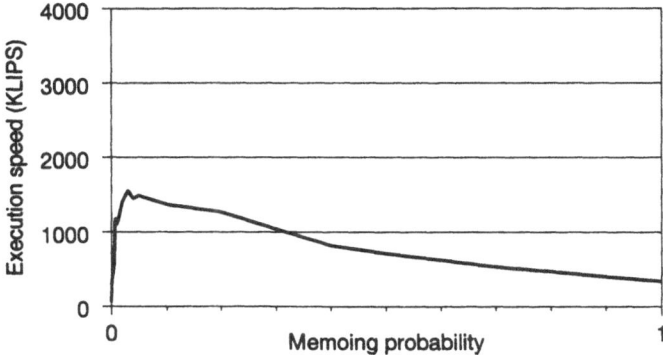

Figure 1: Execution speed of the Delphi lemmas w.r.t. the probability.

6.4   Indexed Delphi lemmas

By combining Delphi lemmas with length-indexing we can see a cumulative
positive speed-up. Computing the length can be partially evaluated away as a
small extra effort for the host predicate. Here is the code obtained for nrev/2.

```
:- ensure_loaded(library(random)).

nrev_lemma(Xs,Ys,Xs1,Ys1,L):-
   nrev_fact(L,Xs,Ys,Xs1,Ys1), !.
nrev_lemma(Xs,Ys,Xs1,Ys1,L):-
   nrev(Xs,Ys,Xs1,Ys1,L),
   make_nrev_lemma(L,Xs1,Ys1).

make_nrev_lemma(L,Xs1,Ys1):-random(X), X>0.04,!.
make_nrev_lemma(L,Xs1,Ys1):-
   copy_term(Xs1+Ys1,Xs2+Ys2),
   asserta(nrev_fact(L,Xs1,Ys1,Xs2,Ys2)).

app([],Ys,Ys,[],Ys1,Ys1).
app([A|Xs],Ys,[A|Zs],[A1|Xs1],Ys1,[A1|Zs1]):-
   app(Xs,Ys,Zs,Xs1,Ys1,Zs1).

nrev([],[],[],[],0).
nrev([X|Xs],R,[X1|Xs1],R1,N):-N1 is N-1,
   nrev_lemma(Xs,T,Xs1,T1,N1),
   app(T,[X],R,T1,[X1],R1).

nrev(Xs,Ys=L+nrev(Xs1,Ys1)):-
   length(Xs,L),
   nrev(Xs,Ys,Xs1,Ys1,L).
```

6.5 Non-copying and lazy-copying techniques

We have also tried to combine Delphi lemmas with BinProlog 1.71's non-copying and lazy-copying blackboard primitives. In BinProlog[6] the programmer has a tighter control on on the copying to the global data area called blackboard.

In the case of **nrev/2**, lemmas are of type 'memoize once, use N times' and are therefore not 'disposable'. However, in the case of more volatile data it is interesting to have lemmas which are used only once. Linear-logic based logic programming languages have the ability to specify this behavior explicitly.

Note that in the absence of backtracking, copying can be avoided if the lemmas are either ground or disposable. In the presence of backtracking, these lemmas must be copied (once) from the heap to the permanent data area (blackboard). Even in this case, structures already on the blackboard are reused by BinProlog's smart copying algorithm.

Hence, in the case of a program that does not backtrack it makes sense to represent lemmas directly as named heap-based data-structures if they are either 'ground' or 'disposable'. This is done easily in BinProlog which replaces **assert** and **retract** by a set of efficient hashing-based 'naming' primitives and a separate set of tunable 'copying' primitives (see [14]).

6.6 Performance results

The execution speeds for the various lemma generation strategies and techniques are given in table 2 normalized from 200 executions on random lists of length 100 with probability 0.04 of Delphi-lemma generation. Although LIPS have no meaning in terms of counting logical inferences (mostly avoided by using the lemmas) we have kept them simply to express the speed-up in familiar terms.

type of lemmas	speed (KLIPS)	speed-up
original **nrev**	145	1.0
naive abstract	358	2.5
length-indexed	1272	8.8
Delphi	1515	10.4
indexed Delphi	1689	11.6
Delphi oracle static code	2525	17.4
human oracle static code	11841	81.7

Table 2: Execution speeds for the abstract lemma techniques on a Sparcstation ELC with Sicstus Prolog 2.1 compact code.

The last two lines are obtained by writing the lemmas to a file and then adding them to the program as static code. They give an idea of the maximum speed-up that can be obtained.

---

[6]a program transformation based continuation passing Prolog compiler available by ftp from clement.info.umoncton.ca.

6.7 Distribution of the generated Delphi lemmas

The probability[7] that a particular lemma is generated is depicted in figure 2. It

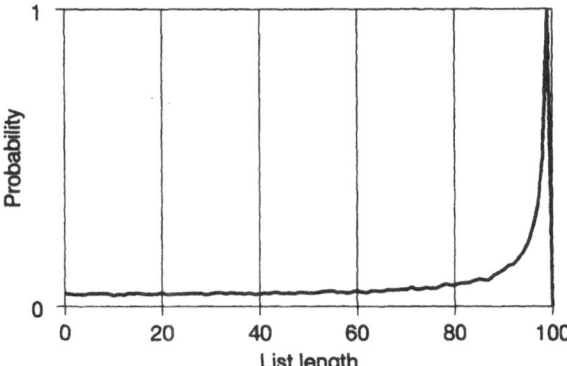

Figure 2: Probability that a lemma of list-length N is generated by the Delphi algorithm.

is obtained with a program running 2 hours and counting lemmas by length. It follows that the Delphi algorithm tends to generate the most efficient lemmas, i.e., the more 'complex' ones in this case with a very high probability. The explanation is basically that for every N, a lemma of length N ensures that no smaller lemmas will be generated while it cannot prevent the generation of larger ones.

7 Extending the approach

We have studied the case of a well-known definite deterministic program as being the simplest instance of this memoing technique. Delphi lemmas have basically the same domain of applicability and limitations as ordinary lemmas. With some care, they can be used in the context of full Prolog, specified as we have suggested by a programmer controlled directive. The program transformations we used should be modified in the case of nondeterministic programs to avoid interference between lemma related pruning and the program's control structure. The concept of abstract answers become also trickier in the presence of Prolog's builtins. Nevertheless, we consider our techniques useful for 'real' programmers as they can accelerate the most critical parts of a program in a significant way and also because they can be fully automated. Delphi lemmas can also complement existing systems with memoing facilities having objectives that are orthogonal to ours, as [17].

---

[7]more precisely: empirical relative frequency

8 Conclusion

We have presented some new memoing techniques and showed their practicality by an empirical study. We do not know about something similar to Delphi-lemmas in functional or procedural languages but the concept can be easily adapted. Although it is a probabilistic concept in the same sense that hashing or Ethernet collision avoidance, it gives very good performances for mostly the same reasons. The technique can be especially beneficial for lemma-intensive theorem proving systems. Future work will focus on integrating our program transformations in BinProlog's preprocessor in a fully automatic way.

Acknowledgement

We are grateful for support from the Canadian National Science and Engineering Research Council (grant OGP0107411) and the FESR of the Université de Moncton. Koen De Bosschere is research assistant with the Belgian National Fund for Scientific Research. Special thanks go to Bart Demoen for pointing out the complexities of lemma generation in the presence of backtracking and his stimulating remarks on a previous version of this paper. We also thank the anonymous referees for their helpful suggestions and constructive criticism.

References

[1] K. Apt. Logic Programming. In J. van Leeuwen, editor, *Handbook of Theoretical Computer Science*, volume B, pages 493–574. Elsevier, North-Holland, 1990.

[2] K. Benkerimi and J. W. Lloyd. A partial evaluation procedure for logic programs. In Debray and Hermenegildo [5], pages 343–358.

[3] M. H. M. Cheng, M. H. van Emden, and B. E. Richards. On Warren's Method for Functional Programming in Logic. In D. H. D. Warren and P. Szeredi, editors, *Proceedings of the Seventh International Conference on Logic Programming*, pages 546–560, Cambridge, Massachusetts London, England, 1990. MIT Press.

[4] M. H. M. Cheng, M. H. van Emden, and P. A. Strooper. Complete Sets of Frontiers in logic-based Program Transformation. In J. W. Lloyd, editor, *Proceedings of the Workshop on Meta-Programming in Logic Programming*, MIT Press Series in Logic Programming, pages 213–225, Cambridge, Massachusetts London, England, 1988. MIT Press.

[5] S. Debray and M. Hermenegildo, editors. *Proceedings of the 1990 North American Conference on Logic Programming*, Cambridge, Massachusetts London, England, 1990. MIT Press.

[6] J. Gallagher and M. Bruynooghe. The derivation of and algorithm for program specialisation. *New Generation Computing*, (9), 1991.

[7] R. S. Kemp and G. A. Ringwood. An Algebraic framework for Abstract Interpretation of Definite Programs. In Debray and Hermenegildo [5], pages 516–530.

[8] H. J. Komorowski. Partial Evaluation as a Means for Inferencing Data Structures in an Applicative Language: A Theory and Implementation in the case of Prolog. In *Proc. of the IXth ACM Symposium on Principles of Programming Languages*. Albuquerque, 1982.

[9] J. W. Lloyd. *Foundations of Logic Programming*. Springer-Verlag, 1987.

[10] J. W. Lloyd and J. C. Shepherdson. Partial evaluation in logic programming. *JLP91*, 11(3,4), October/November 1991.

[11] L. Sterling and E. Shapiro. *The Art of Prolog*. MIT Press, 1986.

[12] H. Tamaki and T. Sato. OLD resolution with tabulation. In E. Shapiro, editor, *Proceedings of the Third International Conference on Logic Programming*, Lecture Notes in Computer Science, pages 84–98, London, 1986. Springer-Verlag.

[13] P. Tarau. *Transformation de programmes logiques. Bases sémantiques et applications*. Phd thesis, Université de Montréal, november 1990.

[14] P. Tarau. Language issues and programming techniques in BinProlog. In D. Sacca, editor, *Proceeding of the GULP'93 Conference*, Gizzeria Lido, Italy, June 1993.

[15] M. H. van Emden. Conditional Answers for Polymorphic Type Inference. In R. A. Kowalski and K. A. Bowen, editors, *Proceedings of the Fifth International Conference and Symposium on Logic Programming*, pages 590–603, Cambridge, Massachusetts London, England, 1988. MIT Press.

[16] D. S. Warren. Memoing for logic programming. *CACM*, 35(3):37–48, March 1992.

[17] D. S. Warren. The XOLDT System. Technical report, SUNY Stony Brook, electronic document: ftp sbcs.sunysb.edu, 1992.

Using Abstract Interpretation for Goal Replacement

Dmitri Boulanger[*]

Department of Computer Science, Katholieke Universiteit Leuven

Heverlee, Belgium

Maurice Bruynooghe[†]

Department of Computer Science, Katholieke Universiteit Leuven

Heverlee, Belgium

Abstract

An abstract interpretation framework for goal replacement in abstract SLD-like derivations is presented. The approach allows to apply correctly goal replacement at static analysis time and to derive non trivial transformations of definite logic programs These transformations are more general than the well known unfold/fold and goal replacement transformations of Tamaki and Sato which are based upon goal replacement in the bodies of clauses. The transformation of a program is controlled by a complete abstract OLDT-like tree. The transformation operations include unfolding/folding and goal replacement.

1 Introduction

The most popular approaches for transforming definite logic programs applying unfold/fold and goal replacement operations on the clauses of a source program. Unfold/fold transformations have been introduced in [4] and were adapted to logic programming in [19, 10, 18]. The recent paper [8][1] revisits the framework developed by Tamaki and Sato.

In this paper we are developing another approach for transforming logic programs. Namely, we split the transformation process in two phases: a first phase performs a complete static data flow analysis of the source program, the second phase uses the results of the first phase to drive the transformation of the source logic program (here we follow some basic ideas of [9]). In [2, 3] we have introduced a rather general and powerful approach to derive unfold/fold transformations of definite logic programs by abstract interpretation. The unfold/fold transformations, which can be obtained in this way, have been shown to be more general than those of Tamaki and Sato. Indeed, as pointed out in [8], SLD-like tree analysis can produce transformations which cannot always be

---

[*]Supported by the Katholieke Universiteit Leuven. Permanent address: Keldysh Institute for Applied Mathematics, Russian Academy of Science, Miusskaya sq., 4, 125047 Moscow, Russia.

[†]Supported by the Belgian National Fund for Scientific Research

[1]The examples presented in this paper show that the approach of Tamaki and Sato is not sound in some cases.

expressed in terms of [19, 10, 18]. However the SLD-like tree analysis of [13, 8] does not allow the derivation of recursive predicates, while in our approach we can easily obtain new recursive predicates generating transformations, which can be better than those of [16, 17]. Moreover, it can be shown that, by restricting the static analysis phase, our transformation algorithm reduces to that [7]. The main motivation of the paper is to facilitate the application of goal replacement operations when constructing the OLDT-like trees during the static analysis phase. This results in a rather powerful framework for transforming logic programs which is based on abstract interpretation.

But there is a serious problem when attempting to incorporate goal replacement operations in our framework. In order to perform the static analysis, we need complete finite SLD-like trees, which are constructed by abstracting or generalising certain parts of the concrete derivations. This creates a problem when attempting to apply goal replacement in partially abstracted derivations.

The problem with goal replacement in partially abstracted OLDT-like derivations is that the conditions for correct goal replacement are very strict. One needs exact information about the binding of certain crucial variables occurring in the goal to be replaced. The latter is not always the case for abstract derivations as described in [3]. Consequently, analysis time can only suggest goal replacement. Some conditions have to be checked at transformation time. Moreover, part of the analysis has to be redone when these conditions are violated. The central idea of our approach is to provide a proof that the crucial variables are not influenced by the abstraction of some parts of the derivation. In order to implement this idea we introduce a special abstract interpretation domain, which includes abstract and concrete variables.

The rest of the paper is organised as follows. After some preliminaries, where we introduce some basic concepts, the conditions for goal replacement in SLD-like derivations are described in section 3. Here we introduce necessary conditions for the soundness and completeness of goal replacement for a special variant of the SLD resolution. Section 4 presents our abstract interpretation technique — we show how the soundness and completeness of the goal replacement can be ensured at static analysis time, i.e. for partially abstracted derivations. An extensive example, which illustrates all the most important details of goal replacement in abstract derivations, can also be found in this section.

2 Preliminaries

In what follows the standard terminology and the basic knowledge of the theory of logic programming, as can be found in [14], is assumed. We will use the standard notions of SLD derivation and refutation, unification and substitution. Some knowledge concerning OLDT resolution [20, 11] and goal replacement [19, 10, 18, 8] will be important.

We consider a definite logic program P to be a collection of definite clauses $\{c_1, \ldots, c_n\}$ equipped with an initial goal G_0. The successive goals in a SLD derivation for the initial goal wrt P will be denoted by G_i, $i = 0, 1, \ldots, n$.

The capital letters B, Q and R will be used to denote conjunctions of atoms, which will be considered as collections and are called *blocks* in the sequel. $B(\overline{X})$ will denote a conjunction of atoms B, where $\overline{X}$ is the set of variables occurring in B. By $var(E)$ we denote the set of variables, occurring in the syntactical object E. The greek letters θ, σ and φ will be used to denote substitutions. Given a substitution θ, $\theta \mid_{var(E)}$ will denote the restriction of the substitution θ to the variables occurring in E.

In the sequel, by equivalent programs we mean programs giving the same computed answer substitutions for the initial goal of the program [15].

3 Goal Replacement for Extended OLD resolution

In this section we discuss goal replacement in SLD-like derivations and the possibility to apply tabulation for this kind of derivations. Extended OLD resolution deviates from standard SLD resolution only by imposing certain restrictions on the computation rule.

Namely, the SLD derivation $G_0 \xrightarrow{c_1 \ \theta_1} G_1 \ldots \xrightarrow{c_n \ \theta_n} G_n$ is an $EOLD$ derivation for the initial goal G_0 wrt a definite logic program P provided that any goal G_i in the derivation is represented as an *ordered* sequence $< B_1, B_2, ..., B_m >$, $m \geq 0$ of conjunctions of atoms (blocks) and the computation rule always selects an atom from the first block. A block will always be considered as a *non empty collection* of atoms. Given a goal G represented as an ordered sequence of blocks, $\|G\|$ will denote the collection of all atoms occurring in G (In OLD resolution [20, 11] blocks have only one atom). In the sequel we do not distinguish atoms, blocks and goals which differ only by a variable renaming. The following definition gives a more precise description of an $EOLD$ resolution step.

Definition 1 *EOLD Resolution Step*
Let G_i be a goal represented as $< B_1, B_2, \ldots, B_m >$, $m \geq 1$, A an atom selected from B_1, c_{i+1} a standardised apart input clause from P and θ_{i+1} the *mgu* of A and the head of the clause c_{i+1}. Then G_{i+1} is derived from G_i and c_{i+1} using *mgu* θ_{i+1} via the $EOLD$ computation rule if G_{i+1} is obtained by applying the following two steps:

- construct the goal $G' = < B_1', \ldots, B_n' >$, where

  if B_1 is singleton and the body of c_{i+1} is empty then $n = m - 1$, $B_i' = B_{i+1}$, $1 \leq i \leq n$
  else $n = m$, $B_1' = B_1$ with A replaced by the body of c_{i+1} and $B_i' = B_i$, $1 \leq i \leq m$

- partition B_1' into arbitrary chosen non empty parts (the new blocks) $B_{11}', \ldots, B_{1k}'$, $k \geq 1$ and let $G_{i+1} = < B_{11}', \ldots, B_{1k}', B_2', \ldots, B_n' > \theta_{i+1}$, i.e. the first block can be splitted in a sequence of new non empty blocks.

□

Notice that if a goal G of the $EOLD$ refutation is splitted in a sequence of several blocks, then atoms not occurring in the first block of G can be selected only after the first block is completely refuted. This property is crucial for the following definition, which will play an important role in the sequel.

Definition 2 *EOLD Subrefutation*

An *EOLD* subderivation of the form $G_i \xrightarrow{c_{i+1} \ \theta_{i+1}} G_{i+1} \ldots \xrightarrow{c_n \ \theta_n} G_n$ is an *EOLD* subrefutation for the first block B_1 of the goal $G_i = < B_1, B_2, \ldots B_k >$, $k \geq 1$ if either $G_n = <>$ and $k = 1$ (i.e. the subderivation is a refutation for B_1) or $\| < B_2, \ldots B_k > \theta_{i+1} \ldots \theta_n \| = \|G_n\|$ and there is no goal G_j, $i < j < n$ having this property in the subderivation. $\square$

This definition implies that a block can be considered as an "extended" atom having a subrefutation including only resolution steps which are necessary to refute atoms occurring in the block. This is a crucial observation when combining *EOLD* resolution with tabulation.

Notice that *EOLD* resolution is sound and complete because soundness and completeness of SLD resolution is independent from the computation rule [14].

In what follows we address the problem of correct goal replacement for *EOLD* derivations. When replacing some atoms of the current goal of a derivation, the connection between variables occurring in these atoms on one hand, and the variables occurring in the initial goal and the remaining part of the current goal on the other hand, are crucial for the correctness of the replacement. The following definition identifies variables which can be safely dropped in a goal replacement operation.

Definition 3 *Local variables in a EOLD derivation*

Given an *EOLD* derivation $G_0 \xrightarrow{c_1 \ \theta_1} G_1 \ldots \xrightarrow{c_n \ \theta_n} G_n$ for the initial goal G_0 and the corresponding accumulated substitution $\sigma_n = \theta_1 \ldots \theta_n$, a variable X occurring in the goal G_n, $n > 0$ is local to G_n iff the variable X does not occur outside the first block of the goal G_n and for all bindings $Y \leftarrow t \in \sigma_n$ holds: $X \in var(Y \leftarrow t)$ implies $var(Y \leftarrow t) \cap var(G_0) = \emptyset$, i.e. X does not occur in $var(G_0)$ and it is *not connected* by the accumulated substitution to the variables of the initial goal.

The set of local variables in the goal G_i of the derivation $G_0 \rightarrow G_1, \ldots, G_i$ will be denoted by $local(G_i)$, $i = 0, \ldots, n$. The set of all non local variables occurring in the goal G_i will be denoted by $\neg local(G_i)$. $\square$

Example 1 Consider the goals in the "skeleton" of an *EOLD* derivation and the corresponding sets of local variables:

- $G_0 = < B_0(X) >$ $local(G_0) = \emptyset$

  ↓ $\theta_1 = \{\}$

- $G_1 = < B_1(Y, Z), B_2(X, Z, U), B_3(X, U) >$ $local(G_1) = \{Y\}$

  ↓ $\theta_2 = \{Y \leftarrow Z\}$

- $G_2 = < B_2(X, Z, U), B_3(X, U) >$ $local(G_2) = \{Z\}$

  ↓ $\theta_3 = \{X \leftarrow f(Z), U \leftarrow g(Z)\}$

- $G_3 = < B_3'(Z) >$ $local(G_3) = \emptyset$

Notice that $G_1 \rightarrow G_2$ is the subrefutation for the block B_1 and $G_2 \rightarrow G_3$ is the subrefutation for block B_2, where $B_3'(Z) = B_3(X, U)\theta_3 = B_3(f(Z), g(Z))$. $\square$

The following definition (it is a slightly weaker version of that [8], see below) simply claims what goals should be considered as equivalent ones.

Definition 4 *Permissible lemma*

Given a definite logic program P, a lemma L of the form

$$Q(\overline{X}, \overline{Y}) \longleftrightarrow R(\overline{X}, \overline{Z}), \ \overline{X} \cap \overline{Y} = \overline{X} \cap \overline{Z} = \overline{Y} \cap \overline{Z} = \emptyset$$

is a permissible lemma wrt P provided that for all substitutions σ

- $P \models \forall Q\sigma$ implies $P \models \forall R\varphi$ for some substitution φ such that $\varphi \mid_{\overline{X}} = \sigma \mid_{\overline{X}}$
- $P \models \forall R\sigma$ implies $P \models \forall Q\varphi$ for some substitution φ such that $\varphi \mid_{\overline{X}} = \sigma \mid_{\overline{X}}$

□

This definition implies that if a permissible lemma is used to reconstruct the current goal of a derivation then the number and the order of the answers for the initial goal is *not* preserved. The preservation of the number and the order of answers is considered to be important when dealing with Prolog programs in the context of partial evaluation (cf. [13]). On the other hand the latter can be very restrictive when deriving non trivial transformations similar to [16, 17, 1, 5].

Example 2 Consider the following definite logic program P

$$app([\ ], L, L).$$
$$app([H|T], L, [H|X]) \leftarrow app(T, L, X).$$

The lemma $L: app(X, [H], D), app(D, L, Y) \longleftrightarrow app(X, [H|L], Y)$ is a permissible lemma wrt P, where $\overline{X} = \{X, Y, L, H\}$, $\overline{Y} = \{D\}$ and $\overline{Z} = \emptyset$. □

In the sequel we will consider definite logic programs P equipped with a set $\mathcal{L}_P$ of lemmas permissible wrt P. We will also assume, that the set of permissible lemmas $\mathcal{L}_P$ satisfies the following simple conditions[2]:

- any lemma $L \in \mathcal{L}_P$ has the "clausal" form $Q \leftarrow R$, i.e. it can only be applied to replace the goal Q by the goal R (cf. def.5 below), but not vice versa.

- for any two lemmas $L, L' \in \mathcal{L}_P$ having the forms $Q \leftarrow R$ and $Q' \leftarrow R'$ respectively holds that Q and Q' are not unifiable.

A lemma can be applied to the first block of the current goal only if it preserves bindings for the variables occurring in the initial goal (def.4 does not ensure this). Consider the following definition:

Definition 5 *Correct lemma application*
Given the current goal $G_n = < Q(\overline{X}, \overline{Y}), B_2, \ldots, B_m >$ of an $EOLD$ derivation wrt a definite logic program P, the replacement of the goal G_n by the goal $G'_n = < R(\overline{X}, \overline{Z}), B_2, \ldots, B_m >$ using a renaming of a permissible lemma from $\mathcal{L}_P$ of the form $Q(\overline{X}, \overline{Y}) \leftarrow R(\overline{X}, \overline{Z})$ is correct if $\overline{Y} \subseteq local(G_n)$ and the variables $\overline{Z}$ are fresh variables. The variables $\overline{Y}$ are said to be *dead end* variables.
□

---

[2] These conditions are not strictly necessary – we use them to simplify the definitions and the proofs below. The first condition is necessary to avoid the introducing of trivial loops by lemma application, while the second one is used to make lemma application deterministic.

The $EOLD$ resolution with correct application of the permissible lemmas is intended to be an extension of the normal $EOLD$ resolution. The definition below gives more details:

Definition 6 *EOLD resolution with lemma application*
Given a definite logic program P, the corresponding set of permissible lemmas $\mathcal{L}_P$ and an initial goal G_0, the $EOLD$ resolution with lemma application deviates from the $EOLD$ resolution (cf. def.1) by imposing the following restriction upon the computation rule: if there exists a renaming of a lemma $L \in \mathcal{L}_P$ having the form $Q \leftarrow R$, such that it can be applied correctly to the first block of the current goal (the latter means that the block has to be identical to Q), then it *has* to be applied (the first block Q has to be replaced by block R), i.e. the clauses of the program P are not allowed to be used for resolving atoms of Q .
$\Box$

Example 3 Consider example 2. Then the following sequence is the part of an $EOLD$ derivation with (correct) lemma application
● $\cdots$
↓ $c_i : \theta_i = \{\ldots\}$
● $G_i = <\ |app(X, [H], D), app(D, L, Y)|\cdots>$
⇓ $L \in \mathcal{L}_P : \theta_{i+1} = \{\}$
● $G_{i+1} = <\ |app(X, [H|L], Y)|\cdots>$
↓
● $\cdots$

provided that the dead end variable D is local to the goal G_i (the blocks in the goals above are separated by the symbol "|"). $\Box$

In the sequel we will denote a definite logic program P equipped with a set of permissible lemmas $\mathcal{L}_P$ by $P \oplus \mathcal{L}_P$. If the set $\mathcal{L}_P$ is empty, then $EOLD$ resolution with lemma application (it will be denoted by $EOLD_{\mathcal{L}}$) wrt $P \oplus \mathcal{L}_P$ is exactly $EOLD$ resolution (def.1), but if the set of lemmas $\mathcal{L}_P$ is not empty, then in general completeness cannot be ensured. The following proposition shows, that permissibility of the lemmas from $\mathcal{L}_P$ and correctness of their application in $EOLD_{\mathcal{L}}$ derivations are sufficient to ensure the soundness of $EOLD_{\mathcal{L}}$ resolution. However, completeness is not ensured as example 4 below shows.

Proposition 1 *Consider a definite logic program P, an initial goal G_0 and a set $\mathcal{L}_P$ of permissible lemmas: if the goal G_0 has an $EOLD_{\mathcal{L}}$ refutation $\mathcal{R}_{\mathcal{L}}$ wrt $P \oplus \mathcal{L}_P$ with computed answer substitution $\theta_{\mathcal{L}}$, then the goal G_0 has an $EOLD$ refutation $\mathcal{R}$ with computed answer substitution θ, such that $G_0\theta = G_0\theta_{\mathcal{L}}$.*
Proof The proof is by induction on the number of lemma application in the refutation $\mathcal{R}_{\mathcal{L}}$.
Base Case. If the refutation $\mathcal{R}_{\mathcal{L}}$ does not contain lemma applications it is a an $EOLD$ refutation. Thus, the proposition holds for $n = 0$.
Induction Step. Assume the proposition holds for $EOLD_{\mathcal{L}}$ refutations with $n-1$ lemma applications. Consider a refutation $\mathcal{R}_{\mathcal{L}}$ with n lemma applications. Let $G_i = < Q(\overline{X}, \overline{Y})|B_2|, \ldots, |B_n| >$ be the goal where the first lemma application is performed with the lemma $Q(\overline{X}, \overline{Y}) \leftarrow R(\overline{X}, \overline{Z})$. Let θ denote the substitution accumulated at G_i. Then we have $G_{i+1} = < R(\overline{X}, \overline{Z})|B_2|, \ldots, |B_n| >$.

After completion of the subrefutation for $R(\overline{X}, \overline{Z})$ with accumulated substitution φ (it has at most $n - 1$ lemma applications) we obtain the goal $G_j = <\ |B_2|, \ldots, |B_n|\ > \varphi$. Because $\overline{Z}$ is local in G_{i+1} we have $\theta\varphi = \theta\varphi|_{\overline{X}}$ and $<\ |B_2|, \ldots, |B_n|\ > \varphi = <\ |B_2|, \ldots, |B_n|\ > \varphi_{\overline{X}}$.

The induction hypothesis is applicable on the subrefutation for $R(\overline{X}, \overline{Z})$, so an $EOLD$ refutation exists for this goal. As the lemma is permissible, there exists an $EOLD$ refutation for $Q(\overline{X}, \overline{Y})$ with accumulated substitution σ such that $\sigma|_{\overline{X}} = \varphi|_{\overline{X}}$.

Now we can change the refutation as follows: starting from the goal G_i, we use the subrefutation for $Q(\overline{X}, \overline{Y})$ with accumulated substitution σ. This leads to the goal $G'_j = <\ |B_2|, \ldots, |B_n|\ > \sigma$. Because $\overline{Y}$ is local in G_i, we have $<\ |B_2|, \ldots, |B_n|\ > \sigma = <\ |B_2|, \ldots, |B_n|\ > \sigma|_{\overline{X}} = G'_j$, and as $\sigma|_{\overline{X}} = \varphi|_{\overline{X}}$, we have $G_j = G'_j$.

Thus from here on we can resume the original refutation as it continued from G_j. With ρ the substitution accumulated in the remainder of the refutation, we obtain correct answer substitution $\theta\sigma\rho|_{var(G_0)} = (\theta\sigma|_{\overline{X}}\rho)|_{var(G_0)}$ which is identical to the $\theta\varphi\rho$ of the original refutation as $\theta\varphi\rho|_{var(G_0)} = (\theta\varphi|_{\overline{X}}\rho)|_{var(G_0)}$ and $\sigma|_{\overline{X}} = \varphi|_{\overline{X}}$.

So we now have an $EOLD_{\mathcal{L}}$ refutation with at most $n - 1$ lemma applications. Applying the induction hypothesis shows that an $EOLD$ refutation exists. This completes the proof. $\square$

The following example shows that the permissibility and correctness of lemma application are not sufficient to ensure the completeness of the $EOLD_{\mathcal{L}}$ resolution. The completeness can be lost due to the "loops" which can be introduced into derivations by lemma application. The following example gives some hints what kind of extra conditions are necessary.

Example 4 Given the definite logic program

$$P : \{\ p(a).\ p(X) \leftarrow q(X).\ q(a).\ q(f(X)) \leftarrow q(X).\ \},$$

the lemma $L : q(X) \leftarrow p(X)$ is a permissible lemma whose application is always correct. However *any* $EOLD_{\mathcal{L}}$ refutation wrt $P \oplus \{q(X) \leftarrow p(X)\}$ for the initial goal $p(X)$ has only $\{X \leftarrow a\}$ as a computed answer substitution, i.e. the set of answer substitutions is not complete for the initial goal $p(X)$. Notice that incompleteness is due to tautologies (or loops) occurring in the derivations with lemma application. $\square$

The following definition introduces extra conditions, which ensure the completeness of the $EOLD_{\mathcal{L}}$ resolution (there is an example below).

Definition 7 *Safe set of lemmas*
A set $\mathcal{L}_P$ of lemmas permissible wrt a definite logic program P is said to be safe if for any lemma $L \in \mathcal{L}_P$ having the form $Q(\overline{X}, \overline{Y}) \longleftarrow R(\overline{X}, \overline{Z})$ holds: if the goal Q has an $EOLD$ refutation with computed answer substitution θ, then the goal R has an $EOLD_{\mathcal{L}}$ refutation wrt $P \oplus \mathcal{L}_P$ with computed answer substitution $\theta_{\mathcal{L}}$ such that $\theta\ |_{\overline{X}} = \theta_{\mathcal{L}}\ |_{\overline{X}}$. $\square$

The condition above is very close to that of [8] and is likely as permissive (a detailed comparison is not possible due to the basic difference in the approaches, see the discussion below).

Notice that for the permissible lemma L: $q(X) \leftarrow p(X)$ from example 4 holds: if $q(X)$ has an $EOLD$ refutation, then $p(X)$ has an $EOLD_{\mathcal{L}}$ refutation. But not all computed answer substitutions of $EOLD$ refutations for $q(X)$ are covered by the $EOLD_{\mathcal{L}}$ refutations of $p(X)$. On the other hand, if the clause $p(f(X)) \leftarrow p(X)$ is added to the program P, the lemma set $\{\ q(X) \leftarrow p(X)\ \}$ is safe and $EOLD_{\mathcal{L}}$ resolution wrt $P \cup \{p(f(X)) \leftarrow p(X)\} \oplus \{q(X) \leftarrow p(X)\}$ becomes complete. Although the lemma L introduces a loop, it is not a dangerous one due to the added clause (The conditions of [8] can be used to produce exactly the same results for this example). Notice that the lemma set $\{\ q(X) \leftarrow p(X)\ \ p(X) \leftarrow q(X)\ \}$ is not safe, i.e. it introduces a "dangerous" loop.

The safety of the set of permissible lemmas combined with the $EOLD$ computation rule ensure the completeness of $EOLD_{\mathcal{L}}$ resolution:

Proposition 2 *Consider a definite logic program P, an initial goal G_0 and a safe set $\mathcal{L}_P$ of lemmas. If the goal G_0 has an $EOLD$ refutation $\mathcal{R}$ with computed answer substitution θ then the goal G_0 has an $EOLD_{\mathcal{L}}$ refutation $\mathcal{R}_{\mathcal{L}}$ wrt $P \oplus \mathcal{L}_P$ with computed answer substitution $\theta_{\mathcal{L}}$, such that $\theta \mid_{var(G_0)} = \theta_{\mathcal{L}} \mid_{var(G_0)}$.*
Proof Let $\mathcal{R}$ be an $EOLD$ refutation for G_0. Consider the first goal G in $\mathcal{R}$ such that its first block Q can be replaced correctly by a permissible lemma L from $\mathcal{L}_P$ (if such goal G does not exist, then $\mathcal{R}$ is an $EOLD_{\mathcal{L}}$ refutation). Then the safety of the set $\mathcal{L}_P$ ensures that the $EOLD$ subrefutation of Q can be replaced by the corresponding $EOLD_{\mathcal{L}}$ subrefutation. The remaining part of $\mathcal{R}$ can be treated in the same way obtaining a derivation, which is an $EOLD_{\mathcal{L}}$ refutation having the desired computed answer substitution.
□

It is important to notice, that the completeness result above relies on the restrictions imposed by the $EOLD$ computation rule (cf. def. 1 and 2). Consider the following example:

Example 5 Given the definite logic program P : $\{\ p(a).\ q(a).\ \}$. The set

$$\{\ L_1 : p(X) \leftarrow q(X) \quad L_2 : q(X), q(Y) \leftarrow p(X), p(Y)\ \}$$

is a safe set $\mathcal{L}_P$ of permissible lemmas wrt P. If $EOLD$ restrictions are dropped, then there exists a computation rule such that the initial goal $q(X), q(Y)$ has only the following infinite derivation wrt $P \oplus \mathcal{L}_P$(it can be considered as a infinitely failed derivation):

$$< \underline{q(X), q(Y)} > \xrightarrow{L_2} < \underline{p(X)}, p(Y) > \xrightarrow{L_1} < q(X), \underline{p(Y)} > \xrightarrow{L_1} < \underline{q(X), q(Y)} > \ldots$$

Notice that the derivation above is not an $EOLD_{\mathcal{L}}$ derivation, because the attempt to refute the atom $p(Y)$ occurring in the third goal is made before the refutation of the firstly selected atom $p(X)$ of the second goal is complete. □

The *EOLD* restrictions upon the computation rule (cf. def. 1) combined with the conditions above, which ensure the soundness and completeness of the EOLDL resolution imply the following proposition:

Proposition 3 *Let P be a definite logic program, G_0 an initial goal and $\mathcal{L}_P$ a safe set of lemmas. Suppose there is an $EOLD_\mathcal{L}$ refutation for $P \oplus \mathcal{L}_P \cup G_0$ with computed answer substitution σ. Then for any $EOLD_\mathcal{L}$ computation rule R (i.e. the specification of the choice of the selected atom in the first block and of the way the first block is splitted in a sequence of new blocks) there exists an $EOLD_\mathcal{L}$ refutation for $P \oplus \mathcal{L}_P \cup G_0$ via R with R-computed answer substitution σ' such that $G_0\sigma = G_0\sigma'$.*
Proof The proof can be obtained from the independence of the computation rule of the *EOLD* resolution combined with the soundness and completeness of the $EOLD_\mathcal{L}$ resolution.
□

In general, the safety conditions for the set of permissible lemmas (def. 7) are rather difficult to verify. So the following definition gives more restrictive conditions, which are still sufficiently interesting for a lot of applications and can be checked more easily:

Definition 8 *Set of non trivial permissible lemmas*
A set $\mathcal{L}_P$ of lemmas permissible wrt a definite logic program P, is said to be a set of non trivial lemmas iff for each lemma $L \in \mathcal{L}_P$ of the form $Q \leftarrow R$ holds:

- Q and R are not unifiable

- there is no *EOLD* derivation of the form $< |R| > \xrightarrow{c_1} \ldots \xrightarrow{c_n} < |Q|, Rest >$

- $EOLD_\mathcal{L}$ derivations of the form $< |R| > \rightarrow \ldots \rightarrow G$ do not contain lemma application steps.

□

It is not difficult to show that any set of non trivial lemmas is a safe set of lemmas. The lemma from example 2 is a non trivial lemma. To be convinced in this it is sufficient to notice that the atom *app* cannot be expanded to *app, app* using clauses of the program P.
The main result of this section is that $EOLD_\mathcal{L}$ resolution can be equipped with a tabulation mechanism, which is applied to blocks in exactly the same way as OLD resolution [20, 11] is equipped with a tabulation mechanism applied to atoms. Def. 1 and 2 ensure that tabulation applied to blocks is sound and complete provided that $EOLD_\mathcal{L}$ resolution is sound and complete wrt the given definite logic program and set of lemmas. Indeed, the *EOLD* restrictions upon the computation rule allow to treat blocks as atoms, while the permissibility and safety conditions allow to treat lemmas as ordinary clauses. The exact proof of the completeness, soundness and independence of the properly restricted computation rule of the $EOLDT_\mathcal{L}$ resolution ($EOLD_\mathcal{L}$ with tabulation) can be obtained by a slight modification of that in [20, 11].
The purpose of the development of the $EOLDT_\mathcal{L}$ resolution mechanism is its application during static analysis to obtain a guide for logic program transformation. This approach allows to integrate powerful unfold/fold transformations with lemma applications. The unfold/fold transformations of definite

logic programs, which can be derived using abstract complete $EOLDT$ tree are described in [2, 3]. This kind of transformations is more powerful than that of [19, 8]. On the other hand, the conditions for correct goal replacement presented above are very close to those of [8]. However our approach has the following advantages when used for program transformations using the finite (abstract) $EOLDT_{\mathcal{L}}$ tree as a guide:

- Our framework makes use of the connectivity of the variables occurring in the derivation preceding a goal replacement step rather than the relations between the variables in the input clause of the resolvent. This makes our conditions less restrictive.

- Taking into account the whole derivation up to the current goal captures implicitly some influence of the initial goal, and thus allows some replacements, which do not satisfy the conditions of [8], because the latter deals with preservation of minimal models rather than preservation of answers wrt the initial goal.

A more detailed and precise comparison with the approaches of [19, 8] is rather difficult, because the latter deals with particular clauses of the source program and addresses the problem of replacing a goal in the body of a clause. In our setting the properties of the derivations are used to ensure equivalence of the source program and the transformed program. The latter allows to apply abstract interpretation for deriving transformations which preserve the set of computed answer substitutions for the variables of the initial goal. The main problem in our approach is to obtain a finite complete abstract $EOLD_{\mathcal{L}}$ tree, which is a correct representation of the concrete one (the latter can be infinite). The next section is devoted to the abstract interpretation framework based upon $EOLDT_{\mathcal{L}}$ resolution and presents an example of the transformation based upon unfold/fold and goal replacement operations, which are derived from the abstract finite $EOLDT_{\mathcal{L}}$ tree.

4 Deriving Transformations Using Abstract Interpretation

In this section we introduce a special abstract interpretation framework which is based upon $EOLDT_{\mathcal{L}}$ resolution and suitable for lemma application during static analysis of definite logic programs. It is developed keeping the conditions for correct lemma application in mind. The basic abstract interpretation device is $EOLD$ resolution equipped with a tabulation mechanism and applied to an abstract domain, which includes abstract and concrete terms.

The abstract finite $EOLDT_{\mathcal{L}}$ tree constructed for a program P, initial goal G_0 with (possible) applications of lemmas from $\mathcal{L}_P$ can be used to derive the corresponding transformation of P. This transformation preserves the set of answer substitutions for the variables of the initial goal provided that abstract interpretation represents the concrete one. So the main topic of this section is the development of conditions for correct abstract interpretation. (The framework which does not allow lemma application during abstract interpretation was introduced in [2, 3].) We start with a presentation of a special abstract interpretation domain.

4.1 Mixed Abstract Terms and Substitutions

Given a countable set of *concrete variables* $\mathcal{V}$ and a finite set of function symbols $\mathcal{F}$, the set of concrete terms *Term* is defined as usual [14]. We extend the notion of terms by introducing a countable set of *abstract variables* $\mathcal{W}$ such that $\mathcal{V} \cap \mathcal{W} = \emptyset$. The central idea of the framework is to distinguish at compile time between abstract variables which are intended to be used for representation of imprecise information about the possible bindings, and concrete variables with the real run-time bindings. An superscript α will be used to distinguish abstract variables, for example W^α.

The *set of mixed abstract terms* $Term^{mix}$ is constructed from the set of function symbols $\mathcal{F}$ and the set of variables $\mathcal{V} \cup \mathcal{W}$. *Mixed abstract expressions* over the set $Term^{mix}$ are defined in the standard way.

Definition 9 *Recognition*
A legal assignment for mixed abstract term t^{mix} with a set of abstract variables $W_1^\alpha, \ldots, W_n^\alpha$ is a substitution $\rho = \{W_1^\alpha \leftarrow t_1, \ldots, W_n^\alpha \leftarrow t_n\}$ such that

$$var(t^{mix}) \cap var\{t_1, \ldots, t_n\} = \emptyset.$$

A legal assignment ρ maps a mixed abstract term t^{mix} into a concrete term $t^{mix}\rho$. □

The *concretization* of a mixed abstract term t^{mix} can be defined as follows: $\gamma(t^{mix}) = \{t \in Term \mid t^{mix} \text{ recognises } t \text{ via some legal assignment}\}$.

A *mixed abstract substitution* is a mapping $\theta^{mix} : \mathcal{W} \cup \mathcal{V} \mapsto Term^{mix}$ such that the domain $dom(\theta^{mix}) = \{U \in \mathcal{W}_T \cup \mathcal{V} \mid \theta^{mix}(U) \neq U\}$ is finite. The application of a substitution to a mixed abstract term $t\theta^{mix}$ (or to a mixed abstract expression) is defined as usual.

Definition 10 *Preorder on the set of mixed abstract terms and substitutions*
Given mixed abstract terms t, t_1, t_2 and mixed abstract substitutions θ_1, θ_2

- $t_1 \unlhd t_2$ if and only if $\gamma(t_1) \subseteq \gamma(t_2)$

- $t_1 \sim t_2$ if and only if $t_1 \unlhd t_2$ and $t_2 \unlhd t_1$.

- $\theta_1 \unlhd \theta_2$ if and only if for any mixed abstract term t holds $t\theta_1 \unlhd t\theta_2$ (θ_2 is said to be *more general* than θ_1)

- $\theta_1 \sim \theta_2$ if and only if $\theta_1 \unlhd \theta_2$ and $\theta_2 \unlhd \theta_1$.

□

A safe abstract interpretation mechanism is based on the notions of unifier and most general unifier. Namely, we have the following property for mixed abstract terms: given two mixed abstract terms t_1 and t_2 such that the concrete terms $\rho_1(t_1)$ and $\rho_2(t_2)$ are unifiable for some legal assignments ρ_1 and ρ_2, there exists a mixed abstract substitution σ such that $t_1\sigma = t_2\sigma$ (the *mixed abstract unifier* of t_1 and t_2) and there exist a unique, up to the variable renaming, most general mixed abstract unifier σ' such that it is more general than any other unifier σ of t_1 and t_2. Then the following proposition is obvious:

Proposition 4 *Given two mixed abstract terms t_1 and t_2 with mgu σ. Any pair of mixed abstract terms t'_1 and t'_2 such that $t_1 \trianglelefteq t'_1$ and $t_2 \trianglelefteq t'_2$ have a mgu σ' such that $\sigma \trianglelefteq \sigma'$.* $\square$

The following example illustrates the notion of most general unifier:

Example 6 $\sigma = mgu(W^\alpha, X) = \{X \leftarrow W^\alpha\}$ and $\sigma' = \{W^\alpha \leftarrow X\}$ is only a unifier of X and W^α because $X \trianglelefteq W^\alpha$. $\square$

4.2 Mixed Abstract EOLD Resolution with Lemma Application

Before introducing our correct goal replacement technique in abstract $EOLD_{\mathcal{L}}$ derivations we introduce some basic notions, such as mixed abstract program and set of mixed abstract lemmas.

A *mixed abstract definite logic program* P^{mix} is a set of mixed abstract clauses (mixed abstract expressions) over the set of terms $Term^{mix}$. For example, $\{p(U^\alpha) \leftarrow true\}$, is a mixed abstract definite logic program. The program $P^{mix} = \{c_1^{mix}, \ldots, c_n^{mix}\}$ recognises the concrete program $P = \{c_1, \ldots, c_n\}$, i.e $P \in \gamma(P^{mix})$, if there exist legal assignments $\rho_1, \ldots, \rho_n$, such that $c_i = \rho_i(c_i^{mix})$, $i = 1, \ldots n$. A *set of mixed abstract lemmas* $\mathcal{L}_P^{mix}$ is defined in exactly the same way.

Given a mixed abstract program P^{mix} and a mixed abstract initial goal G_0^{mix}, a mixed abstract $EOLD$ derivation is the same as an $EOLD$ derivation provided that the notions of mixed abstract term and the corresponding notion of most general unifier are used (cf. def. 1). The definition of subrefutation (def. 2) is also applicable without any modifications. The proposition 4 ensures correctness of these definitions.

As could be seen from section 3, correct lemma application requires special conditions to be satisfied. The following definition prevents the abstraction of dead end variables.

Definition 11 *Local variables of mixed abstract EOLD derivation*

Given a mixed abstract $EOLD$ derivation $G_0^{mix} \xrightarrow{c_1^{mix} \ \theta_1^{mix}} G_1^{mix} \ldots \xrightarrow{c_n^{mix} \ \theta_n^{mix}} G_n^{mix}$ with accumulated substitution σ_n^{mix}, a variable V occurring in the goal G_n^{mix} is a local variable if it is a concrete variable and if:

- the variable V is not connected via σ_n^{mix} to any non local variable occurring in the initial goal G_0^{mix}

- the variable V does not occur outside the first block of the goal G_n^{mix}

- the variable V is not connected via σ_n^{mix} to any abstract variable occurring in the derivation

$\square$

The main property of a mixed abstract $EOLD$ resolution is its correctness wrt the concrete one. The following proposition is an immediate consequence of the proposition 4 and the definition above:

Proposition 5 *Given a mixed abstract definite logic program P^{mix} with a mixed abstract initial goal G_0^{mix}, a concrete program $P \in \gamma(P^{mix})$ with a concrete initial goal $G_0 \in \gamma(G_0^{mix})$. If there is a concrete EOLD derivation $\mathcal{D}$ of the form*

$$G_0 \xrightarrow{c_1 \ \theta_1} G_1 \ldots \xrightarrow{c_n \ \theta_n} G_n,$$

then there exists a mixed abstract EOLD derivation $\mathcal{D}^{mix}$ of the form

$$G_0^{mix} \xrightarrow{c_1^{mix} \ \theta_1^{mix}} G_1^{mix} \ldots \xrightarrow{c_n^{mix} \ \theta_n^{mix}} G_n^{mix},$$

and a legal assignment ρ such that $c_i = \rho(c_i^{mix})$, $G_i = \rho(G_i^{mix})$, $local(G_i) \supseteq local(G_i^{mix})$ and $\theta_i \trianglelefteq \theta_i^{mix}$ for all $i = 0, 1, \ldots, n$. The derivation $\mathcal{D}$ is said to be represented by the derivation $\mathcal{D}^{mix}$.

Proof The proof is a standard one (see, for example, [9]) and can be obtained by induction on the length of the derivations, if the following property of the proposed abstract interpretation framework is taken into account: a legal assignment always introduces fresh variables (see def. 9).
□

Let us provide some important remarks concerning the proposition above. Firstly, notice that the recognition is basically a recognition of the derivation as a whole, i.e. multiple occurrences of variables in the goals have to be concretized simultaneously. Secondly, if there is an occurrence of a local variable in the mixed abstract derivation then this variable always is a local variable in the corresponding concrete derivation. The latter observation is crucial for correct lemma application during abstract interpretation. The following definition gives the properties of the lemmas which should be used during abstract interpretation:

Definition 12 *Permissible mixed abstract lemma*
A permissible mixed abstract lemma L^{mix} wrt a program P^{mix} is a mixed abstract expression such that any of its concretization $L \in \gamma(L^{mix})$ is a permissible lemma wrt any concrete logic program $P \in \gamma(P^{mix})$. □

Example 7 Given the definite logic program P defined in example 2, the mixed abstract lemma L^{mix}

$$app(X^\alpha, [H^\alpha], D), app(D, L^\alpha, Y) \longleftarrow app(X^\alpha, [H^\alpha | L^\alpha], Y)$$

is a permissible mixed abstract lemma wrt P. Notice that the dead end variable D is a concrete variable. This is crucial when applying lemmas in abstract derivations — the dead end variables cannot be influenced by the abstraction.
□

The condition for correct lemma application in a mixed abstract *EOLD* resolution is exactly the same as for a concrete one (cf. def. 5 and 6). Thus, we have the following proposition, which can be considered as a "soundness" result for lemma application in the mixed abstract *EOLD* derivations:

Proposition 6 *Given a mixed abstract definite logic program P^{mix} with a mixed abstract initial goal G_0^{mix}, a set of permissible lemmas $\mathcal{L}_P^{mix}$ and a* *concrete program $P \in \gamma(P^{mix})$ with a concrete initial goal $G_0 \in \gamma(G_0^{mix})$. If there exist a mixed abstract EOLD derivation with lemma application of the form*

$$G_0^{mix} \xrightarrow{s_1^{mix} \; \theta_1^{mix}} G_1^{mix} \ldots \xrightarrow{s_n^{mix} theta_n^{mix}} G_n^{mix}, n \geq 0$$

where s_i^{mix} denotes a clause or a lemma, then there exists a concrete derivation of the form

$$G_0 \xrightarrow{s_1 \; \theta_1} G_1 \ldots \xrightarrow{s_m \; \theta_m} G_m, 0 \leq m \leq n$$

and a legal assignment ρ such that $s_i = \rho(s_i^{mix})$, $G_i = \rho(G_i^{mix})$, $local(G_i) \supseteq local(G_i^{mix})$ and $\theta_i \trianglelefteq \theta_i^{mix}$ for all $i = 0, 1, \ldots, m$, where either $m = n$ or $G_{m+1} = fail$

Proof The proof can also be obtained by induction on the length of the derivations. Note that if there is a correct application of a permissible lemma in the abstract derivation, then any of its concretizations can be applied to the corresponding concretization of the current goal.
□

Notice that the proposition above *does not ensure* that in general any $EOLD_{\mathcal{L}}$ refutation can be represented by a mixed abstract one because some local variables occurring in the concrete refutation can be lost (i.e. they can be represented as abstract ones) in the abstract derivation. However, the proposition 2 ensure soundness in the following sense: if there is $EOLD_{\mathcal{L}}^{mix}$ derivation, then any corresponding concrete derivation is a derivation with correct lemma application. Moreover, if "completeness" is ensured (see def. 13 and discussion below), then proposition 1 ensures that any $EOLD^{mix}$ refutation is covered by some $EOLD_{\mathcal{L}}^{mix}$ refutation.

In order to have "completeness" of abstract mixed $EOLD$ resolution with lemma application we need the following definition:

Definition 13 *Safe set of mixed abstract permissible lemmas*
A set $\mathcal{L}_P^{mix}$ of lemmas permissible wrt a definite logic program P^{mix} is said to be safe iff for any lemma $L^{mix} \in \mathcal{L}_P^{mix}$ of the form $Q^{mix}(\overline{X}, \overline{Y}) \leftarrow R^{mix}(\overline{X}, \overline{Z})$ holds: if the goal Q^{mix} has an $EOLD$ refutation with computed answer substitution θ^{mix}, then the goal R^{mix} has an $EOLD_{\mathcal{L}}^{mix}$ refutation wrt $P^{mix} \oplus \mathcal{L}_P^{mix}$ with computed answer substitution $\theta_{\mathcal{L}}^{mix}$ such that $\theta_{mix} |_{\overline{X}} = \theta_{\mathcal{L}}^{mix} |_{\overline{X}}$. □

It is important to notice that the conditions above are much weaker than those for abstract permissibility (cf. def. 12). The permissibility of abstract lemma requires that *all* concretizations should be permissible, while the safety condition does not refer to concrete derivations. It the set $\mathcal{L}_P^{mix}$ is safe, then abstract $EOLD_{\mathcal{L}}$ resolution is complete in abstract form, i.e. proposition 2 is true for abstract $EOLD_{\mathcal{L}}$ resolution. The latter implies the following: If there exists an $EOLD$ refutation for the initial goal, then it is represented by some $EOLD^{mix}$ refutation (cf. proposition 1). The safety condition ensures existence of the corresponding $EOLD_{\mathcal{L}}^{mix}$ refutation. Thus, the proposed abstract interpretation schema is correct.

Our purpose is to ensure correctness of lemma application in abstract form combined with a tabulation mechanism (the $EOLDT_{\mathcal{L}}^{mix}$ resolution). Its correctness follows immediately from the discussion above. The $EOLDT_{\mathcal{L}}^{mix}$ resolution can be used to construct finite abstract trees which correctly represent the concrete ones. Moreover, lemmas can be used to construct these trees. The next section gives an example of the compilation of a mixed abstract $EOLDT_{\mathcal{L}}^{mix}$ tree into a program, which is equivalent to the source one wrt the set of computed answer substitutions for the variables of the initial goal and has the behaviour, which is prescribed by the abstract tree.

Example 8 Given the definite logic program P:

$$c_1 : \quad rev([],[]).$$
$$c_2 : \quad rev([H|T], Y) \leftarrow rev(T, R), app(R, [H], Y).$$
$$c_3 : \quad app([], L, L).$$
$$c_4 : \quad app([H|T], L, [H|X]) \leftarrow app(T, L, X).$$

and the mixed abstract initial goal $G_0^{mix} = rev(X_0^\alpha, Y_0)$, the following mixed abstract $EOLD$ derivation is correct

- $G_0^{mix} = < |\underline{rev}(X_0^\alpha, Y_0)| >$

  $\downarrow$ $\qquad\qquad\qquad\qquad\qquad\qquad c_2 : \theta_1^{mix} = \{X_0^\alpha \leftarrow [H_1^\alpha | T_1^\alpha]\}$

- $G_1^{mix} = < |\underline{rev}(T_1^\alpha, R_1), app(R_1, [H_1^\alpha], Y_0)| >$

  $\downarrow$ $\qquad\qquad\qquad\qquad\qquad\qquad c_2 : \theta_2^{mix} = \{T_1^\alpha \leftarrow [H_2^\alpha | T_2^\alpha]\}$

- $G_2^{mix} = < |\underline{rev(T_2^\alpha, R_2), app(R_2, [H_2^\alpha], R_1), app(R_1, [H_1^\alpha], Y_0)}| >$

  $\Downarrow$ $\qquad\qquad\qquad\qquad\qquad\qquad L^{mix} : \theta_3^{mix} = \{\}$

- $G_3^{mix} = < |rev(T_2^\alpha, R_2), app(R_2, [H_2^\alpha, H_1^\alpha], Y_0)| >$

where the permissible mixed abstract lemma L^{mix} wrt P has been obtained from the lemma given in example 7 by the following obvious specialisation: given the permissible lemma of the from $Q(\overline{X}, \overline{Y}) \longleftarrow R(\overline{X}, \overline{Z})$, the lemma $B(\overline{X})Q(\overline{X}, \overline{Y})\sigma \longleftarrow B(\overline{X})R(\overline{X}, \overline{Z})\sigma$ is also permissible lemma provided that $dom(\sigma) \subseteq \overline{X}$. In fact, the mixed abstract derivation $\mathcal{D}^{mix}$ apparently is a proof that the dead end variable R_1 cannot be disturbed by the abstracted parts of the program, and, thus, the lemma application in abstract form is correct, i.e. given a concrete derivation $\mathcal{D}$ represented by the mixed abstract derivation $\mathcal{D}^{mix}$ the application of the corresponding lemma $L \in \gamma(L^{mix})$ is correct for $\mathcal{D}$. Notice that the lemma used is a non trivial lemma. $\square$

4.3 Logic Program Transformation using Abstract EOLDT resolution

In this section we show how an $EOLDT_{\mathcal{L}}^{mix}$ tree can be used to perform a transformation of the source logic program. The transformation algorithm is presented by an example. Its precise version is the straightforward extension of the algorithm in [2, 3] provided that the correctness of lemma application for $EOLDT_{\mathcal{L}}^{mix}$ resolution is taken into account.

Before going into details, we need some simple definitions. Any expression equivalent (up to renaming of variables) to the first block B of the goal G is said to be the *extended call* of the goal. Given a subrefutation of the first block of the goal G having the first block B and the corresponding sequence of substitutions $\theta_1, \ldots, \theta_n$, the *extended answer* for the call is any expression equivalent (up to renaming of variables) to $A = B\theta_1 \cdots \theta_n$.

The simple definitions above are used to reconstruct the mixed abstract derivation given in example 8 as follows:

- $G_0^{mix} =< |\underline{rev}(X_0^\alpha, Y_0)| >$

$\downarrow$ $\qquad\qquad c_2 : \theta_1^{mix} = \{X_0^\alpha \leftarrow [H_1^\alpha | T_1^\alpha]\}$

- $G_1^{mix} =< |\underline{rev}(T_1^\alpha, R_1), app(R_1, L_1^\alpha|) >$

$\downarrow$ $\qquad\qquad c_2 : \theta_2^{mix} = \{T_1^\alpha \leftarrow [H_2^\alpha | T_2^\alpha]\}$

- $G_2^{mix} =< |\underline{rev}(T_2^\alpha, R_2), app(R_2, [H_2^\alpha], R_1), app(R_1, L_1^\alpha, Y_0)| >$

$\Downarrow$ $\qquad\qquad L^{mix} : \theta_3^{mix} = \{\}$

- $G_3^{mix} =< |\underline{rev}(T_2^\alpha, R_2), app(R_2, L_2^\alpha, Y_0)| >$

$\downarrow$ $\qquad\qquad A^{mix} : \theta_4^{mix} = \{R_2 \leftarrow W_1^\alpha, T_2^\alpha \leftarrow W_1^\alpha, Y_0 \leftarrow W_2^\alpha\}$

- $G_4^{mix} =<>$

The goals G_1^{mix} and G_3^{mix} were obtained by the obvious *generalisation* of the corresponding goal in the derivation of example 8. The goal G_4^{mix} was obtained by application of *abstract tabulation* (the details can be found in [20, 11, 9, 2, 3]) using the following algorithm. Firstly notice that there exists a mixed subrefutation for the first block of the goal G_1^{mix}

- $G_1^{mix} =< |\underline{rev}(T_1^\alpha, R_1), app(R_1, L_1^\alpha, Y_0)| >$

$\downarrow$ $\qquad\qquad c_1 : \theta_5^{mix} = \{T_1^\alpha \leftarrow [], R_1 \leftarrow []\}$

- $G_5^{mix} =< |\underline{app}([], L_1^\alpha, Y_0)| >$

$\downarrow$ $\qquad\qquad c_3 : \theta_6^{mix} = \{Y_0 \leftarrow L_1^\alpha\}$

- $G_6^{mix} =<>$

with the *generalised* abstract extended answer

$$A^{mix} = rev(W_1^\alpha, W_2^\alpha), app(W_2^\alpha, W_3^\alpha, W_4^\alpha)$$

Notice also that the abstract extended calls of the goals G_1^{mix} and G_3^{mix} are equivalent to $rev(X^\alpha, D), app(D, W^\alpha, Y)$. This allows to extend the first block of G_3^{mix} by the mixed abstract answer A^{mix} applying it as the input pseudo clause, i.e using a mixed abstract $EOLD$ resolution step for the block as a whole. This does not create new answers for the abstract call of the goal G_1^{mix} due to the chosen generalisation algorithm. The construction of the mixed abstract tree can be completed by noticing that there exists one more simple refutation

- $G_0^{mix} =< |\underline{rev}(X_0^\alpha, Y_0)| >$

$\downarrow$ $\qquad\qquad c_1 : \theta_7^{mix} = \{X_0^\alpha \leftarrow [], Y_0 \leftarrow []\}$

- $G_7^{mix} =<>$

This example shows the importance of lemma application in mixed abstract derivation. In fact, to make the tree finite we *have* to generalise goals and apply generalised abstract answers, which can introduce abstract variables. On the other hand, generalisation should be done as precise as possible keeping in mind the conditions for lemma application. Thus the correct lemma application after several applications of abstract answers needs the proof that dead end variables are not influenced by the abstract answers. This consideration is the main extension of the algorithm presented in [2, 3]. The goal transformation by lemma application is a powerful tool to construct efficient abstract trees (notice that the abstract tree above does not use clause $c4$ and corresponds to the program, which uses an accumulating parameter). Thus, it seems reasonable to apply a rather complex abstract interpretation technique to ensure the correctness of lemma application during static analysis time.

The second important information in the tree is the following: the variable R_1 occurring in the goal G_1^{mix} is a local variable. Thus, it can be dropped during the transformation of the source program (this is the second improvement of the algorithm of [2, 3]).

The tree presented above can be used to obtain the following program

$$c_1 : \quad rev([], []).$$
$$c_2 : \quad rev([H|T], Y) \leftarrow \pi_3(T, [H], Y).$$
$$c_3 : \quad \pi_3([], L, L).$$
$$c_4 : \quad \pi_3([H|T], L, Y) \leftarrow \pi_3(T, [H|L], Y).$$

by the transformation algorithm given in [2, 3] with the extension that local variables are dropped when generating definitions for the new program. This program is equivalent to the source one wrt the initial goal. In general, the transformations of the source definite logic program, which can be obtained using the presented framework, preserve the set of computed answer substitutions for the variables of the initial goal.

5   Conclusion and Related Work

The presented framework is aimed at deriving complex logic program transformations based upon goal replacement and unfold/fold operations (the latter were described in details in [2, 3]). Our approach makes use of a complete flow analysis of the source definite logic program as a pretransformation phase (here we follow the basic ideas of [9]).

This approach is more powerful than that of [19, 10, 18, 12] because as it was pointed out in [13, 8] the unfold/fold transformations, which can be derived from the SLD-like tree analysis cannot always be expressed in terms of Tamaki and Sato transformations. On the other hand, in our settings recursive predicates can be derived (this is not possible using the framework of [13, 8]). Moreover, it can be shown that our unfold/fold transformations can be easily reduced by restricting abstract interpretation algorithms to obtain exactly the algorithm of [7] (this can be done by allowing only singleton blocks and only one answer for each call when applying tabulation). So the main motivation of the paper is to combine this technique with the goal replacement operations through the lemma application.

Firstly we have presented conditions for the goal replacement in the SLD-like derivations. This approach differs significantly from that of [8] (the latter should be considered as the most advanced in the scope of the goal replacement) because the latter deals with goal replacement in the clause bodies and aimed to preserve the minimal model rather than the set of computed answer substitutions for certain variables of the initial goal. On the other hand our conditions combined with the subsequent transformation algorithms seem to be as permissible as those of [8]. Unfortunately the precise comparison is rather difficult, although it is possible to show that our approach is capable to produce the same results for several interesting examples.

Secondly, in order to derive the transformations we have to construct a finite complete abstract tree, what in general cannot be achieved without abstraction or generalisation. Thus, the main problem in our approach is the correct lemma application for the partially abstracted derivations. As it could be seen from above, the conditions for the goal replacement are very strict, i.e. they require rather precise information about the current goal and its relation with the initial goal, what is not always the case in the abstracted derivations. So we have proposed a special abstract interpretation schema which allows to construct finite complete abstract trees using abstract tabulation mechanism combined with correct lemma application. As a result, our framework allows to derive non trivial transformations of definite logic programs which could be more powerful than those of [16, 17, 6, 7] because we provide more flexible unfold/fold transformations combined with goal replacement.

Acknowledgements We are grateful to the referees for several accurate remarks and questions.

References

[1] Bruynooghe,M., De Schreye,D., Krekels,B., Compiling Control, J. Logic Programming, 1989, Vol.6, Nos.2-3, 135-162.

[2] Boulanger,D., Bruynooghe,M., Deriving Transformations of Logic Programs using Abstract Interpretation, Logic Program Synthesis and Transformation (LOPSTR'92), eds. K.K. Lau and T. Clement, Workshops in Computing, Springer-Verlag, 1993, 99-117.

[3] Boulanger,D., Bruynooghe,M., Deriving Fold/Unfold Transformations of Logic Programs Using Extended OLDT-based Abstract Interpretation, J. Symbolic Computation, 1993, Vol.15, 495-521.

[4] Burstall,R., Darlington,J., A Transformation System for Developing Recursive Programs, JACM, Jan.1977, Vol.24, No.1, 44-67.

[5] De Schreye,D., Martens,B., Sablon,G., Bruynooghe,M., Compiling Bottom-Up and Mixed Derivations into Top-Down Executable Logic Programs, J. Automated Reasoning, 1991, Vol.7, 337-358.

[6] Gallagher,J., Bruynooghe,M., Some Low Level Transformations of Logic Programs, Proc. 2nd Workshop in Meta-Programming in Logic, Leuven, 1990, 229-244.

[7] Gallagher,J., Bruynooghe,M., The Derivation of an Algorithm for Program Specialisation, New Generation Computing, 1991, Vol.9, 305-333.

[8] Gardner, P., Shepherdson, J., Unfold/Fold Transformations of Logic Programs, Computational Logic, Essays in Honour of Alan Robinson, eds. J.L.Lassez and G.Plotkin, MIT Press, 1991, 565-583.

[9] Gallagher, J., Codish M., Shapiro E., Specialisation of Prolog and FCP Programs Using Abstract Interpretation, New Generation Computing, 1988, Vol.6, Nos.2-3, 159-186.

[10] Kawamura, T., Kanamori, T., Preservation of Stronger Equivalence in Unfold/Fold Logic Program Transformation, Proc. 4th Int. Conf. on FGCS, Tokyo,1988.

[11] Kanamori, T., Kawamura, T., Abstract Interpretation Based on OLDT Resolution, J. Logic Programming, Vol.15, Nos. 1-2, 1-30 1993 .

[12] Kawamura, T., Derivation of Efficient Logic Programs by Synthesising New Predicates, Proc. 1991 Int. Symp. on Logic Programming, San Diego, 1991, 611-625.

[13] Lloyd,L., Shepherdson,J., Partial Evaluation in Logic Programming, J. Logic Programming, 1991, Vol.11, Nos.3-4, 217-242.

[14] Lloyd,L., Foundations of Logic Programming, Springer-Verlag, Berlin, 1987.

[15] Maher,M., Equivalences of Logic Programs, Foundations of Deductive Databases and Logic Programming, Ed. J.Minker, Morgan-Kaufmann, 1988, 627-658.

[16] Proietti,M., Pettorossi,A., Construction of Efficient Logic Programs by Loop Absorption and Generalisation, Proc. 2nd Workshop in Meta-Programming in Logic, Leuven, 1990, 57-81.

[17] Proietti,M., Pettorossi,A., Unfolding - Definition - Folding, In this Order, For Avoiding Unnecessary Variables in Logic Programs, Proc. 3rd Int. Symp. on Programming Languages Implementation and Logic Programming, Aug. 1991, LNCS No.528, Springer-Verlag, 1991, 347-358.

[18] Seki,H., Unfold/Fold Transformation of stratified programs, J. Theoretical Computer Science, 1991, Vol.86, 107-139.

[19] Tamaki,H., Sato,T., Unfold/Fold Transformation of Logic Programs, Proc. 2nd Int. Conf. on Logic Programming, Uppsala, 1984, 127-138.

[20] Tamaki,H., Sato,T., OLD Resolution with Tabulation, Proc. 3rd Int. Conf. on Logic Programming, London, July 1986, 84-98.

Mechanical Transformation of Logic Definitions augmented with Type Information into Prolog Procedures: Some Experiments

Pierre De Boeck, Baudouin Le Charlier

Institut d'Informatique, University of Namur,
rue Grandgagnage, 21, B-5000 Namur (Belgium)
Email: ble@info.fundp.ac.be

Abstract

This paper describes experiments done with a static type analyser to transform pure logic definitions (the so-called *logic descriptions* [7]) into executable Prolog procedures. The presented static analyser can be used in a final transformation component of a logic program synthesis system such as the systems described in [8, 18]. The paper recalls the notion of a logic description and discusses how type information can be used to relate the logic description to its intended meaning. Then the *analyser* and the underlying notions of *type*, and *abstract substitution* are presented. It is explained how type and *mode* information can be combined to derive Prolog procedures that are correct wrt given *directionalities*. The type analyser is able to derive procedures producing correct and well typed results, by finding correct permutations of literals in clauses. Practicality of the analyser is illustrated on three examples. It is shown that: (1) there are several (more or less clever) ways to combine type and mode information to help the analyser finding solutions, (2) explicit type checking can be avoided most of the time at run-time, (3) the analyser is able to find multidirectional procedures in many cases, (4) *no share* constraints are useful to find more solutions when restricted uses are chosen for the procedures (allowing for elaborate optimizations). The analyser is also useful to combine pure and impure logic procedures as it allows to reuse any Prolog procedure provided that it is given a behaviour.

1   Introduction

Program synthesis is a very challenging field of research since programming is definitely a creative task. Our work is related to logic program synthesis (see for example [1, 8, 9, 14, 18]). However our present aim is not to offer a similar proposal or an improvement to those works. We want to present a complementary tool. This is because most existing works produce as their result "pure logic definitions" which are computable in theory but only by ideal logic languages. However real logic languages and Prolog in particular are very far from this ideal.

The tool that we present in this paper is an attempt to bridge a part of this gap between theory and practice. It allows to transform automatically a class of pure logic descriptions into Prolog procedures which are correct for a class of call patterns defined by means of type and mode information.

It can be argued of course that existing logic languages are unsatisfactory and that new ones must be designed. Nevertheless, a lot of work has been done on Prolog and efficient implementations exist and, therefore, we think that it is interesting to use it as the target language for a logic program synthesis tool.

The paper is organized as follows. Section 2 defines the class of logic definitions we are considering and explains how types can help to relate them to their "intended meaning". Section 3 states the problem of deriving Prolog procedures which implement adequately the logic definitions for a class of input patterns. Section 4 describes our transformation tool. Section 5 reports on a set of experiments made with the tool on three sample problems. Sections 6 and 7 discuss related works and provide the conclusion.

2 Logic Descriptions, Types and Intended Meaning

According to [7], the first step in constructing a logic procedure is to define logically a relation p between arguments $X_1, \ldots, X_n$ ranging on the set of all ground terms (Herbrand universe). This definition is called a logic description in [7], has the form

$$p(X_1, \ldots, X_n) \Leftrightarrow F,$$

where F^1 is a first order logic formula with free variables $X_1, \ldots, X_n$ and is denoted $LD(p)$. It is often convenient to restrict the domain of $X_1, \ldots, X_n$ because we are not interested in the meaning of the relation outside a well-determined subset of the universe. For example, when designing (or synthesizing) the logic description of append, we are only interested in arguments that are *lists*.

Types are useful to express such restrictions as quoted for example by Naish[15]. So a logic description for p should express its *intended meaning* if and only if the following conditions (respectively C1 and C2) hold:

$(t_1, \ldots, t_n) \in p \Leftrightarrow p(t_1, \ldots, t_n)$ is true in any Herbrand model of $LD(p)$ and

$(t_1, \ldots, t_n) \notin p \Leftrightarrow p(t_1, \ldots, t_n)$ is false in any Herbrand model of $LD(p)$,

for all $(t_1, \ldots, t_n)$ such that $t_1 \in T_1, \ldots, t_n \in T_n$ where $T_1, \ldots, T_n$ are the types restricting the range of the arguments.

According to this approach, types play a role similar to preconditions in traditional programming and the logic description has a unique meaning when restricted to the types. However a major problem arises from the fact that the Prolog procedure to be derived from the logic description is required to be executable with non ground arguments. For example, a variable logically stands for all possible ground terms. The computed answer substitutions for the call $p(t1, \ldots, tn)$ should cover the set of all ground instances $p(d1, \ldots, dn)$

---

[1]In [7], F is assumed to be arbitrary. In this paper however, we assume, for the sake of simplicity, that F is an existentially quantified disjunction of conjunctions of literals.

such that $(d1,\ldots,dn) \in p \wedge (d1,\ldots,dn) \in T1\times\ldots\times Tn$ but what about the ground instances $p(d1,\ldots,dn)$ such that $(d1,\ldots,dn) \notin T1\times\ldots\times Tn$?

Although it can be argued[15] that they are acceptable results that could be discarded afterwards, by a final type-checking literal, we take the point of view that they are incorrect answers. We believe this later approach cleaner and more efficient. So correct procedures will only produce correctly typed results[2].

Given our correctness notion for the Prolog procedures, several approaches remains possible when constructing the logic description. We review three of them which will be considered in the following.

The first approach has already been mentioned. It consists in using the types as preconditions during the construction process. This implies that the types of formal parameters do not have to be checked. However type-checking literals must sometimes be added to ensure type correctness of a recursive call as shown by the logic description of flattree in figure 2: the assumption that T is a tree and L is a list implies that LT and RT are trees and that TAIL is a list. However nothing is known about LLT and LRT, so two type-checking literals are added to ensure that the flattree and append literals have well-defined truth values[3].

Another approach (taken in [7]), consists in building logic descriptions that explicitly check the type of the arguments. This results in the descriptions of figure 3. Type checking literals are still needed, but they are not used in the same way. It is intersesting to see that type-checking literals are now used in base cases instead of recursive cases. In flattree, type-checking literals are no longer required because some type-checking has been added in append.

Finally, a third approach consists in doing no type checking at all because variables are implicitly assumed to range on a given type. The corresponding logic description for append, efface and flattree are the same as previously except that all type checking predicates are removed. This approach is often used by programmers who are reasoning "declaratively" in an "intended" interpretation domain. Such logic descriptions can also be produced by synthesis systems [1] which use types during the synthesis process and subsequently forget the types in the derived logic definition. The resulting logic descriptions do not respect conditions C1 and C2, in general, and type-checking literals must be (re)introduced to ensure correctness at the declarative level. At the Prolog level, however, the type-checking literals can often be dropped because the procedures are intended to be used only in a restricted way.

---

[2]For the sake of simplicity we only consider in the following procedures that produce *ground* results.

[3]In fact, it can be shown that the logic description is still correct without the type checking literals but this requires an extra reasoning about arbitrary terms. Moreover, thanks to the two literals the logic description remains correct if arbitrary conjunctions not respecting the types are added to flattree and append.
E.g.: T=void ∧ L=a for flattree and L1=a ∧ L2=a ∧ LR=[a] for append.

procedure append(L1,L2,LR)
types L1,L2,LR: *list*
relation LR is the concatenation of L1 and L2
directionality in(*any, any, ground*)
               in(*ground, ground, any*)

procedure efface(X,L,LEff)
types X: *term*
      L,LEff: *list*
relation X belongs to L and LEff is L where the first
      occurrence of X has been removed
directionality in(*any, ground, any*)
               in(*ground, any, ground*)

procedure flattree(T,L)
types T: *tree*
      L: *list*
relation L is the list of the elements of the tree T in prefixed order
directionality in(*any, ground*)
               in(*ground, any*)

Figure 1: Specifications for **append**, **efface** and **flattree**.

```
append(L1,L2,LR) ⇔ (L1=[] ∧ L2=LR) ∨
   (L1=[H1|T1] ∧ append(T1,L2,TR) ∧ LR=[H1|TR])
efface(X,L,LEff) ⇔ L=[H|T] ∧ ((X=H ∧ LEff=T) ∨
   (X≠H ∧ efface(X,T,TEff) ∧ LEff=[H|TEff]))
flattree(T,L) ⇔ T=void ∧ L=[] ∨
   (T=tree(R,LT,RT) ∧ L=[R|TAIL] ∧ append(LLT,LRT,TAIL)
   flattree(LT,LLT) ∧ list(LLT)∧ flattree(RT,LRT) ∧ list(LRT))
```

Figure 2: The logic descriptions with types used as preconditions.

```
append(L1,L2,LR) ⇔ (L1=[] ∧ L2=LR ∧ list(LR)) ∨
   (L1=[H1|T1] ∧ append(T1,L2,TR) ∧ LR=[H1|TR])
efface(X,L,LEff) ⇔ L=[H|T] ∧ ((X=H ∧ LEff=T ∧ list(LEff)) ∨
   (X≠H ∧ efface(X,T,TEff) ∧ LEff=[H|TEff]))
flattree(T,L) ⇔ T=void ∧ L=[] ∨
   (T=tree(R,LT,RT) ∧ L=[R|TAIL] ∧ append(LLT,LRT,TAIL)
   flattree(LT,LLT) ∧ flattree(RT,LRT))
```

Figure 3: The logic descriptions with types completely checked.

3 Prolog Procedures, Modes and Specifications

3.1 Modes and Directionalities

Intuitively, a Prolog procedure should be correct wrt an intended meaning iff for any call pattern it returns a sequence of answer substitutions covering exactly the set of ground atoms which agree with the pattern and are true in the intended meaning of the procedure. A procedure enjoying the above property is called a *fully multidirectional* procedure. Experience shows that it is not possible to derive such procedures in general. It is often possible however to derive procedures which behave well for a given class of call (or input) patterns. A large class of input patterns can be specified by means of type and *mode* information [7]. Modes provide information about the instantiation of terms. We only consider three modes here: **ground** representing fully instantiated terms, **var** representing completely uninstantiated terms (variables) and **any** representing all terms (no restriction). A more precise mode system is proposed in [7] but we believe that **ground**, **var** and **any** are the three most interesting modes in practice.

In the following, we focus on the automatic transformation of logic descriptions into Prolog procedures which are correct for a given *directionality*.

Definition 1 (Directionality)
Let p/n, a procedure name. An (input) directionality for p/n is a n-tuple of modes, noted $in(m_1, \ldots, m_n)$. A n-tuple of terms respects a directionality iff each term belongs to the set of terms represented by the corresponding mode.

In [7] input and output directionalities are distinguished. We only specified input directionalities here because we focus on procedures producing **ground** results.

We are now in position to introduce the notion of a *specification*. Note that, at this stage, it is only a conventional notion without a unique precise meaning. The meaning will be discussed later.

Definition 2 (Specification of a Prolog procedure)
A specification consists of four parts:

1. the *head*, of the form $p(X_1, \ldots, X_n)$, where p/n is the name of the procedure and $X_1, \ldots, X_n$ are called the parameters;

2. the *types* of the parameters;

3. the intended *relation* to be implemented by the procedure;

4. one or several *directionalities*

Specifications for the procedures **append**, **efface** and **flattree** are depicted in figure 1.

3.2 Meaning of a Specification

Our specification schema is a simplification of the schema proposed in [7]. However, Deville gives a single meaning to specifications. In this paper we stress that other meanings are worth considering. (Our transformation tool is able to deal with several of them.)

Output patterns As far as output patterns are concerned, the meaning of the specification is simple and unique: ouput patterns must be ground; moreover they have to respect the types and the relation (soundness) and the procedure must succeed for any ground pattern respecting the types and the relation (completeness).

Input patterns Types and directionalities must be combined to define a set of input patterns for which the procedure correctly behaves. Several way to combine types and directionalities are possible. For example, type list combined with mode **any** can mean that any input terms are accepted or that any term instantiable to a list is acceptable[4] or that any term whose all instances are lists is acceptable[5].

One aim of this paper is to compare those different ways to assign a meaning to specifications and to show how this meaning interact with the way types are used to relate the logic descriptions to their intended meaning.

4 Transformation of Logic Descriptions into Prolog Procedures

4.1 The goal to be achieved

Now we turn to the problem of deriving correct Prolog procedures from the logic descriptions.

Note that we are mainly interested in theoretical correctness: that is all solutions and only them are in the SLDNF-tree whose root is a query respecting the *in* part of the directionalities. Other concerns (termination and optimization) are to be dealt with in a subsequent step that we ignore here.

The first step is to derive a Prolog procedure from the logic description. This step is based on a *completion* notion defined in [7]. Syntactic transformations are applied to the logic descriptions resulting in the procedures depicted in figure 4. Taking the completion of those procedures gives back the logic descriptions. Standard results about SLDNF-resolution ensure then that all ground logical consequences of the logic descriptions are in the SLDNF-tree and only them. Finally to prove that the procedures are correct it is sufficient to show that all subgoals in the SLDNF-tree will succeed with correctly typed arguments, because this allows to instantiate all variables in the SLDNF-tree with correctly typed values and hence to prove that any answer substitutions yields a correct result whatever approach was chosen to construct the logic description (see [7]).

---

[4] Such a term is called an **any list** in [7].
[5] Such a term is called an **complete list** in [17].

```
append(L1,L2,LR) ← L1=[],L2=LR,list(LR).
append(L1,L2,LR) ← L1=[H1|T1],append(T1,L2,TR),LR=[H1|TR].

efface(X,L,LEff) ← L=[H|T],X=H,LEff=T,list(LEff).
efface(X,L,LEff) ← L=[H|T],X≠H,efface(X,T,TEff),
                            LEff=[H|TEff].

flattree(T,L) ← T=void,L=[].
flattree(T,L) ← T=tree(R,LT,RT),L=[R|TAIL],
    flattree(LT,LLT),flattree(RT,LRT),append(LLT,LRT,TAIL).
```

Figure 4: The Prolog procedures with types completely checked.

Note that arguments have to respect the types only at success time, not at call time, but in order to prove type-correctness at success time, we need to require some other conditions at call time.

In fact, to prove this property of the SLDNF-tree it is sufficient to find a permutation of the subgoals of each clause such that the directionalities are fulfilled at call time. Moreover at the end of the clause analysis, all arguments must be ground and respect the types of the procedure.

4.2 Types

Our type notion is similar to the notion developed by G. Janssens and M. Bruynooghe[12, 13], although we implement it differently and use it for other purposes.

First, it must be noticed that in the first part of this paper we have been considering *ground* types only. On the contrary, the analyser uses possibly *non ground* types. In fact, combining a (ground) type and a mode will boil down to assign to them a (possibly) non ground type, in the analyser.

Two kinds of types are considered. *Primitive* types are built-in. They include the following: **ground, var, any, integer, constant**, ... Other types are defined by means of so-called *type descriptions* (see below). They are called *user* types.

Internally however, types are represented by *names* (or internal identifiers). The type descriptions are pre-processed (compiled) and transformed in a set of primitive operations working on the type names. Therefore the set of types which are considered during the transformation process is fixed and finite. No type inference is performed. The user has to define a set of "interesting" types before starting the transformation process. Although more limited in theory, this approach is more efficient. Moreover experiments seem to show that it is powerful enough. (The reader is refered to [2, 3, 5, 4, 6, 10] for more information about the design of the analyzer and the handling of types.)

In the following we confuse the types (of the analyser) and their names. Moreover, from now on, we use the word type in the technical sense of type definable in the analyser.

We now give an overview of the type system and of the analyser functionalities.

4.2.1 The type description language

We use a restricted first-order logic language which is equivalent to the type graphs of G. Janssens and M. Bruynooghe.

Definition 3 (Type description) A type description for a type T denoted $TD(T)$ is an iff-formula of the form[6]

$$T(X) \Leftrightarrow C_1 \vee \ldots \vee C_f$$

where each C_i is either a literal $T'(X)$ where T' is a type or a conjunction of the form $X = f(Y_1, \ldots, Y_n) \wedge T_1(Y_{i_1}) \ldots \wedge T_s(Y_{i_s})$ where $Y_1, \ldots, Y_n$ are distinct variables different from X, $T_1, \ldots, T_s$ are types and $i_1, \ldots, i_s$ are different indices greater or equal to 1 and lower or equal to n.

Definition 4 (Set of type descriptions) A description of a set of types denoted STD is a set of type descriptions $TD(T_1), \ldots, TD(T_n)$ such that all T's are distinct and all $TD(T)$'s use only user types $T_1, \ldots, T_n$ or primitive types.

Definition 5 (Denotation of a type) The denotation of a type T of STD denoted $\gamma(T)$ is the set of terms t such that $T(t)$ is true in any Herbrand model[7]

For the sake of safety of our generation scheme (notably the termination of the primitives) we ensure that STD has a unique Herbrand model[8]. Syntactic restrictions on STD are sufficient to ensure this property: in the case of a (possibly indirect) recursive definition, the variable occurring in the recursive call must represent a strict subterm of the term represented by the variable in the head of the definition. (This is not trivially ensured because some C_i can be of the form $T'(X)$.)

Example 6 (Type descriptions)
We give hereunder the definitions of the types **ground list** (gl), **any list** (al) and **complete list** (cl) which will be used in the experiments.

```
gl(X) ⇔
     X=[]
V    X=[H|Tail] ∧ ground(H) ∧ gl(Tail)

al(X) ⇔
     X=[] ∨ var(X)
V    X=[H|Tail] ∧ al(Tail)

cl(X) ⇔
     X=[]
V    X=[H|Tail] ∧ cl(Tail)
```

---

[6] X is a variable universally quantified; the other variables are quantified existentially in their respective conjunction.

[7] The notion of Herbrand model is extended in the usual way to accept any Prolog term in the denotation.

[8] Provided that equality is interpreted as identity on the Herbrand domain

4.3 Abstract substitutions and Behaviours

Analysing a clause consists in labelling each of its execution points with *abstract substitutions* expressing type information about the variables of the clause, given some input abstract substitution. Passing from one execution point to the next one requires some knowledge about the subprocedure at this point. In our system, knowledge about a subprocedure (except $=/2$, handled as a built-in) is expressed by means of a so-called *behaviour*, namely a formal specification in the form of a set of pre-post conditions. Definitions of abstract substitutions and behaviours are given hereafter.

Definition 7 (Typed term) A typed term has one of the two form defined below:

- a term of the form $\$(T,I)$ where T is a type and I is an integer. This term is called an *indexed type*.

- a term of the form $f(tt_1,\ldots,tt_n)$ where $tt_1,\ldots,tt_n$ are typed terms.

The denotation of a typed term tt is the set of all Prolog terms obtained by replacing each of its indexed type $\$(T,I)$ by a Prolog term belonging to $\gamma(T)$; in this process two identical indexed types (same type and same index) must be replaced by the same term.

Example 8 (Typed term)
The typed term $[a,\$(var,1),\$(gl,1)|\$(var,1)]$ denotes the set of terms of the form $[a,X,e|X]$ where X and e are respectively a variable and a ground list.

Definition 9 (Abstract substitution) An abstract substitution is a term of the form $(bind, nosh)$ where

- bind has the form $<X_1/tt_1,\ldots,X_n/tt_n>$ with $X_1,\ldots,X_n$ being distinct variables (the domain of the substitution) and $tt_1,\ldots,tt_n$ being typed terms.

- nosh has the form $<(ita_1,itb_1),\ldots,(ita_f,itb_f)>$ with the ita's, itb's being indexed types used in $tt_1,\ldots,tt_n$. Each couple (ita,itb) specifies a *noshare* constraint (no common variables) between the two indexed types.

The denotation of an abstract substitution is the set of (idempotent) substitutions
$<X_1/t_1,\ldots,X_n/t_n>$ such that $(t_1,\ldots,t_n)$ belongs to the denotation of the typed term $tt_1,\ldots,tt_n$ and respects the noshare constraints specified by nosh.

Example 10 (Abstract substitution) The abstract substitution

$$(< X1/\$(al,1), X2/\$(al,2) >, < (\$(al,1),\$(al,2)) >)$$

denotes all concrete substitutions binding **any lists** to X1, X2 with no possible aliasing between them.

Definition 11 (Behaviour) The behaviour of a procedure p/n is a set of couples *pre::post* of abstract substitutions on the formal parameters (variables in the head) of the procedure.

It means that if the procedure is called with arguments respecting at least one abstract substitution *pre* of its behaviour, then it is ensured to return arguments respecting the corresponding *post* part.

Example 12 (Behaviour) A behaviour for `append(L1,L2,LR)` could be

- `(<L1/$(gl,1),L2/$(gl,2),LR/$(al,1)>,<>)::`
  `(<L1/$(gl,1),L2/$(gl,2),LR/$(gl,3)>,<>)`

- `(<L1/$(al,1),L2/$(al,2),LR/$(gl,1)>,<>)::`
  `(<L1/$(gl,1),L2/$(gl,2),LR/$(gl,3)>,<>)`

Clause analysis based on behaviours offers many advantages with respect to program construction and verification.

efficiency: the analysis of a clause is very fast since the literals of the clause do not require further anlalysis. This is especially important when the analyser is used to analyse all permutations of literals in the clause.

precision: the behaviour of a procedure, when specified by the programmer is often more precise than the information that can be collected thanks to a recursive analysis of the code. This precision requires of course an accurate type system.

hidden code: the ability to analyse a clause without knowing the code of its sub-problems is very important in programming contexts where either this code is not yet constructed or the code exists but cannot be used. For instance, top-down, modular or object-oriented programming are such contexts. In either cases, only the external interface of the subprocedure stating 'how to use it' is supplied.

The clause analyser is now specified more precisely as follows (SLDNF-resolution is assumed). A formal statement of the correctness of the analyser can be found in [2].

Specification 13 (The clause analyser)

- Let `CL` be a Prolog clause $p(X_1,\ldots,X_n) \leftarrow L_1,\ldots,L_f$ where $X_1,\ldots,X_n$ are distinct variables[9] and $L_1,\ldots,L_f$ are literals (including extra-logic ones) specified by their respective behaviours.

- Let as_{in} be the input abstract substitution on $X_1,\ldots,X_n$.

Then the analyser will compute $as_0,\ldots,as_f$ which are all abstract substitutions on *all* the variables of the clause with

- as_0 is the same as as_{in} except that it has been extended to all the variables of `CL`;

- as_i (i>0) is the abstract substitution holding just after the execution of L_i; it is computed with as_{i-1} + the behaviour of L_i + general information about SLDNF-resolution (e.g: the term bound to a variable after a call is an instance of its value before the call).

---

[9] Any Prolog clause can be normalized in this form

4.4 Synthesis of correct clauses

The experiments discussed in the next section were realized with a synthesis tool based on the clause analyser. This tool find all the *correct* permutations of a clause, given some intended *uses* specified as behaviours.

Definition 14 (Correct permutation of the literals in a clause)

Let - CL be a Prolog clause $p(X_1, \ldots, X_n) \leftarrow L_1, \ldots, L_f$
- as_{in}, as_{out} be two abstract substitutions on $X_1, \ldots, X_n$; such a couple determines an intended use of the clause, specifying the input values (as_{in}) and the output values (as_{out}).

The permutation $L_1, \ldots, L_f$ is said to be correct with respect to (as_{in}, as_{out}) iff during any execution of the clause starting with values respecting as_{in} the following two conditions are respected:

1. each literal L_i is called with arguments respecting *at least* one precondition of its respective behaviour;

2. as_{out} is respected at the end of the execution.

The following function *permut/2* enables to compute in a efficient way all the correct permutations of a clause CL, given some use (as_{in}, as_{out}); it is defined by means of the basic operations of the clause analyser described in [2].

Specification 15 (Function *permut/2*)

If - **prefix** is the prefix of some permutation of CL correct with respect to (as_{in},TRUE)
- *as* is an abstract substitution on all the variables of the clause holding at the end of **prefix**

Then *permut(**prefix**, as)* will return all the permutations of CL which are correct with respect to (as_{in}, as_{out}) and that begin with **prefix**. The call *permut(ϕ, as$_0$)* will compute all the permutations of CL, where as_0 is as_{in} extended to all the variables of the clause. This function is defined as follows:

- *permut(**prefix**, as)* = {**prefix**} if **prefix** is a complete permutation and *as* respects as_{out};

- *permut(**prefix**, as)* = ϕ if **prefix** is a complete permutation and *as* does not respect as_{out};

- *permut(**prefix**, as)* = $\bigcup$ *permut(**prefix**.L, as')* if **prefix** is not a complete permutation, where L $\in$ CL but $\notin$ **prefix** and *as* implies at least one precondition of the behaviour of L and *as'* is the abstract substitution derived from *as* and L.

The above scheme is more efficient than a generate-and-test-all process since once a correct prefix has been found, all the correct permutations prefixed with it can be generated without generating and testing the prefix again.

5 Experiments

We now turn to some experiments done with the analyser about the procedures **append**, **efface** and **flattree**. We want the procedures to be correct with respect to the directionalities given in the specifications of figure 1. However clause analysis requires to combine type and mode information of the specification into *pre* part(s) of one or several behaviours.

The right way to do this is not fully obvious. In [7] it is assumed that at least one instance of a given argument must belong to the corresponding type. This leads to the notion of an **any** type. If **T** is a (ground) type, **any T** denotes the set of (non necessarily ground) terms having at least a ground instance in **T**. **Any** modes are thus replaced by **any** types in the behaviours. The following other approaches are worth considering.

1. No type constraint is required at call time. This allows for the broadest use of the procedure. However ill-typed results are more likely to be produced preventing the analyser to find correct permutations.

2. Partially instantiated arguments are forbidden to avoid aliasing problems, so the two previous approaches reduce to two more restrictive ones where an any mode becomes (**ground** type + **variable**) or (**ground** + **variable**) respectively.

3. **Complete** types (that is: *all* ground instances belong to the type) can be considered as a better way to combine a type with the mode **any**, since type preconditions are then implicitly respected by the arguments of the call, but a variable should also be accepted. So the mode **any** yields (**complete** type + **variable**) in the behaviour.

Of course the different points of view can be arbitrarily combined in the behaviours. Moreover no share constraints between non ground arguments can be added. This sometimes allows to find more correct permutations.

We report in tables 1, 2, 3 the number of correct permutations found by the analyser for the proposed directionalities, the different versions of the clauses and the given approaches to combining type and mode information. The symbols **a**, **g**, **al**, **gl**, **clv**, **gv**, **glv**, **at**, **gt**, **ctv**, **gtv** stand for **any term**, **ground term**, **any list**, **ground list**, **complete list** or **variable**, **ground term** or **variable**, **ground list** or **variable**, **any tree**, **ground tree**, **complete tree** or **variable**, **ground tree** or **variable** respectively. cl_i denotes the ith clause of a procedure and cl^{tc} denotes the version of a clause that uses type checking literals. If a column is labelled with *no sharing* no share constraints are added in the behaviours between all non ground arguments. Permuting a sequence of built-in does not affect the correctness of a clause, so all such permutations are counted for a single one. Moreover to ease the comparison between the versions of a clause containing or not a type-checking literal, position of such a literal is not taken into account.

When several permutations are found, some can be better for optimization purposes (tail recursion, cut introduction, ...). This aspect must be taken into account in another, final, step (see [7, 10]).

We also give results about multidirectionality: a row such as (**g/a** , **g/a** , **a/g**) means that the analyser has tried to find permutations which are simultaneously correct with respect to the directionalities **in(ground, ground, any)** and **in(any, any, ground)**.

Different behaviours have been used for **append** when analyzing procedure **flattree** in order to use consistent conventions for combining type and mode information in the behaviours. For example, when type checking of the arguments is the chosen approach for **flattree**, the same approach is taken for **append** (that is the code of **append** contains a type checking litteral). However the code of **append** is not used but we choose the best possible behaviour for **append** (according to the conventions for combining mode and type information used for analysing **flattree**). So when **flattree** is analysed for inputs **T/any term** and **L/ground term**, **append** is given the input behaviours: {**L1/any term, L2/any term, LR/ground term**} and {**L1/ground term, L2 ground term, LR/any term**}. Finally it must be remembered that output parts of the behaviours always assign ground types to arguments.

5.1 Discussion

The following interesting facts can be concluded from the results of the experiments:

1. **Any** types appear not to be very useful to find correct permutations, although it is the proposed solution in [7]. Choosing **any** instead of **any list** or **any tree** always gives better results. More importantly maybe, no multidirectional procedure can be found with that choice although some are found for all others choices (except **flattree**, where no multidirectional procedure is found at all). This is counter intuitive but is explained by the fact that any loss of information may change an **any** type into an **any term**.

2. Correct permutations can always be found for the most general uses (arbitrary term are accepted as inputs) provided that the types are completely checked in the logic descriptions. Moreover the same solutions are found if types are used as preconditions or are not checked at all, provided that *ground* arguments respect the types at call time. In both approaches multidirectional procedures are found except for **flattree** where no permutation of the second clause respects the types for all uses: either recursive calls or the call to **append** produce partially instantiated results.

3. Correct permutations can also be found for more restrictive uses when **any** is replaced by (**ground + variable**) or (**complete + variable**). This is interesting since further optimizations of the clause are then possible (see [7, 10]).

4. No share constraints do not help to find more correct permutations when **any** or **any** types are used. This is because internal sharing in the arguments induces possible sharing between terms through unification. On the contrary, they allow for more correct permutations when restricted uses are considered as examplified by **append** and **efface** (a multidirectional procedure is found only if no share constraints are added).

L1	L2	LR	sharing			no sharing			L1	L2	LR	cl_1	cl_1^{tc}	cl_2
			cl_1	cl_1^{tc}	cl_2	cl_1	cl_1^{tc}	cl_2						
a	a	g	0	1	2	0	1	2	g	g	a	0	1	2
a	a	gl	1	1	2	1	1	2	gl	gl	a	1	1	2
al	al	gl	1	1	1	1	1	1	gl	gl	al	1	1	1
gv	gv	g	0	1	1	0	1	2	g	g	gv	0	1	2
glv	glv	gl	1	1	2	1	1	2	gl	gl	glv	1	1	2
clv	clv	gl	1	1	1	1	1	2	gl	gl	clv	1	1	2
g/a	g/a	a/g	0	1	1	0	1	1						
gl/a	gl/a	a/gl	1	1	1	1	1	1						
gl/al	gl/al	al/gl	1	1	0	1	1	0						
g/gv	g/gv	gv/g	0	1	0	0	1	1						
gl/glv	gl/glv	glv/gl	1	1	0	1	1	1						
gl/clv	gl/clv	clv/gl	0	1	1	1	1	1						

Table 1: Number of correct permutations for **append**

X	L	LEff	cl_1	cl_1^{tc}	cl_2	X	L	LEff	cl_1	cl_1^{tc}	cl_2
a	g	a	0	1	3	g	a	g	0	1	6
a	gl	a	1	1	3	g	a	gl	1	1	6
a	gl	al	1	1	2	g	al	gl	1	1	3
gv	g	gv	0	1	2	g	gv	g	0	1	6
gv	gl	glv	1	1	2	g	glv	gl	1	1	6
a	gl	clv	1	1	3	g	clv	gl	1	1	6

X	L	LEff	sharing			no sharing		
			cl_1	cl_1^{tc}	cl_2	cl_1	cl_1^{tc}	cl_2
a/g	g/a	a/g	0	1	1	0	1	1
a/g	gl/a	a/gl	1	1	1	1	1	1
a/g	gl/al	al/gl	1	1	0	1	1	0
gv/g	g/gv	gv/g	0	1	0	0	1	1
gv/g	gl/glv	glv/gl	1	1	0	1	1	1
a/g	gl/clv	clv/gl	1	1	1	1	1	1

Table 2: Number of correct permutations for **efface**

T	L	type checking		type as precondition		no type checking	
		cl_1	cl_2	cl_1	cl_2	cl_1	cl_2
a	g	1	8	1	0	1	0
a	gl	1	8	1	8	1	8
at	gl	1	2	1	2	1	2
gtv	gl	1	8	1	8	1	8
g	a	1	8	1	8	1	8
gt	a	1	8	1	8	1	8
gt	al	1	2	1	2	1	2
gt	glv	1	8	1	8	1	8
a/g	g/a	1	0	1	0	1	0
a/gt	gl/a	1	0	1	0	1	0
at/gt	gl/al	1	0	1	0	1	0
gtv/gt	gl/glv	1	0	1	0	1	0

Table 3: Number of correct permutations for **flattree**

5. Using `complete` types instead of **any** types gives more solutions in many cases (never less) but is a less good solution than simply using **any**.

6   Related works

Many works have been devoted to Type Analysis in Logic programming (see [16] for a representative account). They are related to correctness and optimization issues or both. Our work can be related to Naish's approach to using types for ensuring correctness. Naish's type notion is more general than ours. However types are not used to perform static analysis but to discard ill-typed results. Although it is argued in [15] that most type correctness problem are undecidable, it appears that our system is able to decide them in many interesting cases (due to the knowledge introduced in the behaviours). It is easy to find examples where a correct permutation exists but the analyser fails to find one. However those examples are rather unnatural since most practical analyses described in [7] can be performed by the analyser.

The way we combine type and mode information is similar to the *integrated types* of M. Bruynooghe and G. Janssens[12, 13]. However they are mostly interested by code optimization. So they use abstract interpretation of the sub-problems instead of behaviours. Another difference is that type graphs are used by primitive operations instead of base information on the types. Our approach allows a faster analysis. However the base information must be computed beforehand.

Our analyser is a major component of an experimental environment for declarative logic programming with Prolog [10]. This environment is open and could be integrated with the synthesis tools described in [8, 18] (among others). For example, Wiggins' system [18] produces typed logic descriptions which are then translated into Gödel [11]. Another approach could be to use our analyser to transform the (typed) descriptions into (untyped) Prolog procedures.

7   Conclusion

We have presented an implemented static type analyser and illustrated its usefulness for transforming pure logic definitions into Prolog procedures.

The system appears to be useful in the final step of a Prolog program synthesis process. We have shown that it can be applied to various form of logic definitions using types in different ways. It is also useful for programmers relying on a declarative approach: using the analyser allows to detect type inconsistencies and to correct them. The system is also useful to combine various approaches in the same program and is powerful enough to deal with bigger examples: some components of the FOLON environment [10] have been checked and optimized with the help of the analyser.

Experiments on three sample procedures have shown that combining mode and type information is essential to get good results. Various heuristics have been illustrated and discussed. Assuming very general preconditions for the calls allows to find multidirectional procedures in many cases. On the contrary restricted uses allow to find procedures more amenable to an optimized version.

References

[1] A. Bundy, A. Smaill, and G. Wiggins. The synthesis of logic programs from inductive proofs. In J.W. Lloyd, editor, *Computational Logic*, Esprit Basic Research Series, 1990.

[2] P. De Boeck and B. Le Charlier. Static type analysis of Prolog procedures for ensuring correctness. In *Proceedings of Programming Language Implementation and Logic Programming (PLILP'90)*, volume 456 of *Lecture Notes in Computer Science*, pages 222–237, Linköping, Sweden, August 1990. Springer-Velag.

[3] P. De Boeck and B. Le Charlier. Automatic construction of Prolog primitives for type checking analysis. unpublished paper, 1991.

[4] P. De Boeck and B. Le Charlier. Automatic construction of Prolog primitives for type checking analysis. In M. Billaud and al., editors, *JTASPEFL'91*, pages 165–172, Bordeaux, France, 1991. Bigre 74.

[5] P. De Boeck and B. Le Charlier. Using static type analysis for constructing correct Prolog procedures. In *ICLP'91 Pre-Conference Workshop on Semantics-Based Analysis of Logic Programs*, INRIA Rocquencourt, France, June 1991.

[6] P. De Boeck and B. Le Charlier. Some lessons drawn from using Type analysis for ensuring correctness of Prolog procedures, March 1992.

[7] Y. Deville. *Logic Programming: Systematic Program Development*. MIT Press, 1990.

[8] P. Flener and Y. Deville. Logic Program Synthesis from Incomplete Specifications. To appear in W. Bibel and A. W. Bierman, editors, *Journal of Symbolic Computation: Special Issue on Automatic Programming*, 1993.

[9] L. Fribourg. Extracting logic programs from proofs that use extended Prolog execution and induction. In *Proceedings of the Seventh International Conference on Logic Programming (ICLP'90)*, Jerusalem, Israel, June 1990. MIT Press.

[10] J. Henrard and B. Le Charlier. FOLON: An environment for Declarative Construction of Logic Programs (extended abstract). In M. Bruynooghe and M. Wirsing, editors, *Proceedings of the Fourth International Workshop on Programming Language Implementation and Logic Programming (PLILP'92)*, Lecture Notes in Computer Science, Leuven, August 1992. Springer-Verlag.

[11] P.M. Hill and J.W. Lloyd. The Gödel report (preliminary version). Technical Report TR-91-02, Computer Science Departement, University of Bristol, March 1991.

[12] G. Janssens. *Deriving Run Time Properties of Logic Programs by Means of Abstract Interpretation*. PhD thesis, Department of Computer Science, Katholieke Universiteit Leuven, Belgium, March 1990.

[13] G. Janssens and M. Bruynooghe. Deriving descriptions of possible values of program variables by means of abstract interpretation. Technical Report CW107, Department of Computer Science, Katholieke Universiteit Leuven, Belgium, March 1990. To appear in Journal of Logic Programming.

[14] K. K. Lau and S. D. Prestwich. Top-down Synthesis of Recursive Logic Procedures from First-order Logic Specifications. In *Proceedings of the Seventh International Conference on Logic Programming (ICLP'90)*, Jerusalem, Israel, June 1990. MIT Press.

[15] L. Naish. Specification = program + types. In K. Nori, editor, *Foundations of Software Technology and Theoretical Computer Science*, number 287 in LNCS. Springer-Verlag, 1987.

[16] F. Pfenning. *Types in Logic Programming*. Logic Programming Series. Addison Wesley, 1992.

[17] L. Sterling and E. Shapiro. *The Art of Prolog: Advanced Programming Techniques*. MIT Press, Cambridge Mass., 1986.

[18] G. A. Wiggins. Synthesis and Transformation of Logic Programs in the Whelk Proof Development System. In *Proc. of the 1992 Joint International Conference and Symposium on Logic Programming*. MIT Press, November 1992.

Author Index

Published in 1990–92

AI and Cognitive Science '89, Dublin City
University, Eire, 14–15 September 1989
A. F. Smeaton and G. McDermott (Eds.)

**Specification and Verification of Concurrent
Systems,** University of Stirling, Scotland,
6–8 July 1988
C. Rattray (Ed.)

Semantics for Concurrency, Proceedings of the
International BCS-FACS Workshop, Sponsored
by Logic for IT (S.E.R.C.), University of
Leicester, UK, 23–25 July 1990
M. Z. Kwiatkowska, M. W. Shields and
R. M. Thomas (Eds.)

Functional Programming, Glasgow 1989
Proceedings of the 1989 Glasgow Workshop,
Fraserburgh, Scotland, 21–23 August 1989
K. Davis and J. Hughes (Eds.)

Persistent Object Systems, Proceedings of the
Third International Workshop, Newcastle,
Australia, 10–13 January 1989
J. Rosenberg and D. Koch (Eds.)

Z User Workshop, Oxford 1989, Proceedings of
the Fourth Annual Z User Meeting, Oxford,
15 December 1989
J. E. Nicholls (Ed.)

**Formal Methods for Trustworthy Computer
Systems (FM89),** Halifax, Canada,
23–27 July 1989
Dan Craigen (Editor) and Karen Summerskill
(Assistant Editor)

Security and Persistence, Proceedings of the
International Workshop on Computer
Architecture to Support Security and Persistence
of Information, Bremen, West Germany,
8–11 May 1990
John Rosenberg and J. Leslie Keedy (Eds.)

**Women into Computing: Selected Papers
1988–1990**
Gillian Lovegrove and Barbara Segal (Eds.)

3rd Refinement Workshop (organised by
BCS-FACS, and sponsored by IBM UK
Laboratories, Hursley Park and the Programming
Research Group, University of Oxford),
Hursley Park, 9–11 January 1990
Carroll Morgan and J. C. P. Woodcock (Eds.)

Designing Correct Circuits, Workshop jointly
organised by the Universities of Oxford and
Glasgow, Oxford, 26–28 September 1990
Geraint Jones and Mary Sheeran (Eds.)

Functional Programming, Glasgow 1990
Proceedings of the 1990 Glasgow Workshop on
Functional Programming, Ullapool, Scotland,
13–15 August 1990
Simon L. Peyton Jones, Graham Hutton and
Carsten Kehler Holst (Eds.)

4th Refinement Workshop, Proceedings of the
4th Refinement Workshop, organised by BCS-
FACS, Cambridge, 9–11 January 1991
Joseph M. Morris and Roger C. Shaw (Eds.)

AI and Cognitive Science '90, University of
Ulster at Jordanstown, 20–21 September 1990
Michael F. McTear and Norman Creaney (Eds.)

Software Re-use, Utrecht 1989, Proceedings of
the Software Re-use Workshop, Utrecht,
The Netherlands, 23–24 November 1989
Liesbeth Dusink and Patrick Hall (Eds.)

Z User Workshop, 1990, Proceedings of the Fifth
Annual Z User Meeting, Oxford,
17–18 December 1990
J.E. Nicholls (Ed.)

IV Higher Order Workshop, Banff 1990
Proceedings of the IV Higher Order Workshop,
Banff, Alberta, Canada, 10–14 September 1990
Graham Birtwistle (Ed.)

ALPUK91, Proceedings of the 3rd UK
Annual Conference on Logic Programming,
Edinburgh, 10–12 April 1991
Geraint A.Wiggins, Chris Mellish and
Tim Duncan (Eds.)

Specifications of Database Systems
International Workshop on Specifications of
Database Systems, Glasgow, 3–5 July 1991
David J. Harper and Moira C. Norrie (Eds.)

**7th UK Computer and Telecommunications
Performance Engineering Workshop**
Edinburgh, 22–23 July 1991
J. Hillston, P.J.B. King and R.J. Pooley (Eds.)

Logic Program Synthesis and Transformation
Proceedings of the LOPSTR 91, International
Workshop on Logic Program Synthesis and
Transformation, University of Manchester,
4–5 July 1991
T.P. Clement and K.-K. Lau (Eds.)

Declarative Programming, Sasbachealden 1991
PHOENIX Seminar and Workshop on Declarative
Programming, Sasbachwalden, Black Forest,
Germany, 18–22 November 1991
John Darlington and Roland Dietrich (Eds.)

Building Interactive Systems:
Architectures and Tools
Philip Gray and Roger Took (Eds.)

Functional Programming, Glasgow 1991
Proceedings of the 1991 Glasgow Workshop on
Functional Programming, Portree, Isle of Skye,
12–14 August 1991
Rogardt Heldal, Carsten Kehler Holst and
Philip Wadler (Eds.)

Object Orientation in Z
Susan Stepney, Rosalind Barden and
David Cooper (Eds.)

Code Generation – Concepts, Tool, Techniques
Proceedings of the International Workshop on Code
Generation, Dagstuhl, Germany, 20–24 May 1991
Robert Giegerich and Susan L. Graham (Eds.)